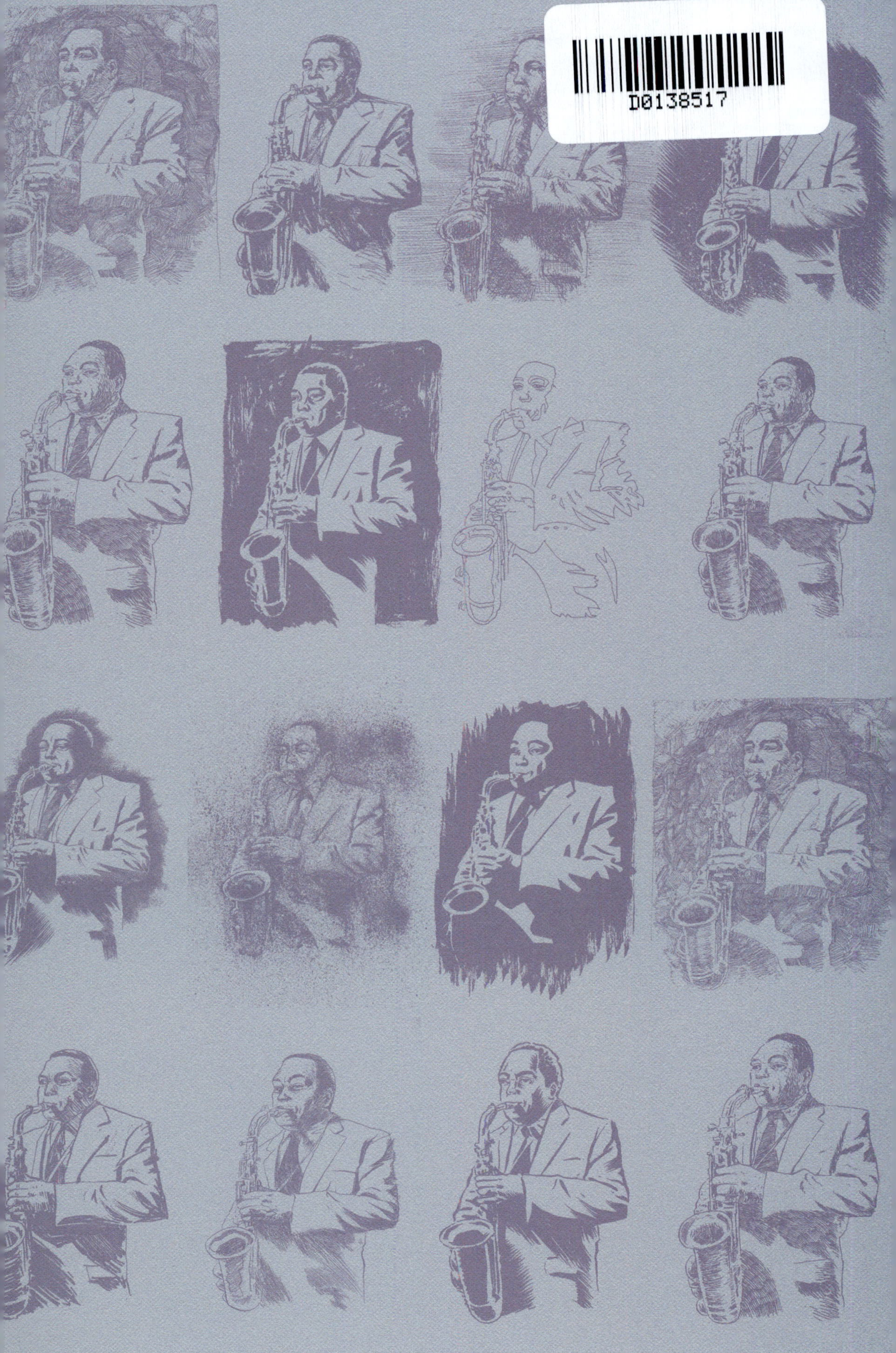

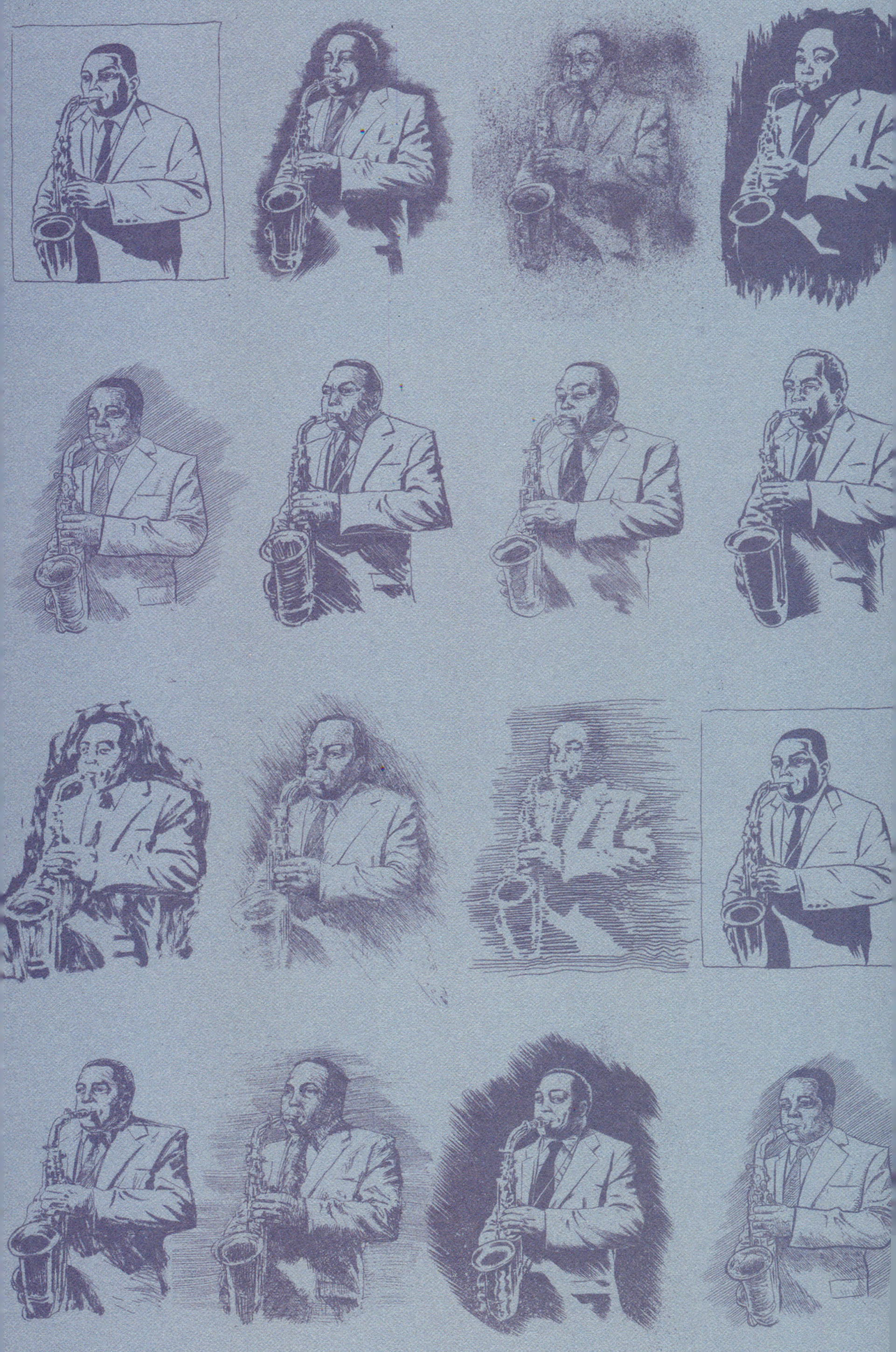

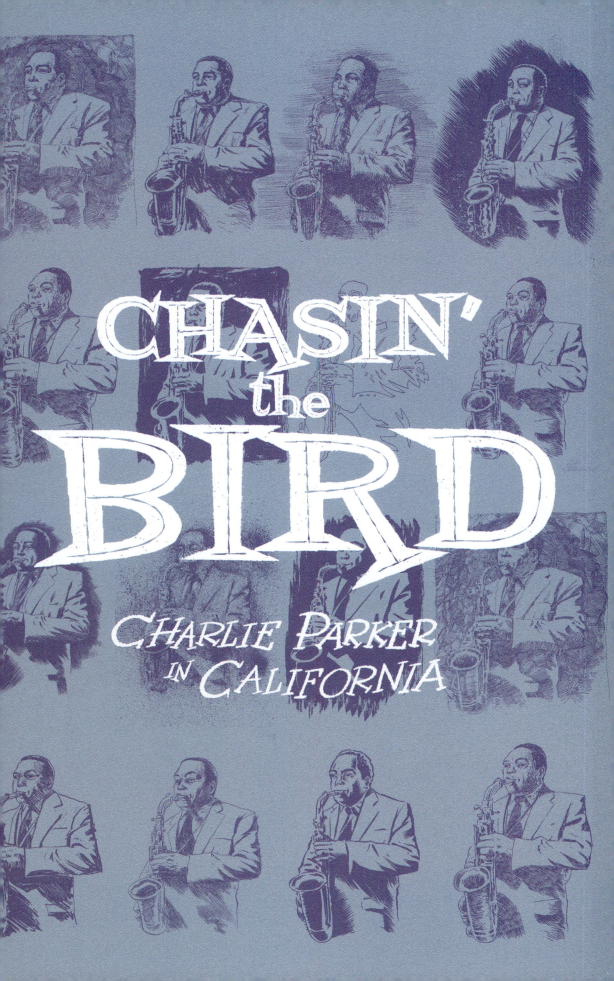

CHASIN' the BIRD

CHARLIE PARKER IN CALIFORNIA

I Hear

Foreword by Kareem Abdul-Jabbar

"I hear..."

You know you've ascended from celebrity to legend when people start a sentence about you with the words **"I hear."** Now they are so ravenous for the sustenance you provide that even the rumors of your movements feed their hope for more. This isn't the **"I hear"** of petty celebrity gossip pin-balling salacious tidbits about sex tapes and break-ups. Rumors about legends are precious information that might explain their performance, their genius. Their ascension. Writer, musician, athlete—why did they rise above all others? And what will be their next great accomplishment that raises us all up with them to another level of perception?

"I hear" is also about how sound affects us: emotionally, spiritually, philosophically. How sound arranged and performed can define who we are, where we came from, and where we want to go. More, what we hear—whether a song by Marvin Gaye or a speech by Martin Luther King Jr.—has the power to change us.

Chasin' the Bird, this phenomenal graphic novel about the groundbreaking jazz musician Charlie "Bird" Parker, begins with a chorus of **"I hear"s** that becomes an archeological dig into the legend that was Bird—and the man that was Charlie Parker. What is especially impressive is how Dave Chisholm and Peter Markowski capture in words and art, the spirit of Bird's music, rooted in the traditions of classic music but reshaped into his own—and their own—personal expression. It is the universal quest each person embarks on to find their unique voice. Most are stifled along the way and so we look to others who, like Bird and Don Quixote, are "willing to march into hell for a heavenly cause."

Even if it destroys them.

For Bird, hell was being black in America. I'm tempted to say things were worse in the 35 years he lived between 1920 and 1955, with open segregation and aggressive Jim Crow laws. But as I write this, black men and women are vigorously protesting in cities across the country after the police killing of George Floyd, who choked out a plea of "I can't breathe," while a white cop kneeled for nine minutes on his neck. We're also in the middle of a nationwide quarantine due to COVID-19, which is killing blacks at three times the rate of whites. And though schools closed and continued their classes online, many black children couldn't afford the computers or had reliable wi-fi to continue classes. Add to that Ahmaud Arbery, a black man out for a jog being ambushed and murdered by white father-and-son vigilantes. So, yeah, 65 years after Bird died, hell is still being black in America. But for Bird, music was the ideal of heaven and while we listened we could experience what heaven might be: intense, carnal, miraculous, celebratory—but fleeting. Ending with the last note. Like life.

Bird preached the gospel of jazz. For him, it wasn't just music, but a language that expressed the spectrum of being black in America: lively, dynamic, innovative, sorrowful, defiant. When we interact with jazz, it teases out of us who we are and projects who we want to be and compresses it then explodes it—all in an instant. A Big Bang of the soul.

The danger with any legend is for the public to deify them because that brushes aside their humanity, the very real suffering they endured that shaped and fueled their talent. Instead, we pay him tribute for being one of us and finding a way to express what it feels like to be us. And that tribute is to say, **"I hear"**—and mean it.

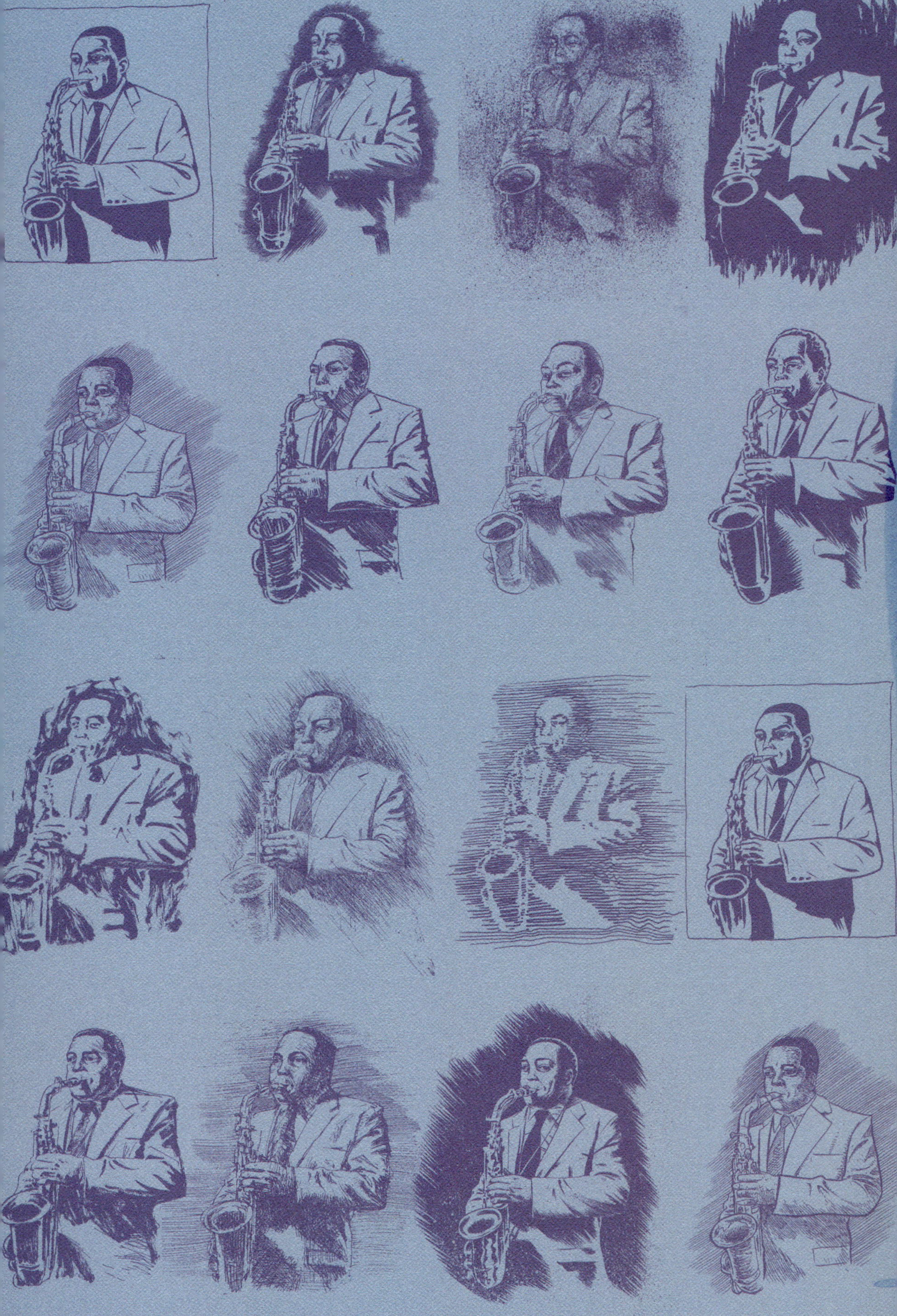

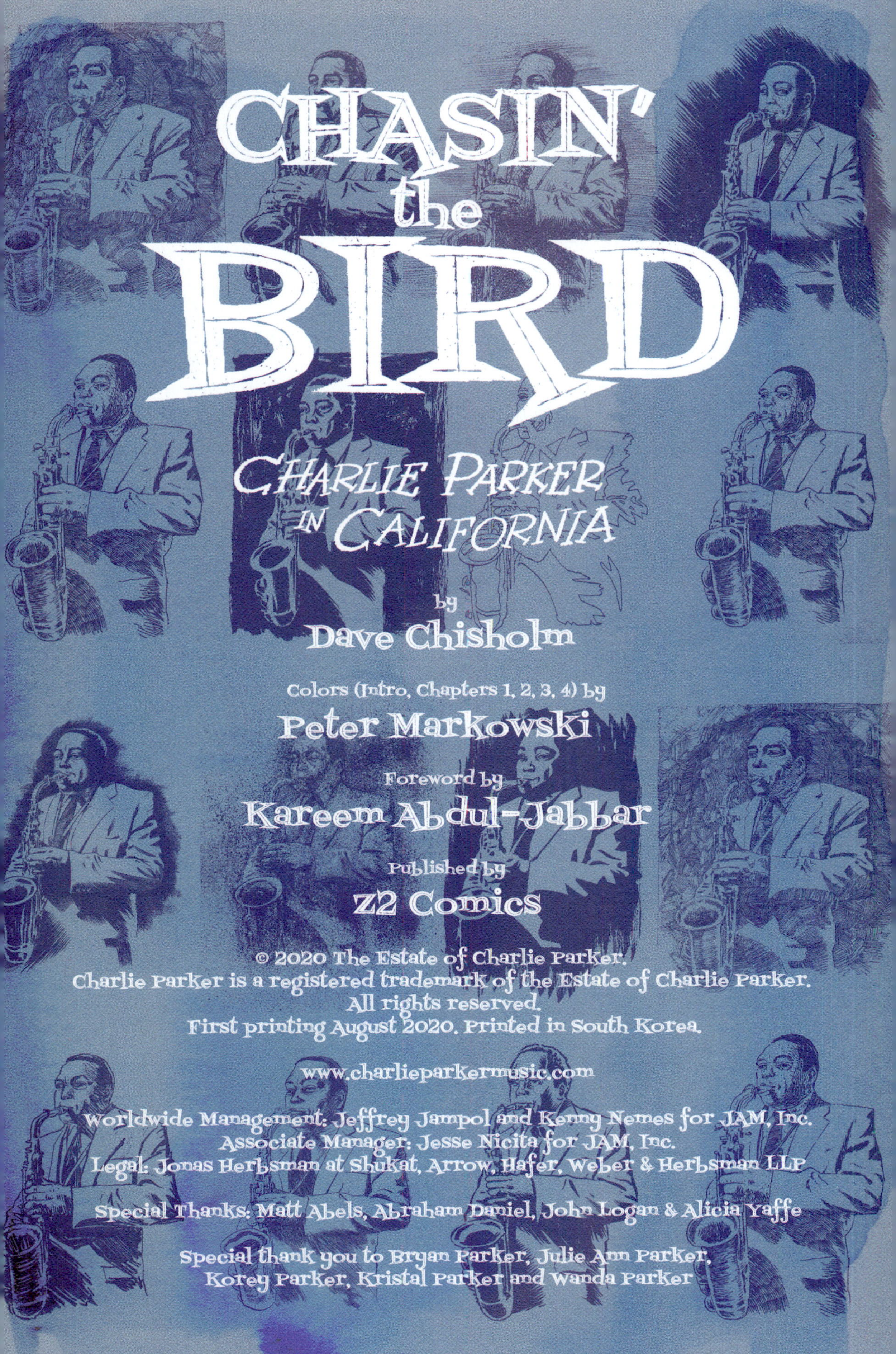

CHASIN' the BIRD

CHARLIE PARKER IN CALIFORNIA

by
Dave Chisholm

Colors (Intro, Chapters 1, 2, 3, 4) by
Peter Markowski

Foreword by
Kareem Abdul-Jabbar

Published by
Z2 Comics

First printing August 2020. Printed in South Korea.

www.charlieparkermusic.com

Worldwide Management: Jeffrey Jampol and Kenny Nemes for JAM, Inc.
Associate Manager: Jesse Nicita for JAM, Inc.
Legal: Jonas Herbsman at Shukat, Arrow, Hafer, Weber & Herbsman LLP

Special Thanks: Matt Abels, Abraham Daniel, John Logan & Alicia Yaffe

Special thank you to Bryan Parker, Julie Ann Parker, Korey Parker, Kristal Parker and Wanda Parker

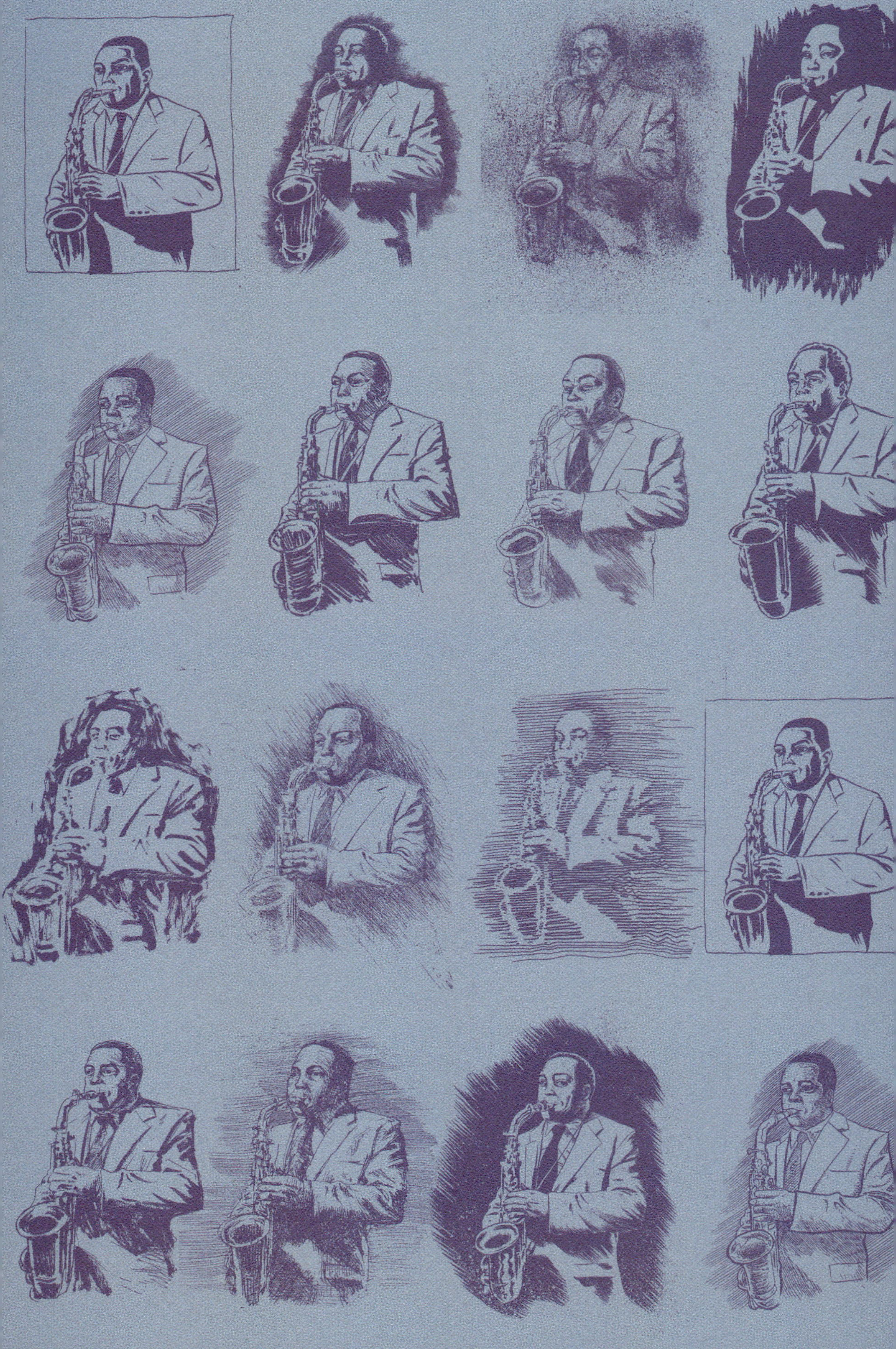

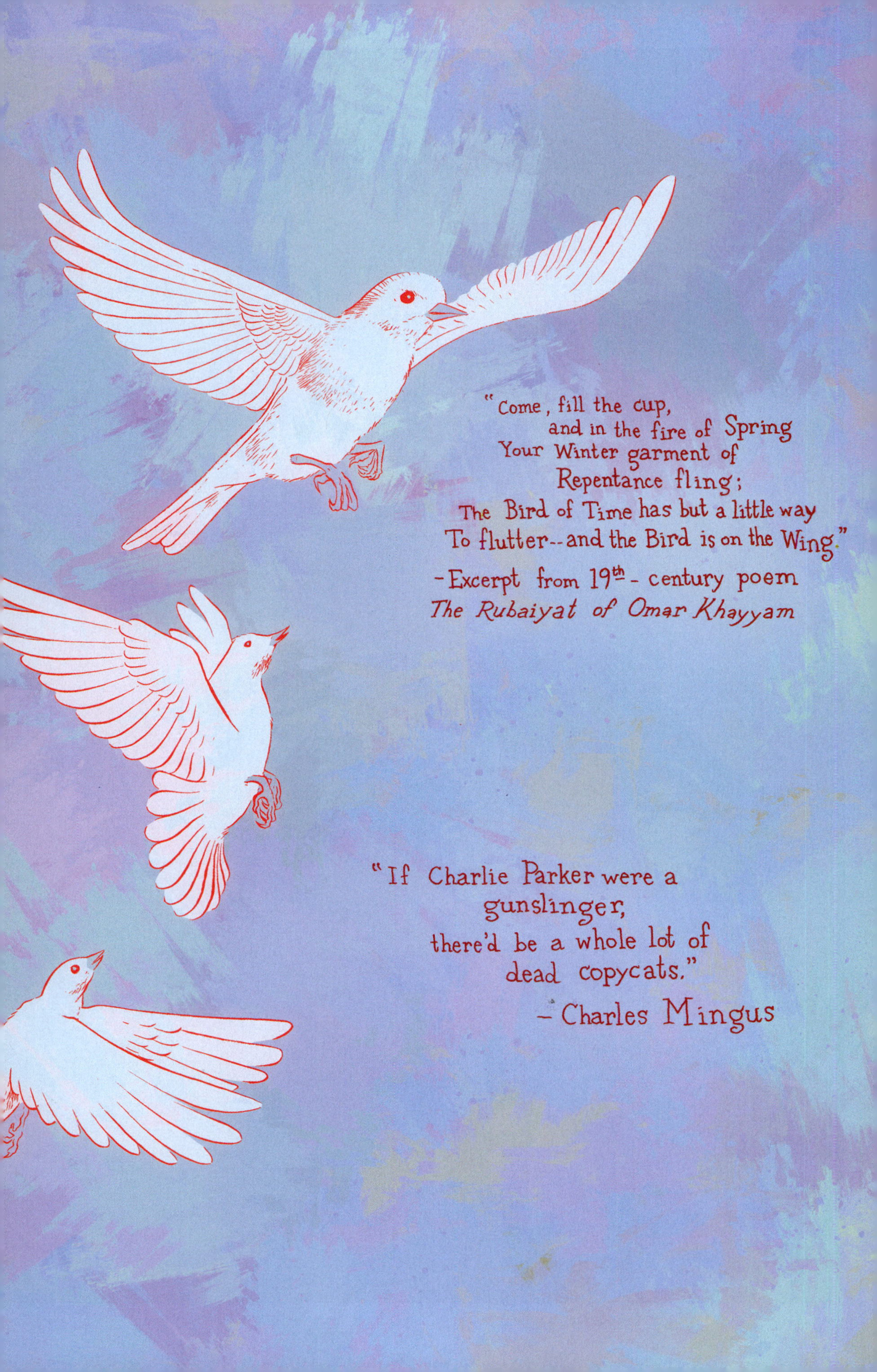

"Come, fill the cup,
and in the fire of Spring
Your Winter garment of
Repentance fling;
The Bird of Time has but a little way
To flutter--and the Bird is on the Wing."

-Excerpt from 19th-century poem
The Rubaiyat of Omar Khayyam

"If Charlie Parker were a
gunslinger,
there'd be a whole lot of
dead copycats."

– Charles Mingus

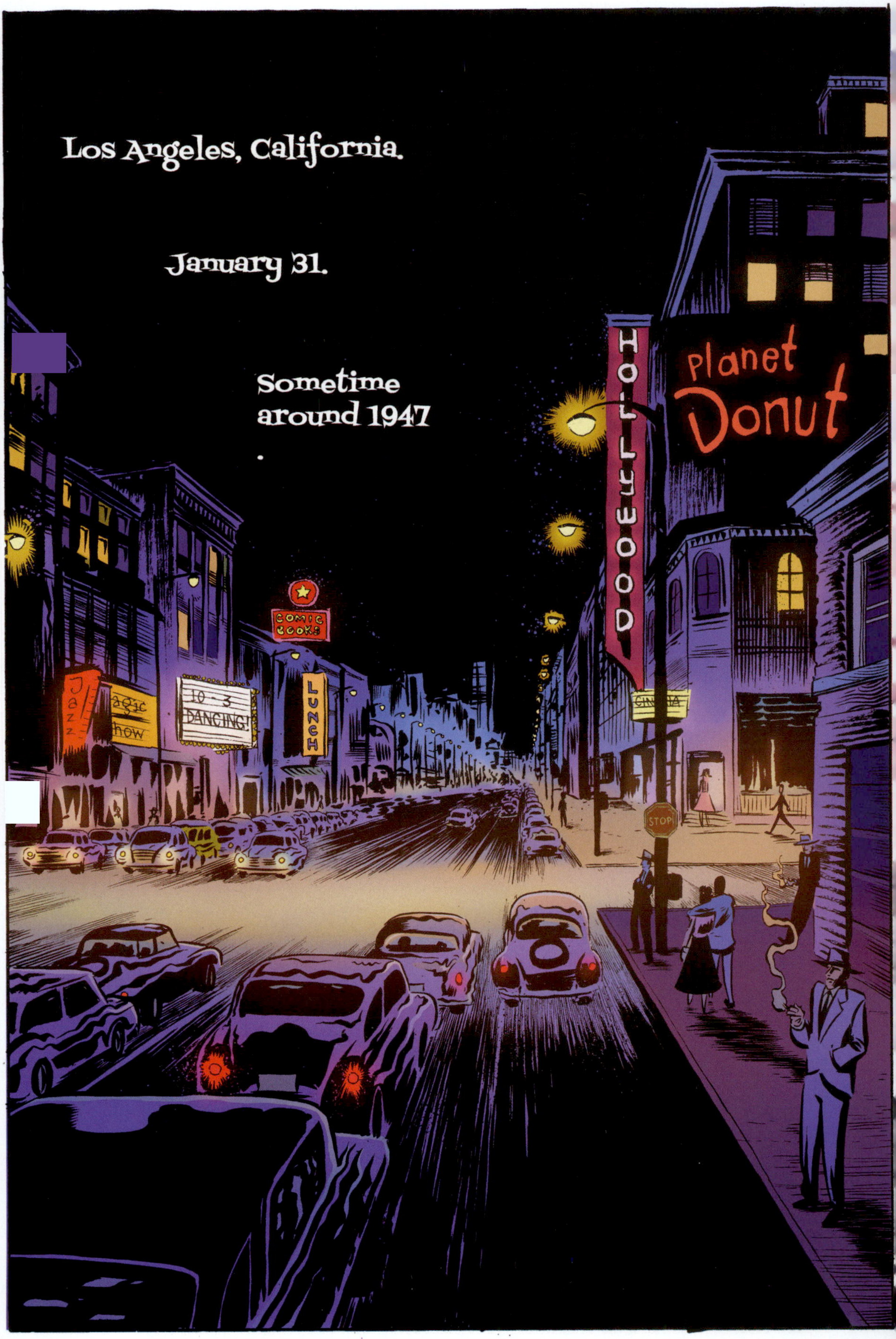
Los Angeles, California.
January 31.
Sometime around 1947
.
Planet Donut
HOLLYWOOD
COMIC BOOKS
Jazz
10-3 DANCING!
LUNCH
STOP!

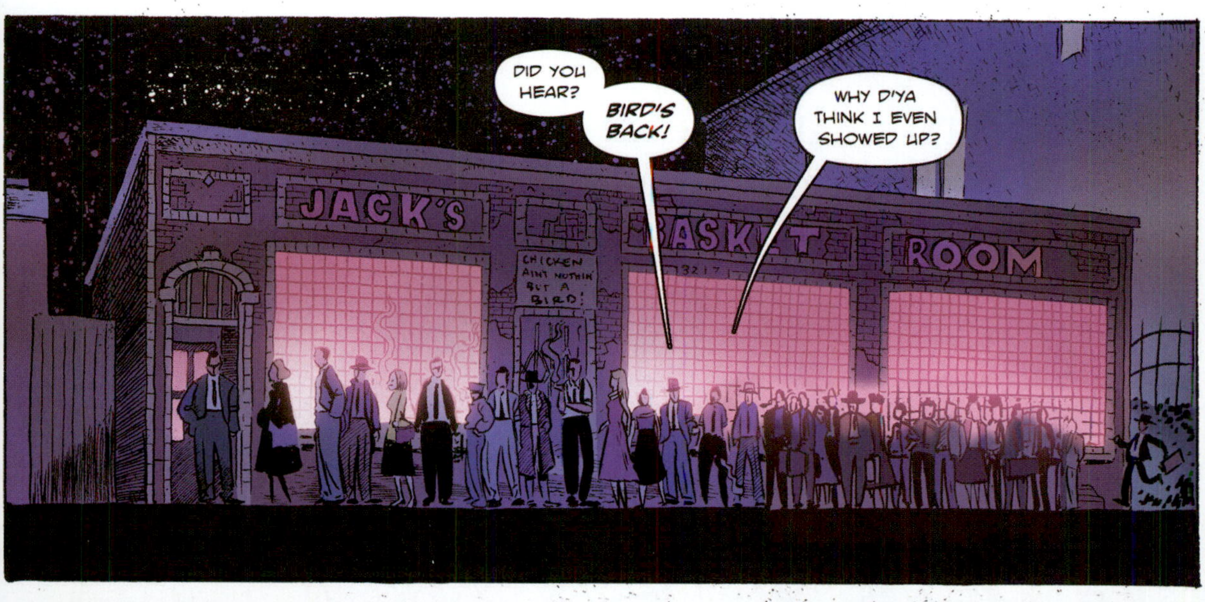
DID YOU HEAR?
BIRD'S BACK!
WHY D'YA THINK I EVEN SHOWED UP?
JACK'S
ROOM
CHICKEN AINT NUTHIN' BUT A BIRD!

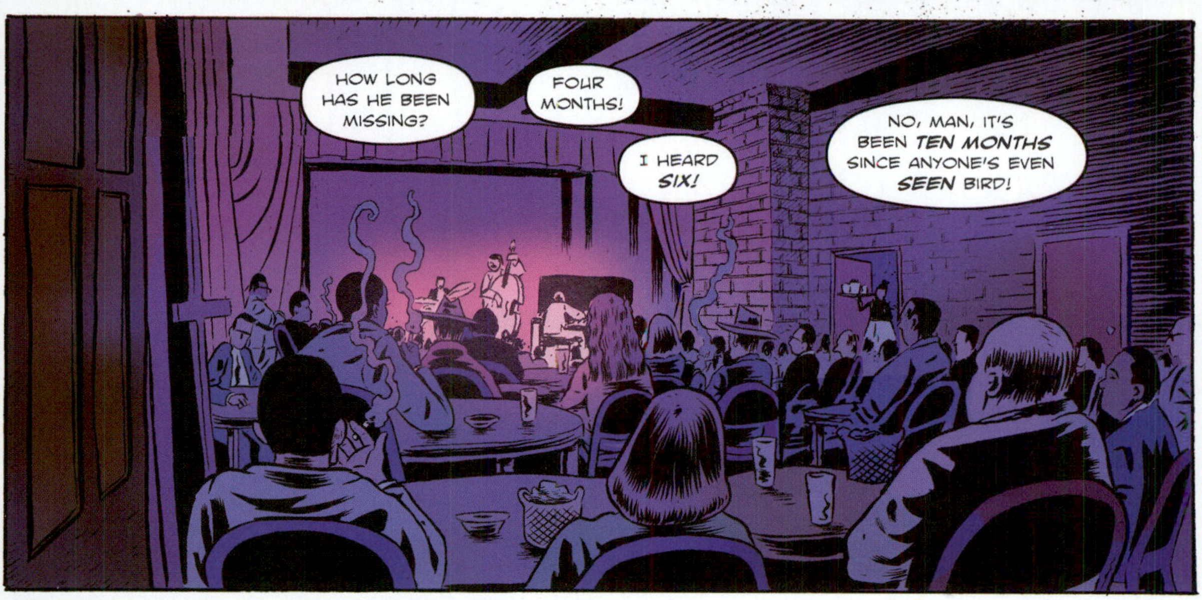
HOW LONG HAS HE BEEN MISSING?
FOUR MONTHS!
I HEARD SIX!
NO, MAN, IT'S BEEN TEN MONTHS SINCE ANYONE'S EVEN SEEN BIRD!

A group of blind men heard that a strange animal called an elephant had been brought to their remote town, but none of them were aware of its shape and form.

They sought it out, and when they found it, overwhelmed with curiosity, they touched it.

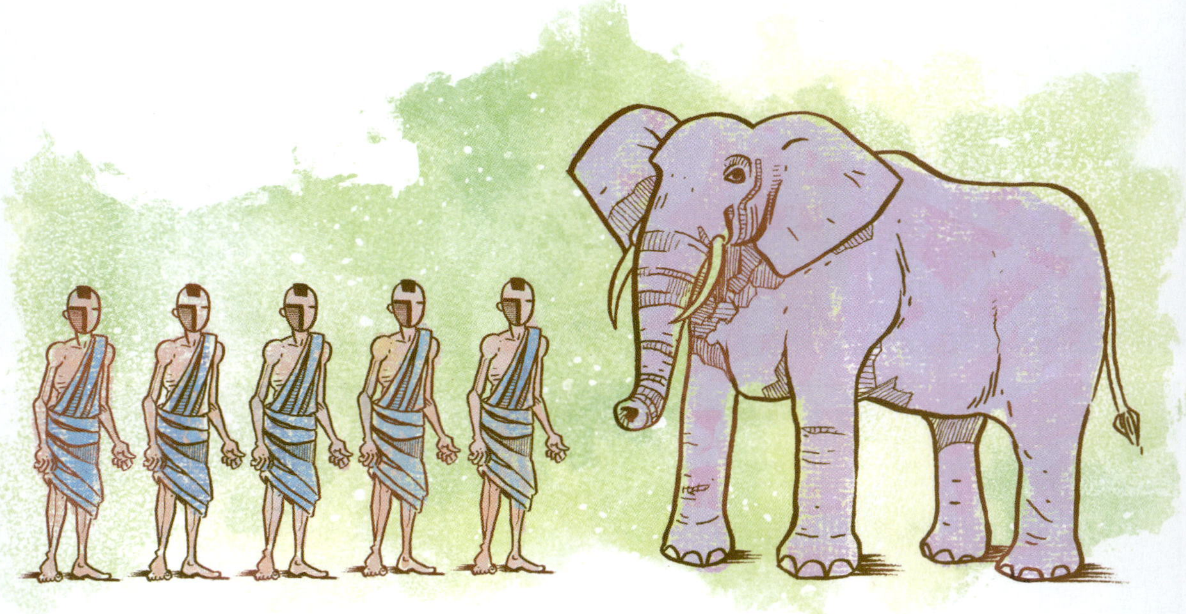

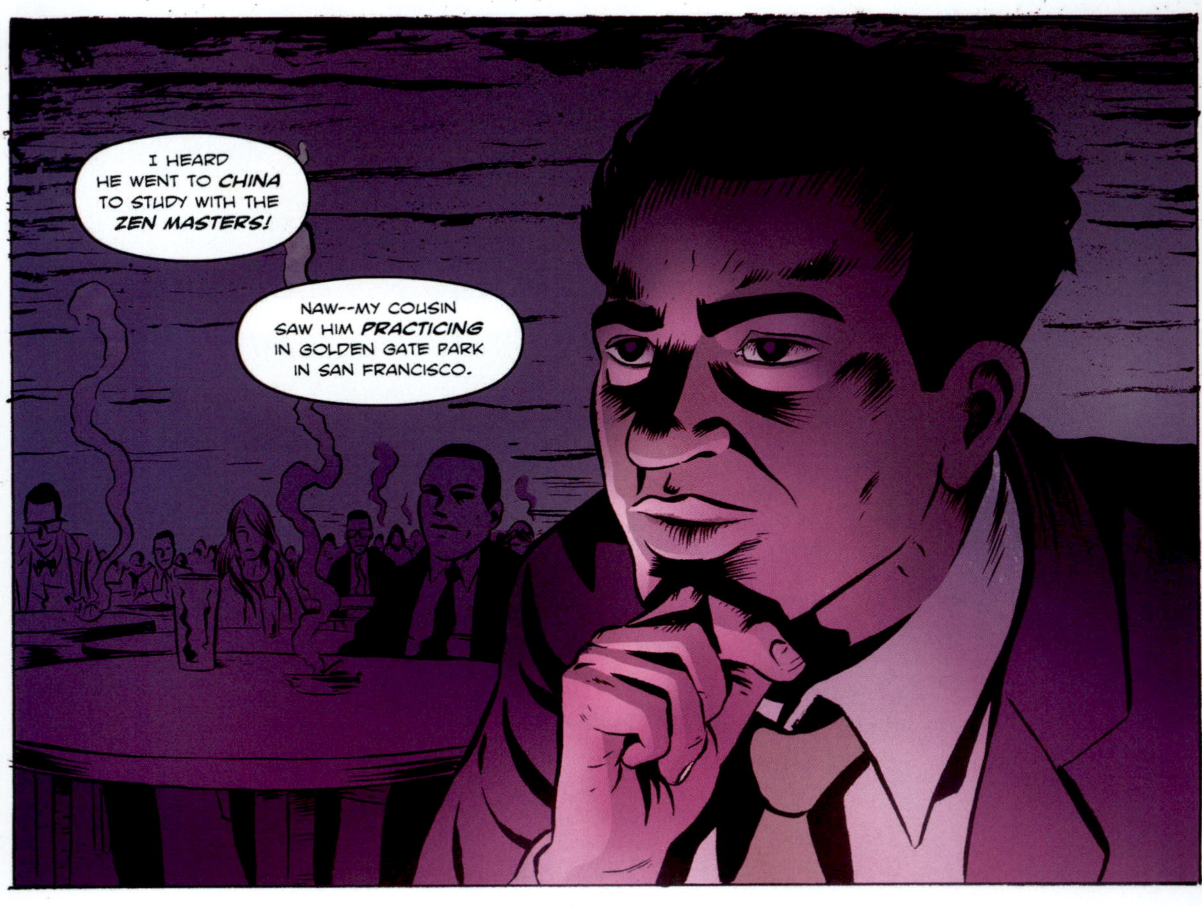
I HEARD HE WENT TO CHINA TO STUDY WITH THE ZEN MASTERS!
NAW--MY COUSIN SAW HIM PRACTICING IN GOLDEN GATE PARK IN SAN FRANCISCO.

In the case of the first person,
whose hand landed on the trunk,
said, "This is a thick rope."

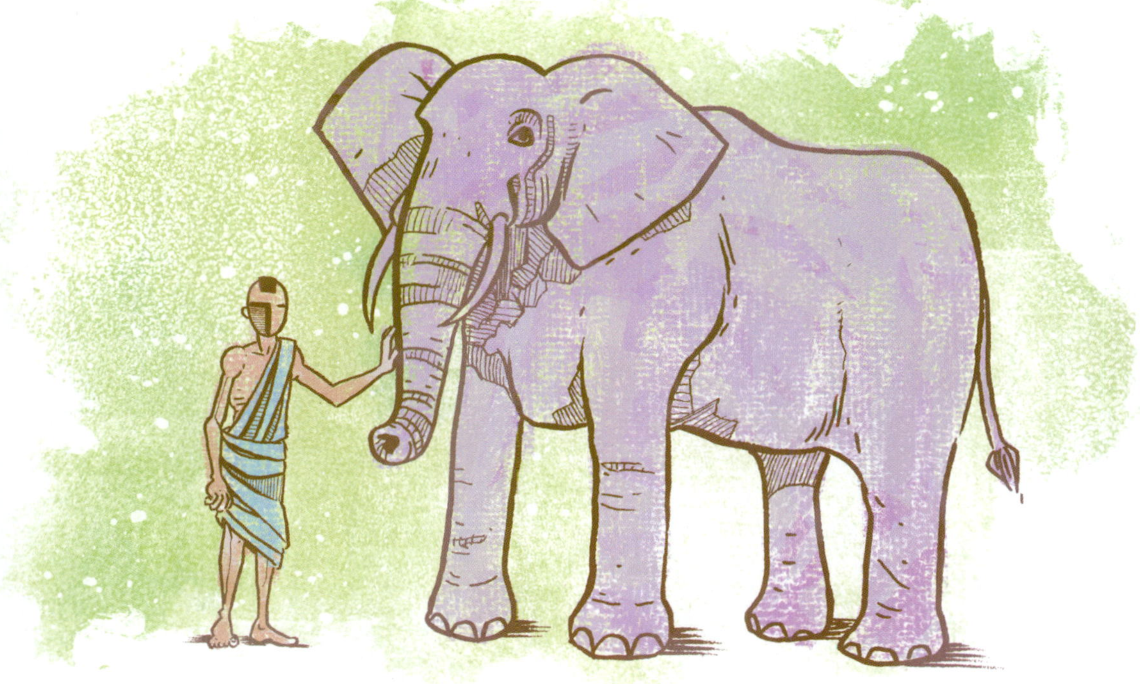

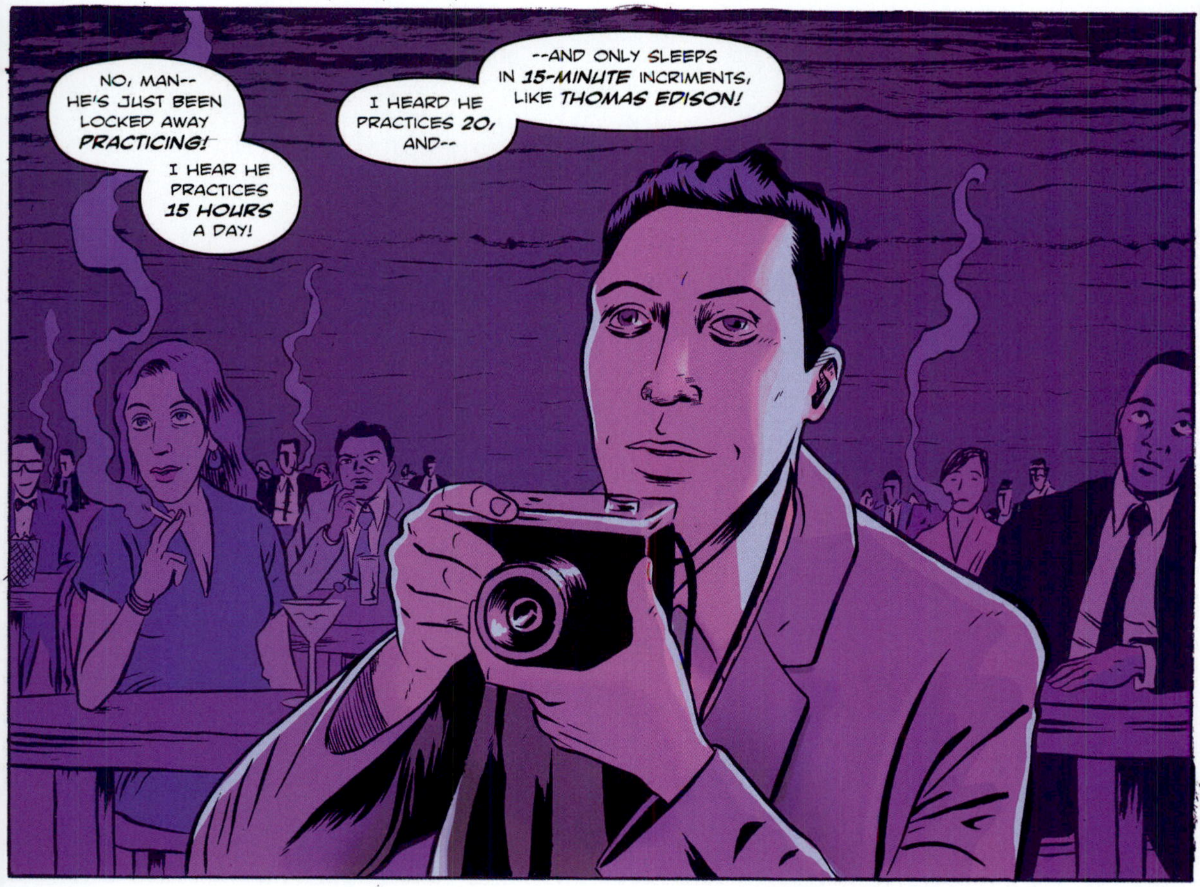
NO, MAN-- HE'S JUST BEEN LOCKED AWAY PRACTICING!
I HEAR HE PRACTICES 15 HOURS A DAY!
I HEARD HE PRACTICES 20, AND--
--AND ONLY SLEEPS IN 15-MINUTE INCRIMENTS, LIKE THOMAS EDISON!

The second person,
whose hand reached its ear,
said, "This is a type of fan."

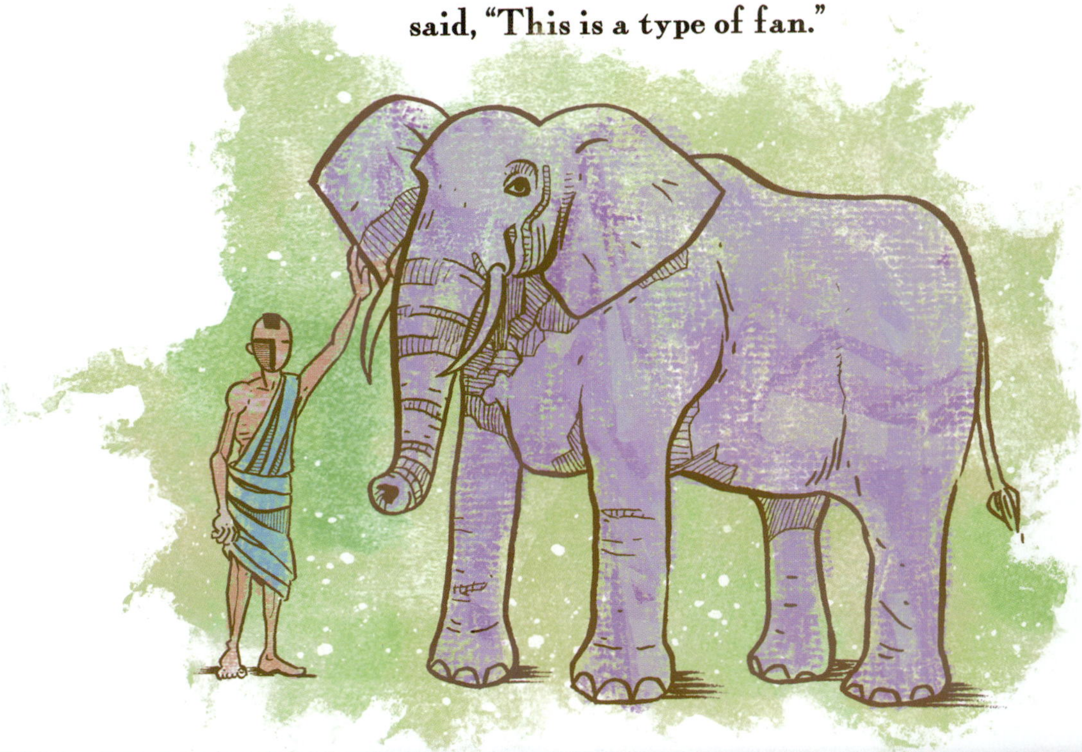

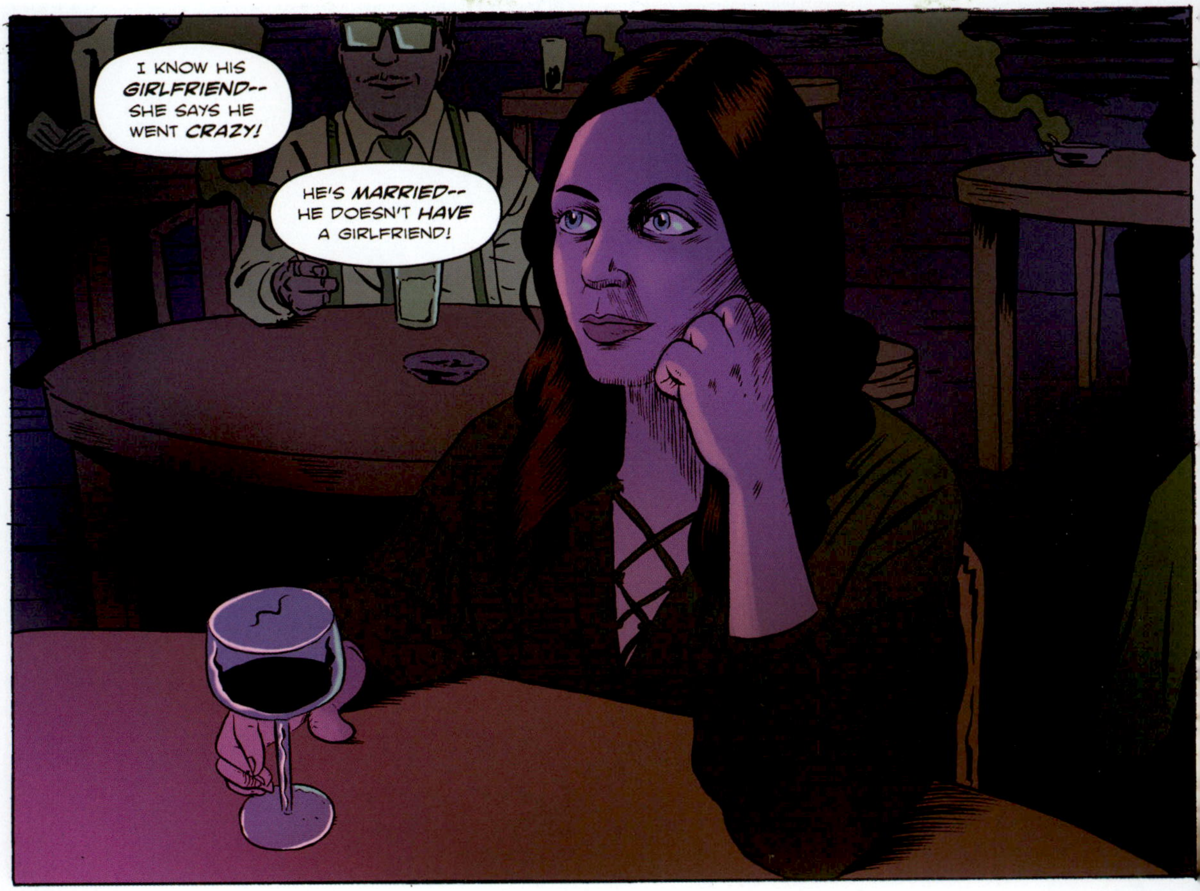
I KNOW HIS *GIRLFRIEND*-- SHE SAYS HE WENT *CRAZY*!
HE'S *MARRIED*-- HE DOESN'T *HAVE* A GIRLFRIEND!

"The third person,
whose hand reached its leg,
said, "This is a tree."

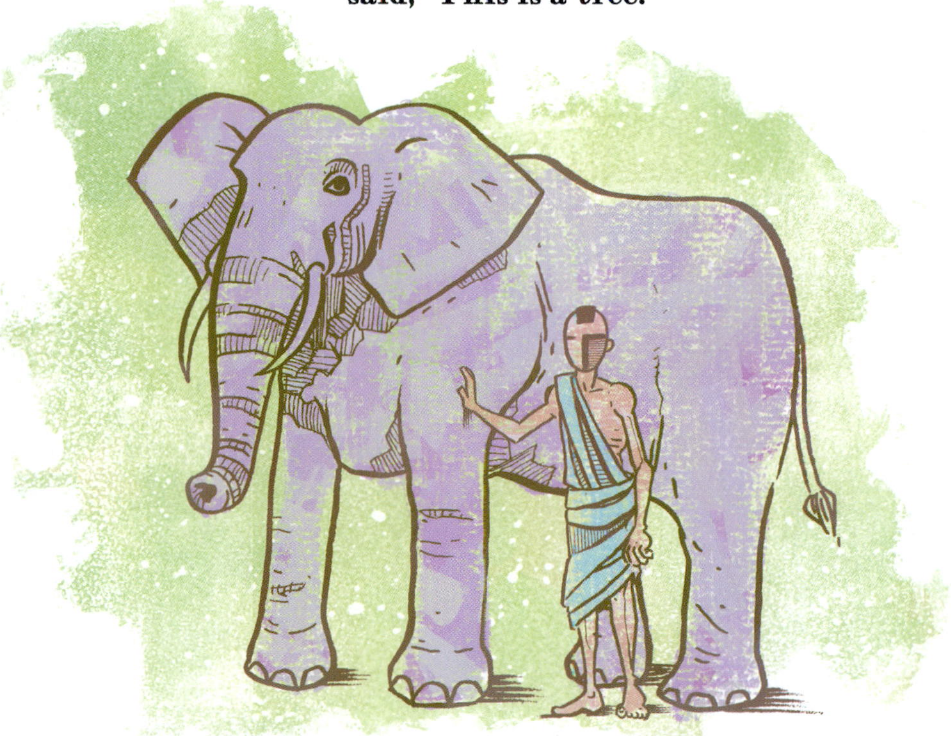

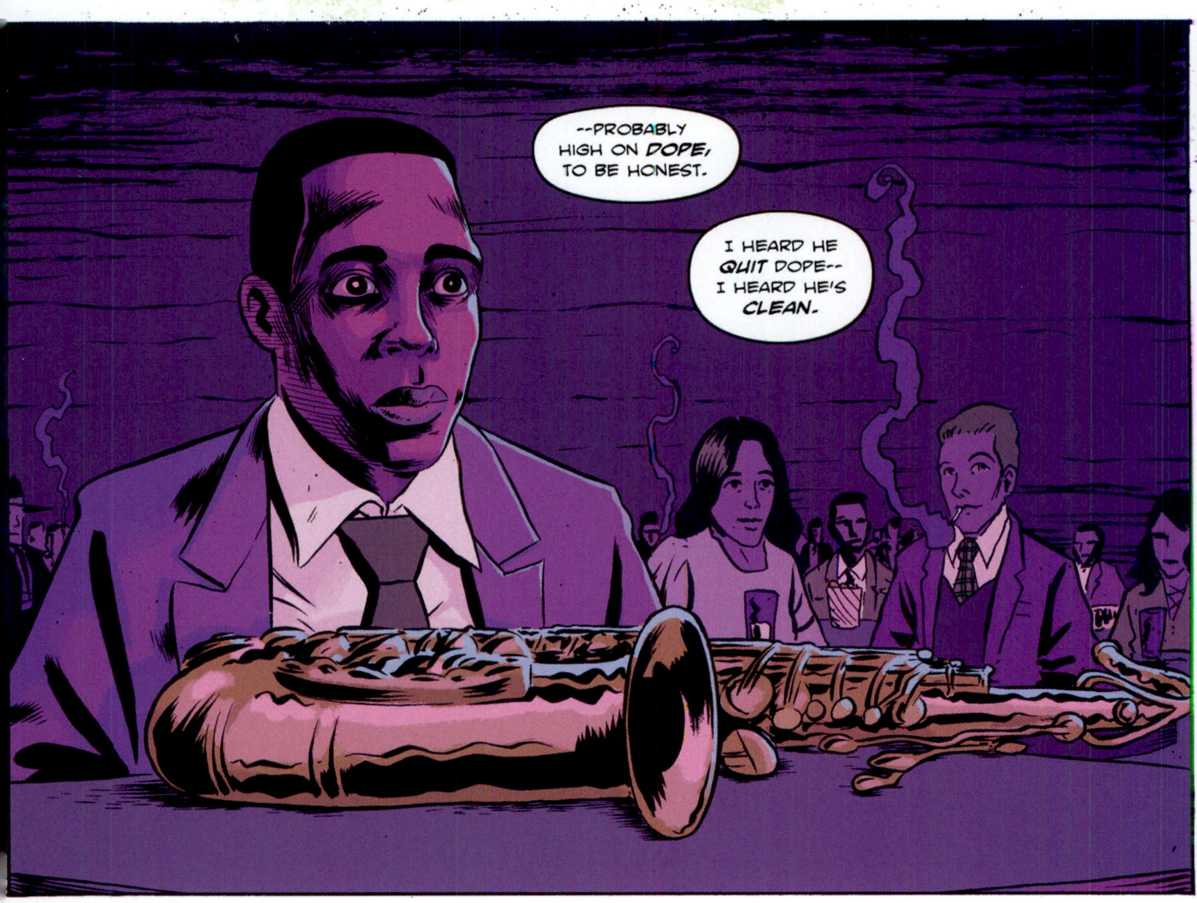
--PROBABLY HIGH ON DOPE, TO BE HONEST.
I HEARD HE QUIT DOPE-- I HEARD HE'S CLEAN.

The fourth person,
whose hand reached the side of the elephant,
said, "This is a wall."

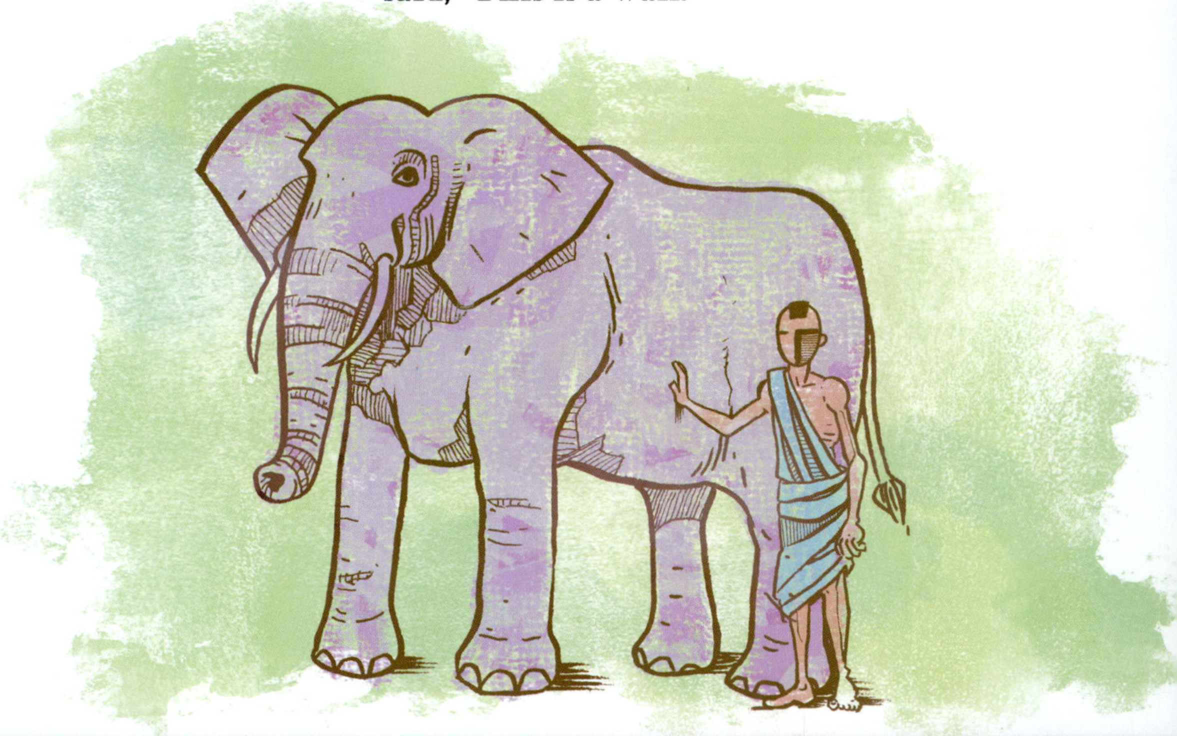

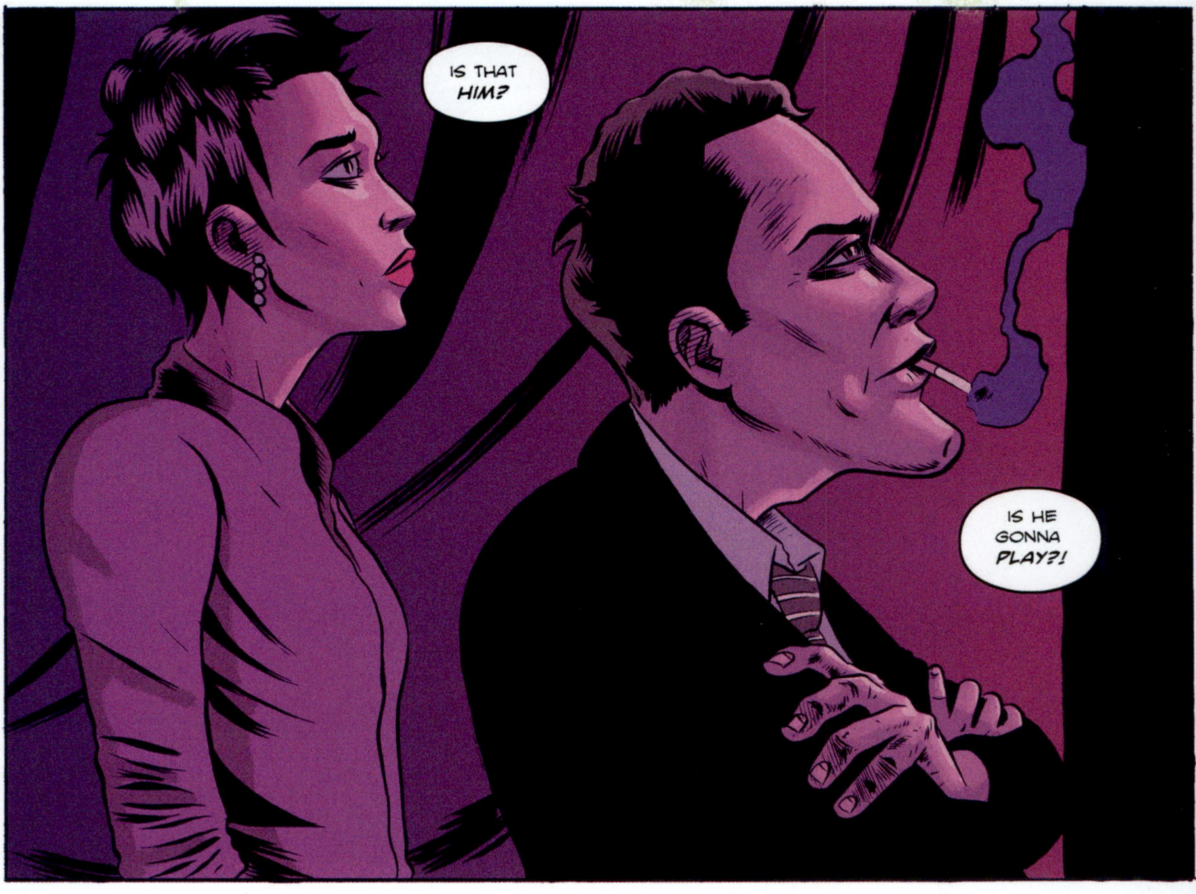
IS THAT *HIM?*
IS HE GONNA *PLAY?!*

The fifth person,
whose hand reached the tusk,
said, "This is a spear."

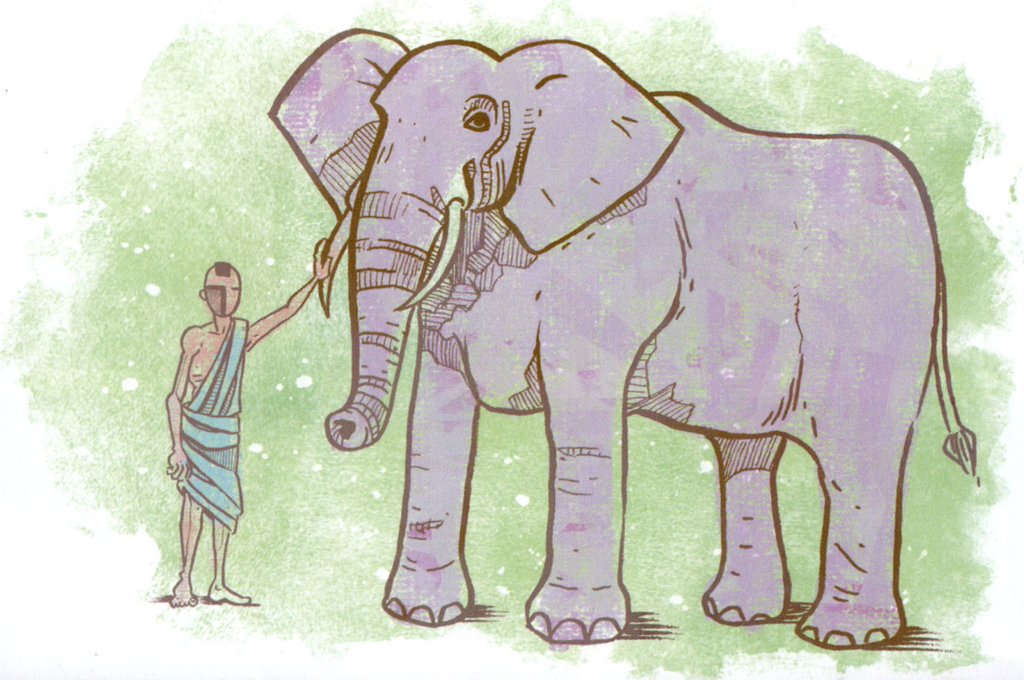

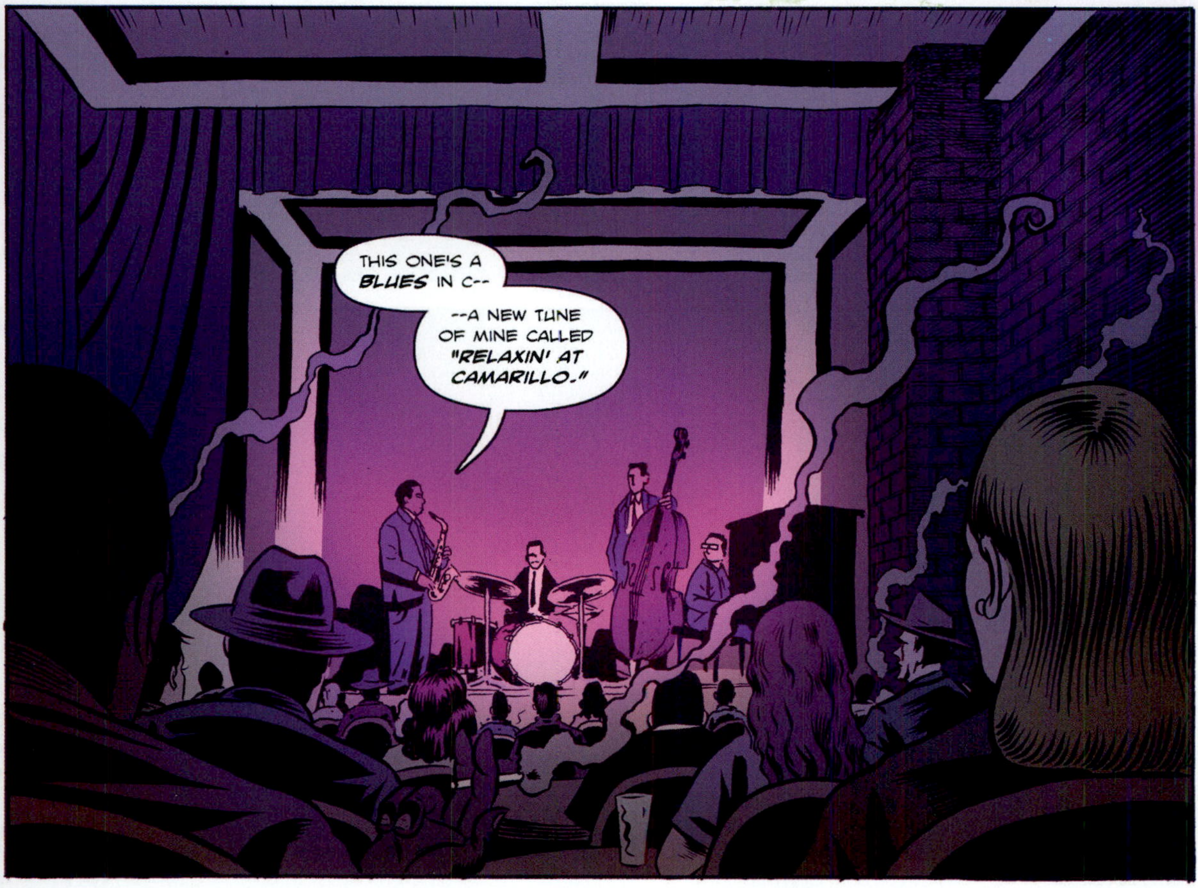
THIS ONE'S A *BLUES* IN C--
--A NEW TUNE OF MINE CALLED *"RELAXIN' AT CAMARILLO."*

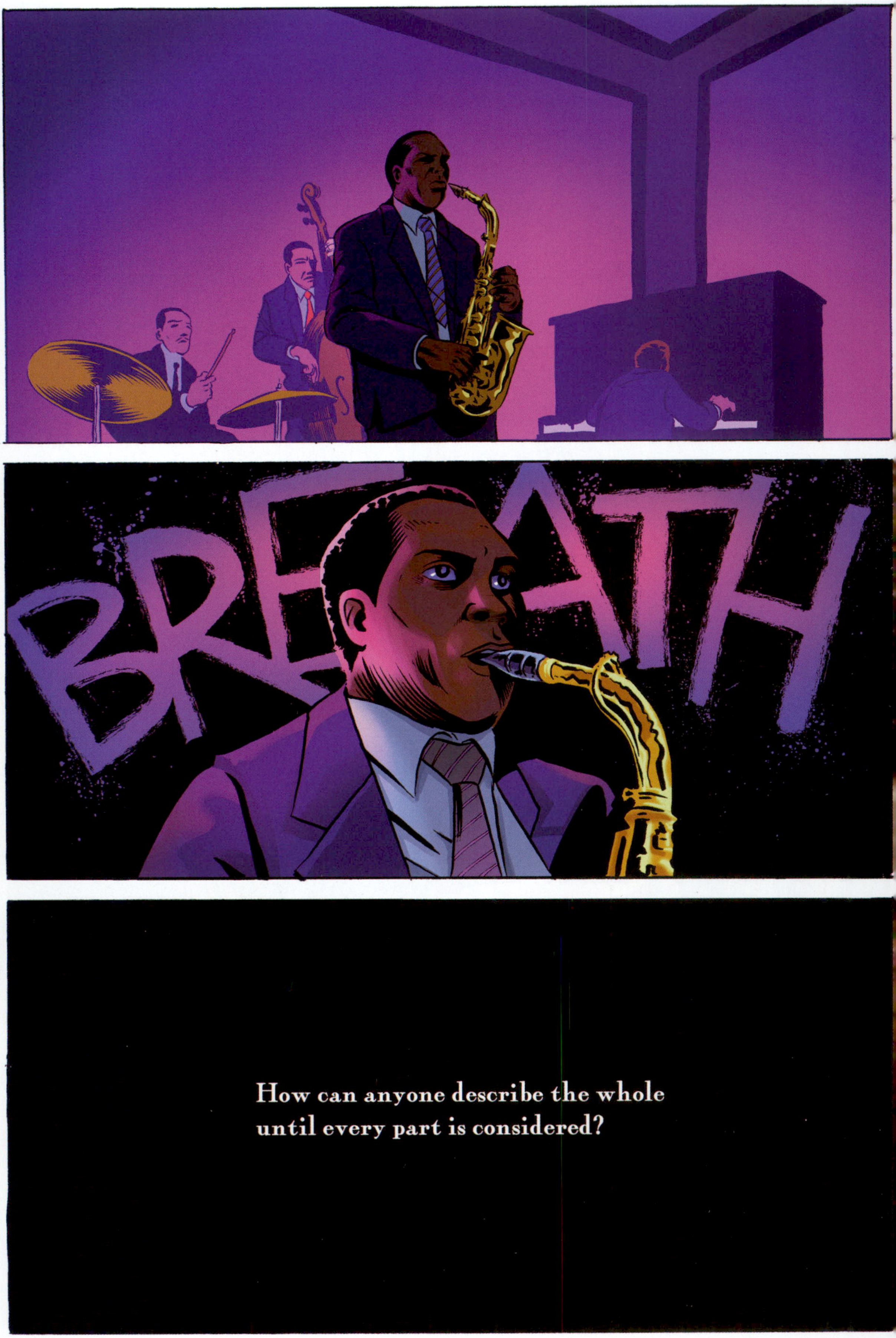
BREATH
How can anyone describe the whole until every part is considered?

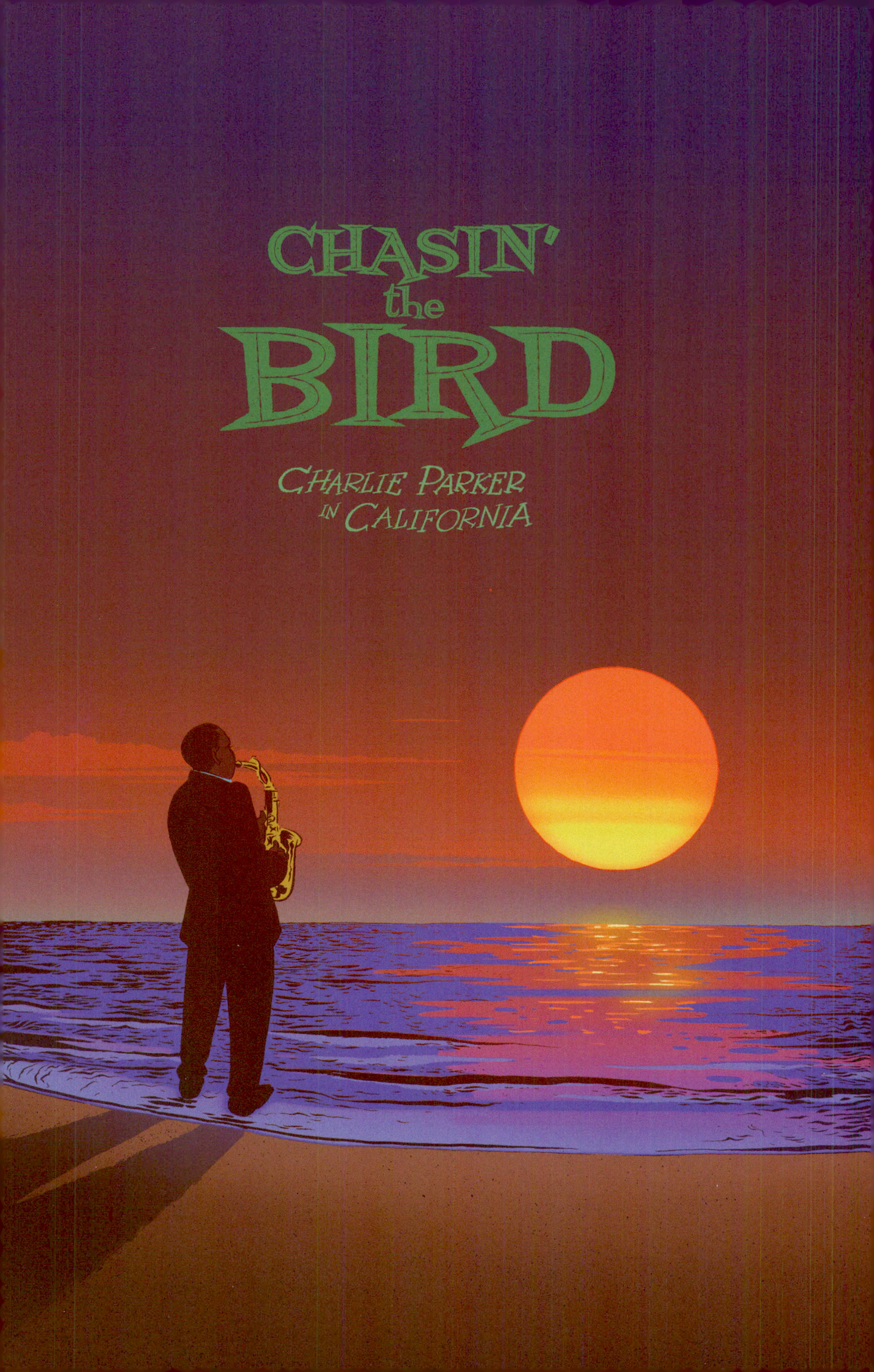
CHASIN' the BIRD
CHARLIE PARKER IN CALIFORNIA

CHORUS 1:

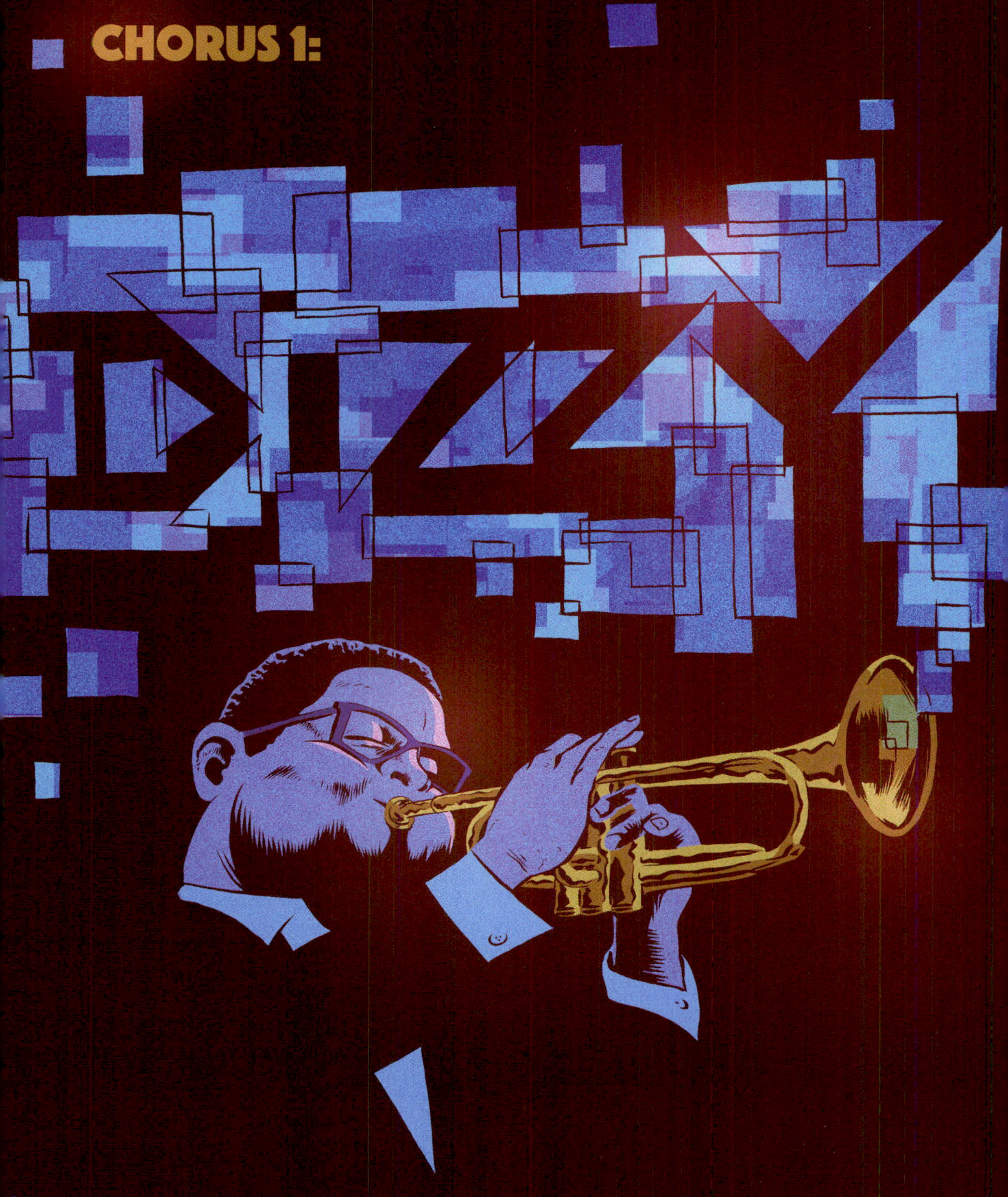
DIZZY

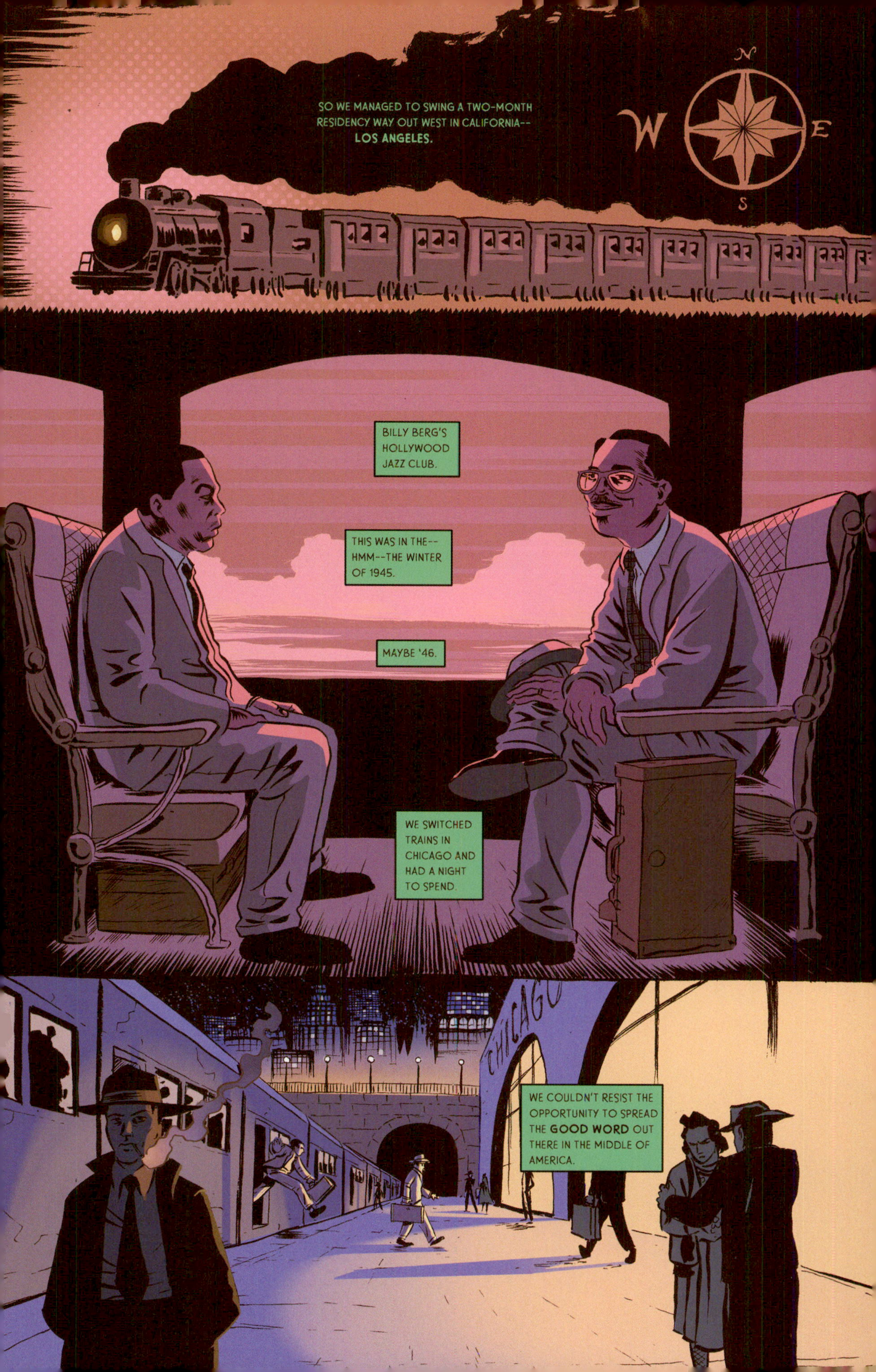

W
E
N
S
SO WE MANAGED TO SWING A TWO-MONTH RESIDENCY WAY OUT WEST IN CALIFORNIA-- **LOS ANGELES.**
BILLY BERG'S HOLLYWOOD JAZZ CLUB.
THIS WAS IN THE-- HMM--THE WINTER OF 1945.
MAYBE '46.
WE SWITCHED TRAINS IN CHICAGO AND HAD A NIGHT TO SPEND.
CHICAGO
WE COULDN'T RESIST THE OPPORTUNITY TO SPREAD THE **GOOD WORD** OUT THERE IN THE MIDDLE OF AMERICA.

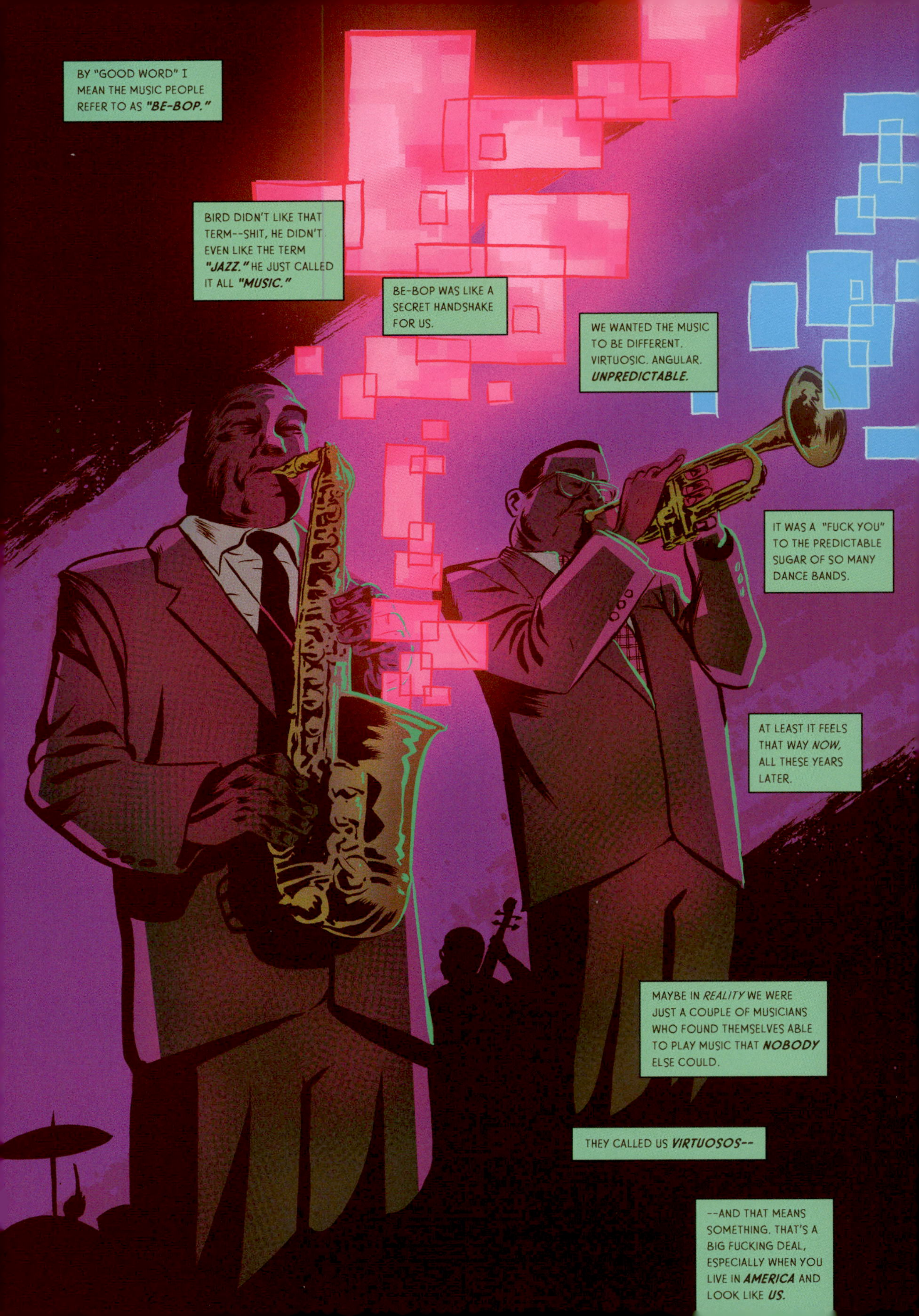

BY "GOOD WORD" I MEAN THE MUSIC PEOPLE REFER TO AS ***"BE-BOP."***
BIRD DIDN'T LIKE THAT TERM--SHIT, HE DIDN'T EVEN LIKE THE TERM ***"JAZZ."*** HE JUST CALLED IT ALL ***"MUSIC."***
BE-BOP WAS LIKE A SECRET HANDSHAKE FOR US.
WE WANTED THE MUSIC TO BE DIFFERENT. VIRTUOSIC. ANGULAR. ***UNPREDICTABLE.***
IT WAS A "FUCK YOU" TO THE PREDICTABLE SUGAR OF SO MANY DANCE BANDS.
AT LEAST IT FEELS THAT WAY *NOW,* ALL THESE YEARS LATER.
MAYBE IN *REALITY* WE WERE JUST A COUPLE OF MUSICIANS WHO FOUND THEMSELVES ABLE TO PLAY MUSIC THAT ***NOBODY*** ELSE COULD.
THEY CALLED US ***VIRTUOSOS--***
--AND THAT MEANS SOMETHING. THAT'S A BIG FUCKING DEAL, ESPECIALLY WHEN YOU LIVE IN ***AMERICA*** AND LOOK LIKE ***US.***

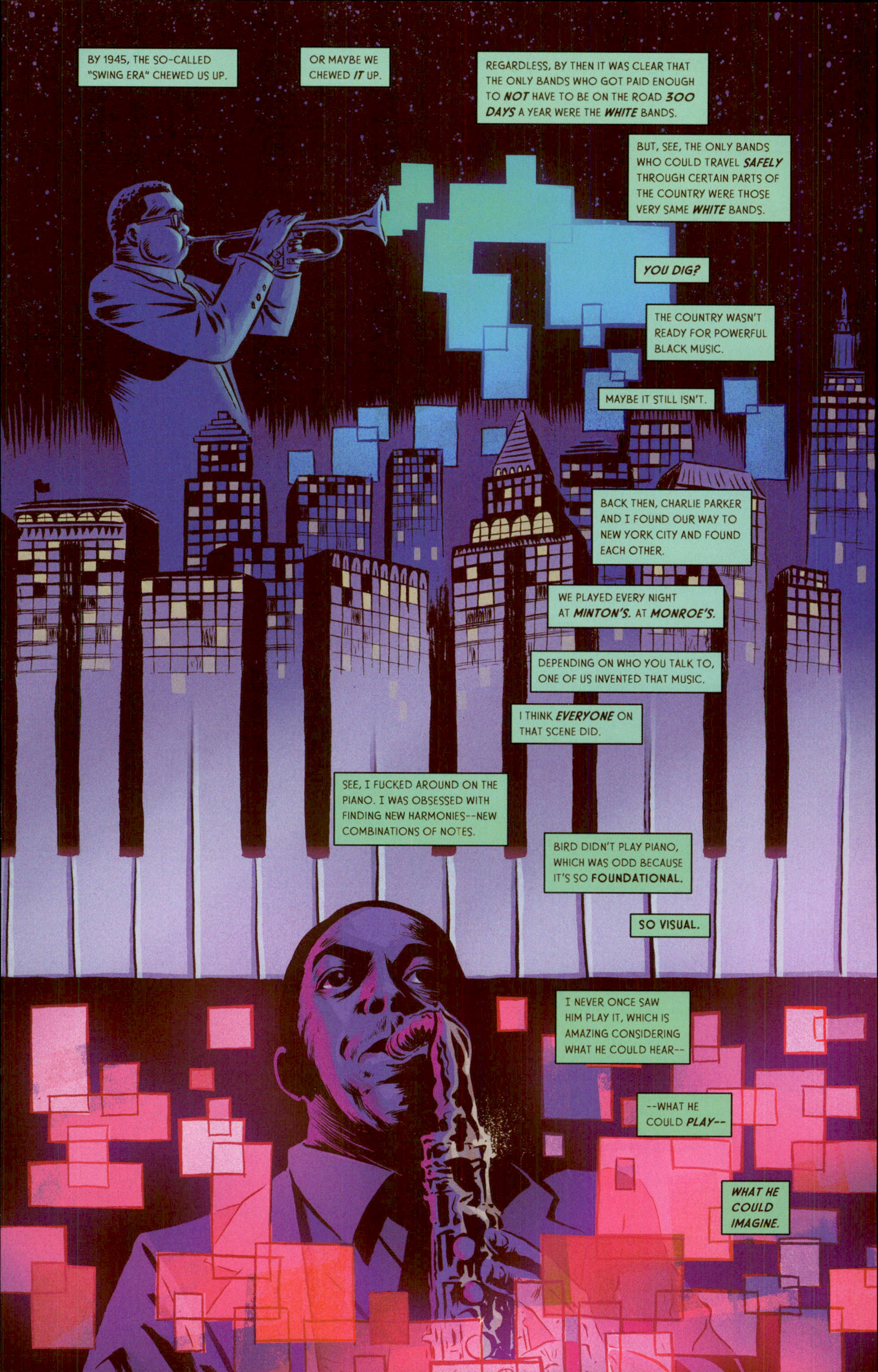
BY 1945, THE SO-CALLED "SWING ERA" CHEWED US UP.
OR MAYBE WE CHEWED IT UP.
REGARDLESS, BY THEN IT WAS CLEAR THAT THE ONLY BANDS WHO GOT PAID ENOUGH TO NOT HAVE TO BE ON THE ROAD 300 DAYS A YEAR WERE THE WHITE BANDS.
BUT, SEE, THE ONLY BANDS WHO COULD TRAVEL SAFELY THROUGH CERTAIN PARTS OF THE COUNTRY WERE THOSE VERY SAME WHITE BANDS.
YOU DIG?
THE COUNTRY WASN'T READY FOR POWERFUL BLACK MUSIC.
MAYBE IT STILL ISN'T.
BACK THEN, CHARLIE PARKER AND I FOUND OUR WAY TO NEW YORK CITY AND FOUND EACH OTHER.
WE PLAYED EVERY NIGHT AT MINTON'S. AT MONROE'S.
DEPENDING ON WHO YOU TALK TO, ONE OF US INVENTED THAT MUSIC.
I THINK EVERYONE ON THAT SCENE DID.
SEE, I FUCKED AROUND ON THE PIANO. I WAS OBSESSED WITH FINDING NEW HARMONIES--NEW COMBINATIONS OF NOTES.
BIRD DIDN'T PLAY PIANO, WHICH WAS ODD BECAUSE IT'S SO FOUNDATIONAL.
SO VISUAL.
I NEVER ONCE SAW HIM PLAY IT, WHICH IS AMAZING CONSIDERING WHAT HE COULD HEAR--
--WHAT HE COULD PLAY--
WHAT HE COULD IMAGINE.

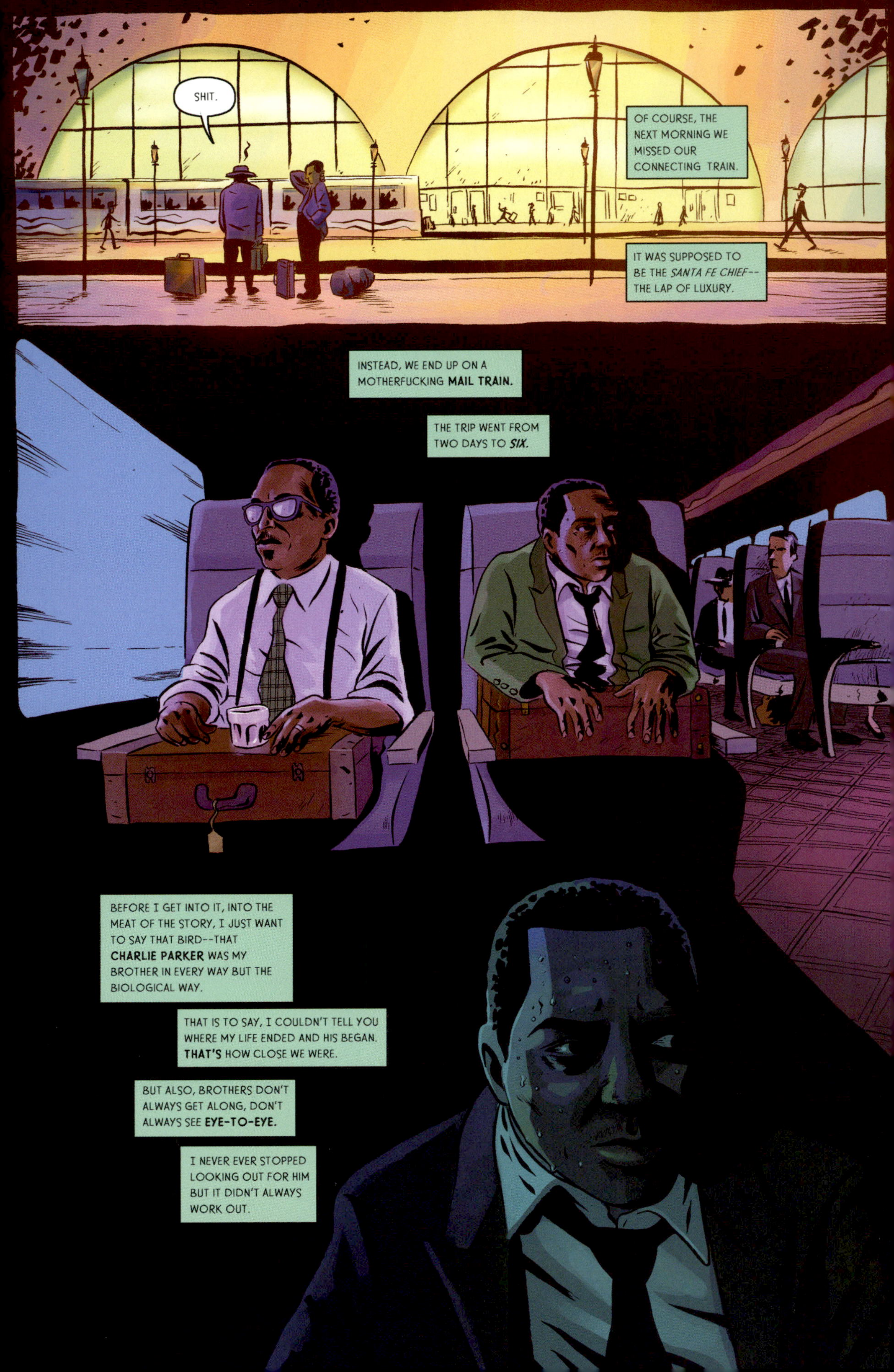

SHIT.
OF COURSE, THE NEXT MORNING WE MISSED OUR CONNECTING TRAIN.
IT WAS SUPPOSED TO BE THE SANTA FE CHIEF-- THE LAP OF LUXURY.
INSTEAD, WE END UP ON A MOTHERFUCKING MAIL TRAIN.
THE TRIP WENT FROM TWO DAYS TO SIX.
BEFORE I GET INTO IT, INTO THE MEAT OF THE STORY, I JUST WANT TO SAY THAT BIRD--THAT CHARLIE PARKER WAS MY BROTHER IN EVERY WAY BUT THE BIOLOGICAL WAY.
THAT IS TO SAY, I COULDN'T TELL YOU WHERE MY LIFE ENDED AND HIS BEGAN. THAT'S HOW CLOSE WE WERE.
BUT ALSO, BROTHERS DON'T ALWAYS GET ALONG, DON'T ALWAYS SEE EYE-TO-EYE.
I NEVER EVER STOPPED LOOKING OUT FOR HIM BUT IT DIDN'T ALWAYS WORK OUT.

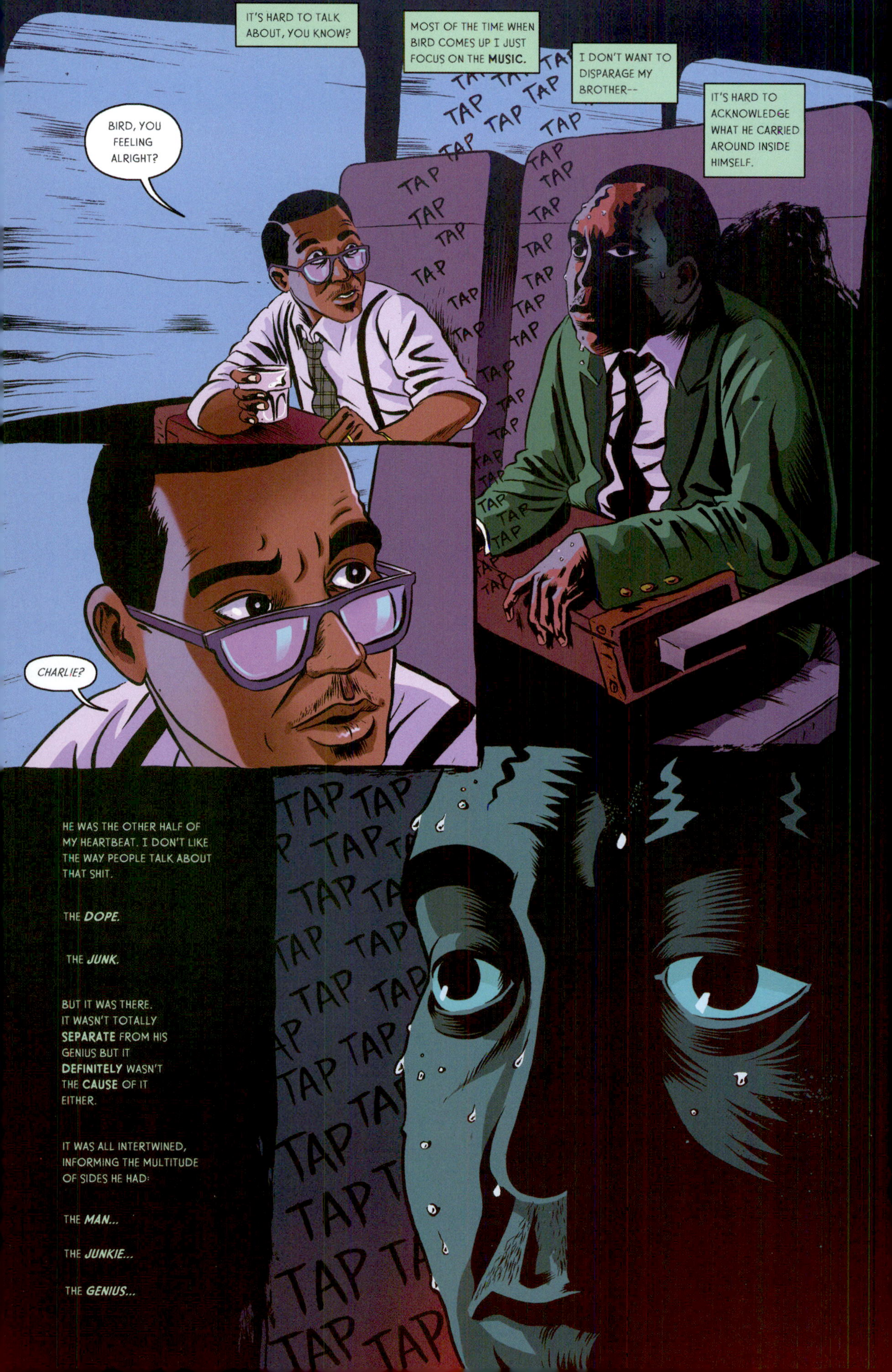
IT'S HARD TO TALK ABOUT, YOU KNOW?
MOST OF THE TIME WHEN BIRD COMES UP I JUST FOCUS ON THE MUSIC.
I DON'T WANT TO DISPARAGE MY BROTHER--
IT'S HARD TO ACKNOWLEDGE WHAT HE CARRIED AROUND INSIDE HIMSELF.
BIRD, YOU FEELING ALRIGHT?
TAP TAP TAP TAP TAP TAP TAP TAP TAP TAP TAP TAP TAP TAP TAP TAP TAP TAP TAP TAP TAP
CHARLIE?
HE WAS THE OTHER HALF OF MY HEARTBEAT. I DON'T LIKE THE WAY PEOPLE TALK ABOUT THAT SHIT.
THE DOPE.
THE JUNK.
BUT IT WAS THERE. IT WASN'T TOTALLY SEPARATE FROM HIS GENIUS BUT IT DEFINITELY WASN'T THE CAUSE OF IT EITHER.
IT WAS ALL INTERTWINED, INFORMING THE MULTITUDE OF SIDES HE HAD:
THE MAN...
THE JUNKIE...
THE GENIUS...
TAP TAP TAP TAP TAP TAP TAP TAP TAP TAP TAP TAP TAP TAP TAP

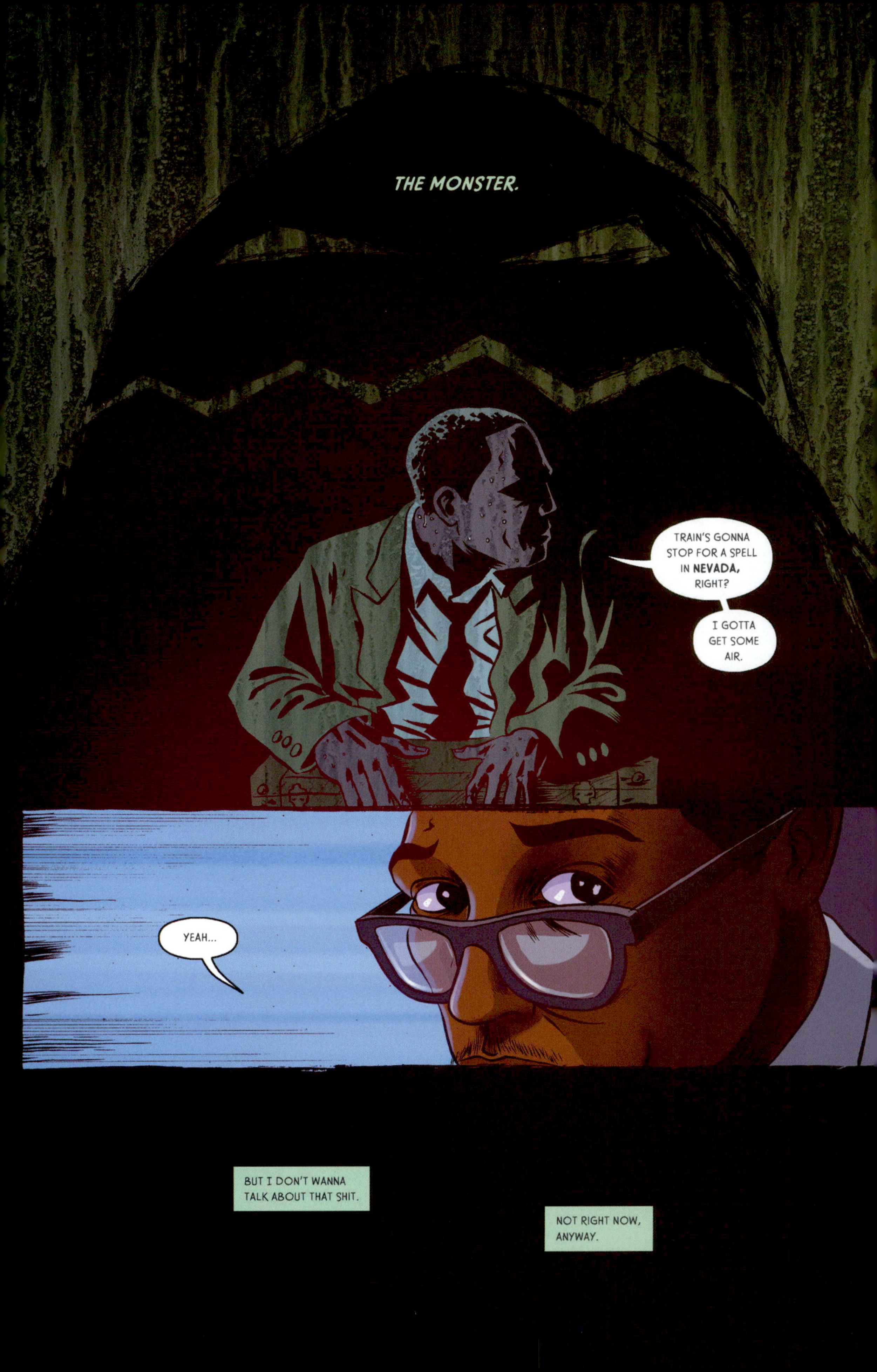
THE MONSTER.
TRAIN'S GONNA STOP FOR A SPELL IN **NEVADA,** RIGHT?
I GOTTA GET SOME AIR.
YEAH...
BUT I DON'T WANNA TALK ABOUT THAT SHIT.
NOT RIGHT NOW, ANYWAY.

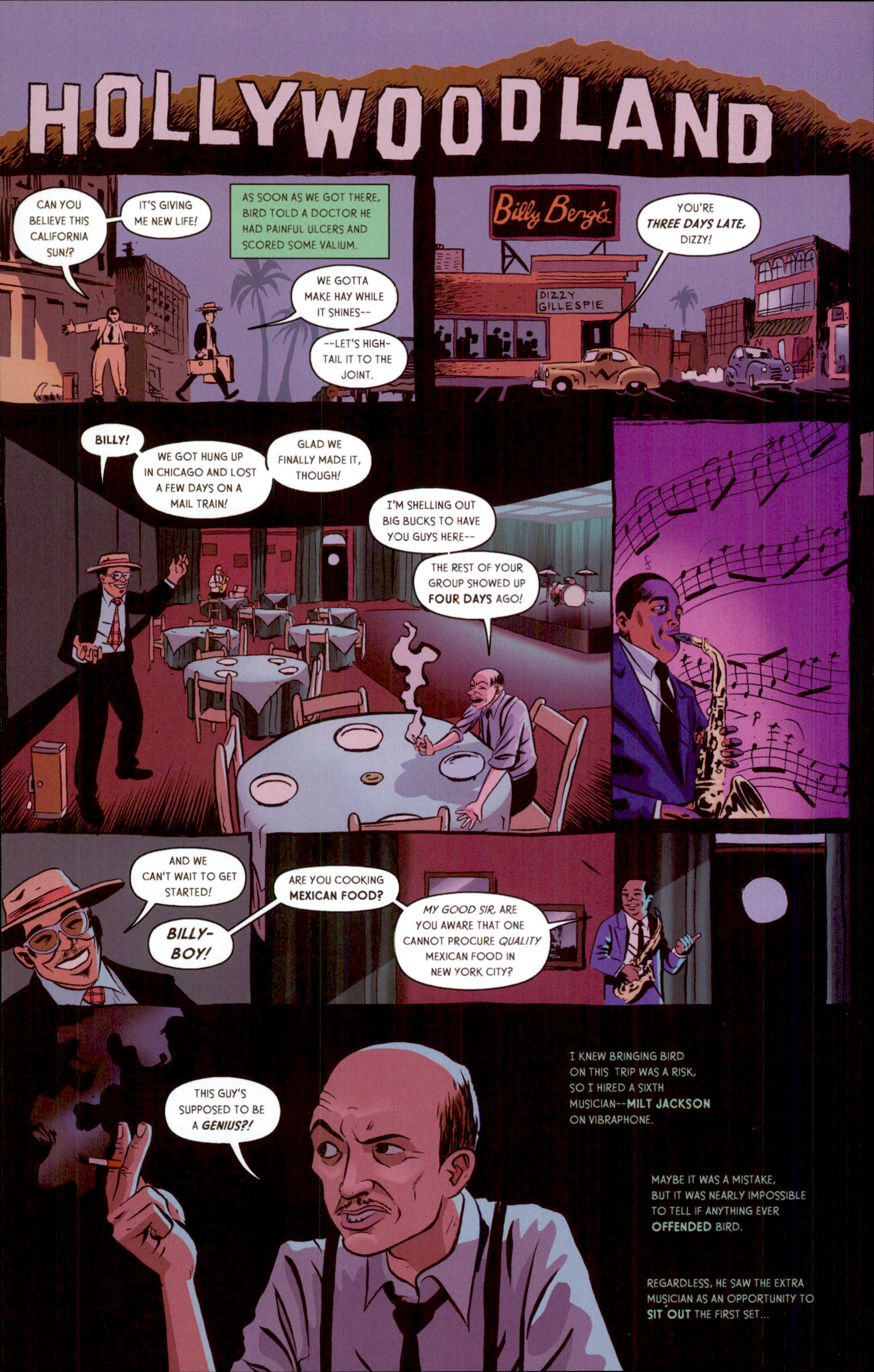
HOLLYWOODLAND
CAN YOU BELIEVE THIS CALIFORNIA SUN!?
IT'S GIVING ME NEW LIFE!
AS SOON AS WE GOT THERE, BIRD TOLD A DOCTOR HE HAD PAINFUL ULCERS AND SCORED SOME VALIUM.
WE GOTTA MAKE HAY WHILE IT SHINES--
--LET'S HIGH-TAIL IT TO THE JOINT.
Billy Berg's
DIZZY GILLESPIE
YOU'RE THREE DAYS LATE, DIZZY!
BILLY!
WE GOT HUNG UP IN CHICAGO AND LOST A FEW DAYS ON A MAIL TRAIN!
GLAD WE FINALLY MADE IT, THOUGH!
I'M SHELLING OUT BIG BUCKS TO HAVE YOU GUYS HERE--
THE REST OF YOUR GROUP SHOWED UP FOUR DAYS AGO!
AND WE CAN'T WAIT TO GET STARTED!
BILLY-BOY!
ARE YOU COOKING MEXICAN FOOD?
MY GOOD SIR, ARE YOU AWARE THAT ONE CANNOT PROCURE QUALITY MEXICAN FOOD IN NEW YORK CITY?
THIS GUY'S SUPPOSED TO BE A GENIUS?!
I KNEW BRINGING BIRD ON THIS TRIP WAS A RISK, SO I HIRED A SIXTH MUSICIAN--MILT JACKSON ON VIBRAPHONE.
MAYBE IT WAS A MISTAKE, BUT IT WAS NEARLY IMPOSSIBLE TO TELL IF ANYTHING EVER OFFENDED BIRD.
REGARDLESS, HE SAW THE EXTRA MUSICIAN AS AN OPPORTUNITY TO SIT OUT THE FIRST SET...

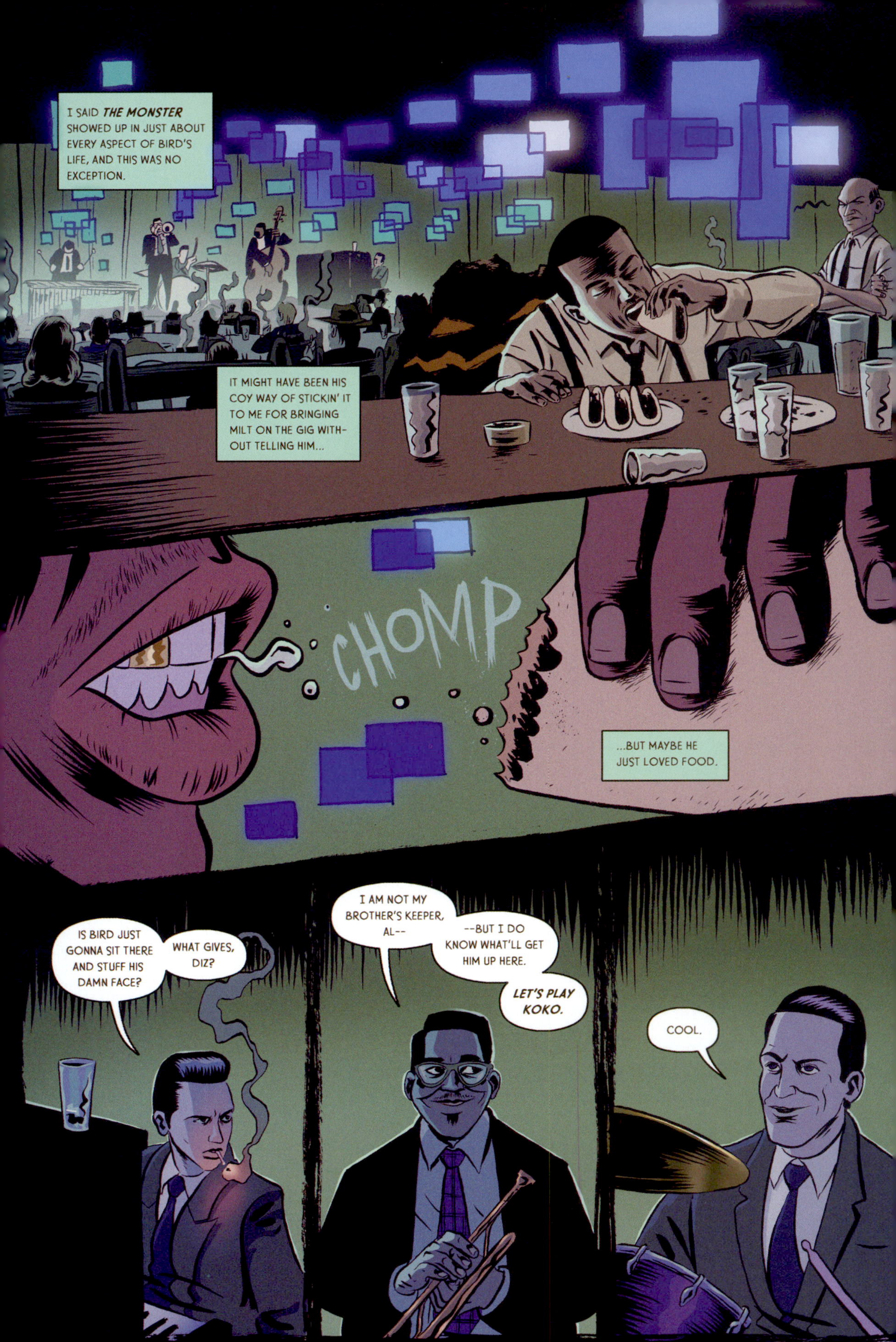
I SAID ***THE MONSTER*** SHOWED UP IN JUST ABOUT EVERY ASPECT OF BIRD'S LIFE, AND THIS WAS NO EXCEPTION.
IT MIGHT HAVE BEEN HIS COY WAY OF STICKIN' IT TO ME FOR BRINGING MILT ON THE GIG WITH-OUT TELLING HIM...
CHOMP
...BUT MAYBE HE JUST LOVED FOOD.
IS BIRD JUST GONNA SIT THERE AND STUFF HIS DAMN FACE?
WHAT GIVES, DIZ?
I AM NOT MY BROTHER'S KEEPER, AL--
--BUT I DO KNOW WHAT'LL GET HIM UP HERE.
LET'S PLAY KOKO.
COOL.

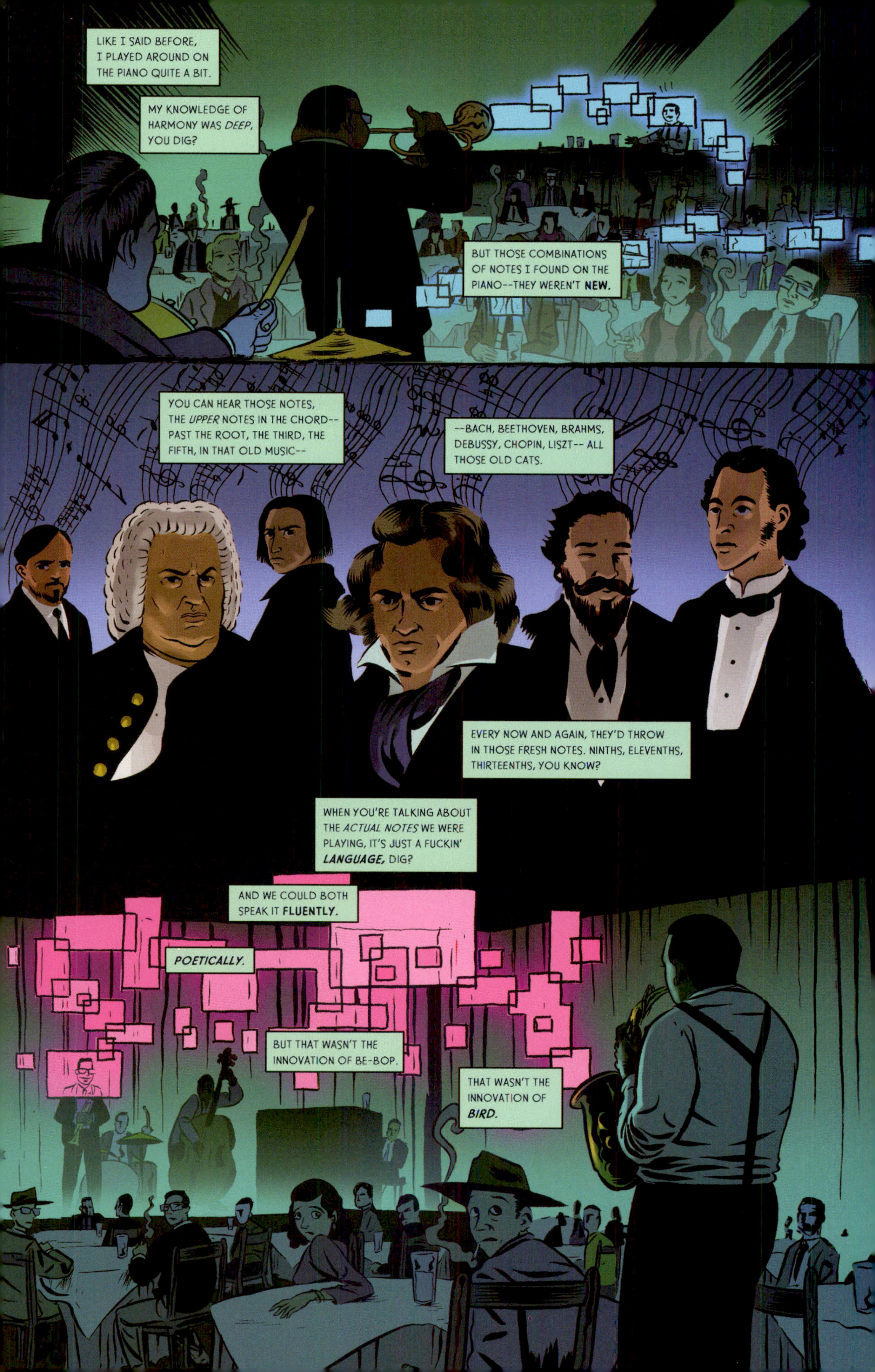
LIKE I SAID BEFORE, I PLAYED AROUND ON THE PIANO QUITE A BIT.
MY KNOWLEDGE OF HARMONY WAS *DEEP*, YOU DIG?
BUT THOSE COMBINATIONS OF NOTES I FOUND ON THE PIANO--THEY WEREN'T **NEW.**
YOU CAN HEAR THOSE NOTES, THE *UPPER* NOTES IN THE CHORD--PAST THE ROOT, THE THIRD, THE FIFTH, IN THAT OLD MUSIC--
--BACH, BEETHOVEN, BRAHMS, DEBUSSY, CHOPIN, LISZT-- ALL THOSE OLD CATS.
EVERY NOW AND AGAIN, THEY'D THROW IN THOSE FRESH NOTES. NINTHS, ELEVENTHS, THIRTEENTHS, YOU KNOW?
WHEN YOU'RE TALKING ABOUT THE *ACTUAL NOTES* WE WERE PLAYING, IT'S JUST A FUCKIN' ***LANGUAGE,*** DIG?
AND WE COULD BOTH SPEAK IT **FLUENTLY.**
POETICALLY.
BUT THAT WASN'T THE INNOVATION OF BE-BOP.
THAT WASN'T THE INNOVATION OF ***BIRD.***

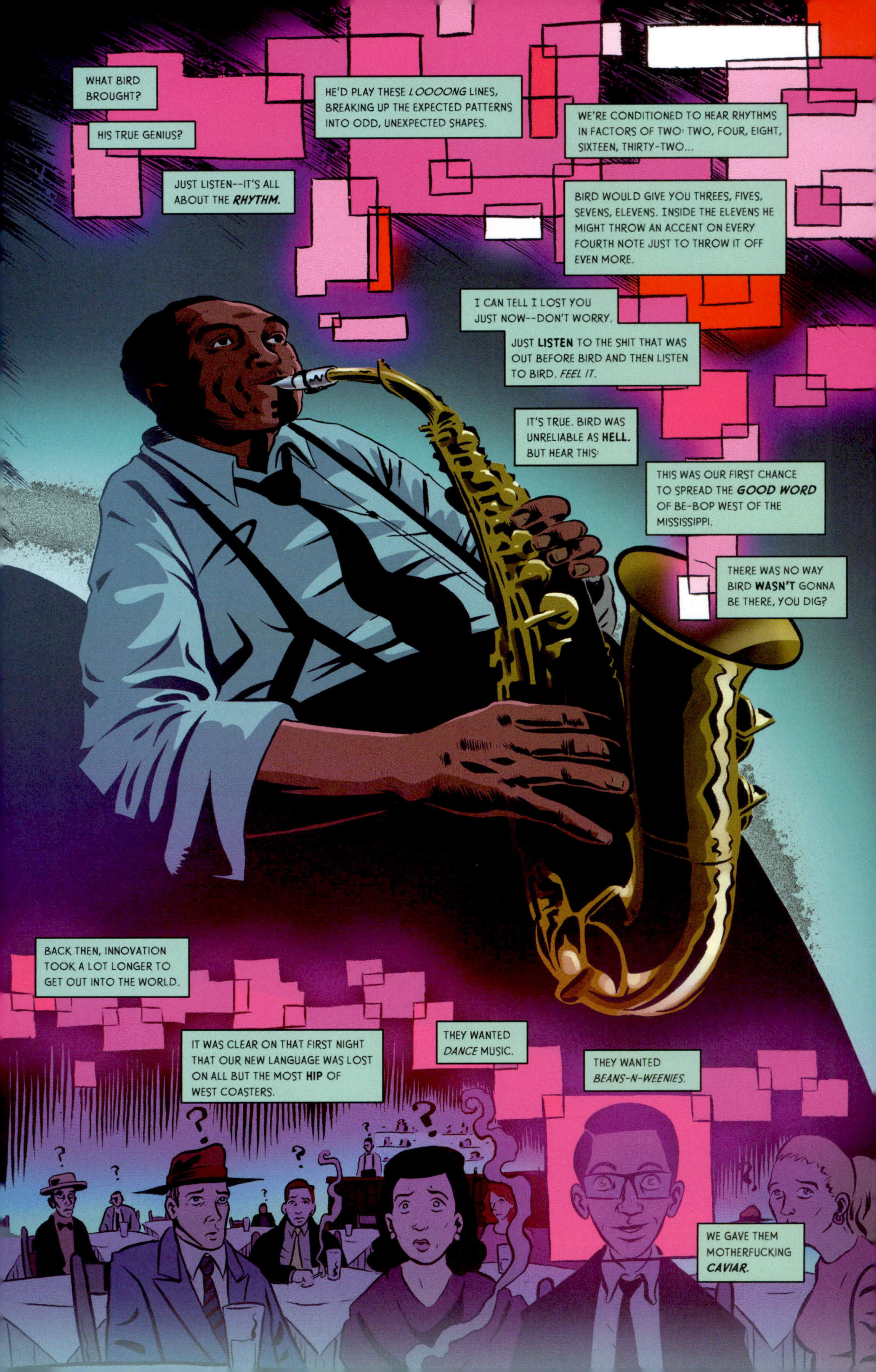
WHAT BIRD BROUGHT?
HIS TRUE GENIUS?
JUST LISTEN--IT'S ALL ABOUT THE *RHYTHM.*
HE'D PLAY THESE *LOOOONG* LINES, BREAKING UP THE EXPECTED PATTERNS INTO ODD, UNEXPECTED SHAPES.
WE'RE CONDITIONED TO HEAR RHYTHMS IN FACTORS OF TWO: TWO, FOUR, EIGHT, SIXTEEN, THIRTY-TWO...
BIRD WOULD GIVE YOU THREES, FIVES, SEVENS, ELEVENS. INSIDE THE ELEVENS HE MIGHT THROW AN ACCENT ON EVERY FOURTH NOTE JUST TO THROW IT OFF EVEN MORE.
I CAN TELL I LOST YOU JUST NOW--DON'T WORRY.
JUST **LISTEN** TO THE SHIT THAT WAS OUT BEFORE BIRD AND THEN LISTEN TO BIRD. *FEEL IT.*
IT'S TRUE. BIRD WAS UNRELIABLE AS **HELL.** BUT HEAR THIS:
THIS WAS OUR FIRST CHANCE TO SPREAD THE ***GOOD WORD*** OF BE-BOP WEST OF THE MISSISSIPPI.
THERE WAS NO WAY BIRD **WASN'T** GONNA BE THERE, YOU DIG?
BACK THEN, INNOVATION TOOK A LOT LONGER TO GET OUT INTO THE WORLD.
IT WAS CLEAR ON THAT FIRST NIGHT THAT OUR NEW LANGUAGE WAS LOST ON ALL BUT THE MOST **HIP** OF WEST COASTERS.
THEY WANTED *DANCE* MUSIC.
THEY WANTED *BEANS-N-WEENIES.*
WE GAVE THEM MOTHERFUCKING ***CAVIAR.***

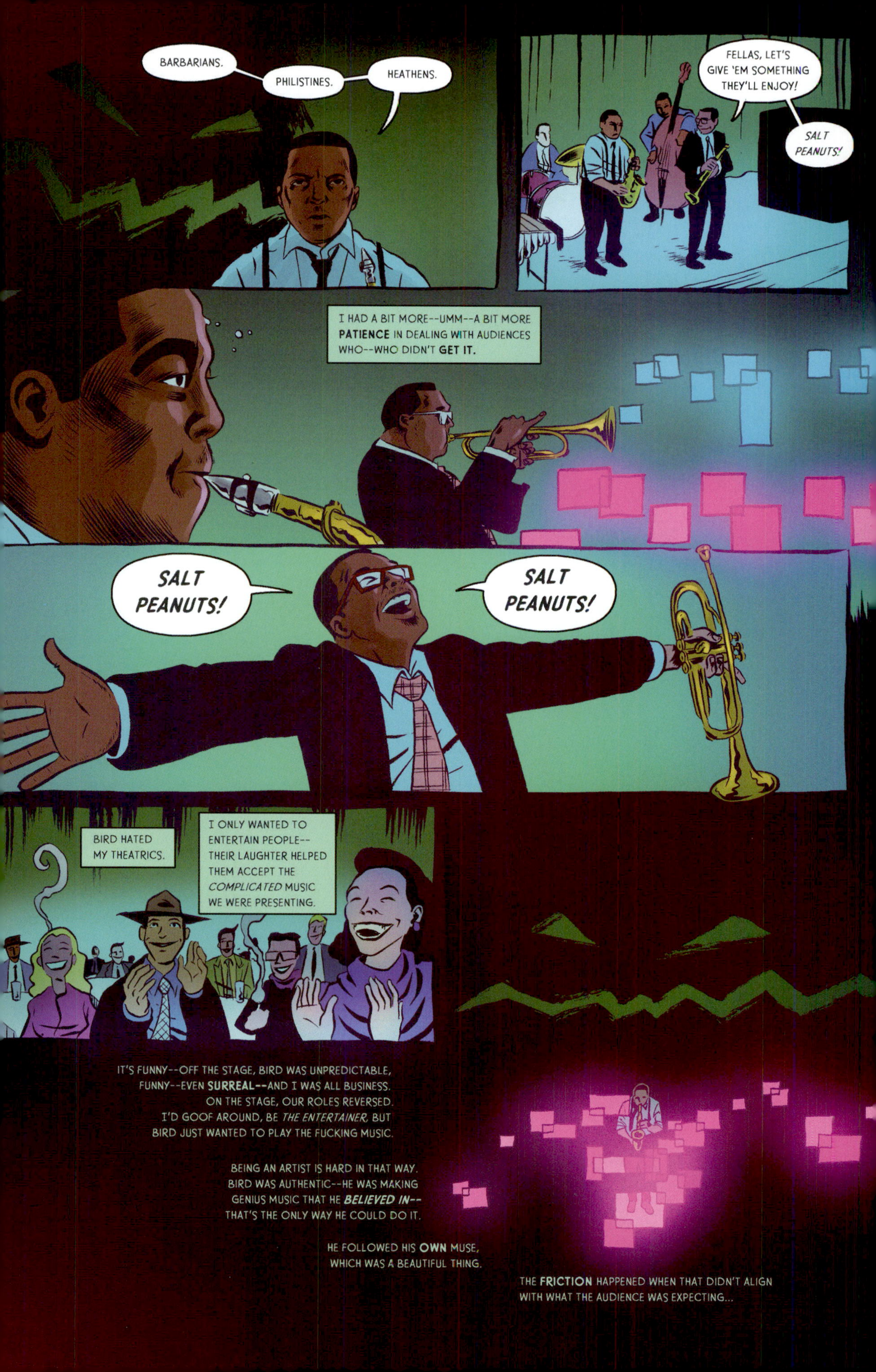
BARBARIANS.
PHILISTINES.
HEATHENS.
FELLAS, LET'S GIVE 'EM SOMETHING THEY'LL ENJOY!
SALT PEANUTS!
I HAD A BIT MORE--UMM--A BIT MORE PATIENCE IN DEALING WITH AUDIENCES WHO--WHO DIDN'T GET IT.
SALT PEANUTS!
SALT PEANUTS!
BIRD HATED MY THEATRICS.
I ONLY WANTED TO ENTERTAIN PEOPLE--THEIR LAUGHTER HELPED THEM ACCEPT THE COMPLICATED MUSIC WE WERE PRESENTING.
IT'S FUNNY--OFF THE STAGE, BIRD WAS UNPREDICTABLE, FUNNY--EVEN SURREAL--AND I WAS ALL BUSINESS. ON THE STAGE, OUR ROLES REVERSED. I'D GOOF AROUND, BE THE ENTERTAINER, BUT BIRD JUST WANTED TO PLAY THE FUCKING MUSIC.
BEING AN ARTIST IS HARD IN THAT WAY. BIRD WAS AUTHENTIC--HE WAS MAKING GENIUS MUSIC THAT HE BELIEVED IN--THAT'S THE ONLY WAY HE COULD DO IT.
HE FOLLOWED HIS OWN MUSE, WHICH WAS A BEAUTIFUL THING.
THE FRICTION HAPPENED WHEN THAT DIDN'T ALIGN WITH WHAT THE AUDIENCE WAS EXPECTING...

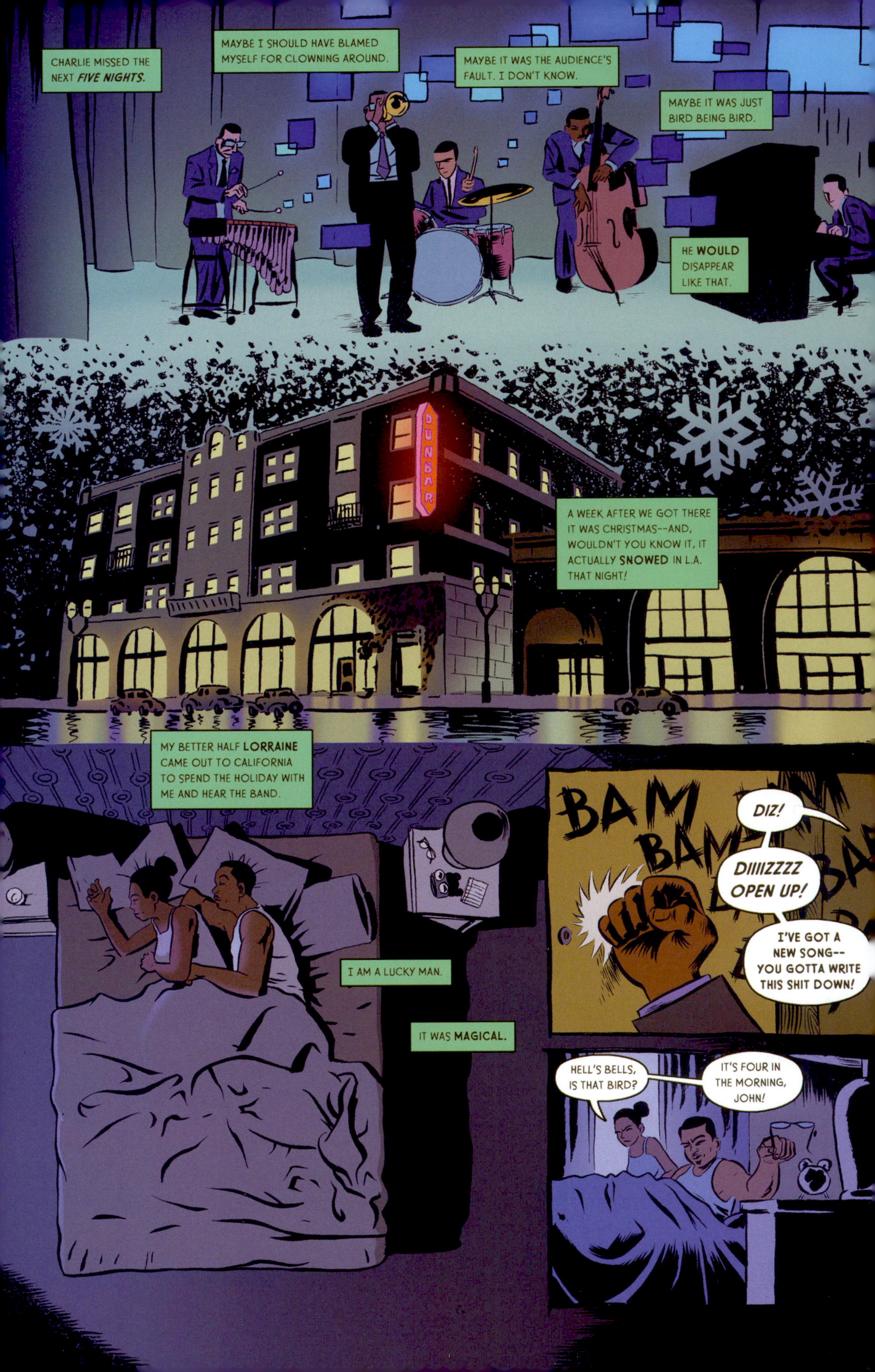

CHARLIE MISSED THE NEXT FIVE NIGHTS.
MAYBE I SHOULD HAVE BLAMED MYSELF FOR CLOWNING AROUND.
MAYBE IT WAS THE AUDIENCE'S FAULT. I DON'T KNOW.
MAYBE IT WAS JUST BIRD BEING BIRD.
HE WOULD DISAPPEAR LIKE THAT.
DUNBAR
A WEEK AFTER WE GOT THERE IT WAS CHRISTMAS--AND, WOULDN'T YOU KNOW IT, IT ACTUALLY SNOWED IN L.A. THAT NIGHT!
MY BETTER HALF LORRAINE CAME OUT TO CALIFORNIA TO SPEND THE HOLIDAY WITH ME AND HEAR THE BAND.
I AM A LUCKY MAN.
IT WAS MAGICAL.
BAM
BAM
DIZ!
DIIIIZZZZ OPEN UP!
I'VE GOT A NEW SONG-- YOU GOTTA WRITE THIS SHIT DOWN!
HELL'S BELLS, IS THAT BIRD?
IT'S FOUR IN THE MORNING, JOHN!

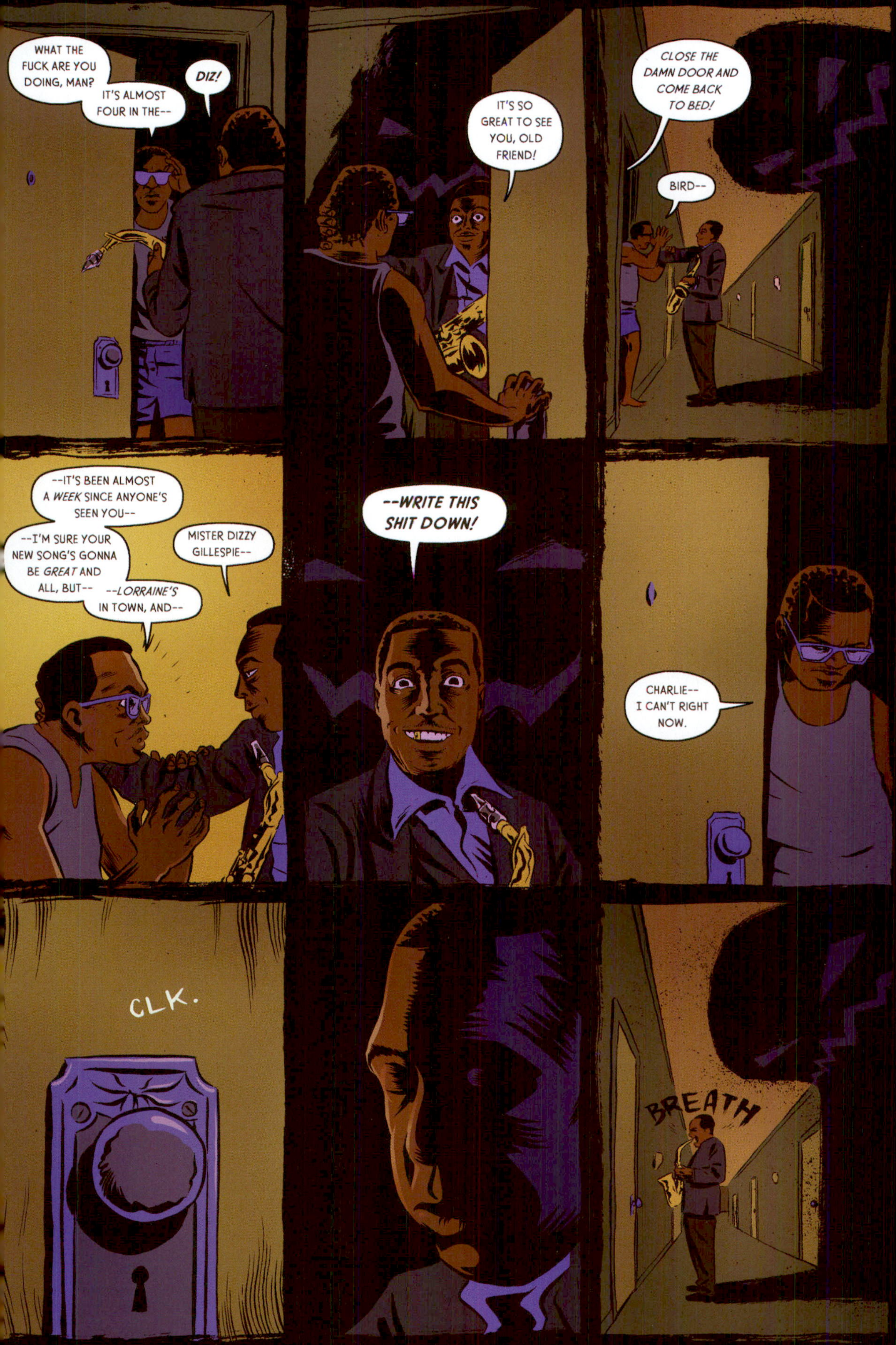
WHAT THE FUCK ARE YOU DOING, MAN?
IT'S ALMOST FOUR IN THE--
DIZ!
IT'S SO GREAT TO SEE YOU, OLD FRIEND!
CLOSE THE DAMN DOOR AND COME BACK TO BED!
BIRD--
--IT'S BEEN ALMOST A *WEEK* SINCE ANYONE'S SEEN YOU--
--I'M SURE YOUR NEW SONG'S GONNA BE *GREAT* AND ALL, BUT--
--*LORRAINE'S* IN TOWN, AND--
MISTER DIZZY GILLESPIE--
--WRITE THIS SHIT DOWN!
CHARLIE-- I CAN'T RIGHT NOW.
CLK.
BREATH

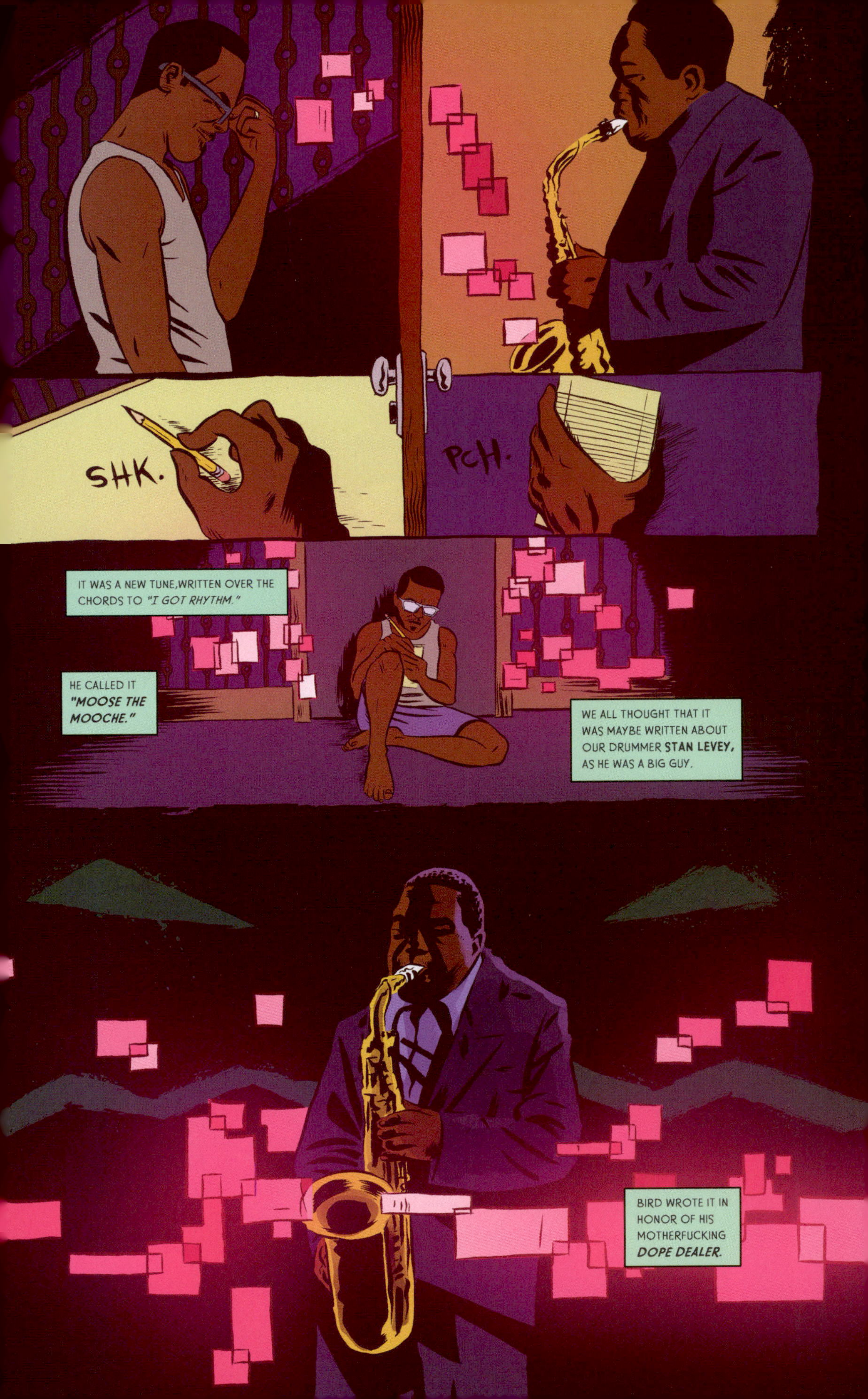
SHK.
PCH.
IT WAS A NEW TUNE, WRITTEN OVER THE CHORDS TO "I GOT RHYTHM."
HE CALLED IT "MOOSE THE MOOCHE."
WE ALL THOUGHT THAT IT WAS MAYBE WRITTEN ABOUT OUR DRUMMER STAN LEVEY, AS HE WAS A BIG GUY.
BIRD WROTE IT IN HONOR OF HIS MOTHERFUCKING DOPE DEALER.

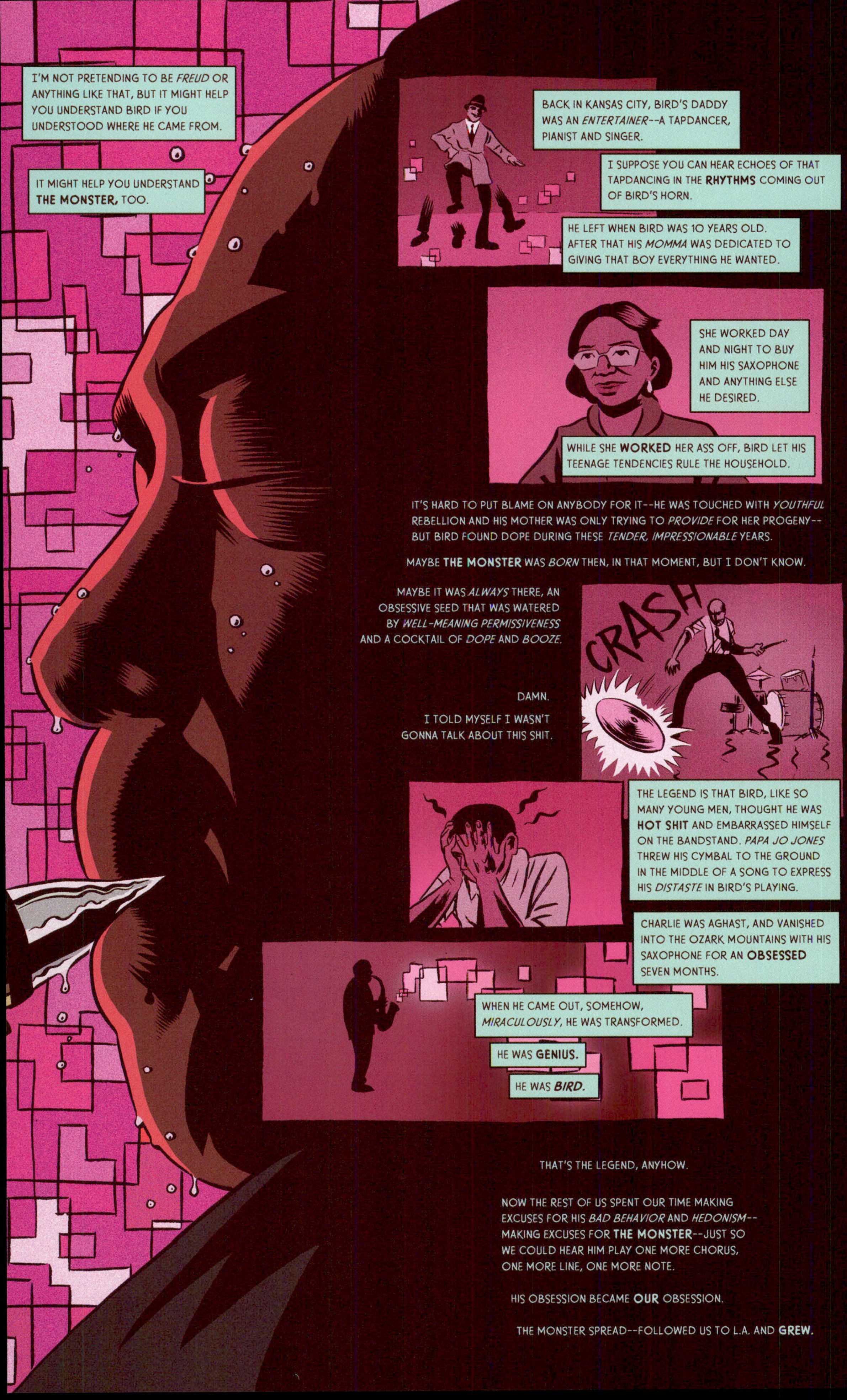

I'M NOT PRETENDING TO BE FREUD OR ANYTHING LIKE THAT, BUT IT MIGHT HELP YOU UNDERSTAND BIRD IF YOU UNDERSTOOD WHERE HE CAME FROM.
IT MIGHT HELP YOU UNDERSTAND THE MONSTER, TOO.
BACK IN KANSAS CITY, BIRD'S DADDY WAS AN ENTERTAINER--A TAPDANCER, PIANIST AND SINGER.
I SUPPOSE YOU CAN HEAR ECHOES OF THAT TAPDANCING IN THE RHYTHMS COMING OUT OF BIRD'S HORN.
HE LEFT WHEN BIRD WAS 10 YEARS OLD. AFTER THAT HIS MOMMA WAS DEDICATED TO GIVING THAT BOY EVERYTHING HE WANTED.
SHE WORKED DAY AND NIGHT TO BUY HIM HIS SAXOPHONE AND ANYTHING ELSE HE DESIRED.
WHILE SHE WORKED HER ASS OFF, BIRD LET HIS TEENAGE TENDENCIES RULE THE HOUSEHOLD.
IT'S HARD TO PUT BLAME ON ANYBODY FOR IT--HE WAS TOUCHED WITH YOUTHFUL REBELLION AND HIS MOTHER WAS ONLY TRYING TO PROVIDE FOR HER PROGENY--BUT BIRD FOUND DOPE DURING THESE TENDER, IMPRESSIONABLE YEARS.
MAYBE THE MONSTER WAS BORN THEN, IN THAT MOMENT, BUT I DON'T KNOW.
MAYBE IT WAS ALWAYS THERE, AN OBSESSIVE SEED THAT WAS WATERED BY WELL-MEANING PERMISSIVENESS AND A COCKTAIL OF DOPE AND BOOZE.
CRASH
DAMN.
I TOLD MYSELF I WASN'T GONNA TALK ABOUT THIS SHIT.
THE LEGEND IS THAT BIRD, LIKE SO MANY YOUNG MEN, THOUGHT HE WAS HOT SHIT AND EMBARRASSED HIMSELF ON THE BANDSTAND. PAPA JO JONES THREW HIS CYMBAL TO THE GROUND IN THE MIDDLE OF A SONG TO EXPRESS HIS DISTASTE IN BIRD'S PLAYING.
CHARLIE WAS AGHAST, AND VANISHED INTO THE OZARK MOUNTAINS WITH HIS SAXOPHONE FOR AN OBSESSED SEVEN MONTHS.
WHEN HE CAME OUT, SOMEHOW, MIRACULOUSLY, HE WAS TRANSFORMED.
HE WAS GENIUS.
HE WAS BIRD.
THAT'S THE LEGEND, ANYHOW.
NOW THE REST OF US SPENT OUR TIME MAKING EXCUSES FOR HIS BAD BEHAVIOR AND HEDONISM--MAKING EXCUSES FOR THE MONSTER--JUST SO WE COULD HEAR HIM PLAY ONE MORE CHORUS, ONE MORE LINE, ONE MORE NOTE.
HIS OBSESSION BECAME OUR OBSESSION.
THE MONSTER SPREAD--FOLLOWED US TO L.A. AND GREW.

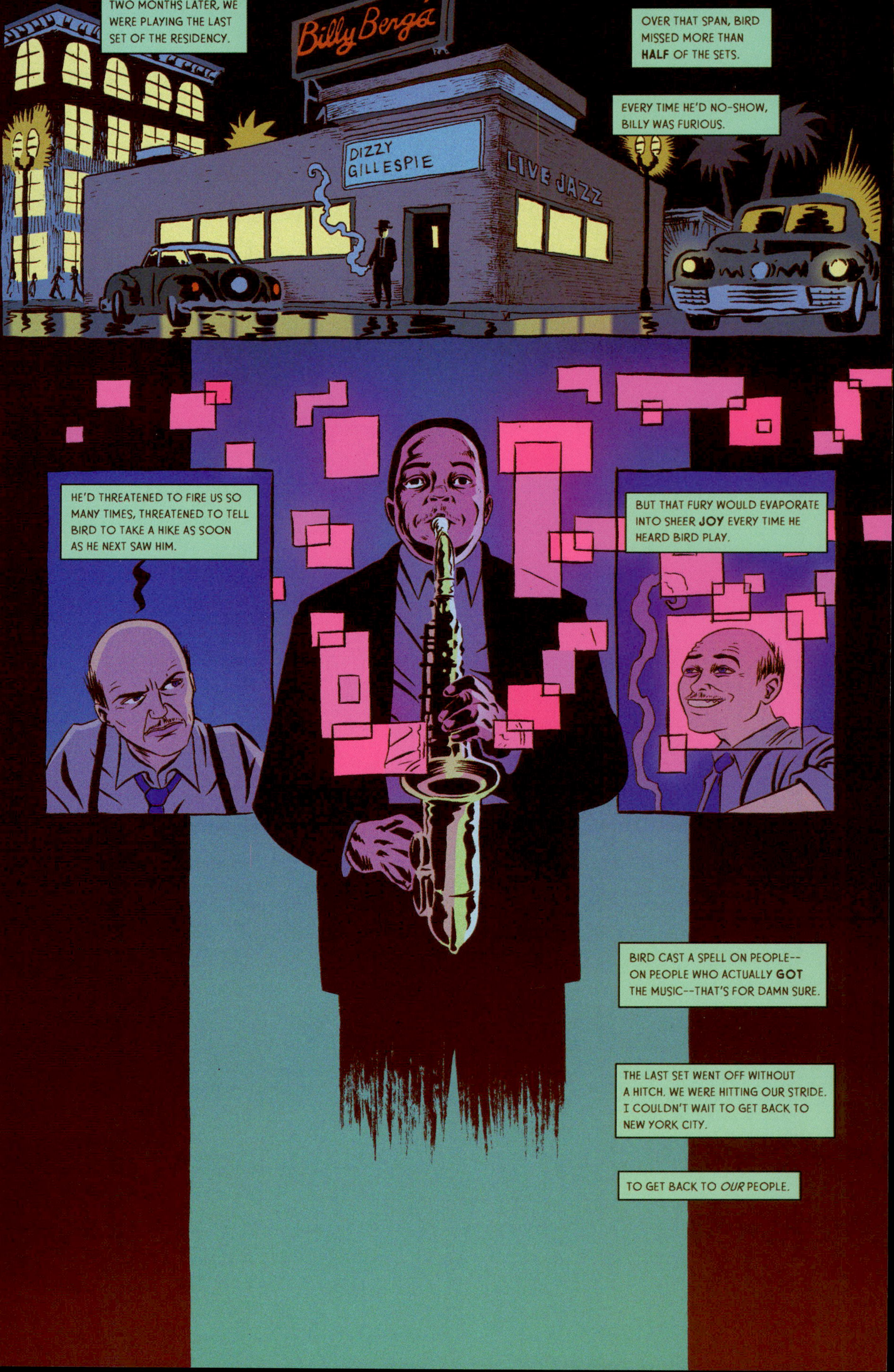

TWO MONTHS LATER, WE WERE PLAYING THE LAST SET OF THE RESIDENCY.
Billy Berg's
OVER THAT SPAN, BIRD MISSED MORE THAN **HALF** OF THE SETS.
EVERY TIME HE'D NO-SHOW, BILLY WAS FURIOUS.
DIZZY GILLESPIE
LIVE JAZZ
HE'D THREATENED TO FIRE US SO MANY TIMES, THREATENED TO TELL BIRD TO TAKE A HIKE AS SOON AS HE NEXT SAW HIM.
BUT THAT FURY WOULD EVAPORATE INTO SHEER **JOY** EVERY TIME HE HEARD BIRD PLAY.
BIRD CAST A SPELL ON PEOPLE-- ON PEOPLE WHO ACTUALLY **GOT** THE MUSIC--THAT'S FOR DAMN SURE.
THE LAST SET WENT OFF WITHOUT A HITCH. WE WERE HITTING OUR STRIDE. I COULDN'T WAIT TO GET BACK TO NEW YORK CITY.
TO GET BACK TO *OUR* PEOPLE.

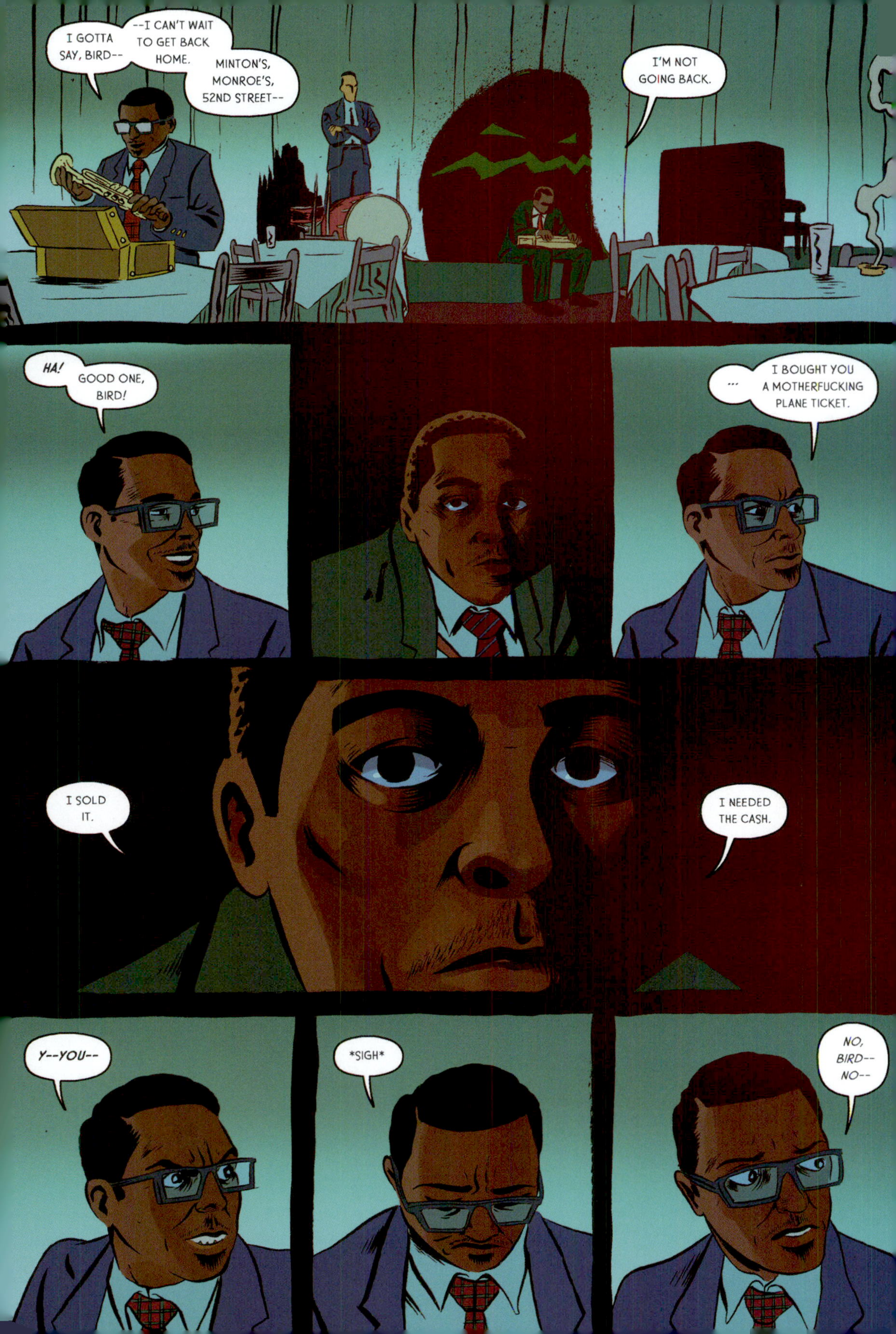
I GOTTA SAY, BIRD--
--I CAN'T WAIT TO GET BACK HOME.
MINTON'S, MONROE'S, 52ND STREET--
I'M NOT GOING BACK.
HA! GOOD ONE, BIRD!
...
I BOUGHT YOU A MOTHERFUCKING PLANE TICKET.
I SOLD IT.
I NEEDED THE CASH.
Y--YOU--
SIGH
NO, BIRD-- NO--

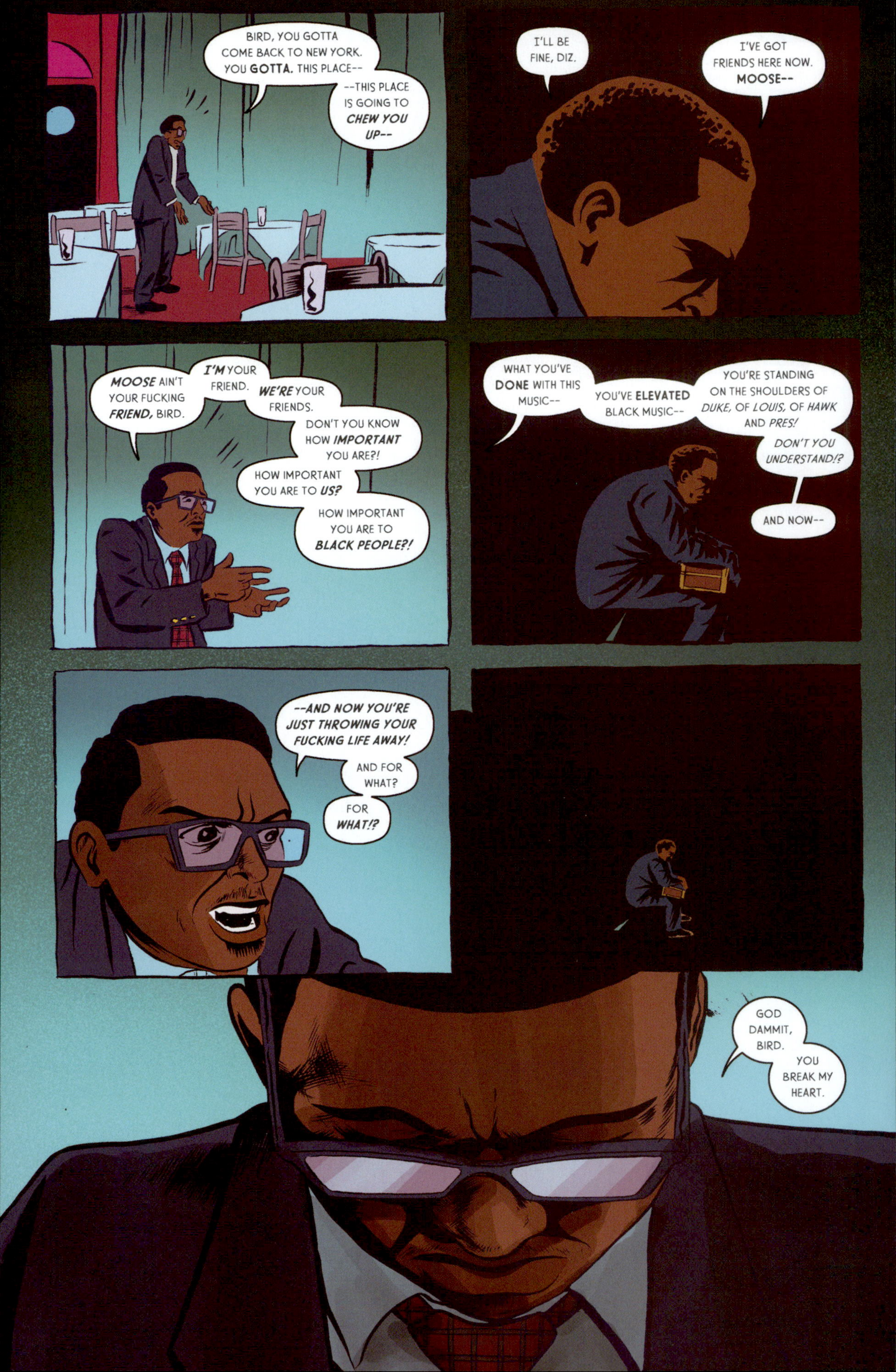
BIRD, YOU GOTTA COME BACK TO NEW YORK. YOU GOTTA. THIS PLACE--
--THIS PLACE IS GOING TO CHEW YOU UP--
I'LL BE FINE, DIZ.
I'VE GOT FRIENDS HERE NOW. MOOSE--
MOOSE AIN'T YOUR FUCKING FRIEND, BIRD.
I'M YOUR FRIEND.
WE'RE YOUR FRIENDS.
DON'T YOU KNOW HOW IMPORTANT YOU ARE?!
HOW IMPORTANT YOU ARE TO US?
HOW IMPORTANT YOU ARE TO BLACK PEOPLE?!
WHAT YOU'VE DONE WITH THIS MUSIC--
YOU'VE ELEVATED BLACK MUSIC--
YOU'RE STANDING ON THE SHOULDERS OF DUKE, OF LOUIS, OF HAWK AND PRES!
DON'T YOU UNDERSTAND!?
AND NOW--
--AND NOW YOU'RE JUST THROWING YOUR FUCKING LIFE AWAY!
AND FOR WHAT?
FOR WHAT!?
GOD DAMMIT, BIRD.
YOU BREAK MY HEART.

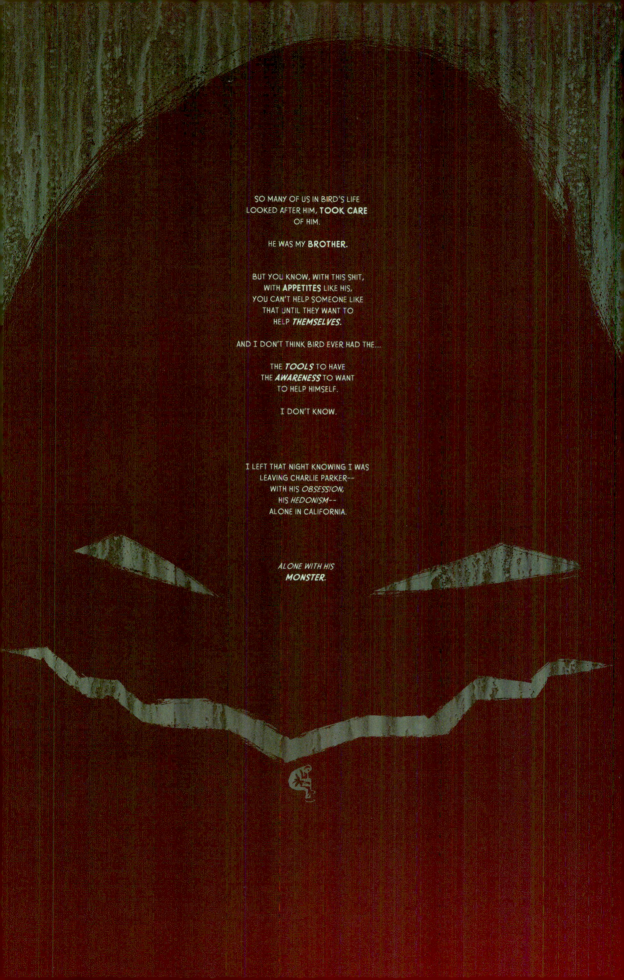

SO MANY OF US IN BIRD'S LIFE
LOOKED AFTER HIM, **TOOK CARE**
OF HIM.

HE WAS MY **BROTHER.**

BUT YOU KNOW, WITH THIS SHIT,
WITH **APPETITES** LIKE HIS,
YOU CAN'T HELP SOMEONE LIKE
THAT UNTIL THEY WANT TO
HELP *THEMSELVES.*

AND I DON'T THINK BIRD EVER HAD THE...

THE **TOOLS** TO HAVE
THE **AWARENESS** TO WANT
TO HELP HIMSELF.

I DON'T KNOW.

I LEFT THAT NIGHT KNOWING I WAS
LEAVING CHARLIE PARKER--
WITH HIS *OBSESSION,*
HIS *HEDONISM--*
ALONE IN CALIFORNIA.

ALONE WITH HIS
MONSTER.

CHORUS 2:
ZORTHIAN

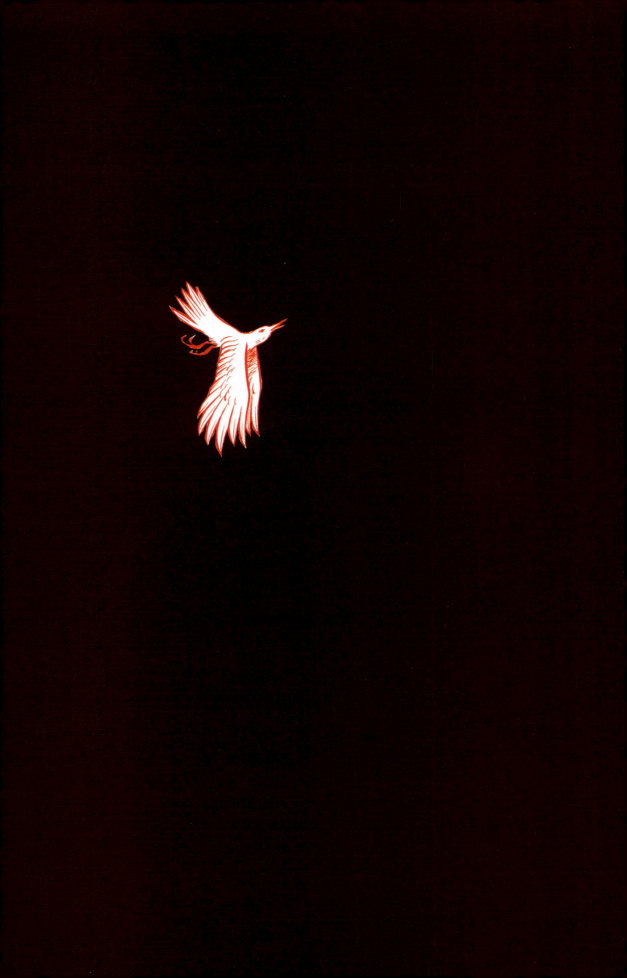

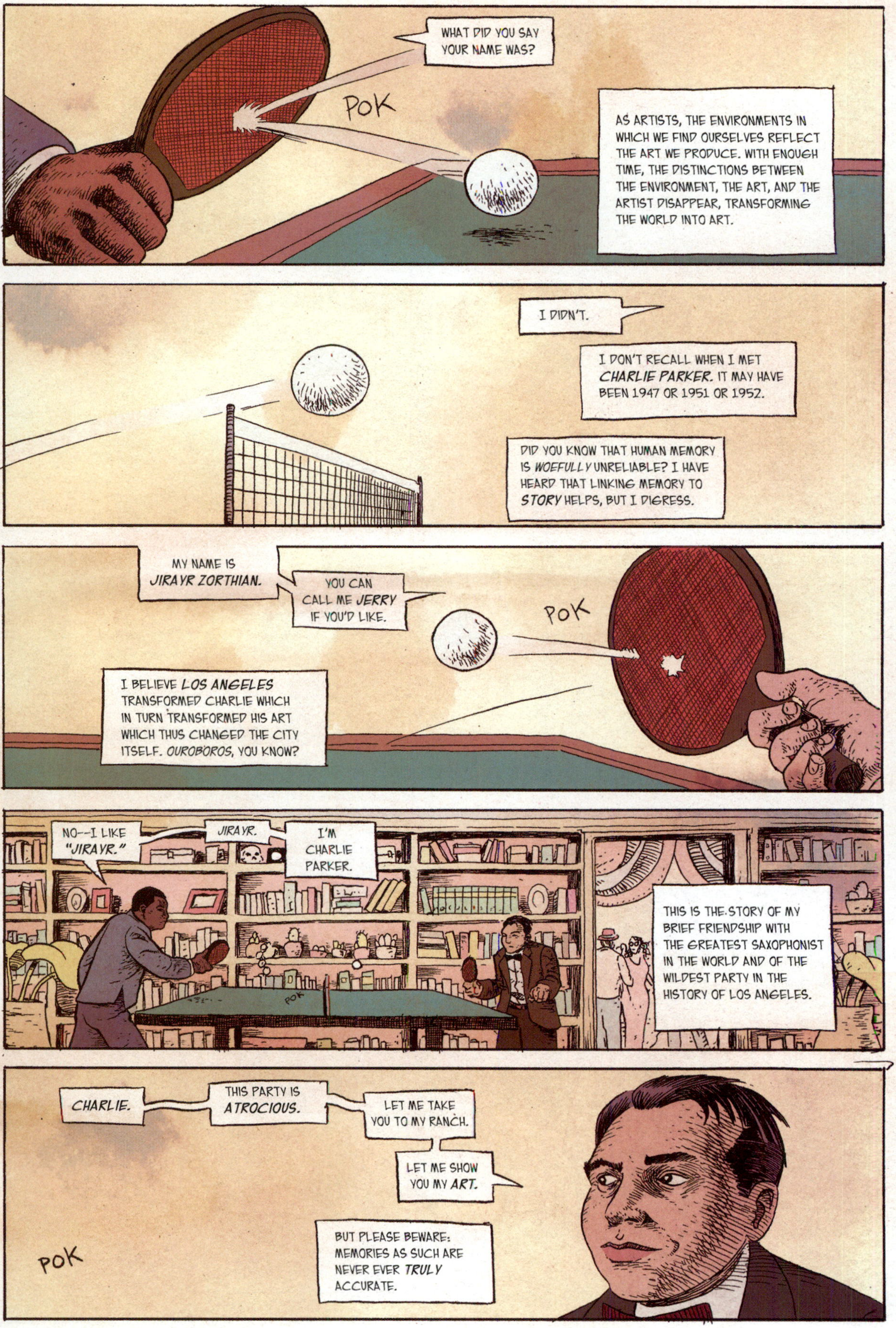
WHAT DID YOU SAY YOUR NAME WAS?
POK
AS ARTISTS, THE ENVIRONMENTS IN WHICH WE FIND OURSELVES REFLECT THE ART WE PRODUCE. WITH ENOUGH TIME, THE DISTINCTIONS BETWEEN THE ENVIRONMENT, THE ART, AND THE ARTIST DISAPPEAR, TRANSFORMING THE WORLD INTO ART.
I DIDN'T.
I DON'T RECALL WHEN I MET *CHARLIE PARKER.* IT MAY HAVE BEEN 1947 OR 1951 OR 1952.
DID YOU KNOW THAT HUMAN MEMORY IS *WOEFULLY* UNRELIABLE? I HAVE HEARD THAT LINKING MEMORY TO *STORY* HELPS, BUT I DIGRESS.
MY NAME IS *JIRAYR ZORTHIAN.*
YOU CAN CALL ME *JERRY* IF YOU'D LIKE.
POK
I BELIEVE *LOS ANGELES* TRANSFORMED CHARLIE WHICH IN TURN TRANSFORMED HIS ART WHICH THUS CHANGED THE CITY ITSELF. *OUROBOROS,* YOU KNOW?
NO--I LIKE *"JIRAYR."*
JIRAYR.
I'M CHARLIE PARKER.
POK
THIS IS THE STORY OF MY BRIEF FRIENDSHIP WITH THE GREATEST SAXOPHONIST IN THE WORLD AND OF THE WILDEST PARTY IN THE HISTORY OF LOS ANGELES.
CHARLIE.
THIS PARTY IS *ATROCIOUS.*
LET ME TAKE YOU TO MY RANCH.
LET ME SHOW YOU MY *ART.*
BUT PLEASE BEWARE: MEMORIES AS SUCH ARE NEVER EVER *TRULY* ACCURATE.
POK

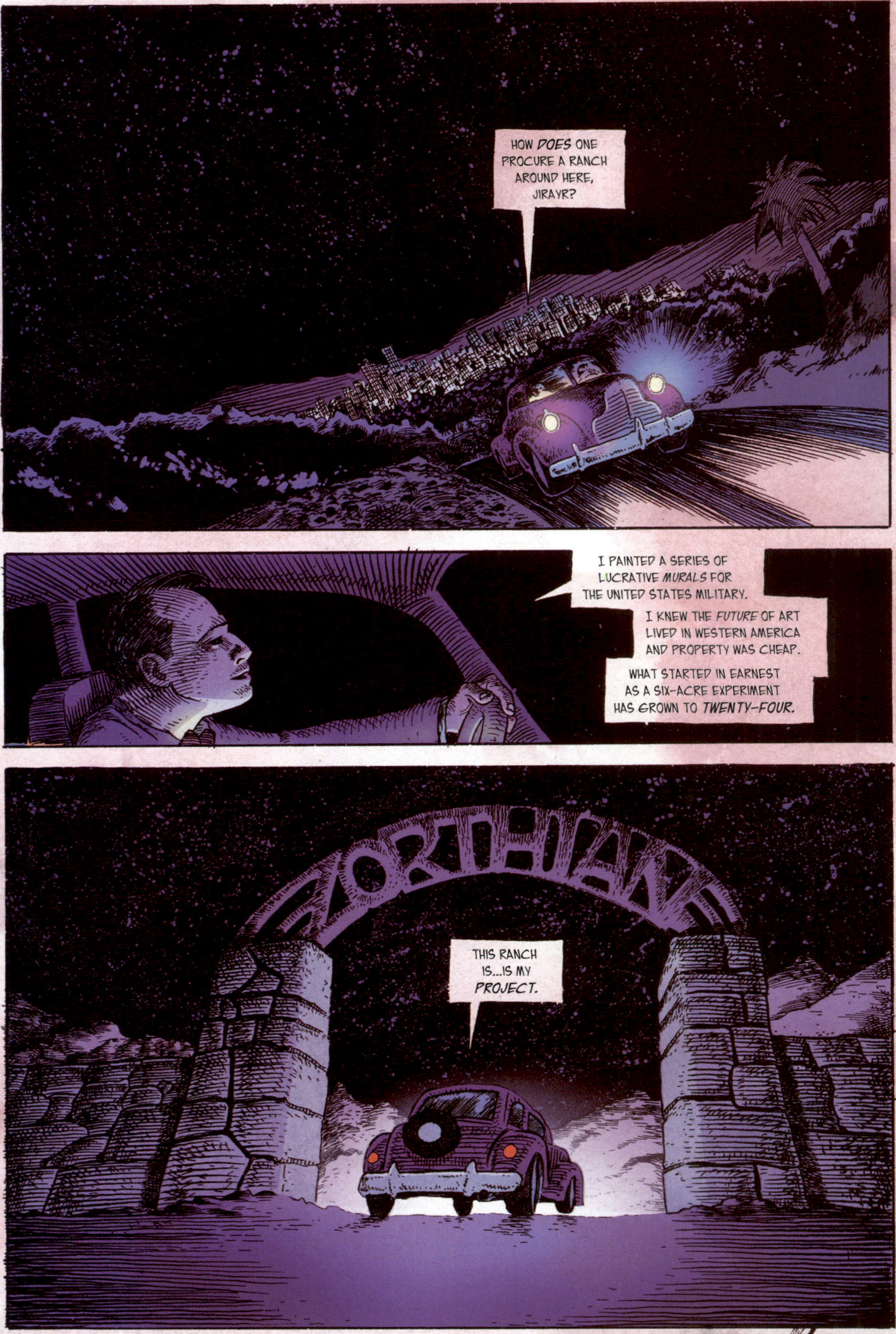

HOW *DOES* ONE PROCURE A RANCH AROUND HERE, JIRAYR?
I PAINTED A SERIES OF LUCRATIVE *MURALS* FOR THE UNITED STATES MILITARY.
I KNEW THE *FUTURE* OF ART LIVED IN WESTERN AMERICA AND PROPERTY WAS CHEAP.
WHAT STARTED IN EARNEST AS A SIX-ACRE EXPERIMENT HAS GROWN TO *TWENTY-FOUR.*
THIS RANCH IS...IS MY *PROJECT.*

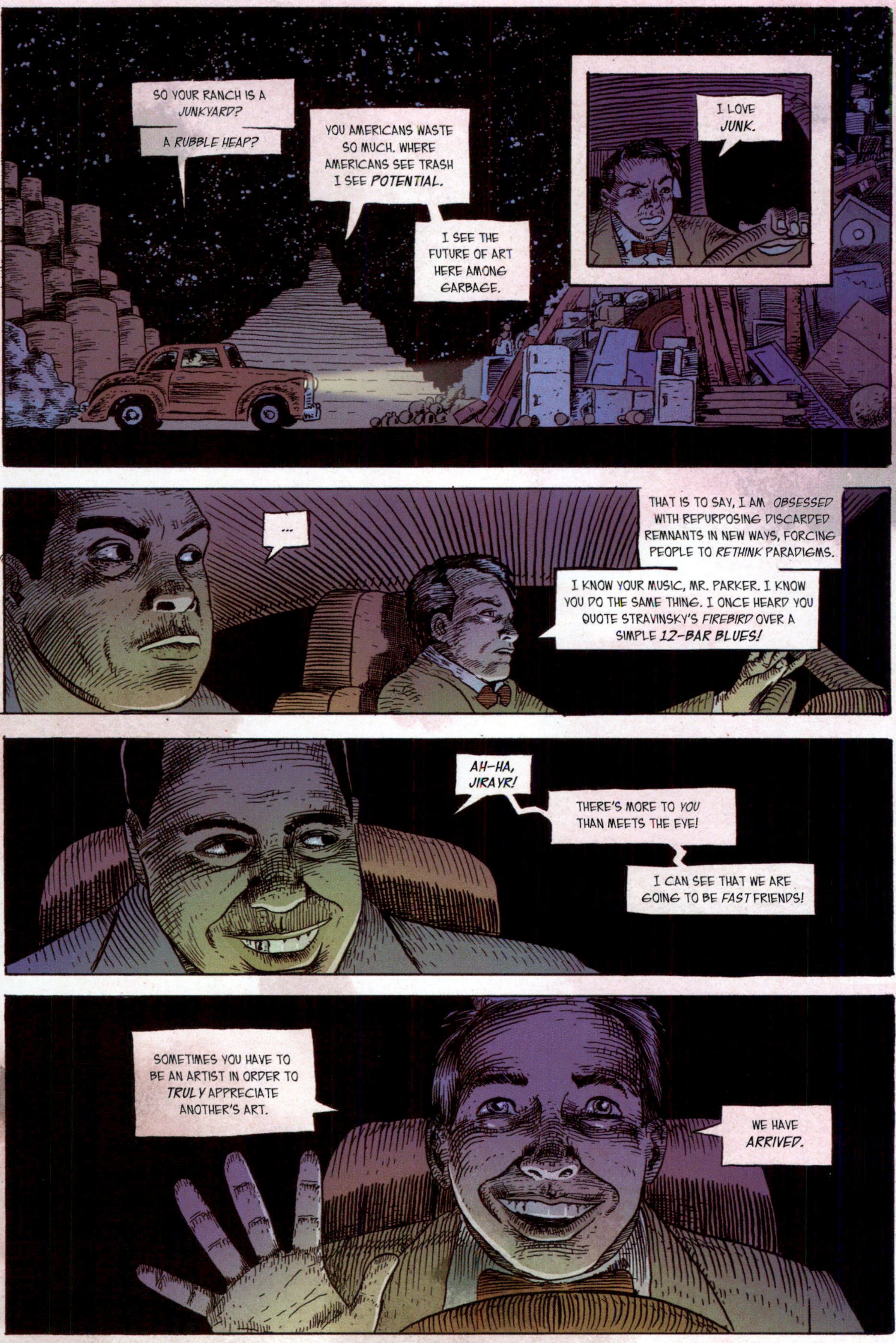
SO YOUR RANCH IS A JUNKYARD?
A RUBBLE HEAP?
YOU AMERICANS WASTE SO MUCH. WHERE AMERICANS SEE TRASH I SEE POTENTIAL.
I SEE THE FUTURE OF ART HERE AMONG GARBAGE.
I LOVE JUNK.
...
THAT IS TO SAY, I AM OBSESSED WITH REPURPOSING DISCARDED REMNANTS IN NEW WAYS, FORCING PEOPLE TO RETHINK PARADIGMS.
I KNOW YOUR MUSIC, MR. PARKER. I KNOW YOU DO THE SAME THING. I ONCE HEARD YOU QUOTE STRAVINSKY'S FIREBIRD OVER A SIMPLE 12-BAR BLUES!
AH-HA, JIRAYR!
THERE'S MORE TO YOU THAN MEETS THE EYE!
I CAN SEE THAT WE ARE GOING TO BE FAST FRIENDS!
SOMETIMES YOU HAVE TO BE AN ARTIST IN ORDER TO TRULY APPRECIATE ANOTHER'S ART.
WE HAVE ARRIVED.

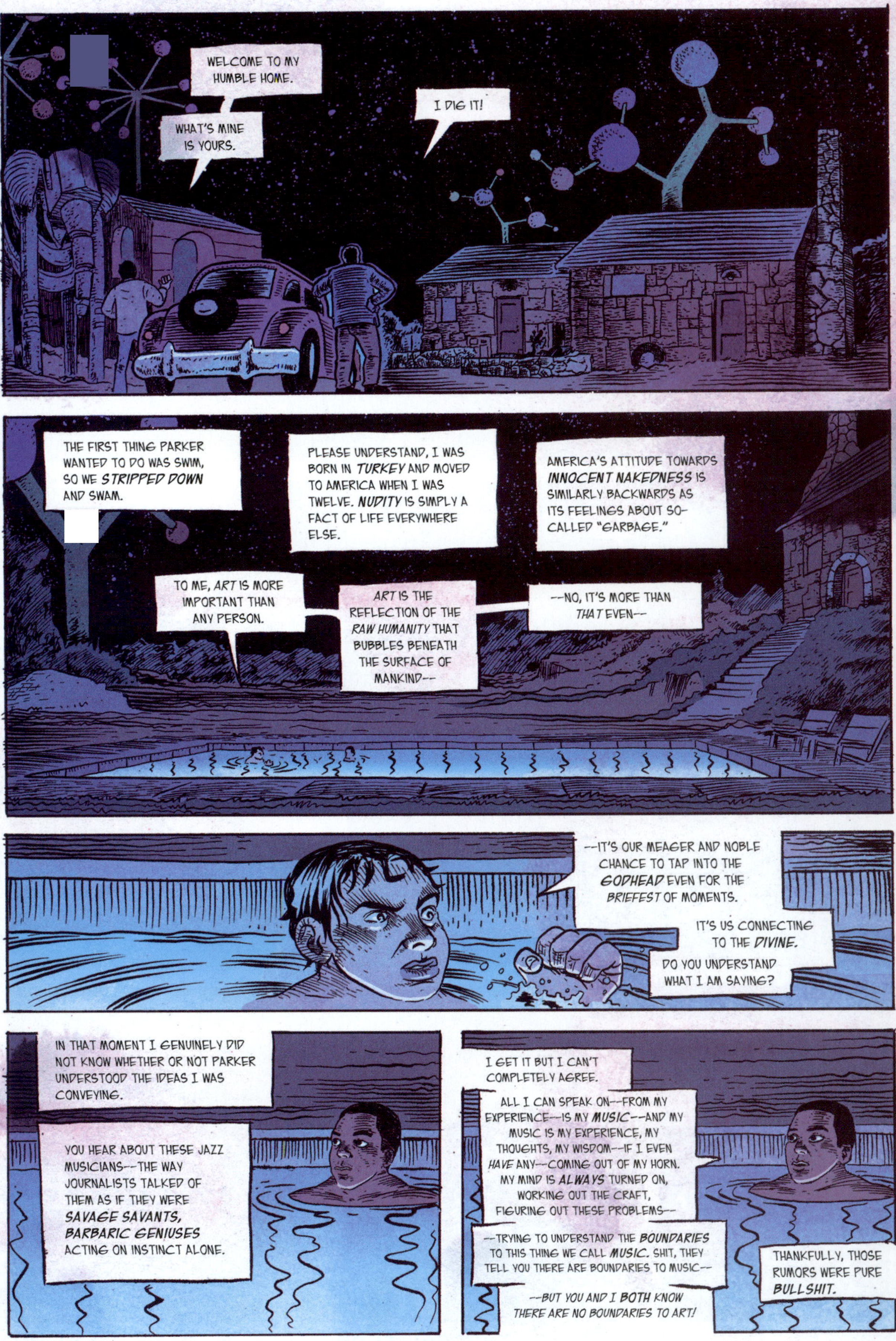
WELCOME TO MY HUMBLE HOME.
WHAT'S MINE IS YOURS.
I DIG IT!
THE FIRST THING PARKER WANTED TO DO WAS SWIM, SO WE STRIPPED DOWN AND SWAM.
PLEASE UNDERSTAND, I WAS BORN IN TURKEY AND MOVED TO AMERICA WHEN I WAS TWELVE. NUDITY IS SIMPLY A FACT OF LIFE EVERYWHERE ELSE.
AMERICA'S ATTITUDE TOWARDS INNOCENT NAKEDNESS IS SIMILARLY BACKWARDS AS ITS FEELINGS ABOUT SO-CALLED "GARBAGE."
TO ME, ART IS MORE IMPORTANT THAN ANY PERSON.
ART IS THE REFLECTION OF THE RAW HUMANITY THAT BUBBLES BENEATH THE SURFACE OF MANKIND--
--NO, IT'S MORE THAN THAT EVEN--
--IT'S OUR MEAGER AND NOBLE CHANCE TO TAP INTO THE GODHEAD EVEN FOR THE BRIEFEST OF MOMENTS.
IT'S US CONNECTING TO THE DIVINE.
DO YOU UNDERSTAND WHAT I AM SAYING?
IN THAT MOMENT I GENUINELY DID NOT KNOW WHETHER OR NOT PARKER UNDERSTOOD THE IDEAS I WAS CONVEYING.
YOU HEAR ABOUT THESE JAZZ MUSICIANS--THE WAY JOURNALISTS TALKED OF THEM AS IF THEY WERE SAVAGE SAVANTS, BARBARIC GENIUSES ACTING ON INSTINCT ALONE.
I GET IT BUT I CAN'T COMPLETELY AGREE.
ALL I CAN SPEAK ON--FROM MY EXPERIENCE--IS MY MUSIC--AND MY MUSIC IS MY EXPERIENCE, MY THOUGHTS, MY WISDOM--IF I EVEN HAVE ANY--COMING OUT OF MY HORN. MY MIND IS ALWAYS TURNED ON, WORKING OUT THE CRAFT, FIGURING OUT THESE PROBLEMS--
--TRYING TO UNDERSTAND THE BOUNDARIES TO THIS THING WE CALL MUSIC. SHIT, THEY TELL YOU THERE ARE BOUNDARIES TO MUSIC--
--BUT YOU AND I BOTH KNOW THERE ARE NO BOUNDARIES TO ART!
THANKFULLY, THOSE RUMORS WERE PURE BULLSHIT.

AFTER SWIMMING, WE RODE HORSES AND TALKED, WAITING FOR THE SUN TO RISE.

CHARLIE HAD NEVER RIDDEN A HORSE BEFORE, BUT WITHIN MINUTES HE HAD IT *COMPLETELY* FIGURED OUT.

TELL ME, JIRAYR: ALL OF THESE SCULPTURES--

--THEY'RE MADE OF DISCARDED PARTS?

YES.

IT'S MY CURRENT OBSESSION.

THAT'S ALL ANYTHING IS, RIGHT?

EVERY PAINTING, EVERY SCULPTURE, EVERY PERSON, EVERY *THING*--

ASSEMBLAGES OF DISCARDED *PARTS.*

HOW DO YOU MEAN?

DO YOU KNOW *PHYSICS?* DO YOU KNOW *SCIENCE?*

I AM FRIENDS WITH MANY SCIENTISTS.

IT MIGHT SEEM STRANGE FOR AN ARTIST, BUT IN THE EXCHANGE OF IDEAS, WE ARE ALL THE SAME.

I TRY TO STAY ABREAST ON AS MANY TOPICS AS POSSIBLE.

YOU ARE FAMILIAR WITH THIS NEW TERM, *"THE BIG BANG,"* THEN?

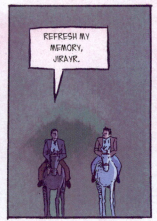

REFRESH MY MEMORY, JIRAYR.

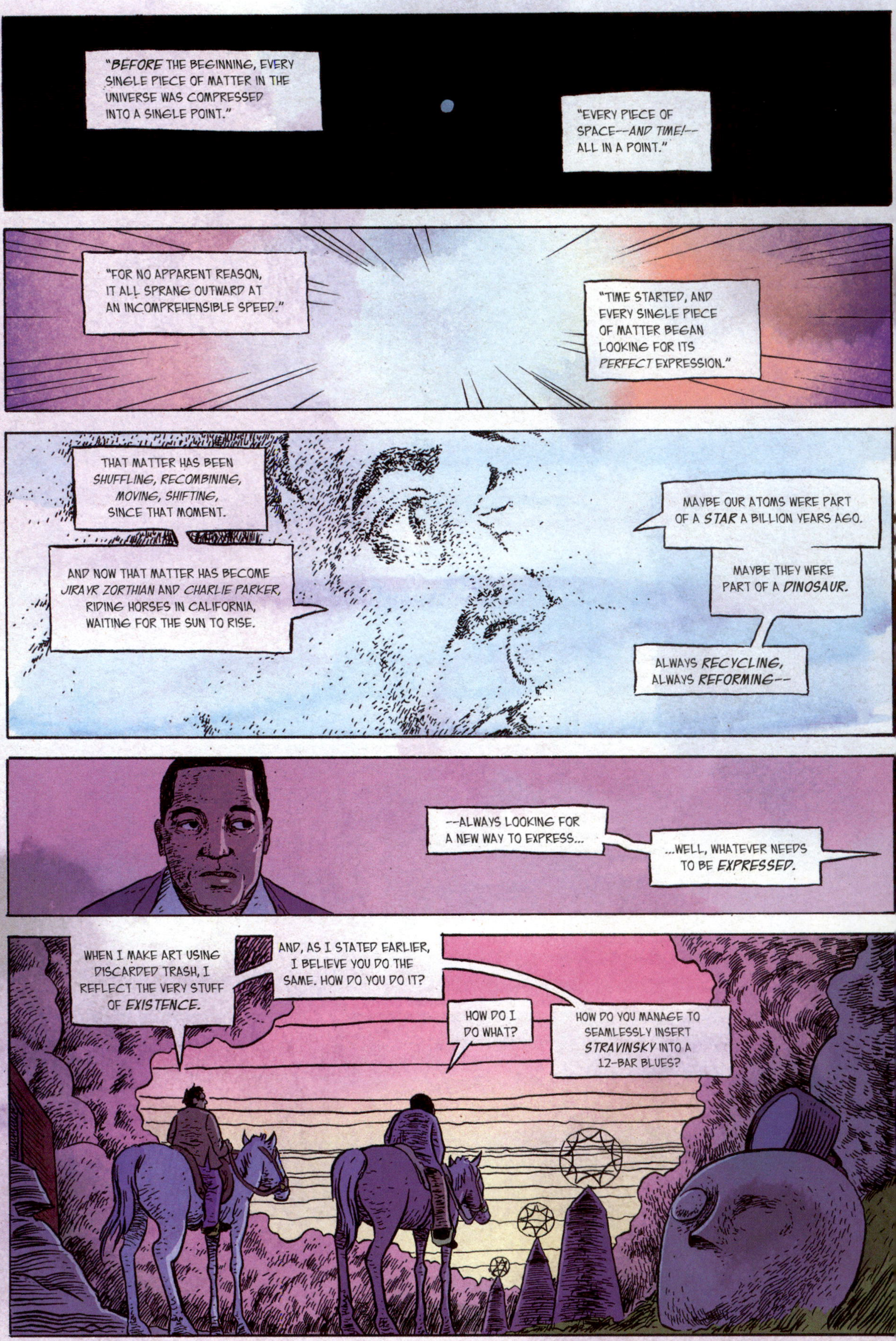
"BEFORE THE BEGINNING, EVERY SINGLE PIECE OF MATTER IN THE UNIVERSE WAS COMPRESSED INTO A SINGLE POINT."
"EVERY PIECE OF SPACE--AND TIME!--ALL IN A POINT."
"FOR NO APPARENT REASON, IT ALL SPRANG OUTWARD AT AN INCOMPREHENSIBLE SPEED."
"TIME STARTED, AND EVERY SINGLE PIECE OF MATTER BEGAN LOOKING FOR ITS PERFECT EXPRESSION."
THAT MATTER HAS BEEN SHUFFLING, RECOMBINING, MOVING, SHIFTING, SINCE THAT MOMENT.
AND NOW THAT MATTER HAS BECOME JIRAYR ZORTHIAN AND CHARLIE PARKER, RIDING HORSES IN CALIFORNIA, WAITING FOR THE SUN TO RISE.
MAYBE OUR ATOMS WERE PART OF A STAR A BILLION YEARS AGO.
MAYBE THEY WERE PART OF A DINOSAUR.
ALWAYS RECYCLING, ALWAYS REFORMING--
--ALWAYS LOOKING FOR A NEW WAY TO EXPRESS...
...WELL, WHATEVER NEEDS TO BE EXPRESSED.
WHEN I MAKE ART USING DISCARDED TRASH, I REFLECT THE VERY STUFF OF EXISTENCE.
AND, AS I STATED EARLIER, I BELIEVE YOU DO THE SAME. HOW DO YOU DO IT?
HOW DO I DO WHAT?
HOW DO YOU MANAGE TO SEAMLESSLY INSERT STRAVINSKY INTO A 12-BAR BLUES?

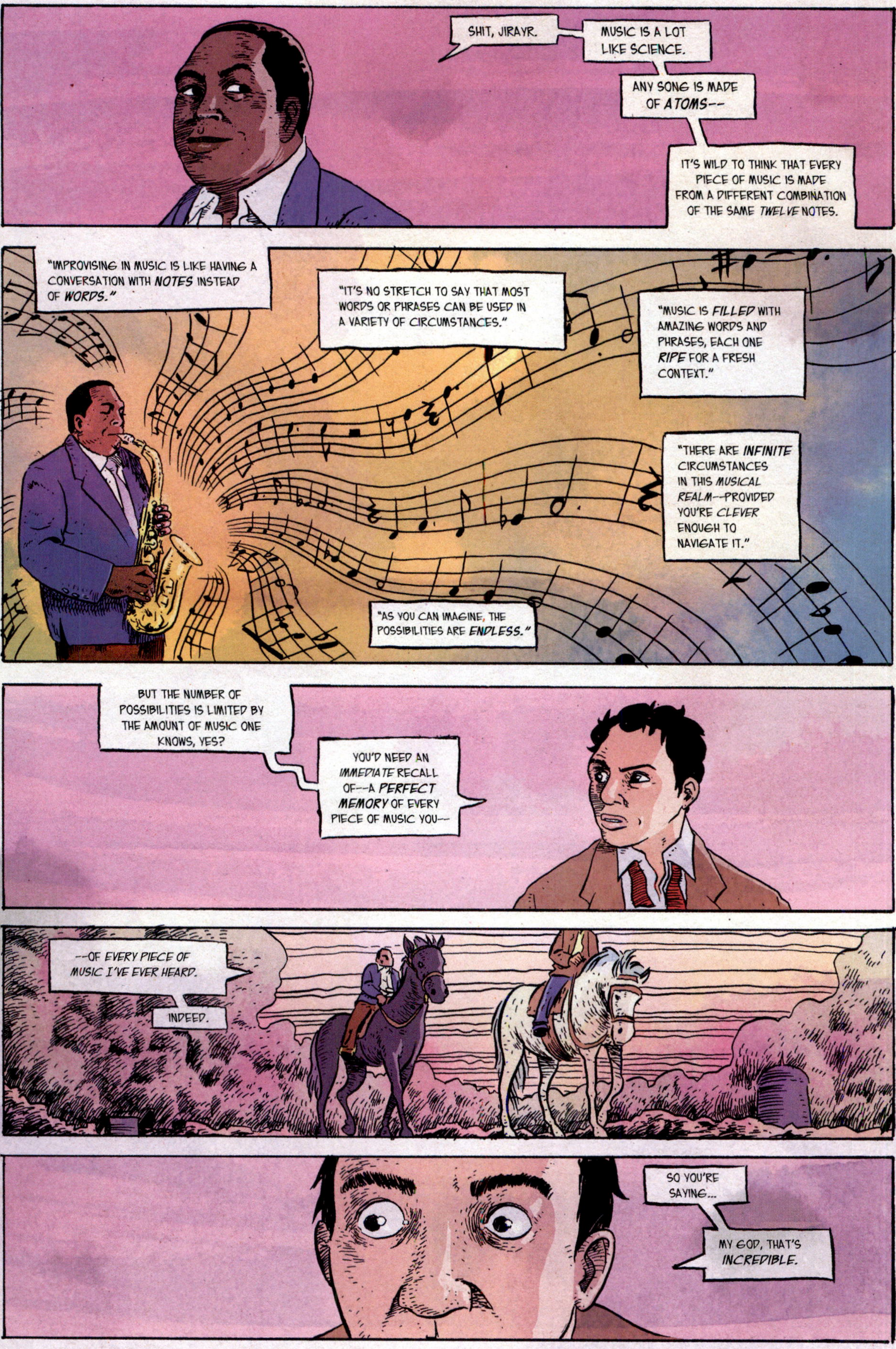
SHIT, JIRAYR.
MUSIC IS A LOT LIKE SCIENCE.
ANY SONG IS MADE OF ATOMS--
IT'S WILD TO THINK THAT EVERY PIECE OF MUSIC IS MADE FROM A DIFFERENT COMBINATION OF THE SAME TWELVE NOTES.
"IMPROVISING IN MUSIC IS LIKE HAVING A CONVERSATION WITH NOTES INSTEAD OF WORDS."
"IT'S NO STRETCH TO SAY THAT MOST WORDS OR PHRASES CAN BE USED IN A VARIETY OF CIRCUMSTANCES."
"MUSIC IS FILLED WITH AMAZING WORDS AND PHRASES, EACH ONE RIPE FOR A FRESH CONTEXT."
"THERE ARE INFINITE CIRCUMSTANCES IN THIS MUSICAL REALM--PROVIDED YOU'RE CLEVER ENOUGH TO NAVIGATE IT."
"AS YOU CAN IMAGINE, THE POSSIBILITIES ARE ENDLESS."
BUT THE NUMBER OF POSSIBILITIES IS LIMITED BY THE AMOUNT OF MUSIC ONE KNOWS, YES?
YOU'D NEED AN IMMEDIATE RECALL OF--A PERFECT MEMORY OF EVERY PIECE OF MUSIC YOU--
--OF EVERY PIECE OF MUSIC I'VE EVER HEARD.
INDEED.
SO YOU'RE SAYING...
MY GOD, THAT'S INCREDIBLE.

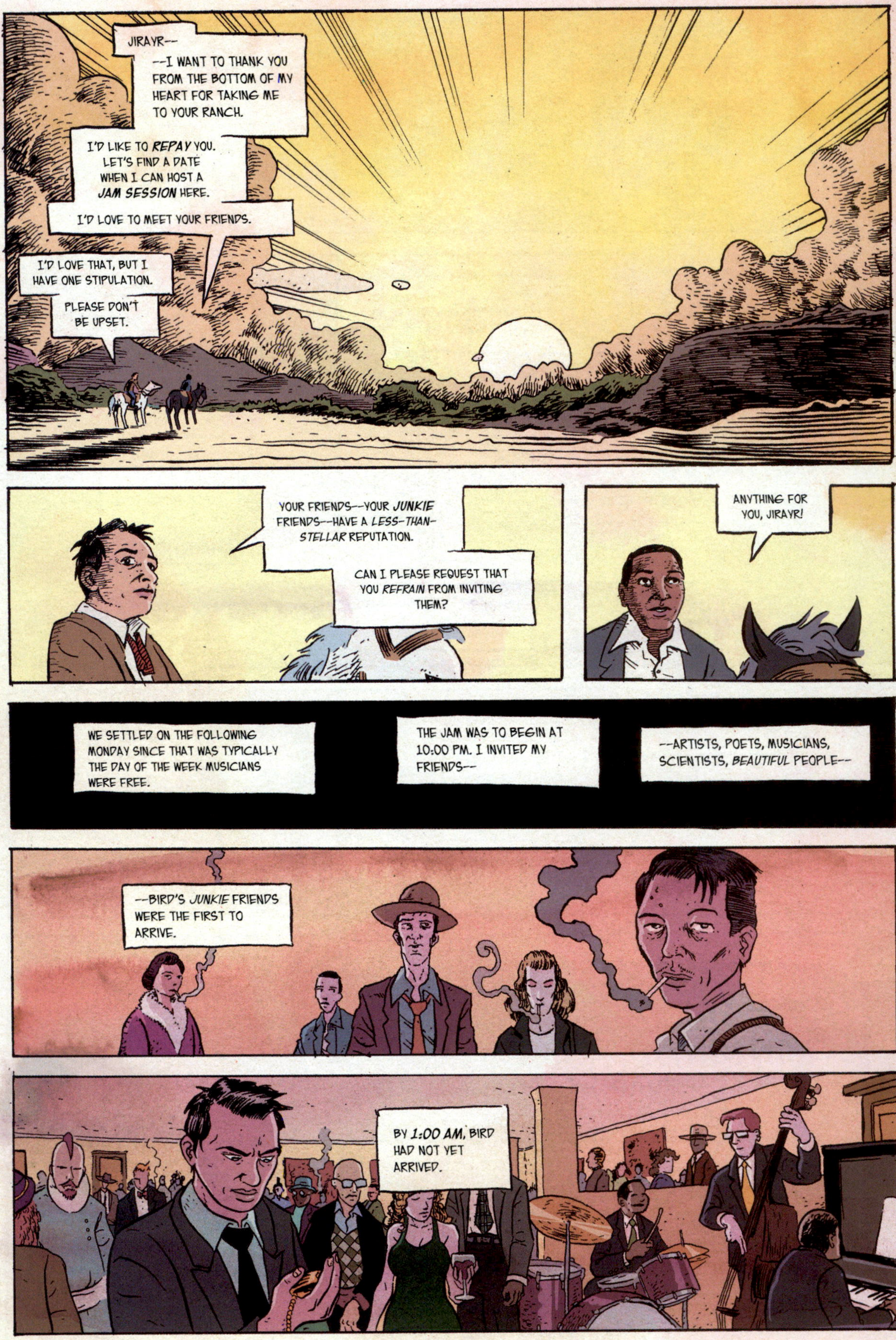
JIRAYR--
--I WANT TO THANK YOU FROM THE BOTTOM OF MY HEART FOR TAKING ME TO YOUR RANCH.
I'D LIKE TO REPAY YOU. LET'S FIND A DATE WHEN I CAN HOST A JAM SESSION HERE.
I'D LOVE TO MEET YOUR FRIENDS.
I'D LOVE THAT, BUT I HAVE ONE STIPULATION.
PLEASE DON'T BE UPSET.
YOUR FRIENDS--YOUR JUNKIE FRIENDS--HAVE A LESS-THAN-STELLAR REPUTATION.
CAN I PLEASE REQUEST THAT YOU REFRAIN FROM INVITING THEM?
ANYTHING FOR YOU, JIRAYR!
WE SETTLED ON THE FOLLOWING MONDAY SINCE THAT WAS TYPICALLY THE DAY OF THE WEEK MUSICIANS WERE FREE.
THE JAM WAS TO BEGIN AT 10:00 PM. I INVITED MY FRIENDS--
--ARTISTS, POETS, MUSICIANS, SCIENTISTS, BEAUTIFUL PEOPLE--
--BIRD'S JUNKIE FRIENDS WERE THE FIRST TO ARRIVE.
BY 1:00 AM, BIRD HAD NOT YET ARRIVED.

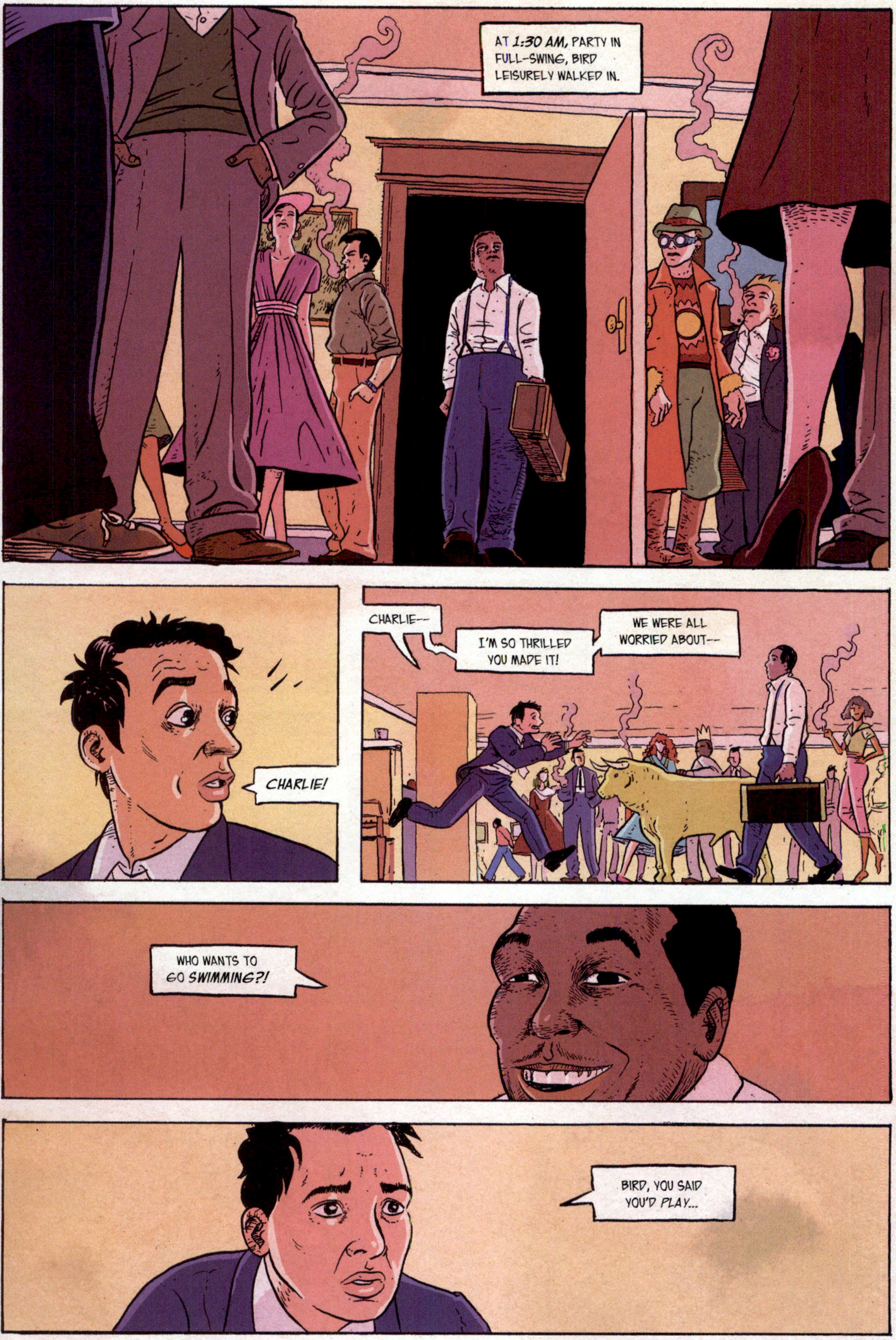
AT 1:30 AM, PARTY IN FULL-SWING, BIRD LEISURELY WALKED IN.
CHARLIE!
CHARLIE--
I'M SO THRILLED YOU MADE IT!
WE WERE ALL WORRIED ABOUT--
WHO WANTS TO GO SWIMMING?!
BIRD, YOU SAID YOU'D PLAY...

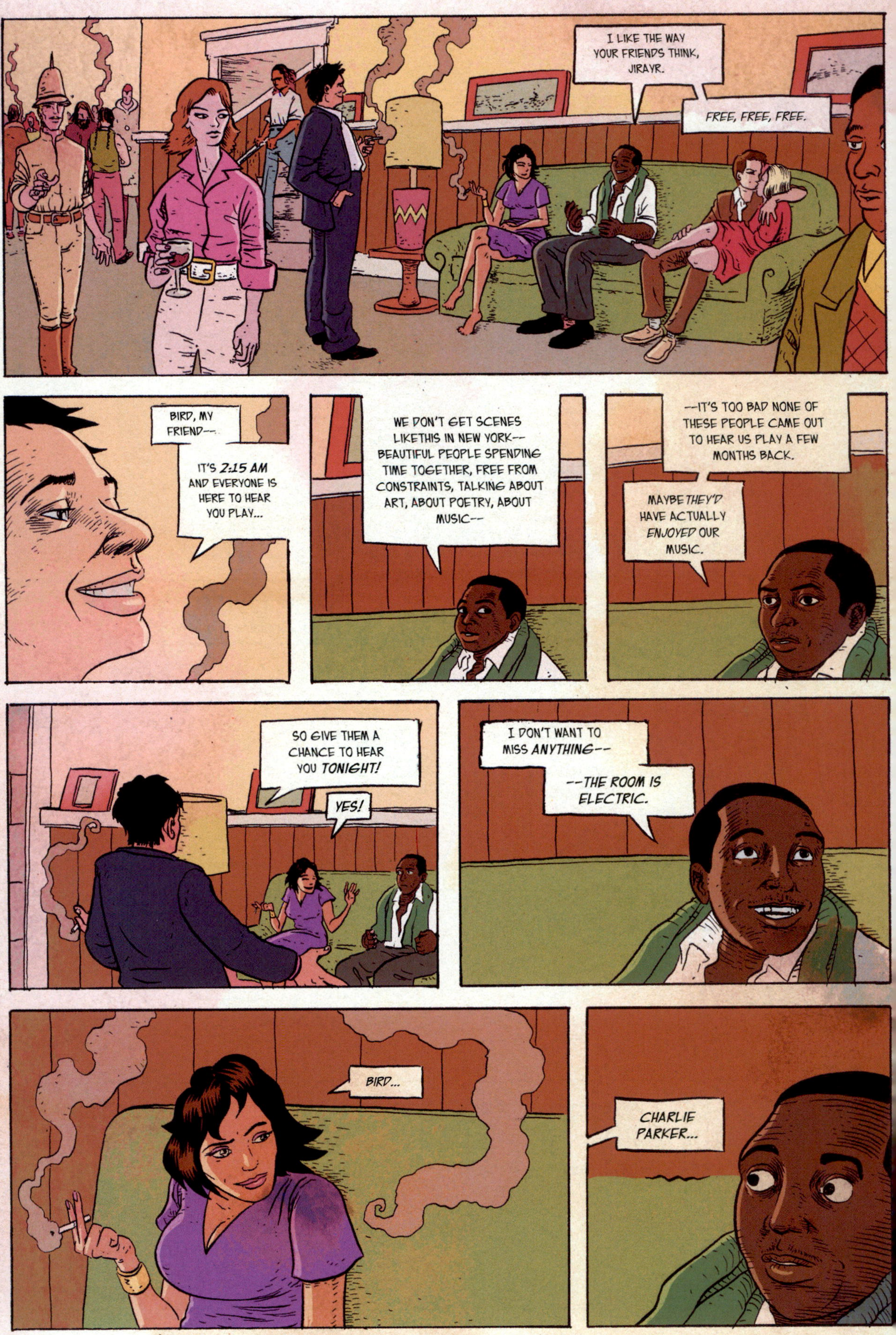
I LIKE THE WAY YOUR FRIENDS THINK, JIRAYR.
FREE, FREE, FREE.
BIRD, MY FRIEND--
IT'S 2:15 AM AND EVERYONE IS HERE TO HEAR YOU PLAY...
WE DON'T GET SCENES LIKETHIS IN NEW YORK-- BEAUTIFUL PEOPLE SPENDING TIME TOGETHER, FREE FROM CONSTRAINTS, TALKING ABOUT ART, ABOUT POETRY, ABOUT MUSIC--
--IT'S TOO BAD NONE OF THESE PEOPLE CAME OUT TO HEAR US PLAY A FEW MONTHS BACK.
MAYBE THEY'D HAVE ACTUALLY ENJOYED OUR MUSIC.
SO GIVE THEM A CHANCE TO HEAR YOU TONIGHT!
YES!
I DON'T WANT TO MISS ANYTHING--
--THE ROOM IS ELECTRIC.
BIRD...
CHARLIE PARKER...

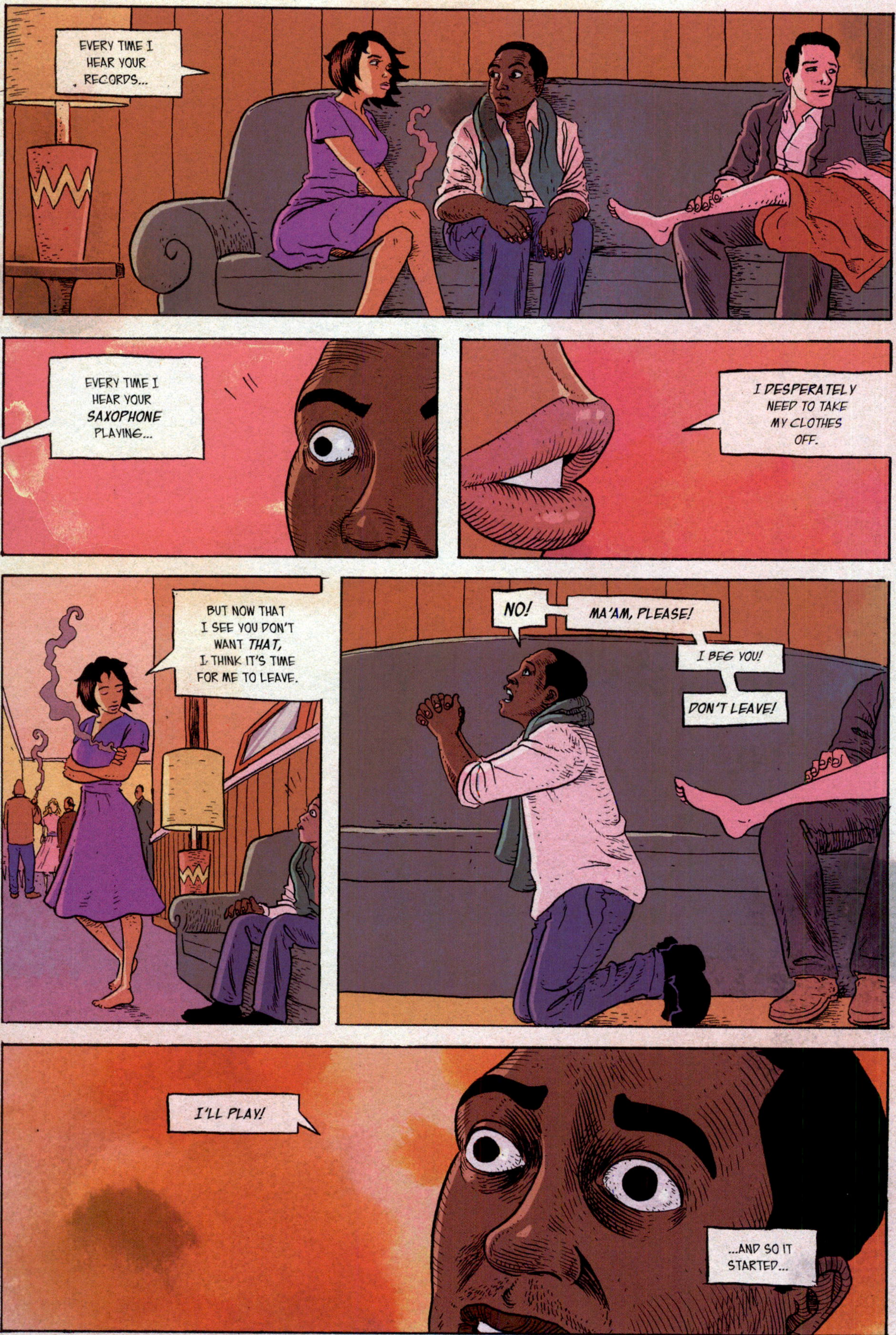
EVERY TIME I HEAR YOUR RECORDS...
EVERY TIME I HEAR YOUR SAXOPHONE PLAYING...
I DESPERATELY NEED TO TAKE MY CLOTHES OFF.
BUT NOW THAT I SEE YOU DON'T WANT THAT, I THINK IT'S TIME FOR ME TO LEAVE.
NO!
MA'AM, PLEASE!
I BEG YOU!
DON'T LEAVE!
I'LL PLAY!
...AND SO IT STARTED...

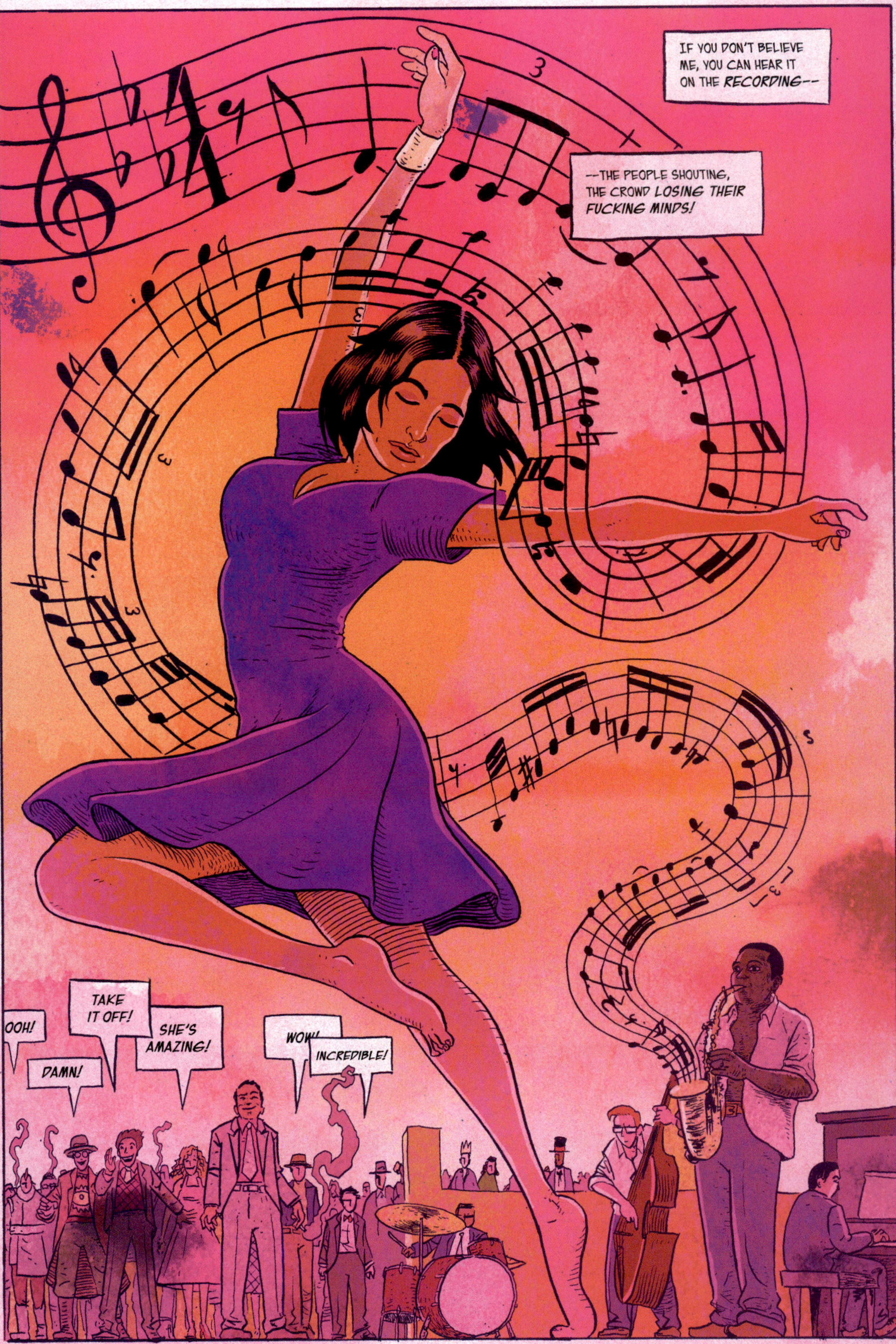
IF YOU DON'T BELIEVE ME, YOU CAN HEAR IT ON THE RECORDING--
--THE PEOPLE SHOUTING, THE CROWD LOSING THEIR FUCKING MINDS!
OOH!
TAKE IT OFF!
DAMN!
SHE'S AMAZING!
WOW!
INCREDIBLE!

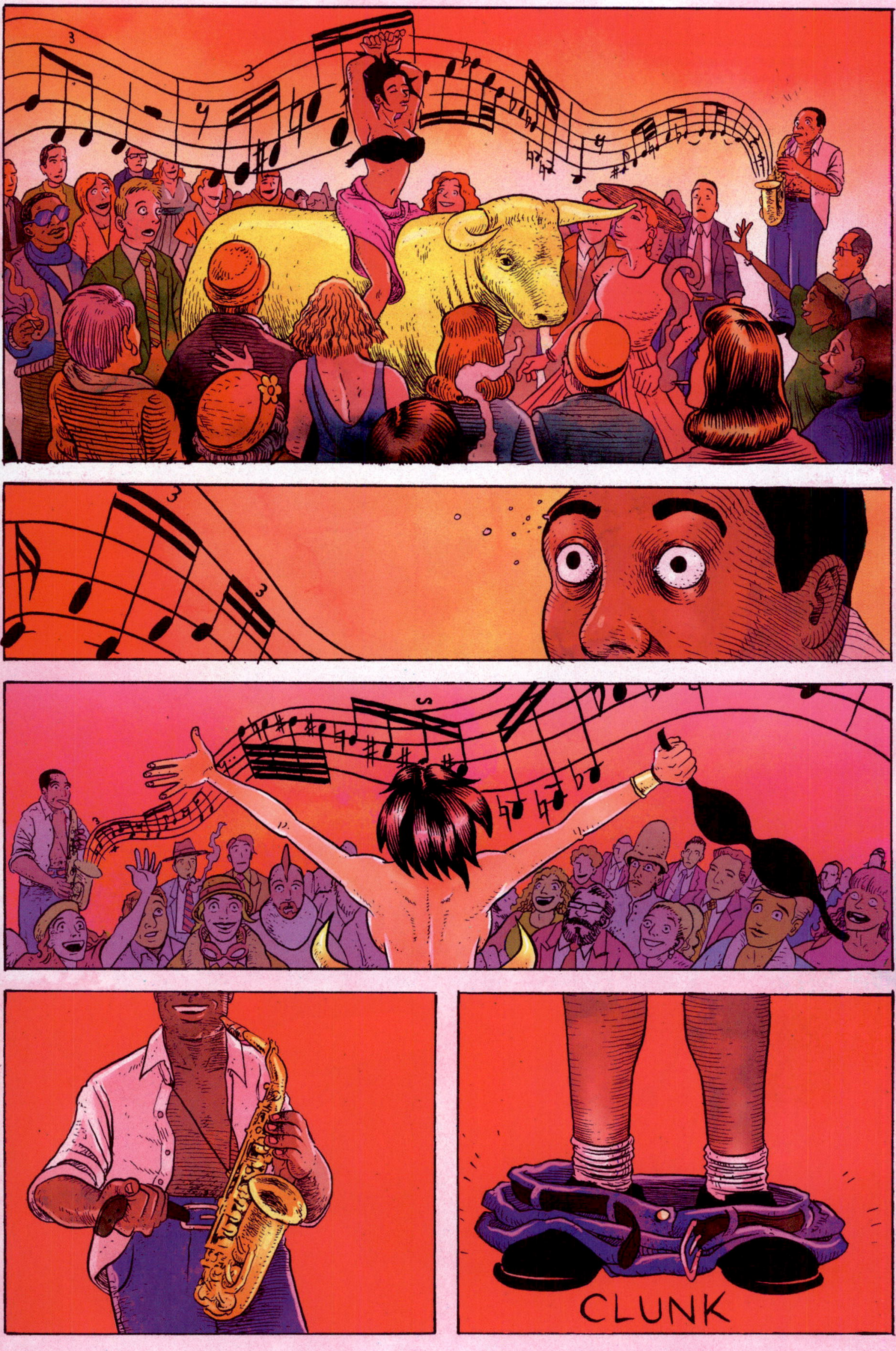
CLUNK

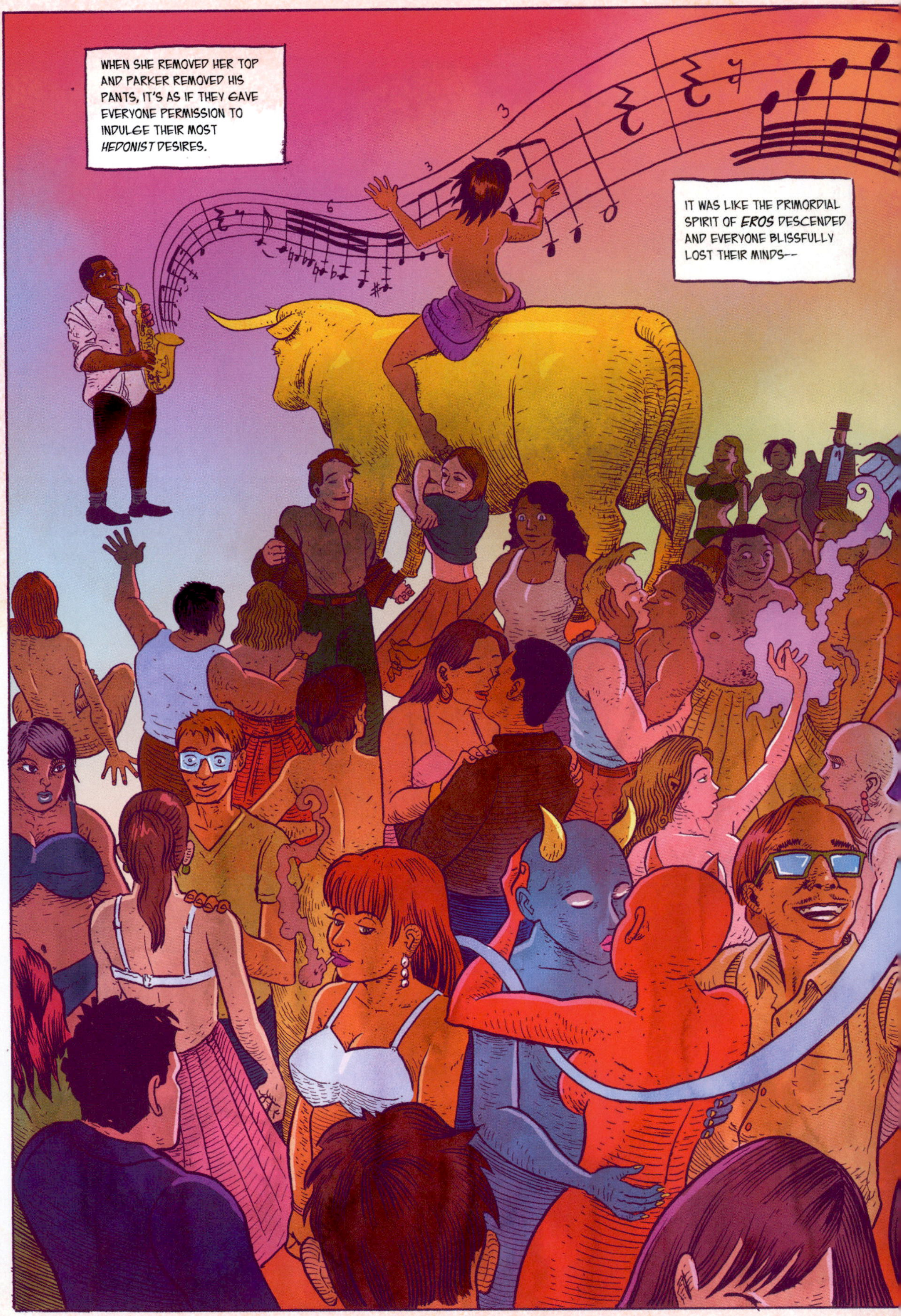
WHEN SHE REMOVED HER TOP AND PARKER REMOVED HIS PANTS, IT'S AS IF THEY GAVE EVERYONE PERMISSION TO INDULGE THEIR MOST *HEDONIST* DESIRES.
IT WAS LIKE THE PRIMORDIAL SPIRIT OF *EROS* DESCENDED AND EVERYONE BLISSFULLY LOST THEIR MINDS--

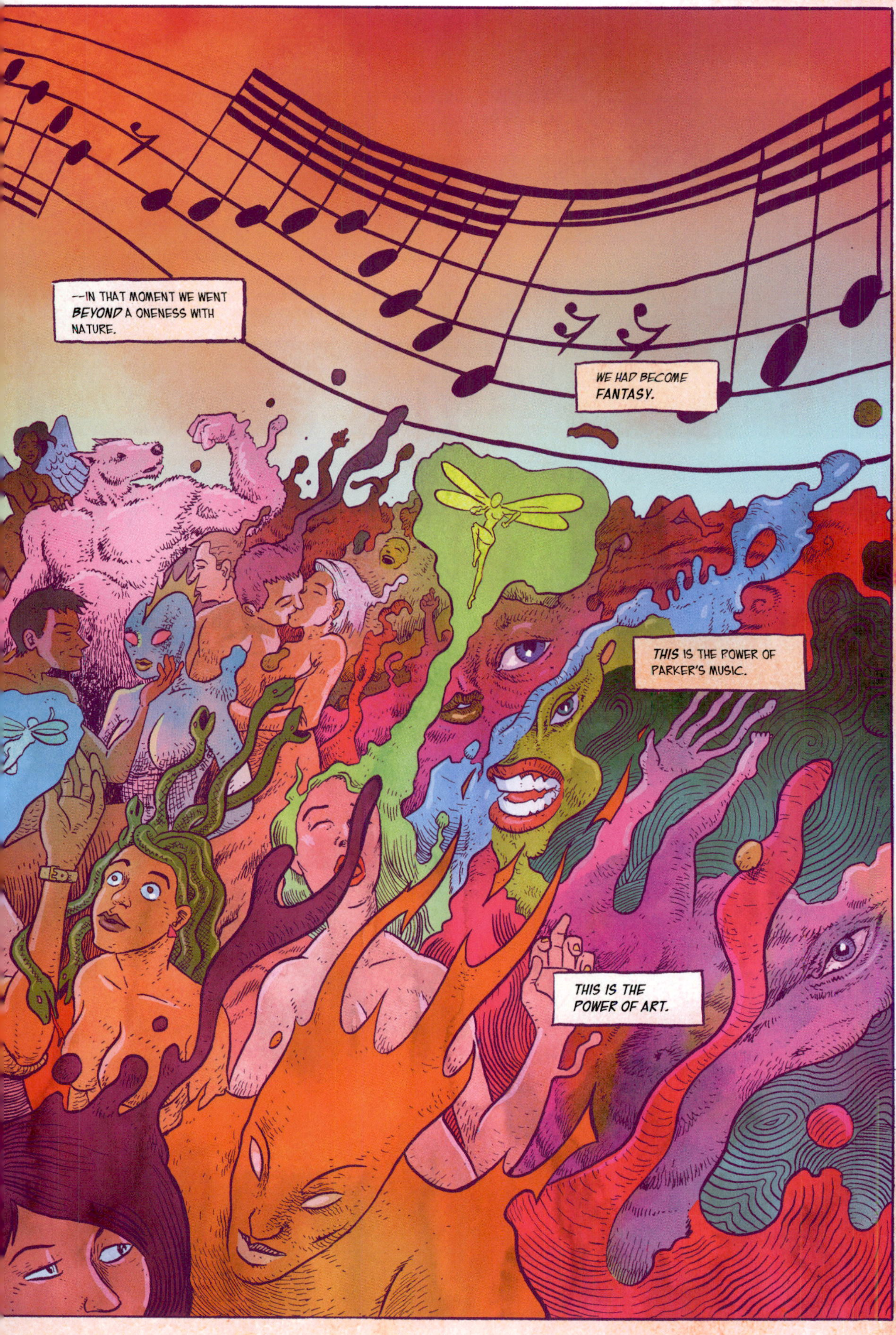
--IN THAT MOMENT WE WENT BEYOND A ONENESS WITH NATURE.
WE HAD BECOME FANTASY.
THIS IS THE POWER OF PARKER'S MUSIC.
THIS IS THE POWER OF ART.

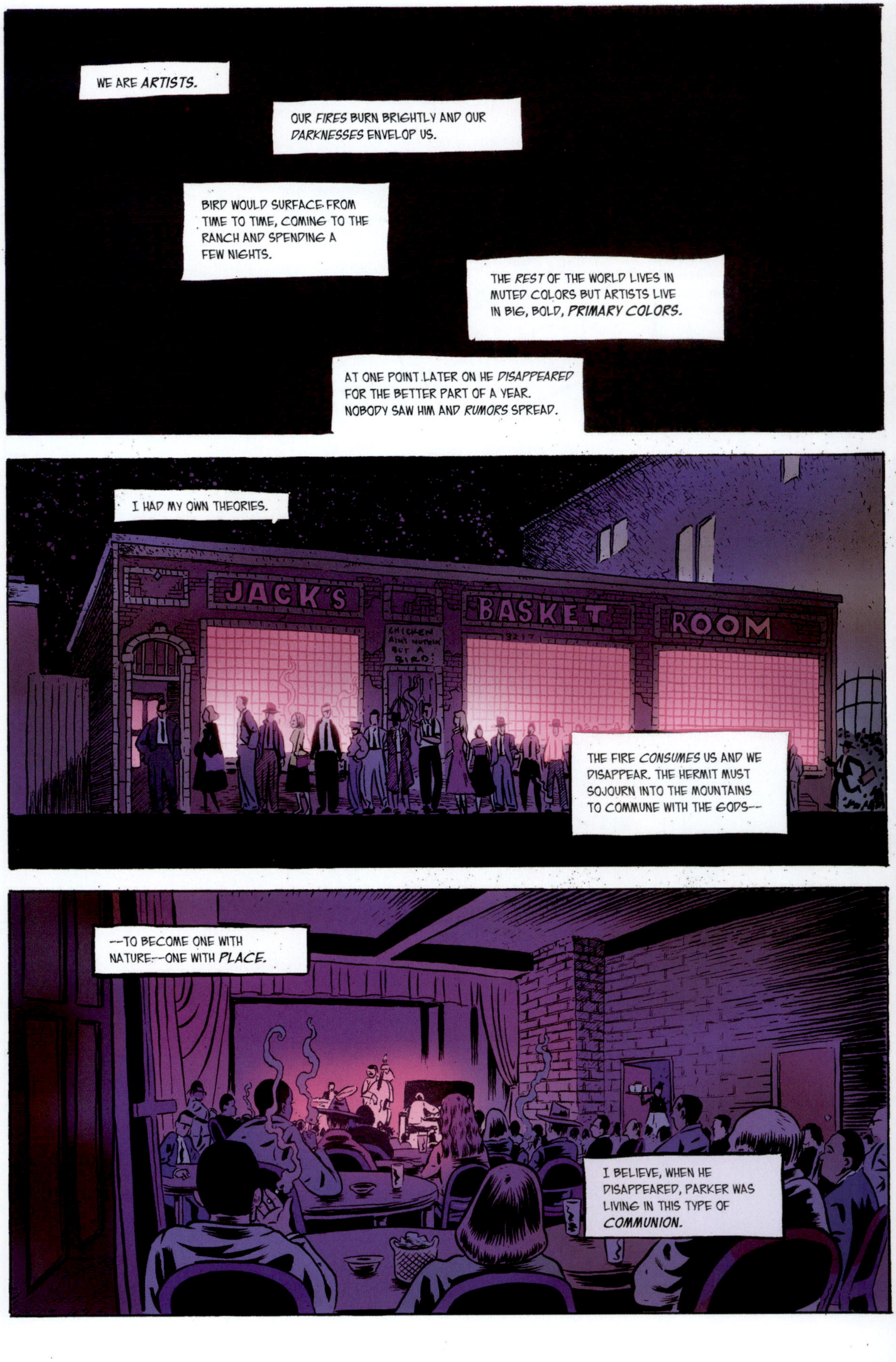
WE ARE *ARTISTS.*
OUR *FIRES* BURN BRIGHTLY AND OUR *DARKNESSES* ENVELOP US.
BIRD WOULD SURFACE FROM TIME TO TIME, COMING TO THE RANCH AND SPENDING A FEW NIGHTS.
THE *REST* OF THE WORLD LIVES IN MUTED COLORS BUT ARTISTS LIVE IN BIG, BOLD, *PRIMARY COLORS.*
AT ONE POINT LATER ON HE *DISAPPEARED* FOR THE BETTER PART OF A YEAR. NOBODY SAW HIM AND *RUMORS* SPREAD.
I HAD MY OWN THEORIES.
JACK'S
BASKET
ROOM
3217
CHICKEN AIN'T NOTHIN' BUT A BIRD!
THE FIRE *CONSUMES* US AND WE DISAPPEAR. THE HERMIT MUST SOJOURN INTO THE MOUNTAINS TO COMMUNE WITH THE GODS--
--TO BECOME ONE WITH NATURE--ONE WITH *PLACE.*
I BELIEVE, WHEN HE DISAPPEARED, PARKER WAS LIVING IN THIS TYPE OF *COMMUNION.*

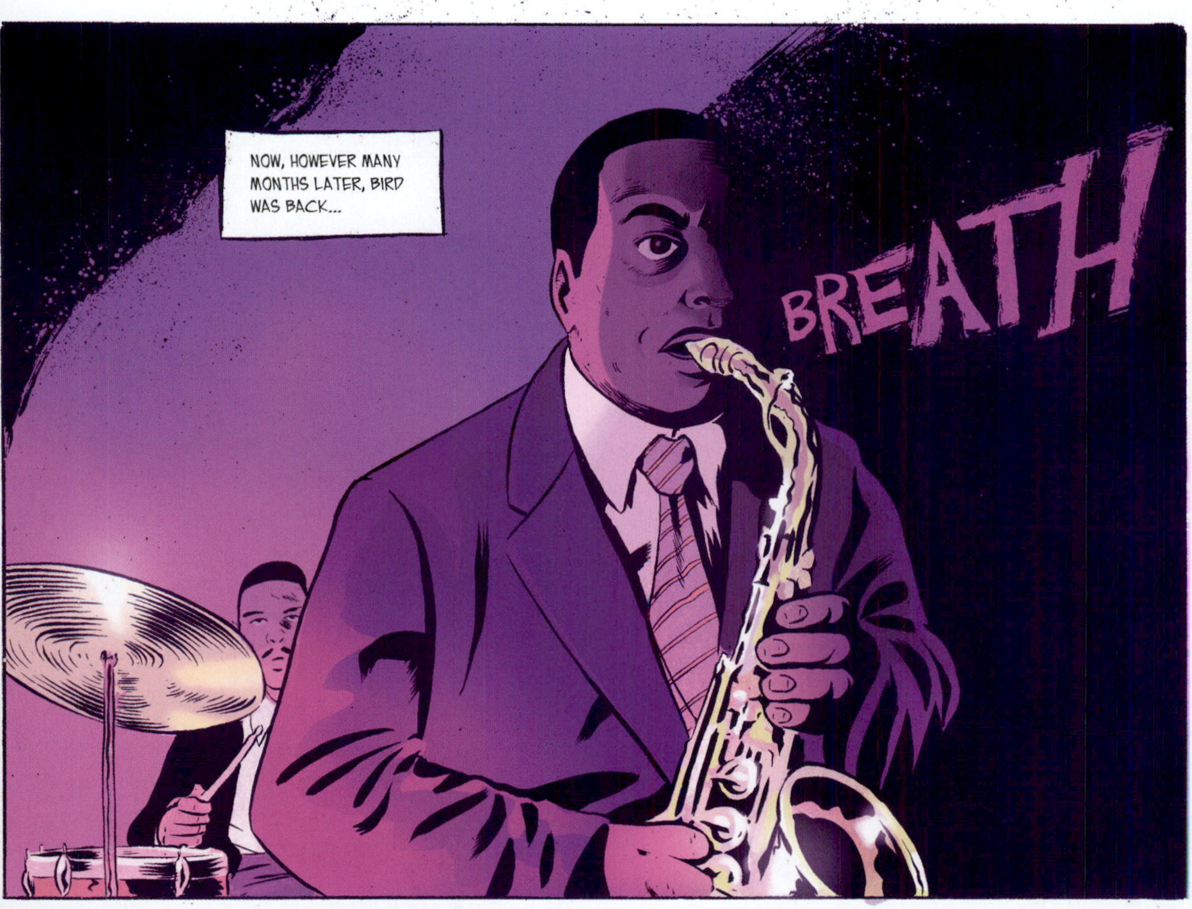
NOW, HOWEVER MANY MONTHS LATER, BIRD WAS BACK...
BREATH

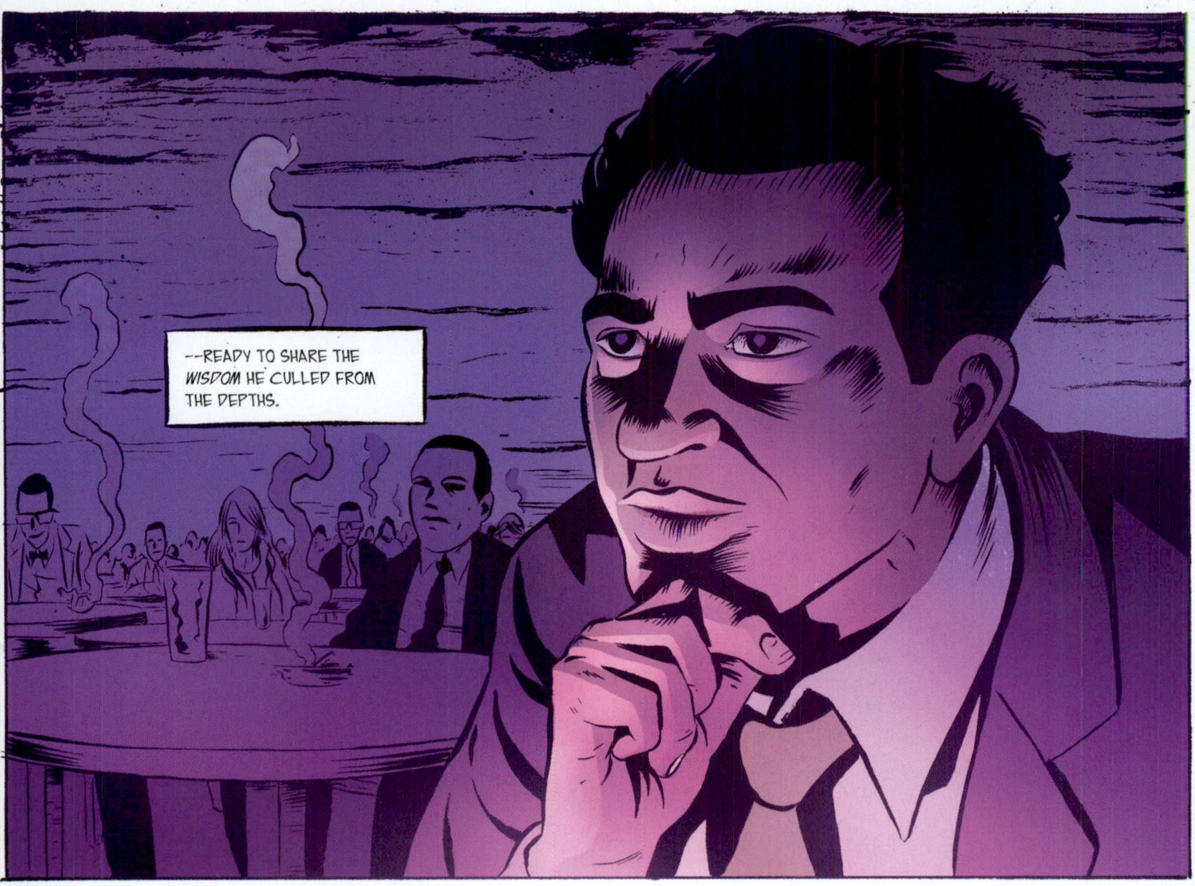
--READY TO SHARE THE *WISDOM* HE CULLED FROM THE DEPTHS.

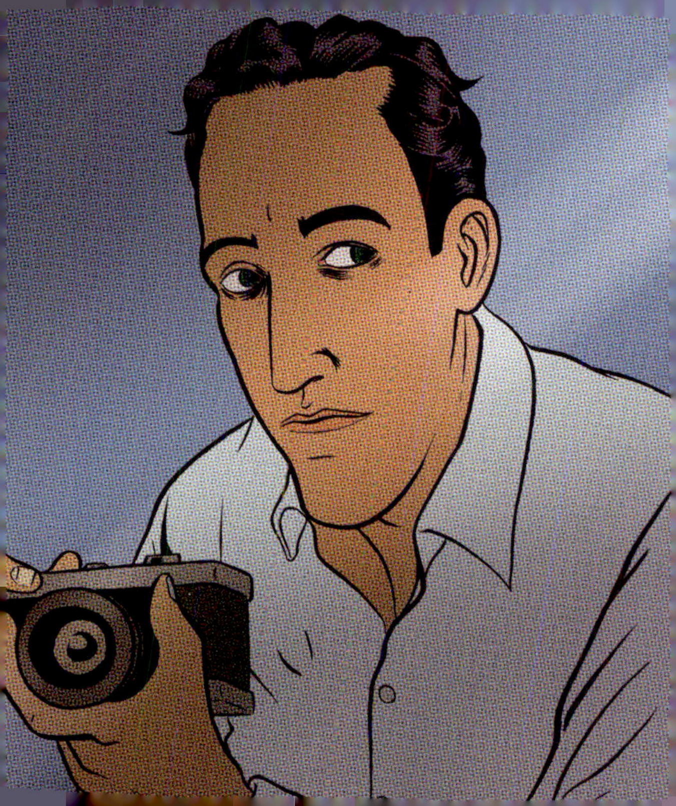

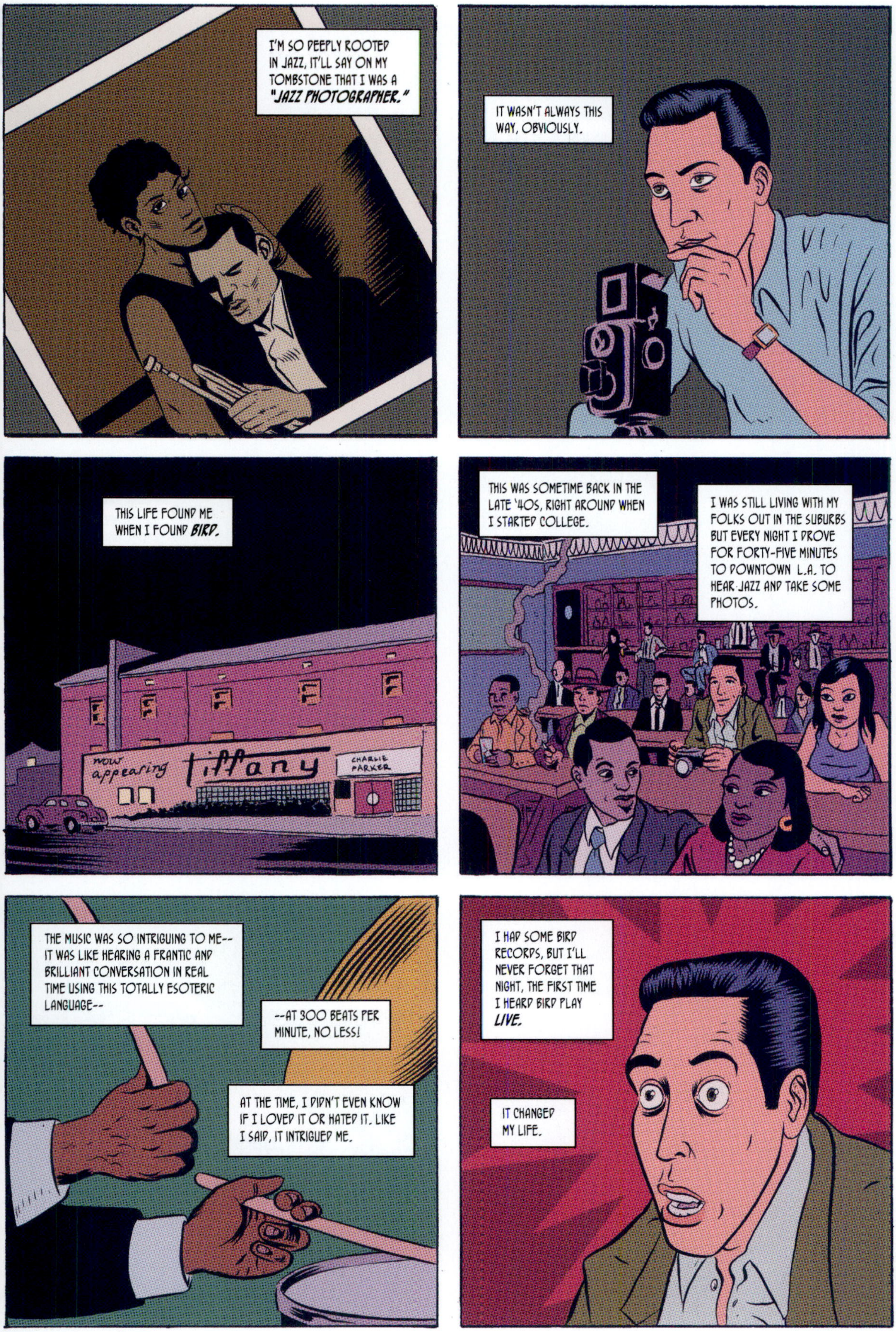
I'M SO DEEPLY ROOTED IN JAZZ, IT'LL SAY ON MY TOMBSTONE THAT I WAS A "JAZZ PHOTOGRAPHER."
IT WASN'T ALWAYS THIS WAY, OBVIOUSLY.
THIS LIFE FOUND ME WHEN I FOUND BIRD.
now appearing
tiffany
CHARLIE PARKER
THIS WAS SOMETIME BACK IN THE LATE '40S, RIGHT AROUND WHEN I STARTED COLLEGE.
I WAS STILL LIVING WITH MY FOLKS OUT IN THE SUBURBS BUT EVERY NIGHT I DROVE FOR FORTY-FIVE MINUTES TO DOWNTOWN L.A. TO HEAR JAZZ AND TAKE SOME PHOTOS.
THE MUSIC WAS SO INTRIGUING TO ME-- IT WAS LIKE HEARING A FRANTIC AND BRILLIANT CONVERSATION IN REAL TIME USING THIS TOTALLY ESOTERIC LANGUAGE--
--AT 300 BEATS PER MINUTE, NO LESS!
AT THE TIME, I DIDN'T EVEN KNOW IF I LOVED IT OR HATED IT. LIKE I SAID, IT INTRIGUED ME.
I HAD SOME BIRD RECORDS, BUT I'LL NEVER FORGET THAT NIGHT, THE FIRST TIME I HEARD BIRD PLAY LIVE.
IT CHANGED MY LIFE.

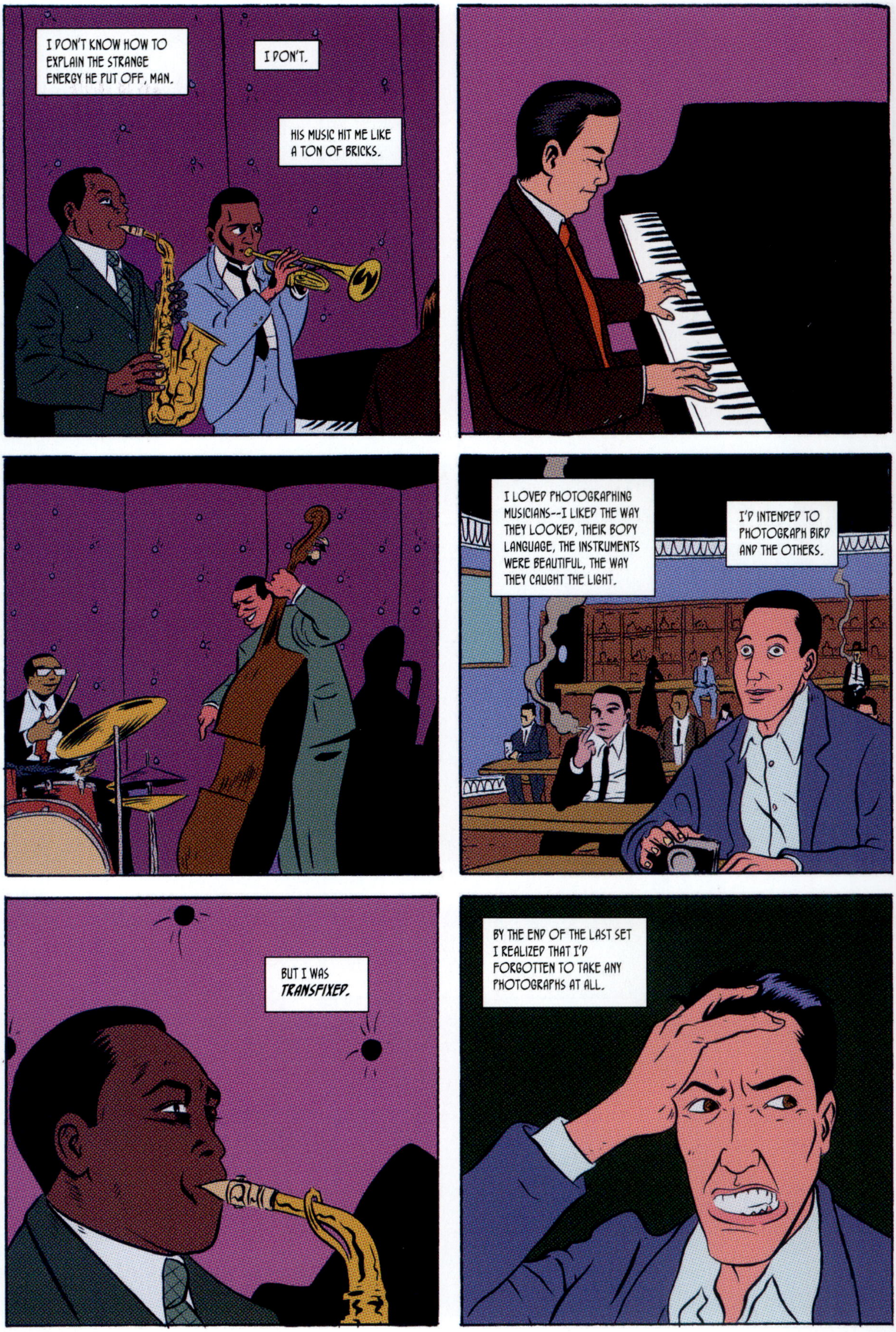
I DON'T KNOW HOW TO EXPLAIN THE STRANGE ENERGY HE PUT OFF, MAN.
I DON'T.
HIS MUSIC HIT ME LIKE A TON OF BRICKS.
I LOVED PHOTOGRAPHING MUSICIANS--I LIKED THE WAY THEY LOOKED, THEIR BODY LANGUAGE, THE INSTRUMENTS WERE BEAUTIFUL, THE WAY THEY CAUGHT THE LIGHT.
I'D INTENDED TO PHOTOGRAPH BIRD AND THE OTHERS.
BUT I WAS *TRANSFIXED.*
BY THE END OF THE LAST SET I REALIZED THAT I'D FORGOTTEN TO TAKE ANY PHOTOGRAPHS AT ALL.

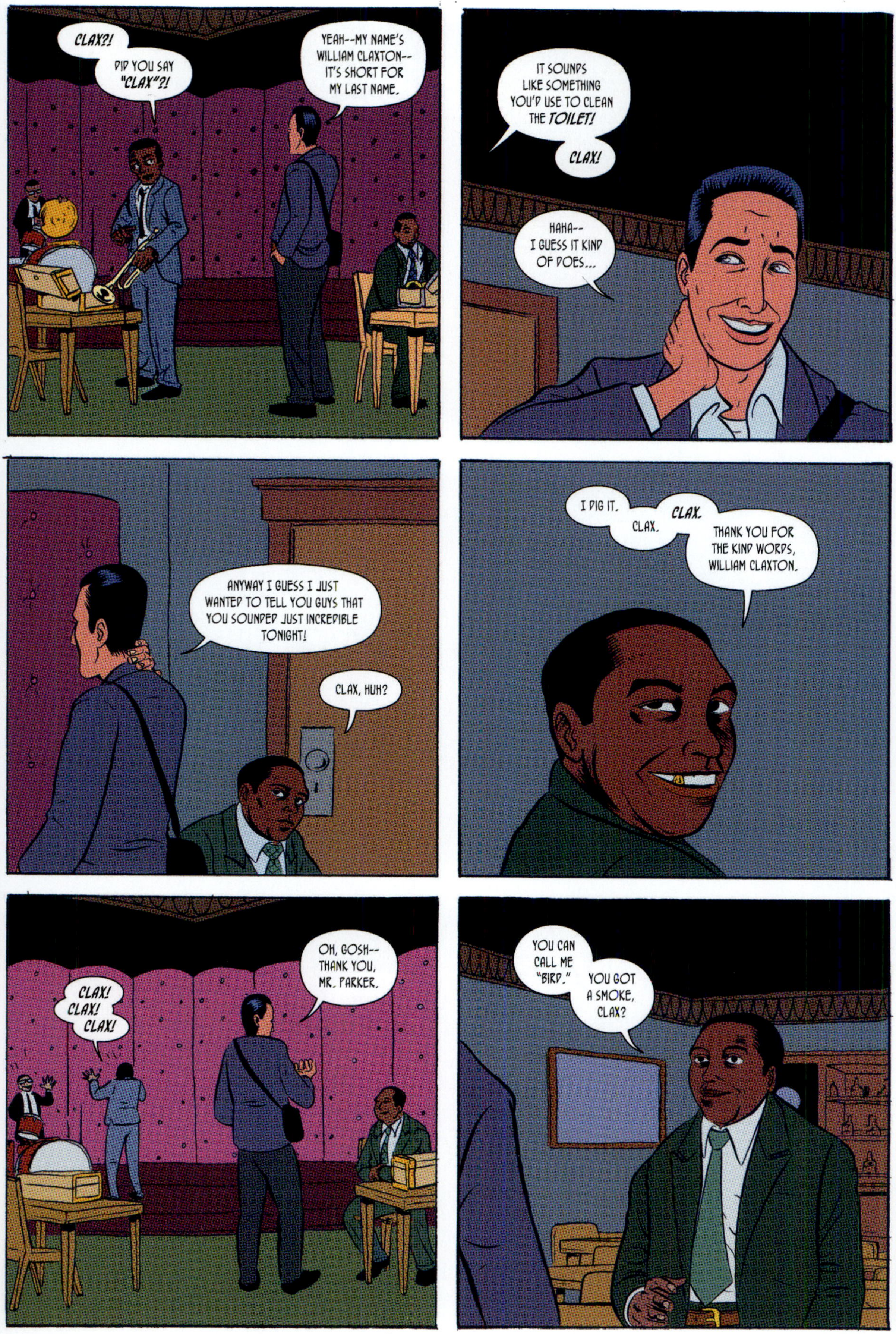
CLAX?!
DID YOU SAY "CLAX"?!
YEAH--MY NAME'S WILLIAM CLAXTON--IT'S SHORT FOR MY LAST NAME.
IT SOUNDS LIKE SOMETHING YOU'D USE TO CLEAN THE TOILET!
CLAX!
HAHA-- I GUESS IT KIND OF DOES...
ANYWAY I GUESS I JUST WANTED TO TELL YOU GUYS THAT YOU SOUNDED JUST INCREDIBLE TONIGHT!
CLAX, HUH?
I DIG IT.
CLAX.
CLAX.
THANK YOU FOR THE KIND WORDS, WILLIAM CLAXTON.
CLAX! CLAX! CLAX!
OH, GOSH-- THANK YOU, MR. PARKER.
YOU CAN CALL ME "BIRD."
YOU GOT A SMOKE, CLAX?

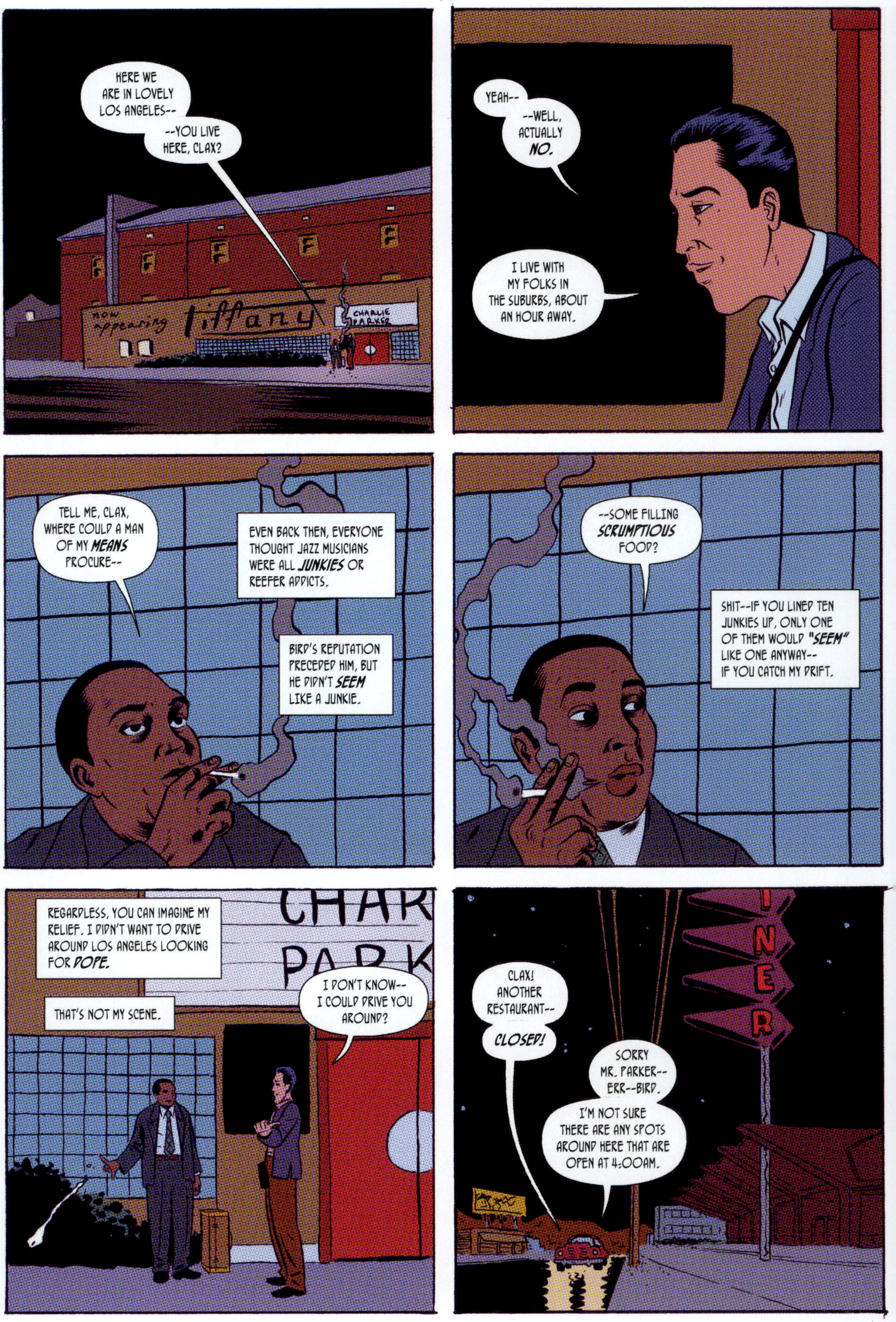
HERE WE ARE IN LOVELY LOS ANGELES--
--YOU LIVE HERE, CLAX?
NOW APPEARING
TIFFANY
CHARLIE PARKER
YEAH--
--WELL, ACTUALLY NO.
I LIVE WITH MY FOLKS IN THE SUBURBS, ABOUT AN HOUR AWAY.
TELL ME, CLAX, WHERE COULD A MAN OF MY MEANS PROCURE--
EVEN BACK THEN, EVERYONE THOUGHT JAZZ MUSICIANS WERE ALL JUNKIES OR REEFER ADDICTS.
BIRD'S REPUTATION PRECEDED HIM, BUT HE DIDN'T SEEM LIKE A JUNKIE.
--SOME FILLING SCRUMPTIOUS FOOD?
SHIT--IF YOU LINED TEN JUNKIES UP, ONLY ONE OF THEM WOULD "SEEM" LIKE ONE ANYWAY-- IF YOU CATCH MY DRIFT.
REGARDLESS, YOU CAN IMAGINE MY RELIEF. I DIDN'T WANT TO DRIVE AROUND LOS ANGELES LOOKING FOR DOPE.
THAT'S NOT MY SCENE.
CHAR
PARK
I DON'T KNOW-- I COULD DRIVE YOU AROUND?
CLAX! ANOTHER RESTAURANT-- CLOSED!
SORRY MR. PARKER-- ERR--BIRD.
I'M NOT SURE THERE ARE ANY SPOTS AROUND HERE THAT ARE OPEN AT 4:00AM.
INER

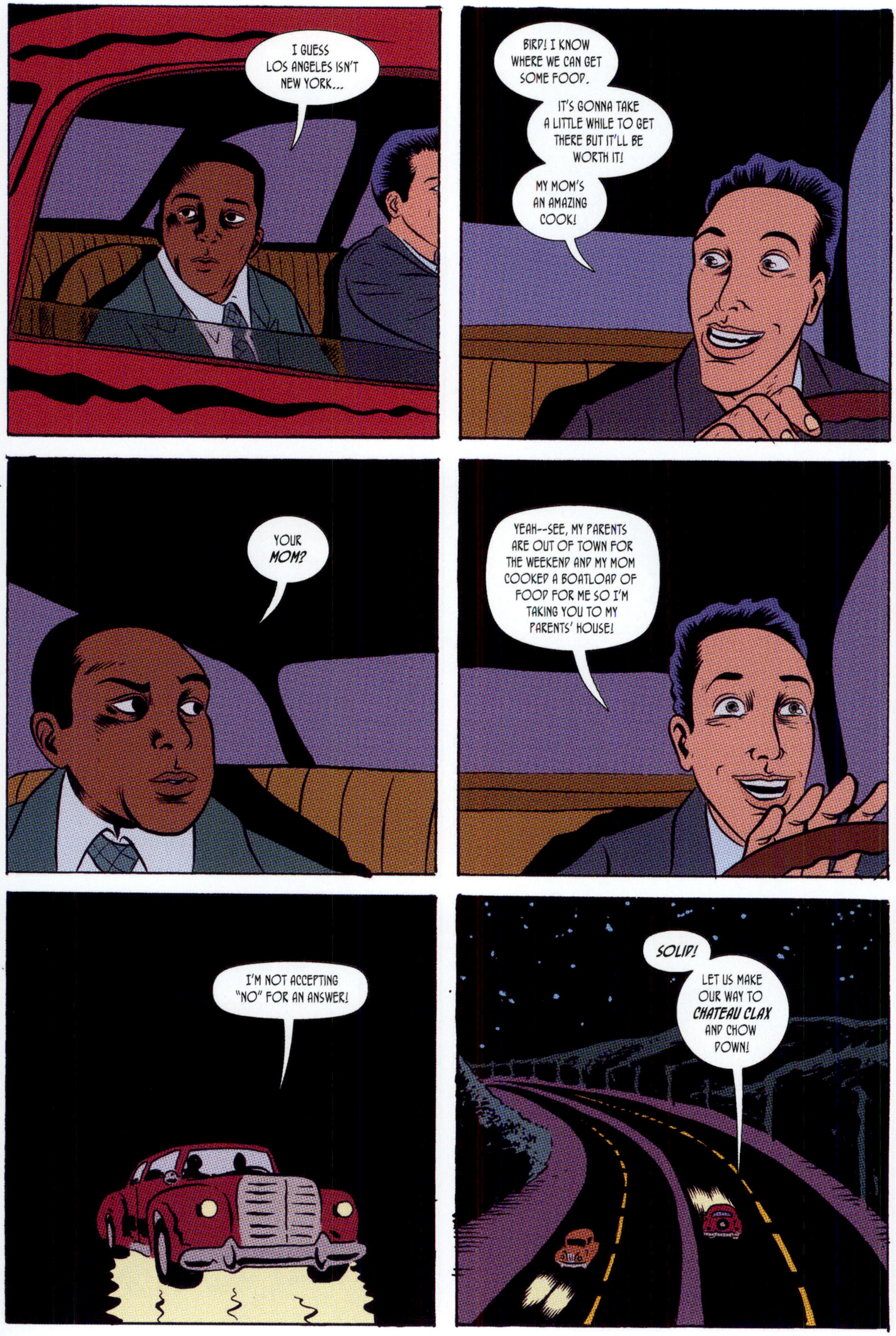
I GUESS LOS ANGELES ISN'T NEW YORK...
BIRD! I KNOW WHERE WE CAN GET SOME FOOD.
IT'S GONNA TAKE A LITTLE WHILE TO GET THERE BUT IT'LL BE WORTH IT!
MY MOM'S AN AMAZING COOK!
YOUR *MOM?*
YEAH--SEE, MY PARENTS ARE OUT OF TOWN FOR THE WEEKEND AND MY MOM COOKED A BOATLOAD OF FOOD FOR ME SO I'M TAKING YOU TO MY PARENTS' HOUSE!
I'M NOT ACCEPTING "NO" FOR AN ANSWER!
SOLID!
LET US MAKE OUR WAY TO *CHATEAU CLAX* AND CHOW DOWN!

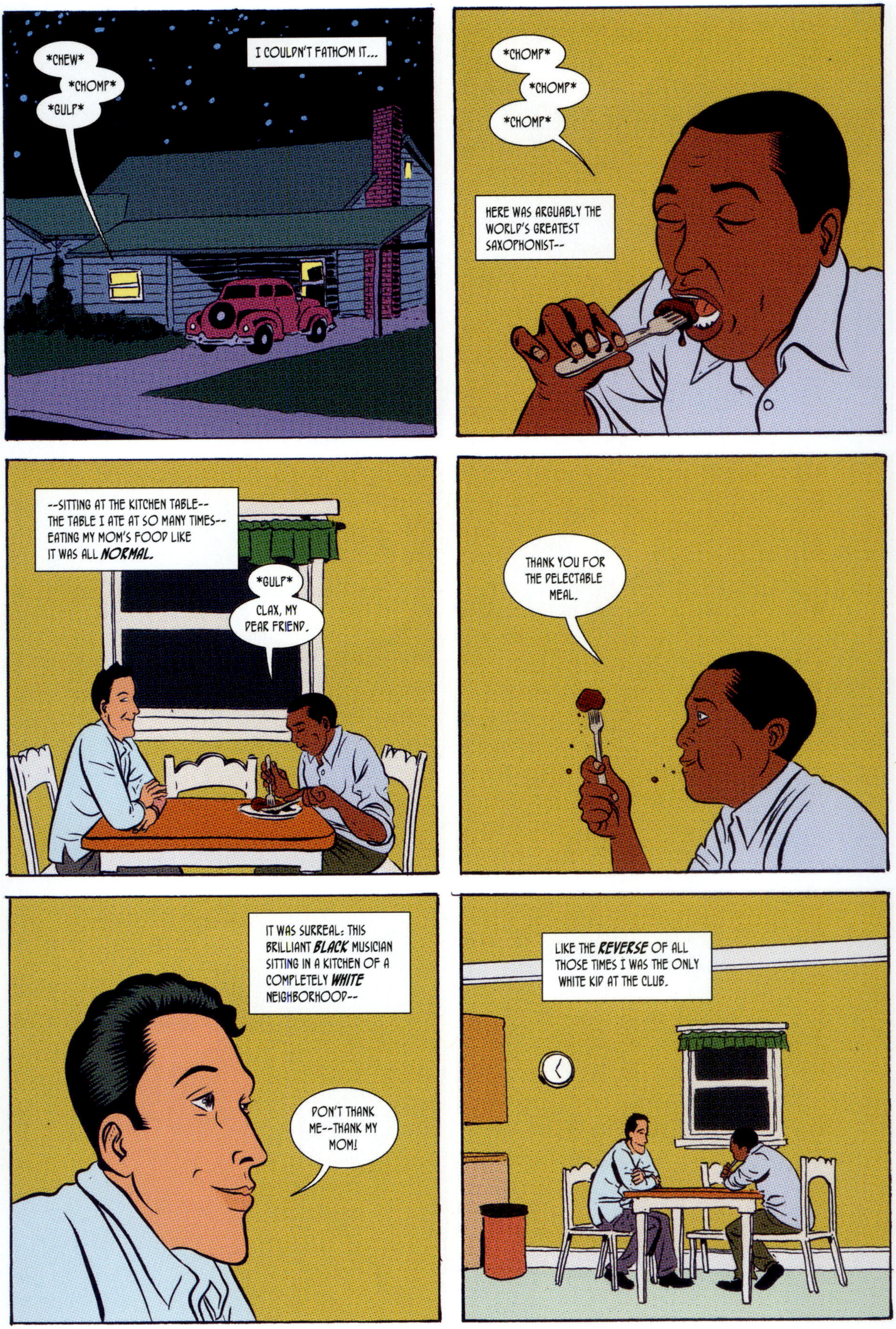
I COULDN'T FATHOM IT...
CHEW
CHOMP
GULP
CHOMP
CHOMP
CHOMP
HERE WAS ARGUABLY THE WORLD'S GREATEST SAXOPHONIST--
--SITTING AT THE KITCHEN TABLE-- THE TABLE I ATE AT SO MANY TIMES-- EATING MY MOM'S FOOD LIKE IT WAS ALL NORMAL.
GULP
CLAX, MY DEAR FRIEND.
THANK YOU FOR THE DELECTABLE MEAL.
IT WAS SURREAL: THIS BRILLIANT BLACK MUSICIAN SITTING IN A KITCHEN OF A COMPLETELY WHITE NEIGHBORHOOD--
DON'T THANK ME--THANK MY MOM!
LIKE THE REVERSE OF ALL THOSE TIMES I WAS THE ONLY WHITE KID AT THE CLUB.

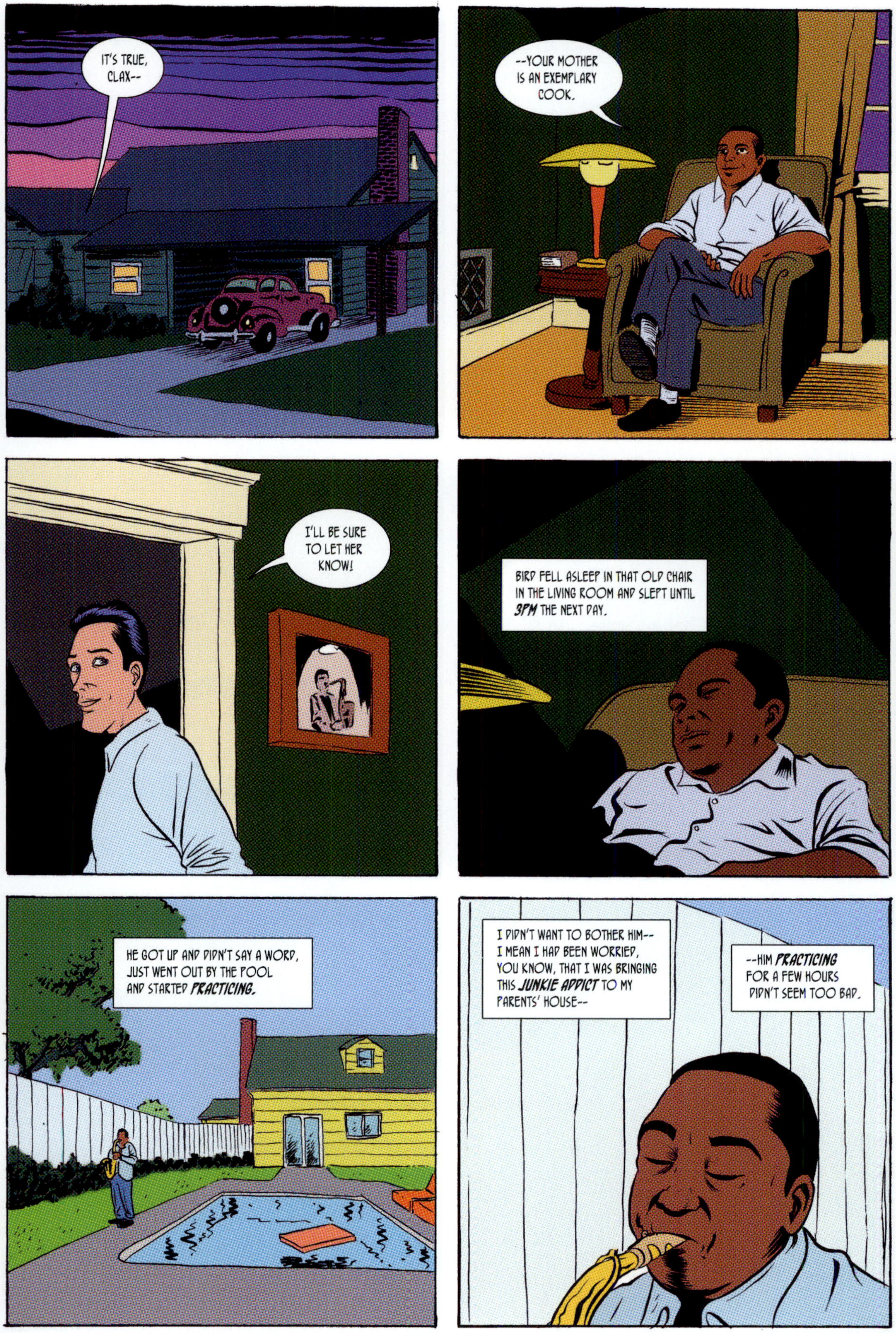
IT'S TRUE, CLAX--
--YOUR MOTHER IS AN EXEMPLARY COOK.
I'LL BE SURE TO LET HER KNOW!
BIRD FELL ASLEEP IN THAT OLD CHAIR IN THE LIVING ROOM AND SLEPT UNTIL 3PM THE NEXT DAY.
HE GOT UP AND DIDN'T SAY A WORD, JUST WENT OUT BY THE POOL AND STARTED PRACTICING.
I DIDN'T WANT TO BOTHER HIM-- I MEAN I HAD BEEN WORRIED, YOU KNOW, THAT I WAS BRINGING THIS JUNKIE ADDICT TO MY PARENTS' HOUSE--
--HIM PRACTICING FOR A FEW HOURS DIDN'T SEEM TOO BAD.

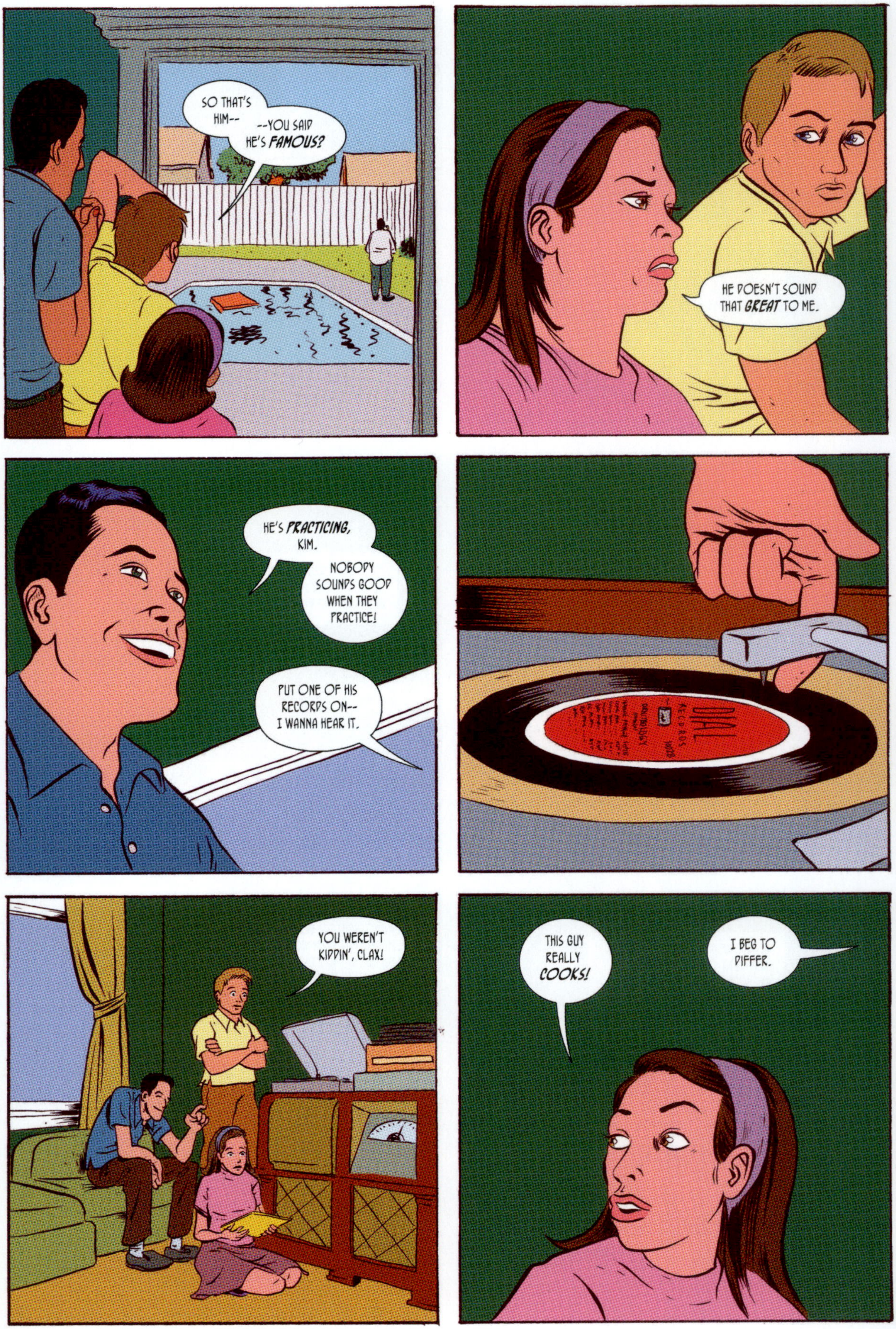
SO THAT'S HIM--
--YOU SAID HE'S FAMOUS?
HE DOESN'T SOUND THAT GREAT TO ME.
HE'S PRACTICING, KIM.
NOBODY SOUNDS GOOD WHEN THEY PRACTICE!
PUT ONE OF HIS RECORDS ON-- I WANNA HEAR IT.
DIAL RECORDS
YOU WEREN'T KIDDIN', CLAX!
THIS GUY REALLY COOKS!
I BEG TO DIFFER.

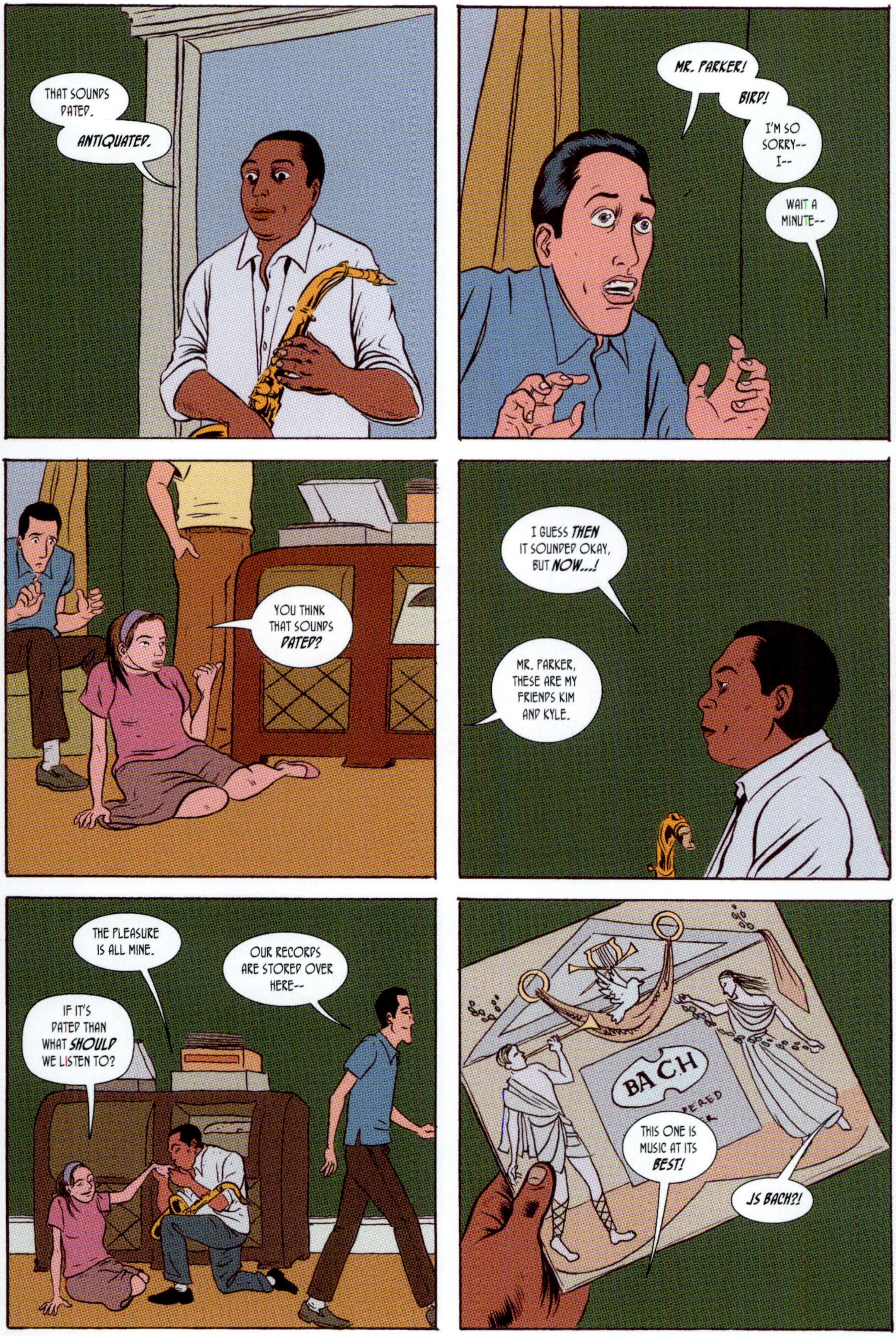
THAT SOUNDS DATED.
ANTIQUATED.
MR. PARKER!
BIRD!
I'M SO SORRY-- I--
WAIT A MINUTE--
YOU THINK THAT SOUNDS DATED?
I GUESS THEN IT SOUNDED OKAY, BUT NOW...!
MR. PARKER, THESE ARE MY FRIENDS KIM AND KYLE.
THE PLEASURE IS ALL MINE.
IF IT'S DATED THAN WHAT SHOULD WE LISTEN TO?
OUR RECORDS ARE STORED OVER HERE--
BACH
THIS ONE IS MUSIC AT ITS BEST!
JS BACH?!

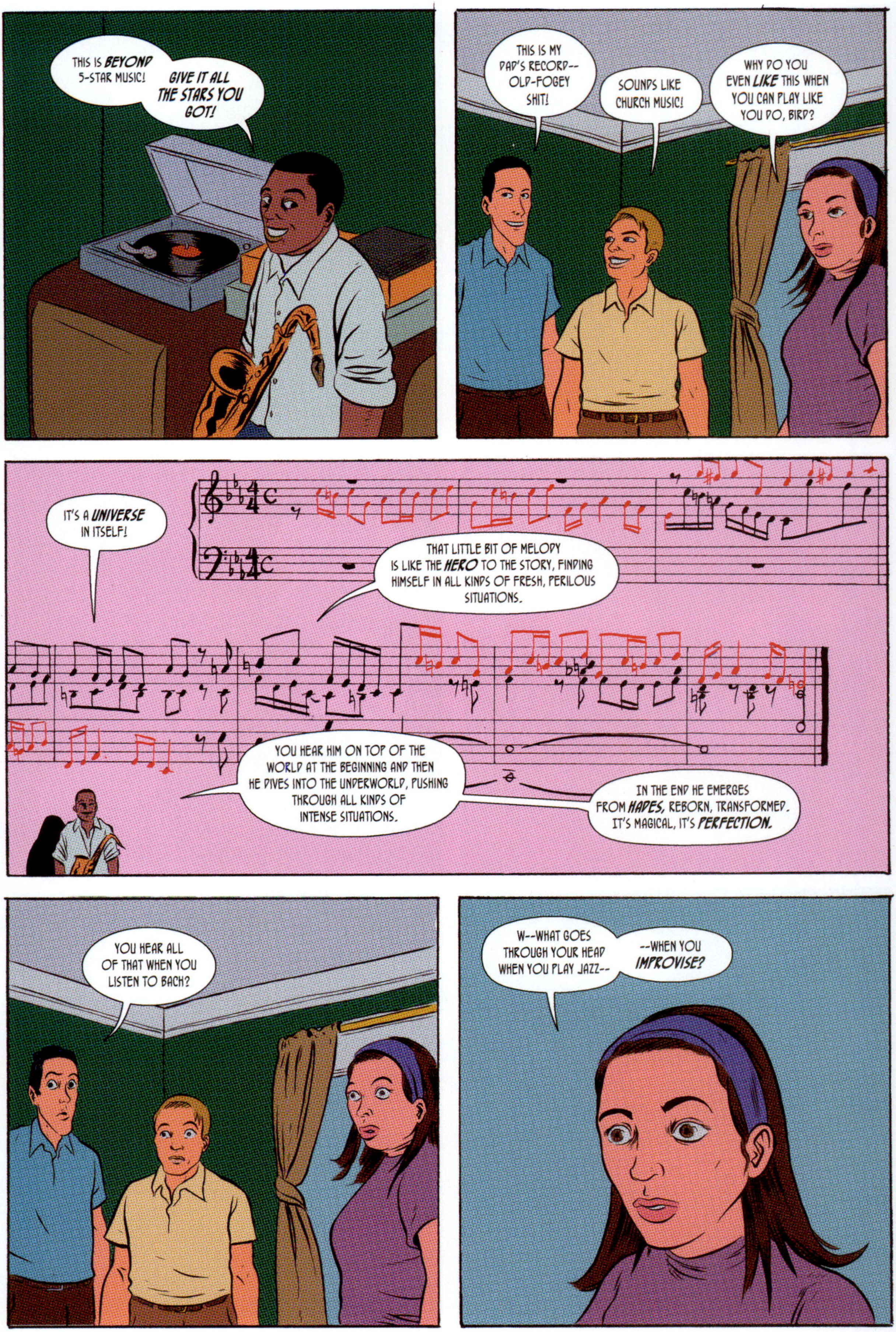
THIS IS BEYOND 5-STAR MUSIC!
GIVE IT ALL THE STARS YOU GOT!
THIS IS MY DAD'S RECORD-- OLD-FOGEY SHIT!
SOUNDS LIKE CHURCH MUSIC!
WHY DO YOU EVEN LIKE THIS WHEN YOU CAN PLAY LIKE YOU DO, BIRD?
IT'S A UNIVERSE IN ITSELF!
THAT LITTLE BIT OF MELODY IS LIKE THE HERO TO THE STORY, FINDING HIMSELF IN ALL KINDS OF FRESH, PERILOUS SITUATIONS.
YOU HEAR HIM ON TOP OF THE WORLD AT THE BEGINNING AND THEN HE DIVES INTO THE UNDERWORLD, PUSHING THROUGH ALL KINDS OF INTENSE SITUATIONS.
IN THE END HE EMERGES FROM HADES, REBORN, TRANSFORMED. IT'S MAGICAL, IT'S PERFECTION.
YOU HEAR ALL OF THAT WHEN YOU LISTEN TO BACH?
W--WHAT GOES THROUGH YOUR HEAD WHEN YOU PLAY JAZZ--
--WHEN YOU IMPROVISE?

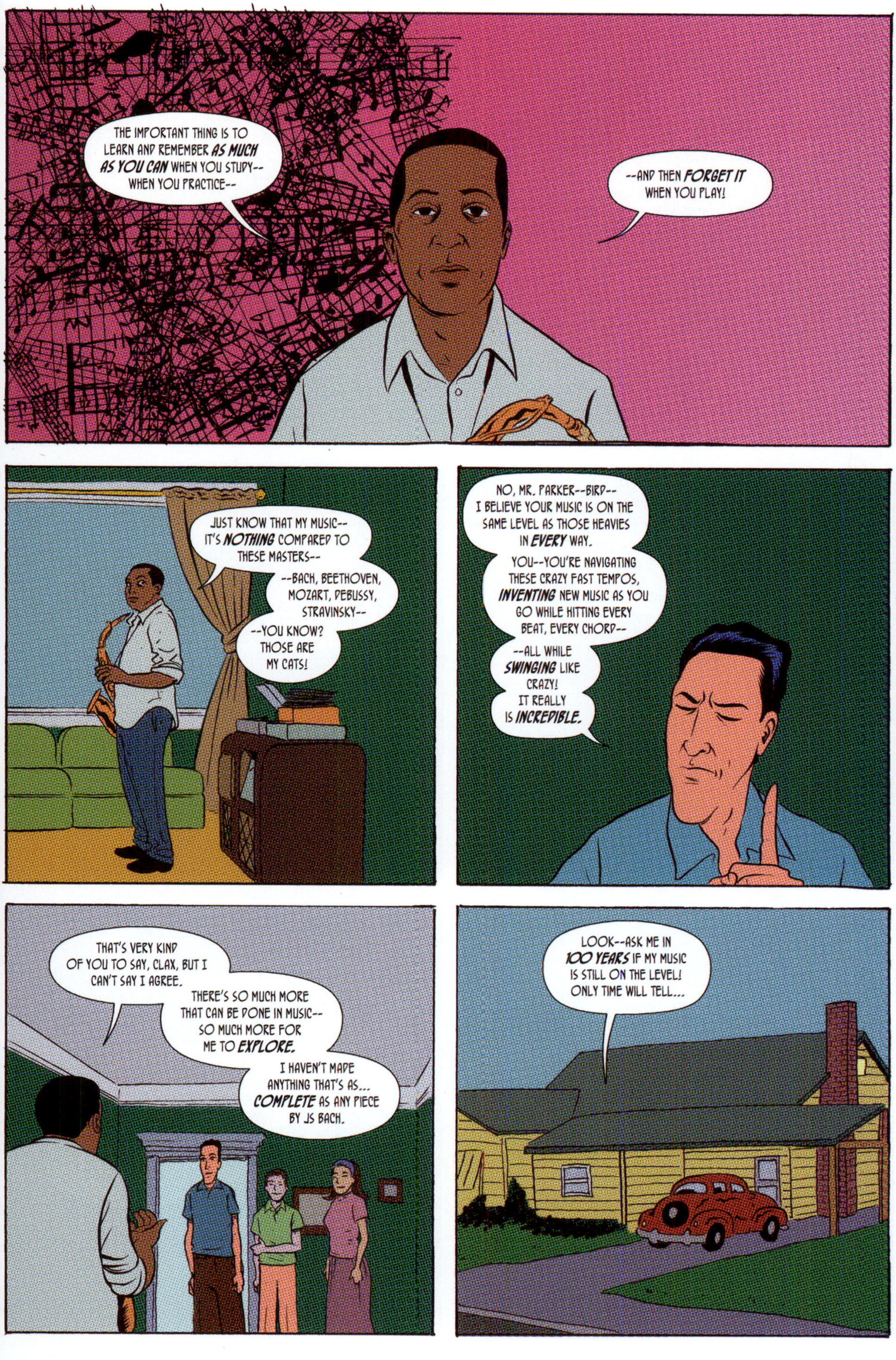
THE IMPORTANT THING IS TO LEARN AND REMEMBER **AS MUCH AS YOU CAN** WHEN YOU STUDY-- WHEN YOU PRACTICE--
--AND THEN **FORGET IT** WHEN YOU PLAY!
JUST KNOW THAT MY MUSIC-- IT'S **NOTHING** COMPARED TO THESE MASTERS--
--BACH, BEETHOVEN, MOZART, DEBUSSY, STRAVINSKY--
--YOU KNOW? THOSE ARE MY CATS!
NO, MR. PARKER--BIRD-- I BELIEVE YOUR MUSIC IS ON THE SAME LEVEL AS THOSE HEAVIES IN **EVERY** WAY.
YOU--YOU'RE NAVIGATING THESE CRAZY FAST TEMPOS, **INVENTING** NEW MUSIC AS YOU GO WHILE HITTING EVERY BEAT, EVERY CHORD--
--ALL WHILE **SWINGING** LIKE CRAZY! IT REALLY IS **INCREDIBLE.**
THAT'S VERY KIND OF YOU TO SAY, CLAX, BUT I CAN'T SAY I AGREE.
THERE'S SO MUCH MORE THAT CAN BE DONE IN MUSIC-- SO MUCH MORE FOR ME TO **EXPLORE.**
I HAVEN'T MADE ANYTHING THAT'S AS... **COMPLETE** AS ANY PIECE BY JS BACH.
LOOK--ASK ME IN **100 YEARS** IF MY MUSIC IS STILL ON THE LEVEL! ONLY TIME WILL TELL...

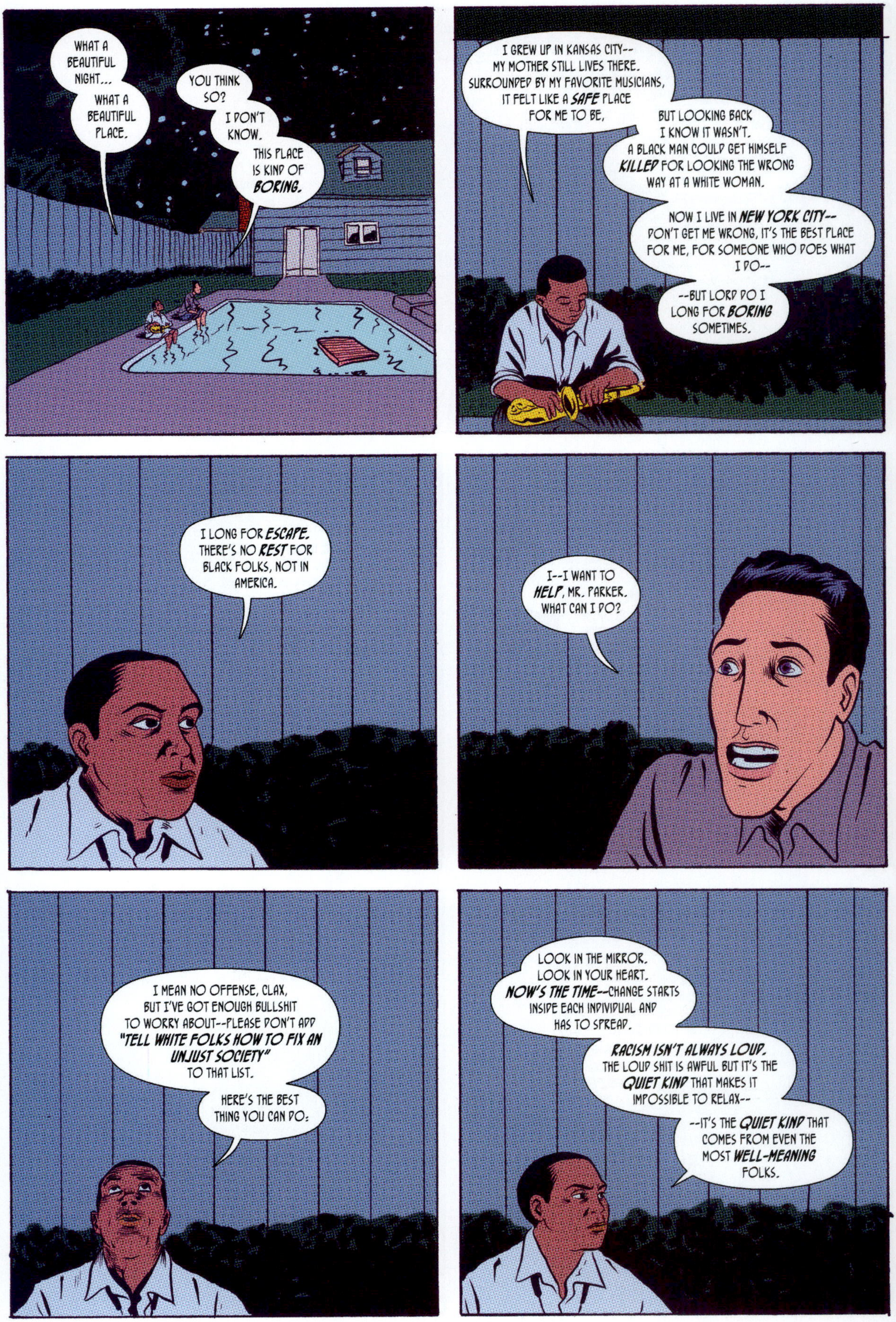

WHAT A BEAUTIFUL NIGHT... WHAT A BEAUTIFUL PLACE.
YOU THINK SO? I DON'T KNOW. THIS PLACE IS KIND OF BORING.
I GREW UP IN KANSAS CITY-- MY MOTHER STILL LIVES THERE. SURROUNDED BY MY FAVORITE MUSICIANS, IT FELT LIKE A SAFE PLACE FOR ME TO BE,
BUT LOOKING BACK I KNOW IT WASN'T. A BLACK MAN COULD GET HIMSELF KILLED FOR LOOKING THE WRONG WAY AT A WHITE WOMAN.
NOW I LIVE IN NEW YORK CITY-- DON'T GET ME WRONG, IT'S THE BEST PLACE FOR ME, FOR SOMEONE WHO DOES WHAT I DO--
--BUT LORD DO I LONG FOR BORING SOMETIMES.
I LONG FOR ESCAPE. THERE'S NO REST FOR BLACK FOLKS, NOT IN AMERICA.
I--I WANT TO HELP, MR. PARKER. WHAT CAN I DO?
I MEAN NO OFFENSE, CLAX, BUT I'VE GOT ENOUGH BULLSHIT TO WORRY ABOUT--PLEASE DON'T ADD "TELL WHITE FOLKS HOW TO FIX AN UNJUST SOCIETY" TO THAT LIST.
HERE'S THE BEST THING YOU CAN DO:
LOOK IN THE MIRROR. LOOK IN YOUR HEART. NOW'S THE TIME--CHANGE STARTS INSIDE EACH INDIVIDUAL AND HAS TO SPREAD.
RACISM ISN'T ALWAYS LOUD. THE LOUD SHIT IS AWFUL BUT IT'S THE QUIET KIND THAT MAKES IT IMPOSSIBLE TO RELAX--
--IT'S THE QUIET KIND THAT COMES FROM EVEN THE MOST WELL-MEANING FOLKS.

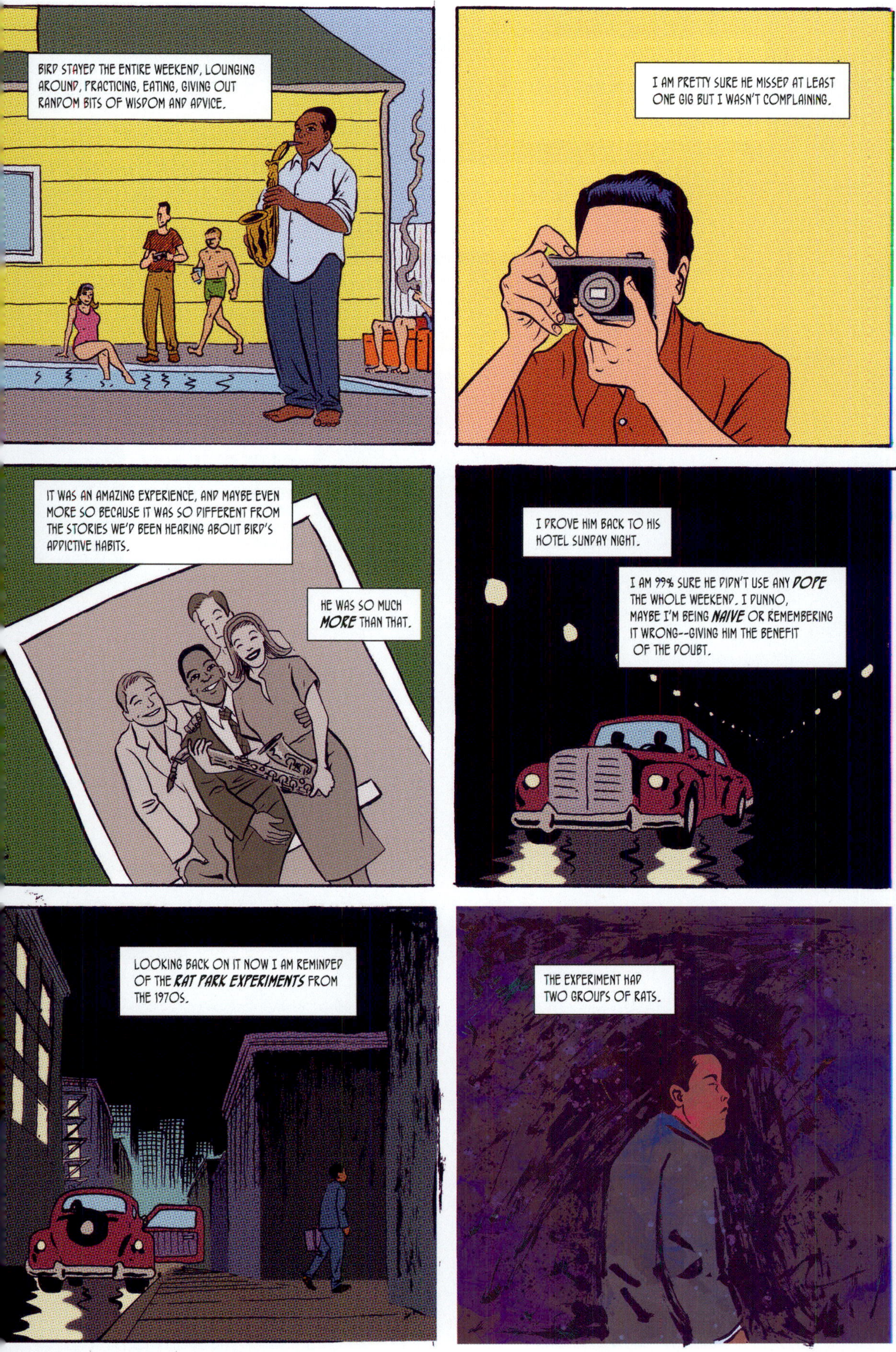
BIRD STAYED THE ENTIRE WEEKEND, LOUNGING AROUND, PRACTICING, EATING, GIVING OUT RANDOM BITS OF WISDOM AND ADVICE.
I AM PRETTY SURE HE MISSED AT LEAST ONE GIG BUT I WASN'T COMPLAINING.
IT WAS AN AMAZING EXPERIENCE, AND MAYBE EVEN MORE SO BECAUSE IT WAS SO DIFFERENT FROM THE STORIES WE'D BEEN HEARING ABOUT BIRD'S ADDICTIVE HABITS.
HE WAS SO MUCH MORE THAN THAT.
I DROVE HIM BACK TO HIS HOTEL SUNDAY NIGHT.
I AM 99% SURE HE DIDN'T USE ANY DOPE THE WHOLE WEEKEND. I DUNNO, MAYBE I'M BEING NAIVE OR REMEMBERING IT WRONG--GIVING HIM THE BENEFIT OF THE DOUBT.
LOOKING BACK ON IT NOW I AM REMINDED OF THE RAT PARK EXPERIMENTS FROM THE 1970S.
THE EXPERIMENT HAD TWO GROUPS OF RATS.

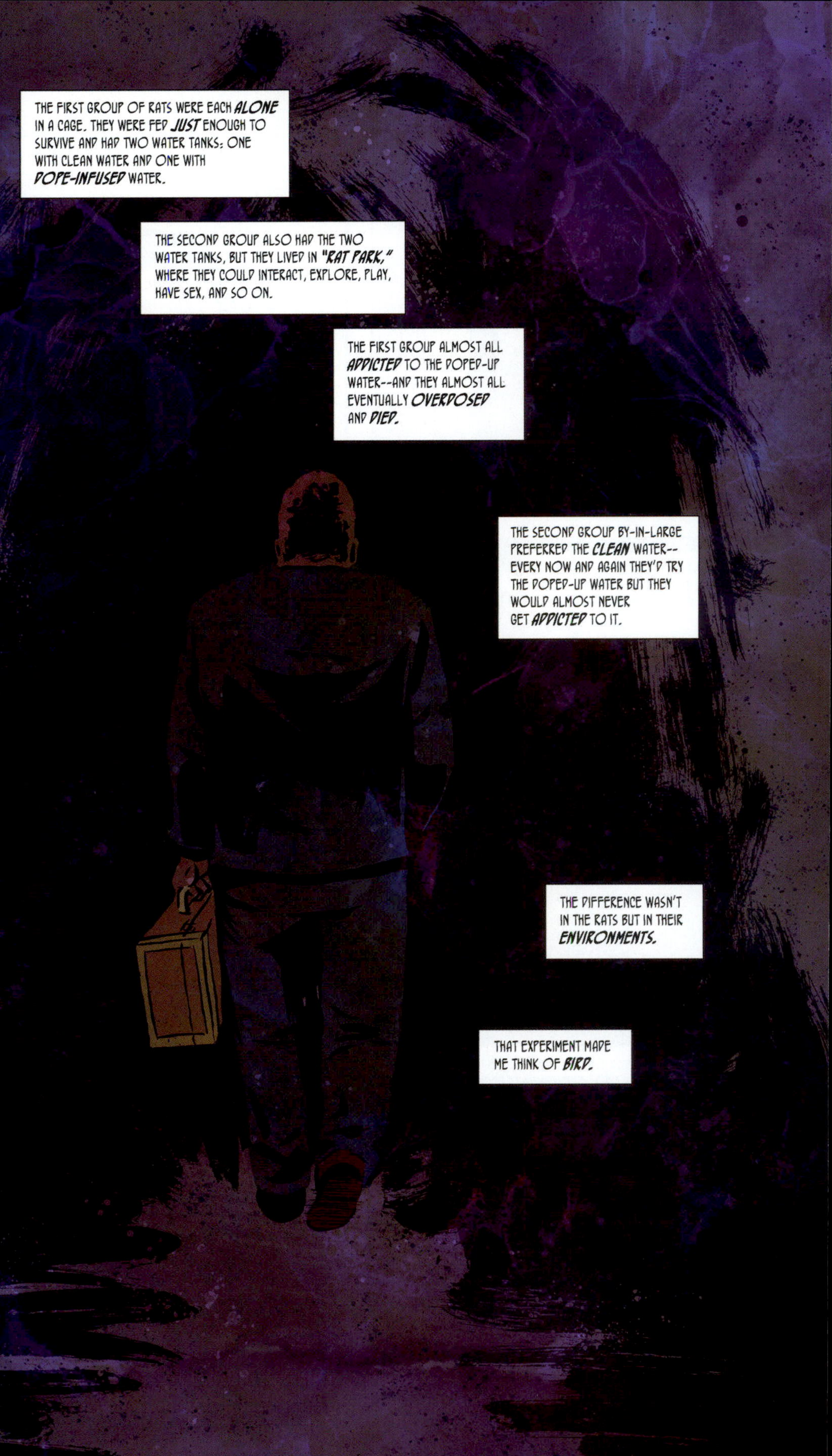
THE FIRST GROUP OF RATS WERE EACH ALONE IN A CAGE. THEY WERE FED JUST ENOUGH TO SURVIVE AND HAD TWO WATER TANKS: ONE WITH CLEAN WATER AND ONE WITH DOPE-INFUSED WATER.
THE SECOND GROUP ALSO HAD THE TWO WATER TANKS, BUT THEY LIVED IN "RAT PARK," WHERE THEY COULD INTERACT, EXPLORE, PLAY, HAVE SEX, AND SO ON.
THE FIRST GROUP ALMOST ALL ADDICTED TO THE DOPED-UP WATER--AND THEY ALMOST ALL EVENTUALLY OVERDOSED AND DIED.
THE SECOND GROUP BY-IN-LARGE PREFERRED THE CLEAN WATER--EVERY NOW AND AGAIN THEY'D TRY THE DOPED-UP WATER BUT THEY WOULD ALMOST NEVER GET ADDICTED TO IT.
THE DIFFERENCE WASN'T IN THE RATS BUT IN THEIR ENVIRONMENTS.
THAT EXPERIMENT MADE ME THINK OF BIRD.

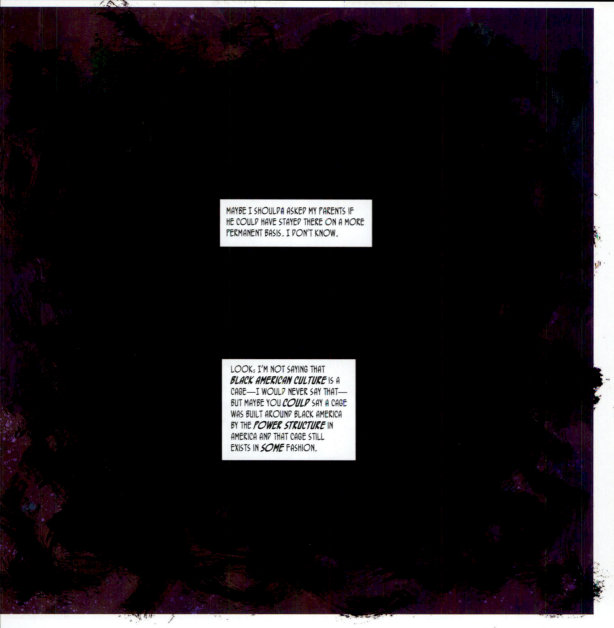

MAYBE I SHOULDA ASKED MY PARENTS IF HE COULD HAVE STAYED THERE ON A MORE PERMANENT BASIS. I DON'T KNOW.

LOOK, I'M NOT SAYING THAT *BLACK AMERICAN CULTURE* IS A CAGE—I WOULD NEVER SAY THAT—BUT MAYBE YOU *COULD* SAY A CAGE WAS BUILT AROUND BLACK AMERICA BY THE *POWER STRUCTURE* IN AMERICA AND THAT CAGE STILL EXISTS IN *SOME* FASHION.

MY PARENTS CAME HOME THE NEXT MORNING.

WILLIAM! WHAT HAPPENED TO ALL OUR FOOD?!

HE DID HAVE AN APPETITE FOR MY MOM'S COOKING!

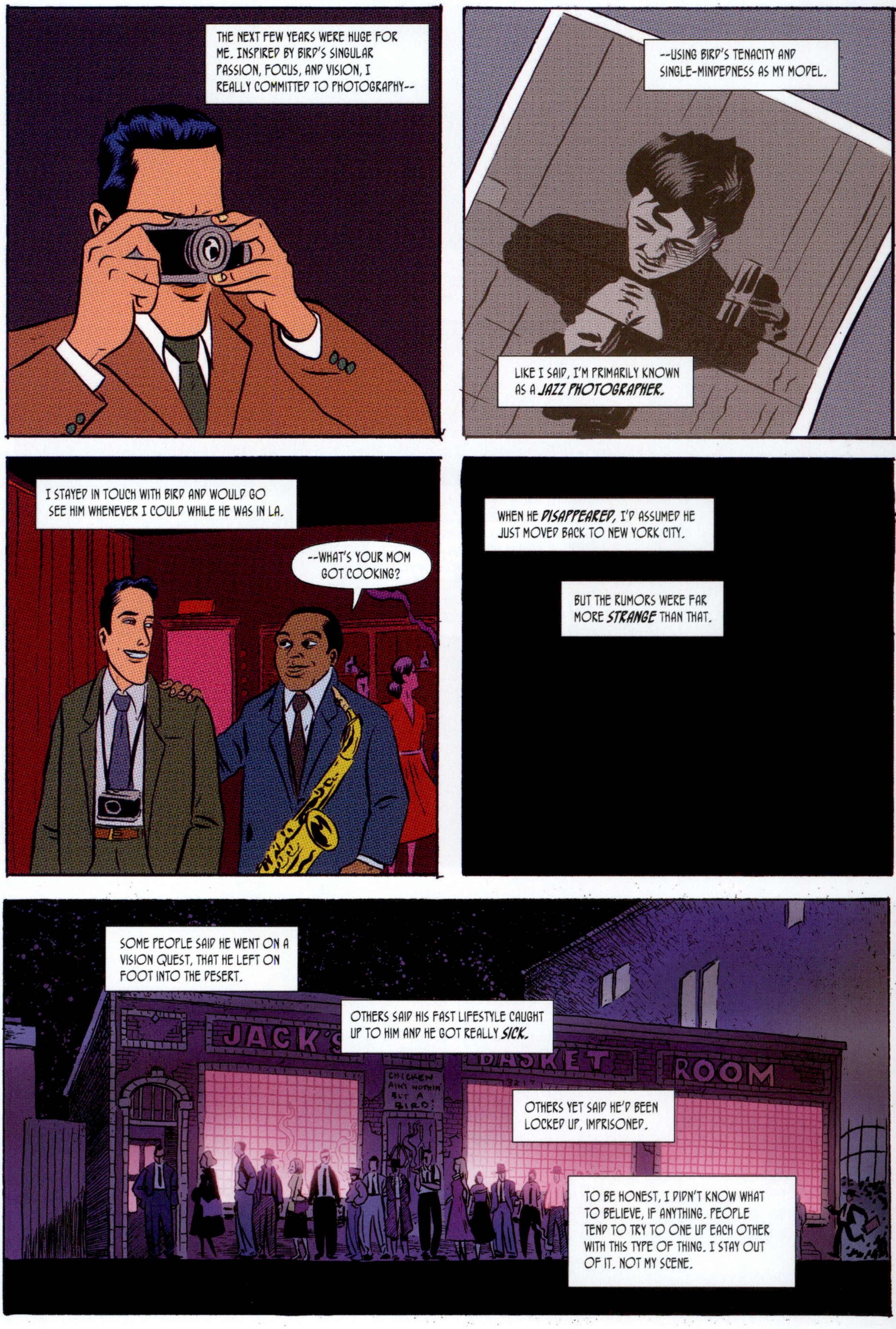
THE NEXT FEW YEARS WERE HUGE FOR ME. INSPIRED BY BIRD'S SINGULAR PASSION, FOCUS, AND VISION, I REALLY COMMITTED TO PHOTOGRAPHY--
--USING BIRD'S TENACITY AND SINGLE-MINDEDNESS AS MY MODEL.
LIKE I SAID, I'M PRIMARILY KNOWN AS A JAZZ PHOTOGRAPHER.
I STAYED IN TOUCH WITH BIRD AND WOULD GO SEE HIM WHENEVER I COULD WHILE HE WAS IN LA.
--WHAT'S YOUR MOM GOT COOKING?
WHEN HE DISAPPEARED, I'D ASSUMED HE JUST MOVED BACK TO NEW YORK CITY.
BUT THE RUMORS WERE FAR MORE STRANGE THAN THAT.
SOME PEOPLE SAID HE WENT ON A VISION QUEST, THAT HE LEFT ON FOOT INTO THE DESERT.
JACK'S
BASKET
ROOM
CHICKEN AIN'T NOTHIN BUT A BIRD!
OTHERS SAID HIS FAST LIFESTYLE CAUGHT UP TO HIM AND HE GOT REALLY SICK.
OTHERS YET SAID HE'D BEEN LOCKED UP, IMPRISONED.
TO BE HONEST, I DIDN'T KNOW WHAT TO BELIEVE, IF ANYTHING. PEOPLE TEND TO TRY TO ONE UP EACH OTHER WITH THIS TYPE OF THING. I STAY OUT OF IT. NOT MY SCENE.

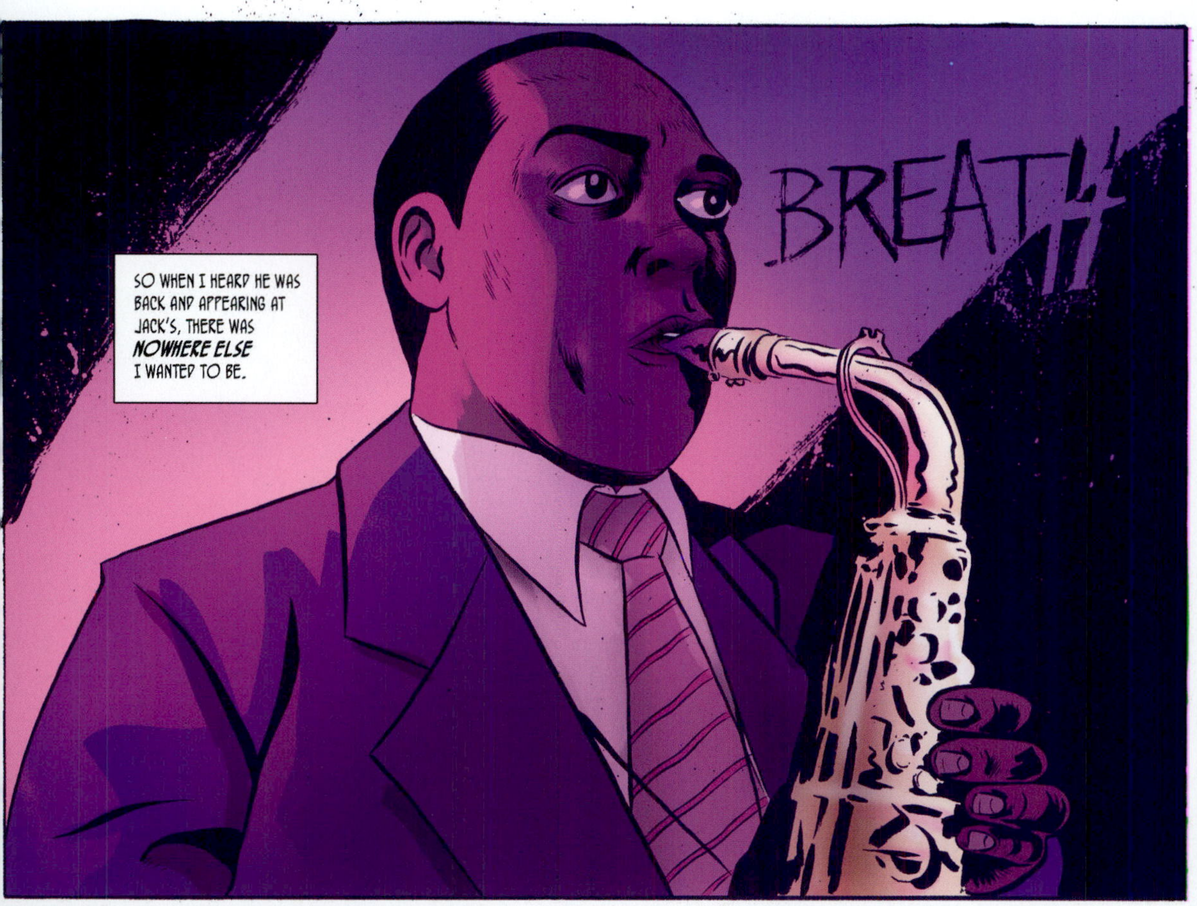
SO WHEN I HEARD HE WAS BACK AND APPEARING AT JACK'S, THERE WAS ***NOWHERE ELSE*** I WANTED TO BE.
BREAT

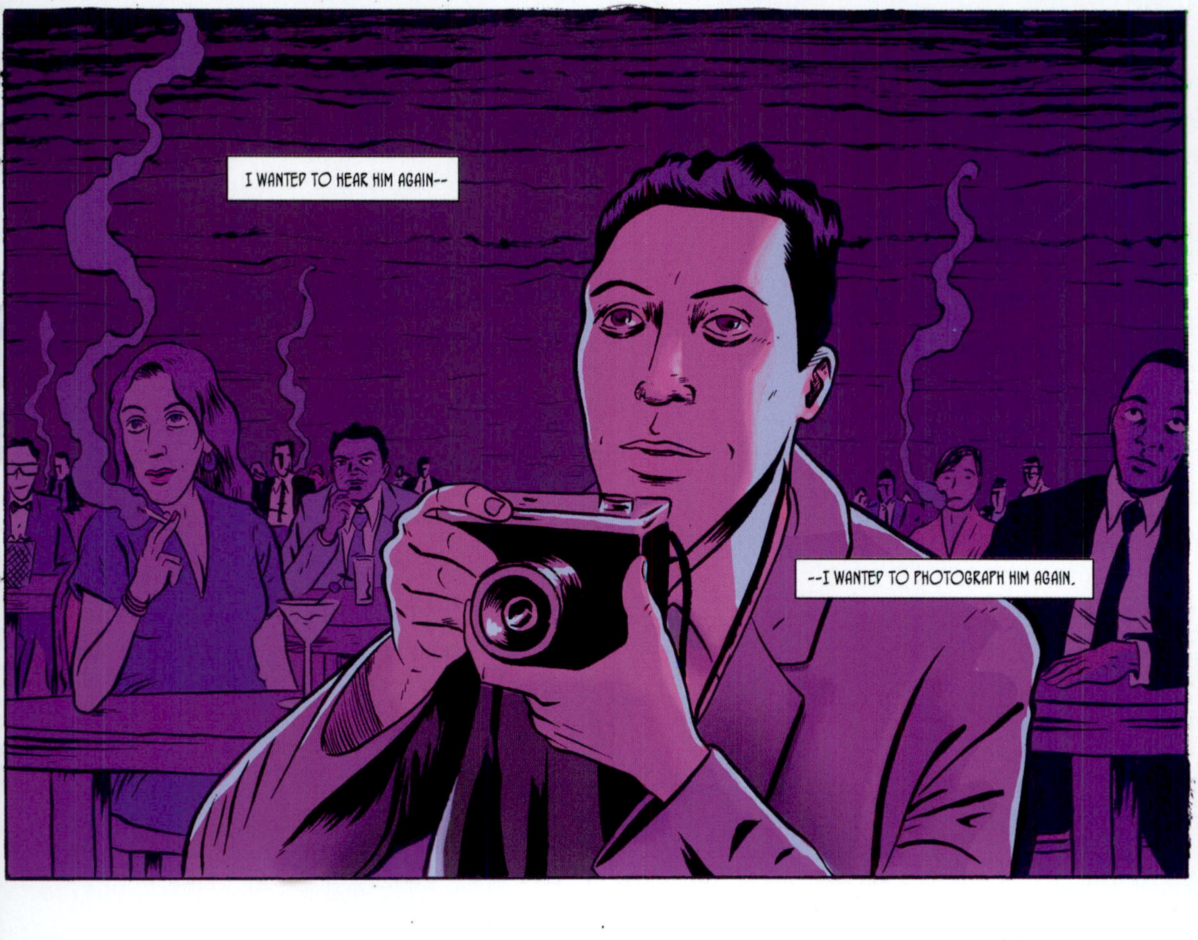
I WANTED TO HEAR HIM AGAIN--
--I WANTED TO PHOTOGRAPH HIM AGAIN.

CHORUS 4:

MacDonald

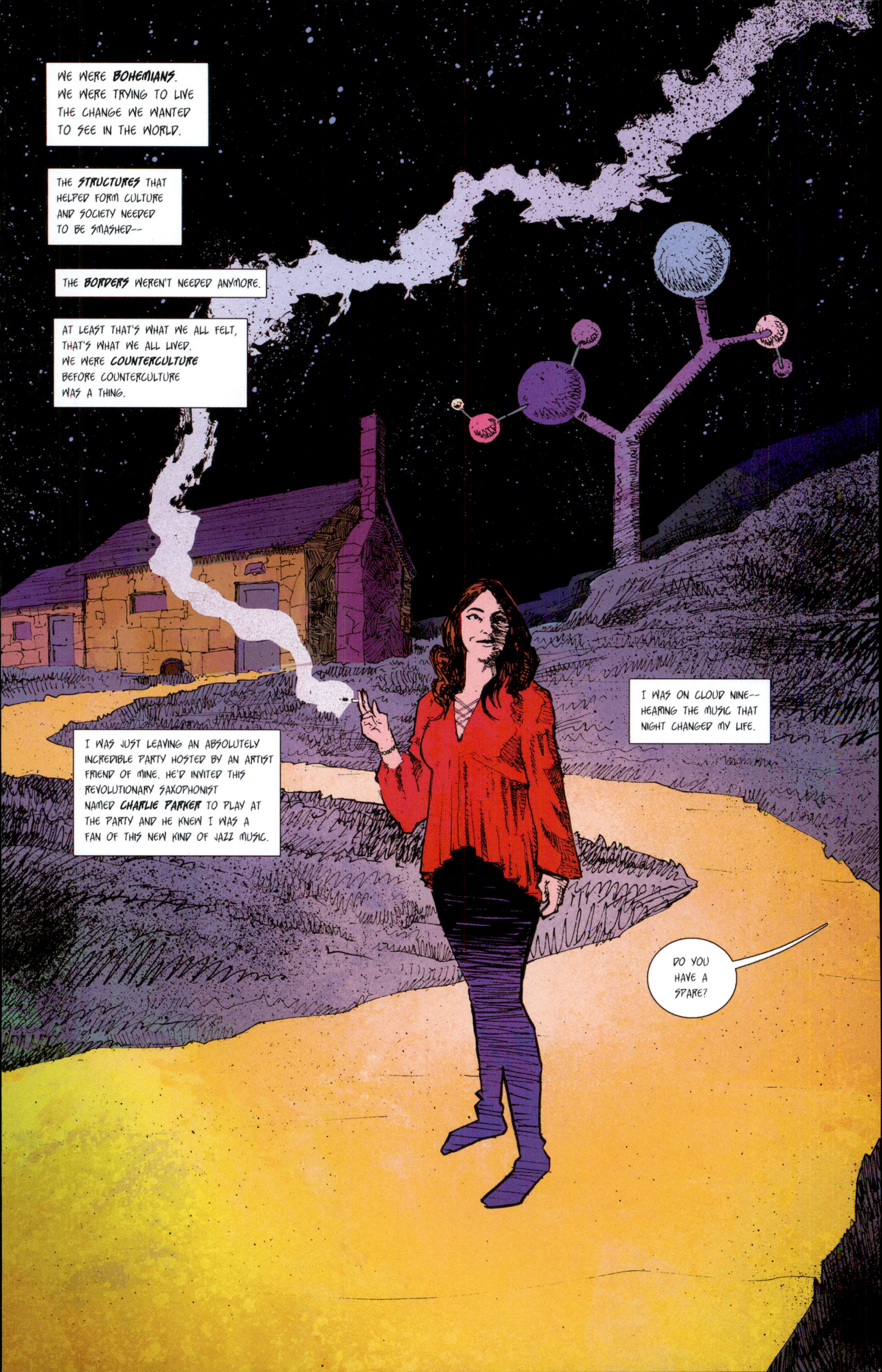
WE WERE **BOHEMIANS**. WE WERE TRYING TO LIVE THE CHANGE WE WANTED TO SEE IN THE WORLD.
THE **STRUCTURES** THAT HELPED FORM CULTURE AND SOCIETY NEEDED TO BE SMASHED--
THE **BORDERS** WEREN'T NEEDED ANYMORE.
AT LEAST THAT'S WHAT WE ALL FELT, THAT'S WHAT WE ALL LIVED. WE WERE **COUNTERCULTURE** BEFORE COUNTERCULTURE WAS A THING.
I WAS JUST LEAVING AN ABSOLUTELY INCREDIBLE PARTY HOSTED BY AN ARTIST FRIEND OF MINE. HE'D INVITED THIS REVOLUTIONARY SAXOPHONIST NAMED **CHARLIE PARKER** TO PLAY AT THE PARTY AND HE KNEW I WAS A FAN OF THIS NEW KIND OF JAZZ MUSIC.
I WAS ON CLOUD NINE-- HEARING THE MUSIC THAT NIGHT CHANGED MY LIFE.
DO YOU HAVE A SPARE?

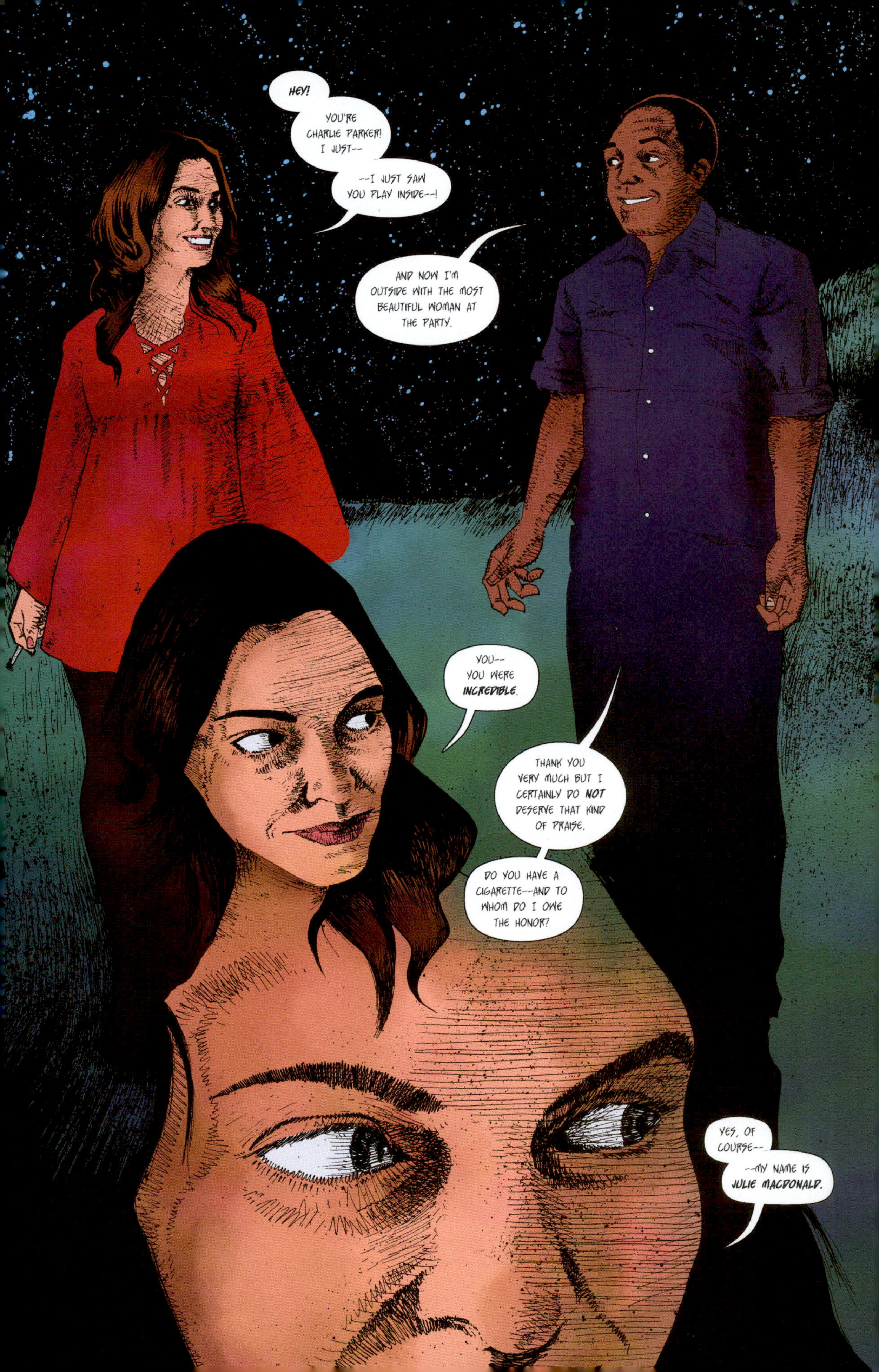
HEY!
YOU'RE CHARLIE PARKER! I JUST--
--I JUST SAW YOU PLAY INSIDE--!
AND NOW I'M OUTSIDE WITH THE MOST BEAUTIFUL WOMAN AT THE PARTY.
YOU-- YOU WERE **INCREDIBLE**.
THANK YOU VERY MUCH BUT I CERTAINLY DO **NOT** DESERVE THAT KIND OF PRAISE.
DO YOU HAVE A CIGARETTE--AND TO WHOM DO I OWE THE HONOR?
YES, OF COURSE--
--MY NAME IS **JULIE MACDONALD**.

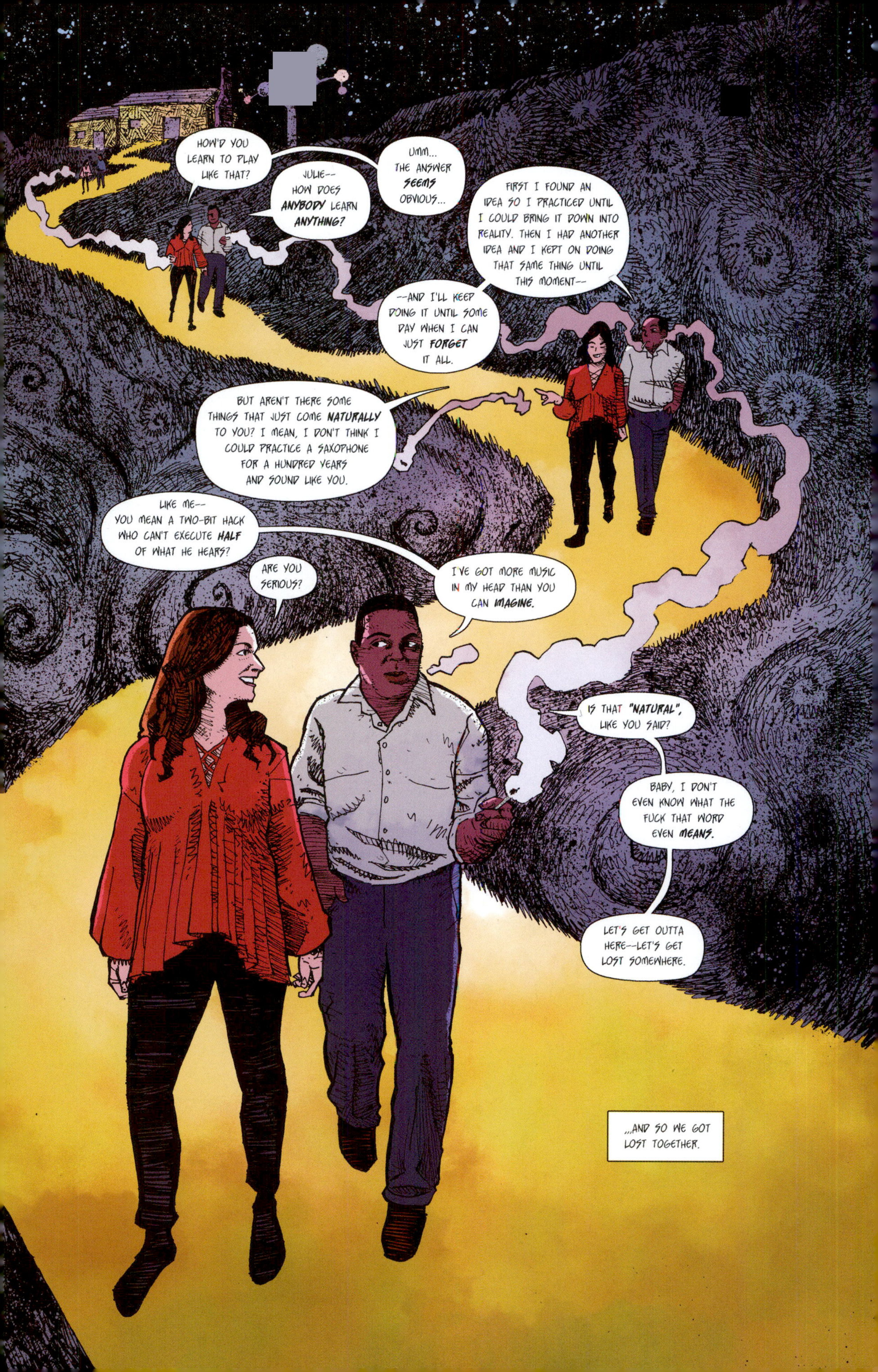
HOW'D YOU LEARN TO PLAY LIKE THAT?
UMM... THE ANSWER SEEMS OBVIOUS...
JULIE-- HOW DOES ANYBODY LEARN ANYTHING?
FIRST I FOUND AN IDEA SO I PRACTICED UNTIL I COULD BRING IT DOWN INTO REALITY. THEN I HAD ANOTHER IDEA AND I KEPT ON DOING THAT SAME THING UNTIL THIS MOMENT--
--AND I'LL KEEP DOING IT UNTIL SOME DAY WHEN I CAN JUST FORGET IT ALL.
BUT AREN'T THERE SOME THINGS THAT JUST COME NATURALLY TO YOU? I MEAN, I DON'T THINK I COULD PRACTICE A SAXOPHONE FOR A HUNDRED YEARS AND SOUND LIKE YOU.
LIKE ME-- YOU MEAN A TWO-BIT HACK WHO CAN'T EXECUTE HALF OF WHAT HE HEARS?
ARE YOU SERIOUS?
I'VE GOT MORE MUSIC IN MY HEAD THAN YOU CAN IMAGINE.
IS THAT "NATURAL", LIKE YOU SAID?
BABY, I DON'T EVEN KNOW WHAT THE FUCK THAT WORD EVEN MEANS.
LET'S GET OUTTA HERE--LET'S GET LOST SOMEWHERE.
...AND SO WE GOT LOST TOGETHER.

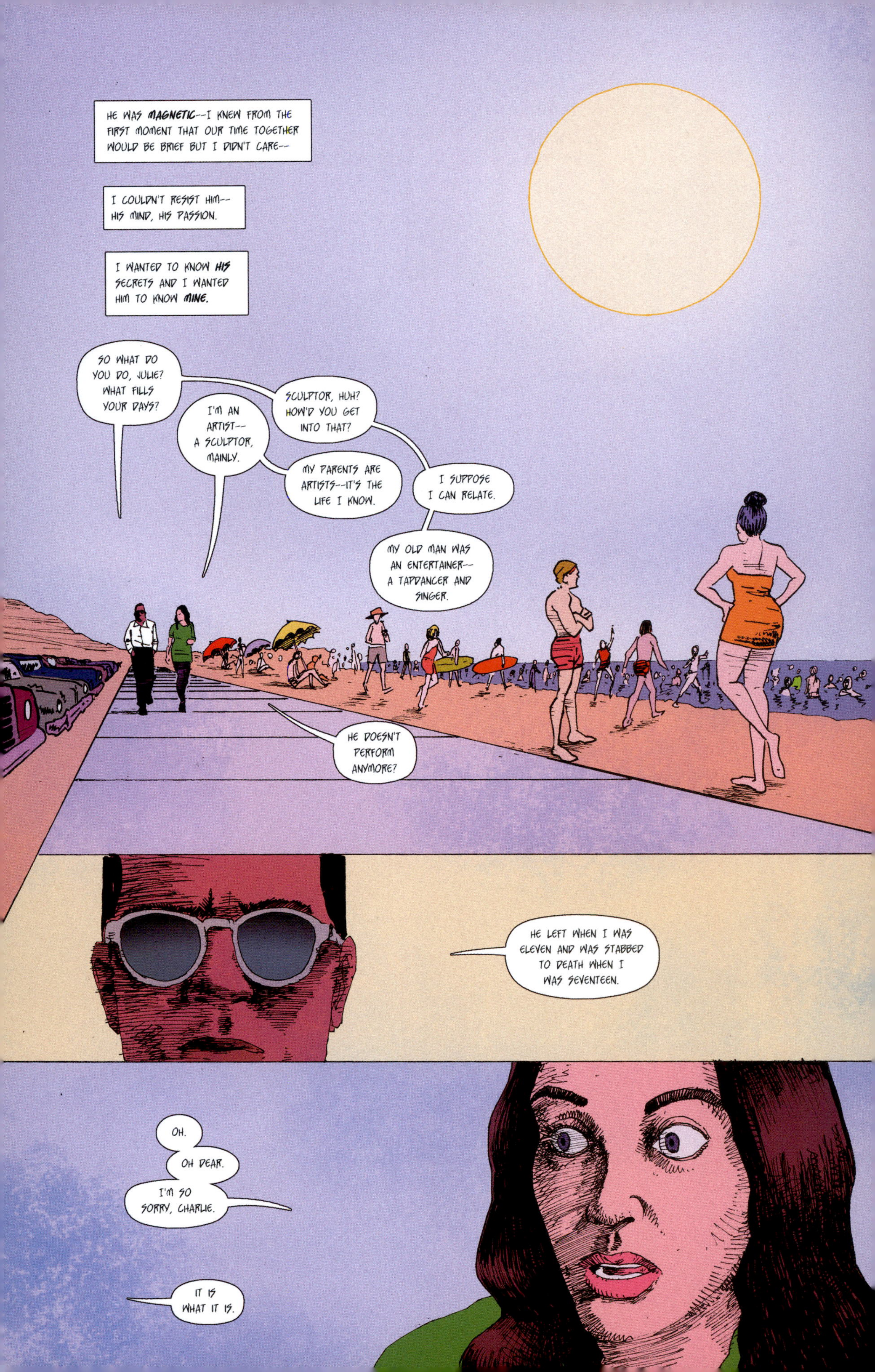
HE WAS MAGNETIC--I KNEW FROM THE FIRST MOMENT THAT OUR TIME TOGETHER WOULD BE BRIEF BUT I DIDN'T CARE--
I COULDN'T RESIST HIM--HIS MIND, HIS PASSION.
I WANTED TO KNOW HIS SECRETS AND I WANTED HIM TO KNOW MINE.
SO WHAT DO YOU DO, JULIE? WHAT FILLS YOUR DAYS?
I'M AN ARTIST--A SCULPTOR, MAINLY.
SCULPTOR, HUH? HOW'D YOU GET INTO THAT?
MY PARENTS ARE ARTISTS--IT'S THE LIFE I KNOW.
I SUPPOSE I CAN RELATE.
MY OLD MAN WAS AN ENTERTAINER--A TAPDANCER AND SINGER.
HE DOESN'T PERFORM ANYMORE?
HE LEFT WHEN I WAS ELEVEN AND WAS STABBED TO DEATH WHEN I WAS SEVENTEEN.
OH.
OH DEAR.
I'M SO SORRY, CHARLIE.
IT IS WHAT IT IS.

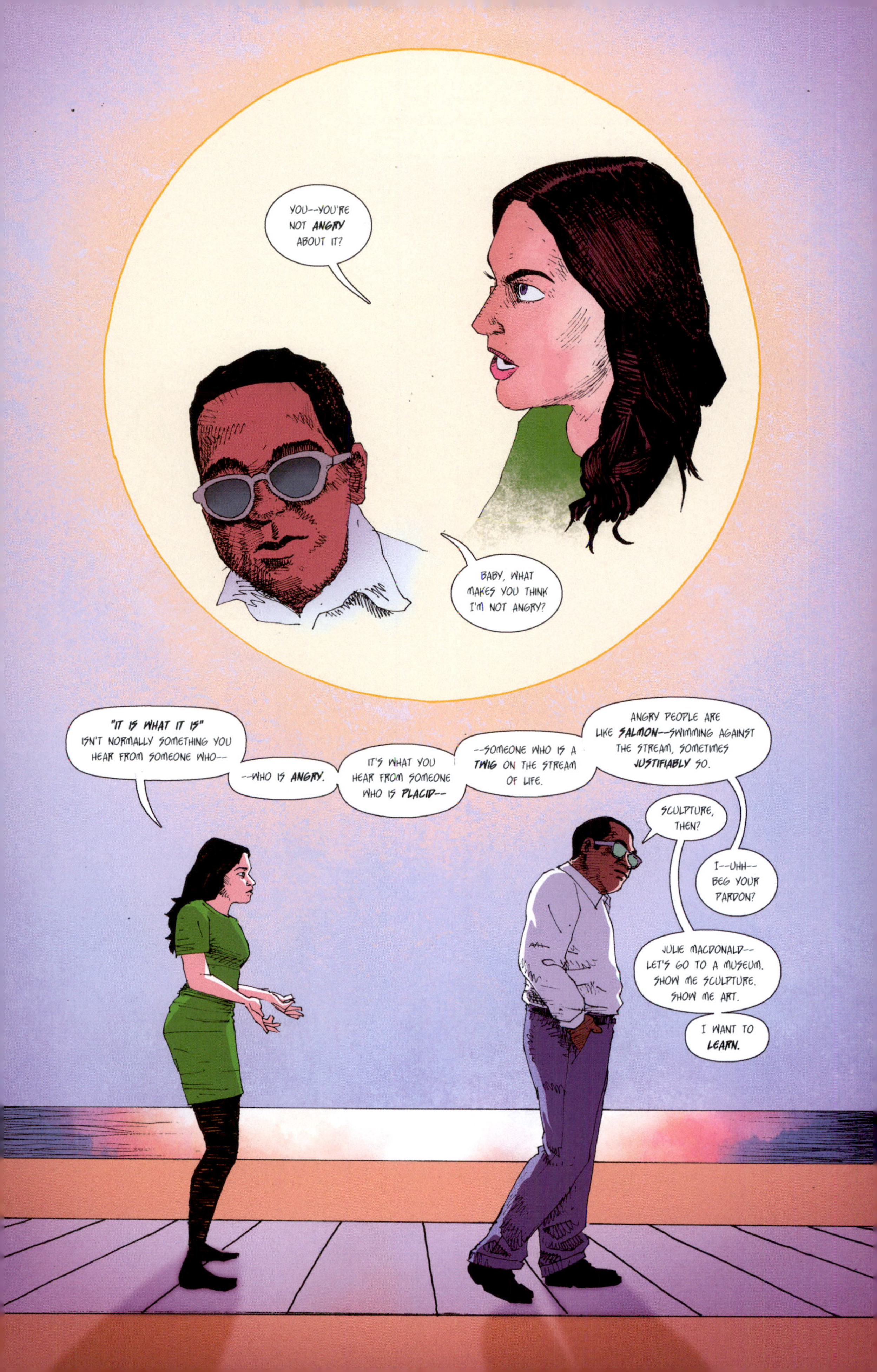
YOU--YOU'RE NOT ANGRY ABOUT IT?
BABY, WHAT MAKES YOU THINK I'M NOT ANGRY?
"IT IS WHAT IT IS" ISN'T NORMALLY SOMETHING YOU HEAR FROM SOMEONE WHO--
--WHO IS ANGRY.
IT'S WHAT YOU HEAR FROM SOMEONE WHO IS PLACID--
--SOMEONE WHO IS A TWIG ON THE STREAM OF LIFE.
ANGRY PEOPLE ARE LIKE SALMON--SWIMMING AGAINST THE STREAM, SOMETIMES JUSTIFIABLY SO.
SCULPTURE, THEN?
I--UHH-- BEG YOUR PARDON?
JULIE MACDONALD-- LET'S GO TO A MUSEUM. SHOW ME SCULPTURE. SHOW ME ART.
I WANT TO LEARN.

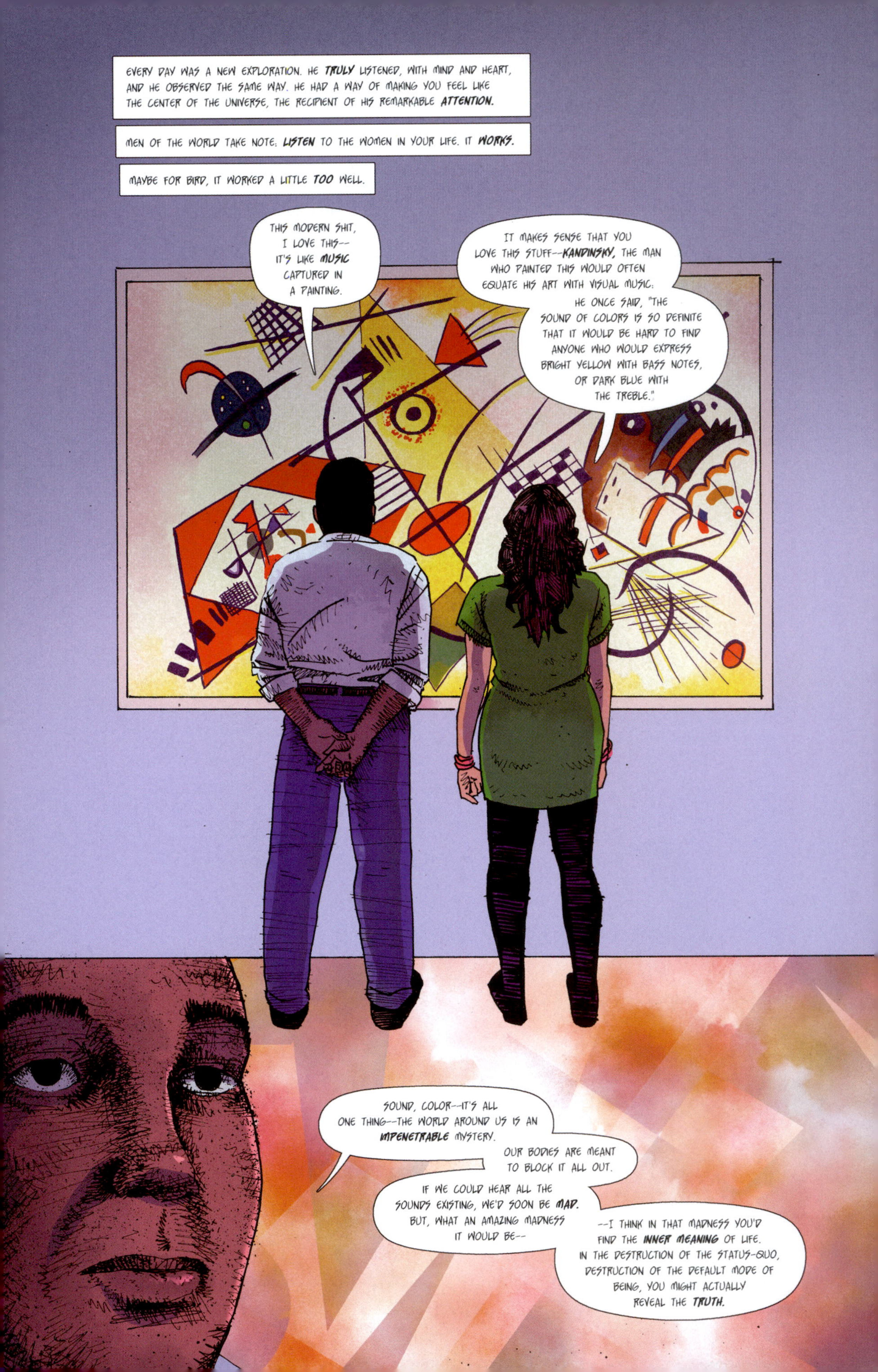
EVERY DAY WAS A NEW EXPLORATION. HE TRULY LISTENED, WITH MIND AND HEART, AND HE OBSERVED THE SAME WAY. HE HAD A WAY OF MAKING YOU FEEL LIKE THE CENTER OF THE UNIVERSE, THE RECIPIENT OF HIS REMARKABLE ATTENTION.
MEN OF THE WORLD TAKE NOTE: LISTEN TO THE WOMEN IN YOUR LIFE. IT WORKS.
MAYBE FOR BIRD, IT WORKED A LITTLE TOO WELL.
THIS MODERN SHIT, I LOVE THIS-- IT'S LIKE MUSIC CAPTURED IN A PAINTING.
IT MAKES SENSE THAT YOU LOVE THIS STUFF--KANDINSKY, THE MAN WHO PAINTED THIS WOULD OFTEN EQUATE HIS ART WITH VISUAL MUSIC.
HE ONCE SAID, "THE SOUND OF COLORS IS SO DEFINITE THAT IT WOULD BE HARD TO FIND ANYONE WHO WOULD EXPRESS BRIGHT YELLOW WITH BASS NOTES, OR DARK BLUE WITH THE TREBLE."
SOUND, COLOR--IT'S ALL ONE THING--THE WORLD AROUND US IS AN IMPENETRABLE MYSTERY.
OUR BODIES ARE MEANT TO BLOCK IT ALL OUT.
IF WE COULD HEAR ALL THE SOUNDS EXISTING, WE'D SOON BE MAD. BUT, WHAT AN AMAZING MADNESS IT WOULD BE--
--I THINK IN THAT MADNESS YOU'D FIND THE INNER MEANING OF LIFE. IN THE DESTRUCTION OF THE STATUS-QUO, DESTRUCTION OF THE DEFAULT MODE OF BEING, YOU MIGHT ACTUALLY REVEAL THE TRUTH.

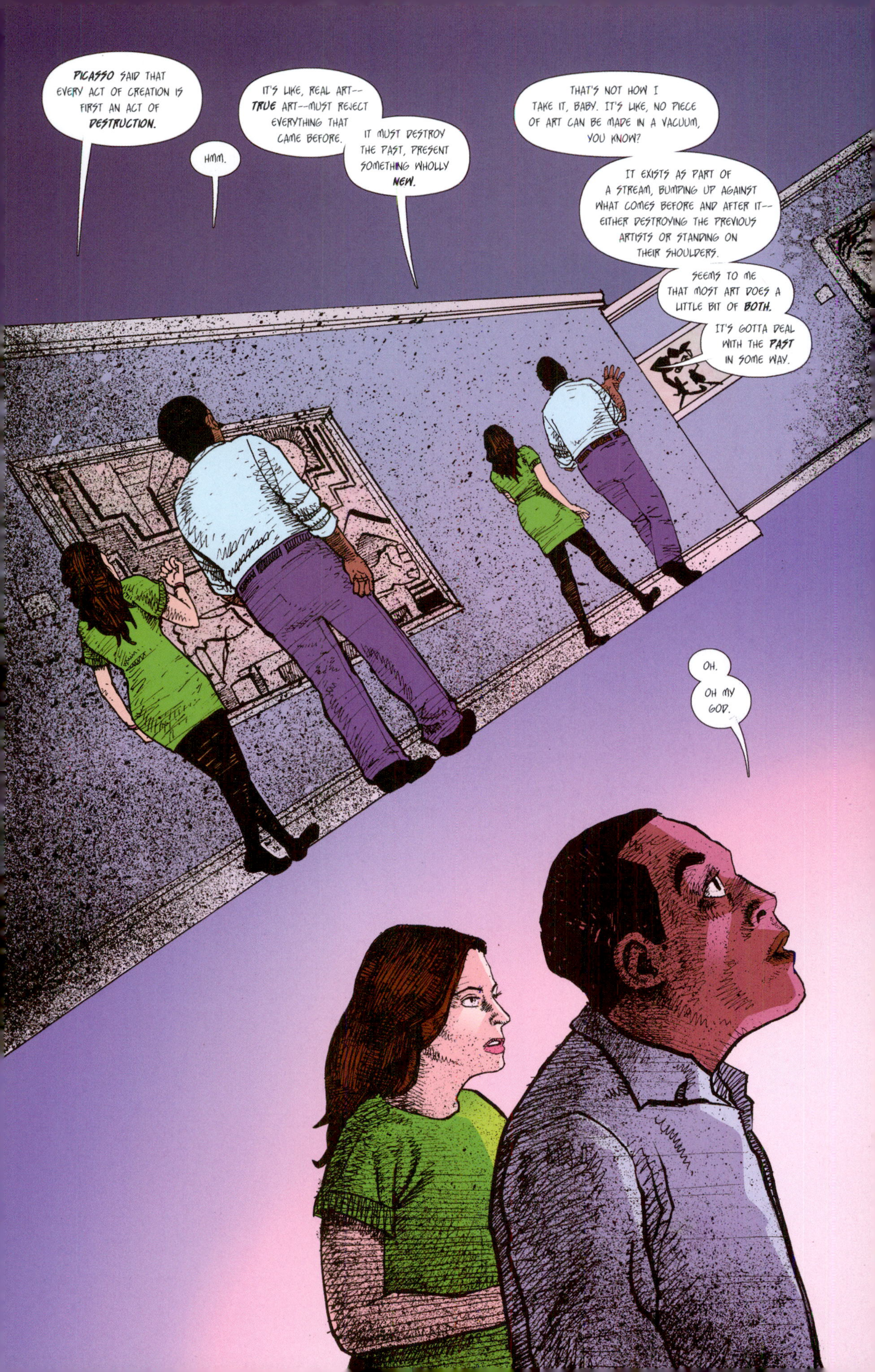
PICASSO SAID THAT EVERY ACT OF CREATION IS FIRST AN ACT OF DESTRUCTION.
HMM.
IT'S LIKE, REAL ART--TRUE ART--MUST REJECT EVERYTHING THAT CAME BEFORE.
IT MUST DESTROY THE PAST, PRESENT SOMETHING WHOLLY NEW.
THAT'S NOT HOW I TAKE IT, BABY. IT'S LIKE, NO PIECE OF ART CAN BE MADE IN A VACUUM, YOU KNOW?
IT EXISTS AS PART OF A STREAM, BUMPING UP AGAINST WHAT COMES BEFORE AND AFTER IT--EITHER DESTROYING THE PREVIOUS ARTISTS OR STANDING ON THEIR SHOULDERS.
SEEMS TO ME THAT MOST ART DOES A LITTLE BIT OF BOTH.
IT'S GOTTA DEAL WITH THE PAST IN SOME WAY.
OH.
OH MY GOD.

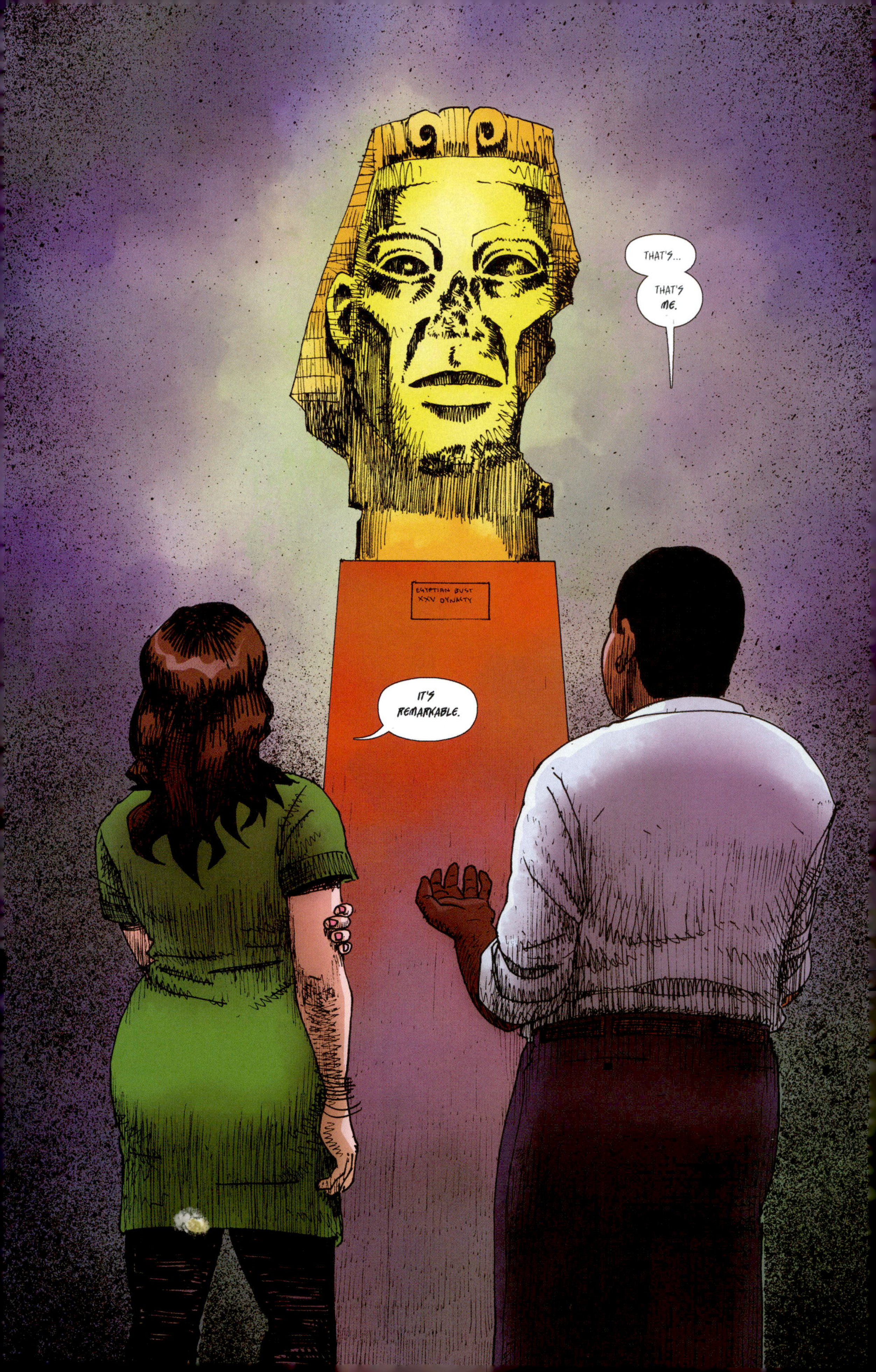
THAT'S...
THAT'S ME.
EGYPTIAN BUST
XXV DYNASTY
IT'S REMARKABLE.

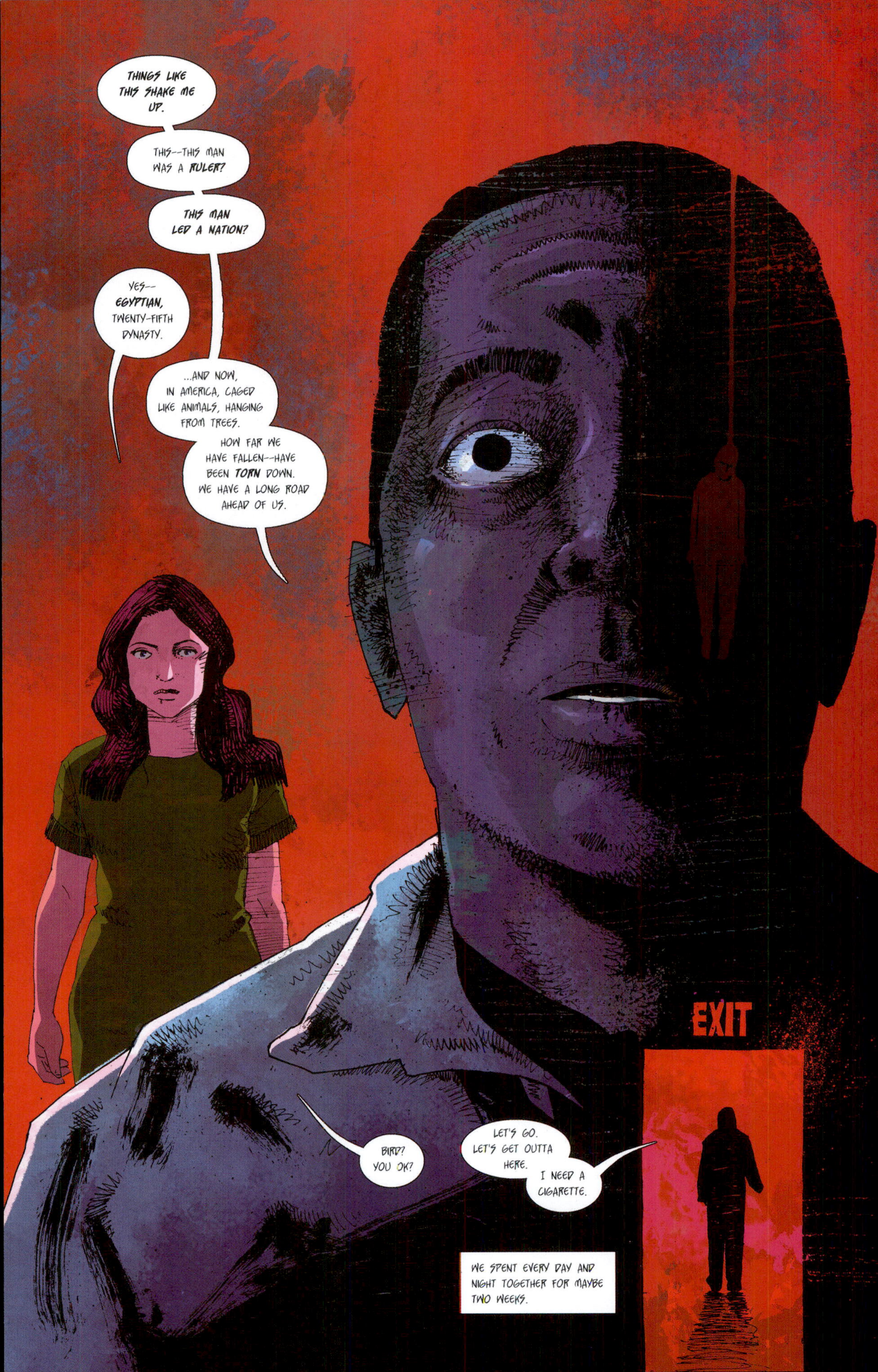
THINGS LIKE THIS SHAKE ME UP.
THIS--THIS MAN WAS A RULER?
THIS MAN LED A NATION?
YES-- EGYPTIAN, TWENTY-FIFTH DYNASTY.
...AND NOW, IN AMERICA, CAGED LIKE ANIMALS, HANGING FROM TREES.
HOW FAR WE HAVE FALLEN--HAVE BEEN TORN DOWN. WE HAVE A LONG ROAD AHEAD OF US.
EXIT
BIRD? YOU OK?
LET'S GO. LET'S GET OUTTA HERE.
I NEED A CIGARETTE.
WE SPENT EVERY DAY AND NIGHT TOGETHER FOR MAYBE TWO WEEKS.

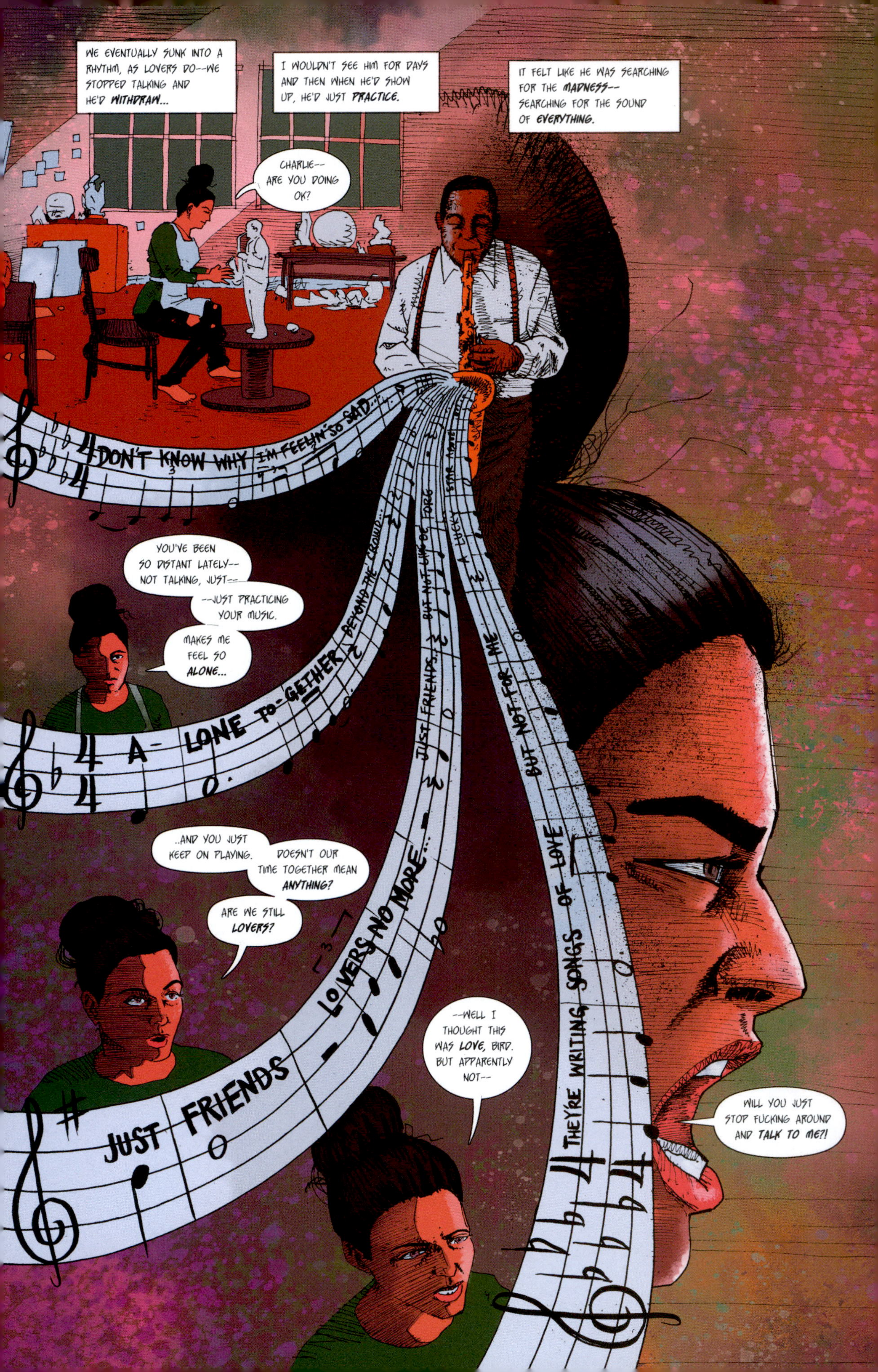

WE EVENTUALLY SUNK INTO A RHYTHM, AS LOVERS DO--WE STOPPED TALKING AND HE'D WITHDRAW...
I WOULDN'T SEE HIM FOR DAYS AND THEN WHEN HE'D SHOW UP, HE'D JUST PRACTICE.
IT FELT LIKE HE WAS SEARCHING FOR THE MADNESS-- SEARCHING FOR THE SOUND OF EVERYTHING.
CHARLIE-- ARE YOU DOING OK?
DON'T KNOW WHY I'M FEELIN' SO SAD...
YOU'VE BEEN SO DISTANT LATELY-- NOT TALKING, JUST--
--JUST PRACTICING YOUR MUSIC.
MAKES ME FEEL SO ALONE...
A- LONE TO- GETHER
BEYOND THE CROWD...
...AND YOU JUST KEEP ON PLAYING.
DOESN'T OUR TIME TOGETHER MEAN ANYTHING?
ARE WE STILL LOVERS?
JUST FRIENDS
LOVERS NO MORE...
JUST FRIENDS, BUT NOT LIKE BE- FORE
BUT NOT FOR ME
THEY'RE WRITING SONGS OF LOVE
--WELL I THOUGHT THIS WAS LOVE, BIRD. BUT APPARENTLY NOT--
WILL YOU JUST STOP FUCKING AROUND AND TALK TO ME?!

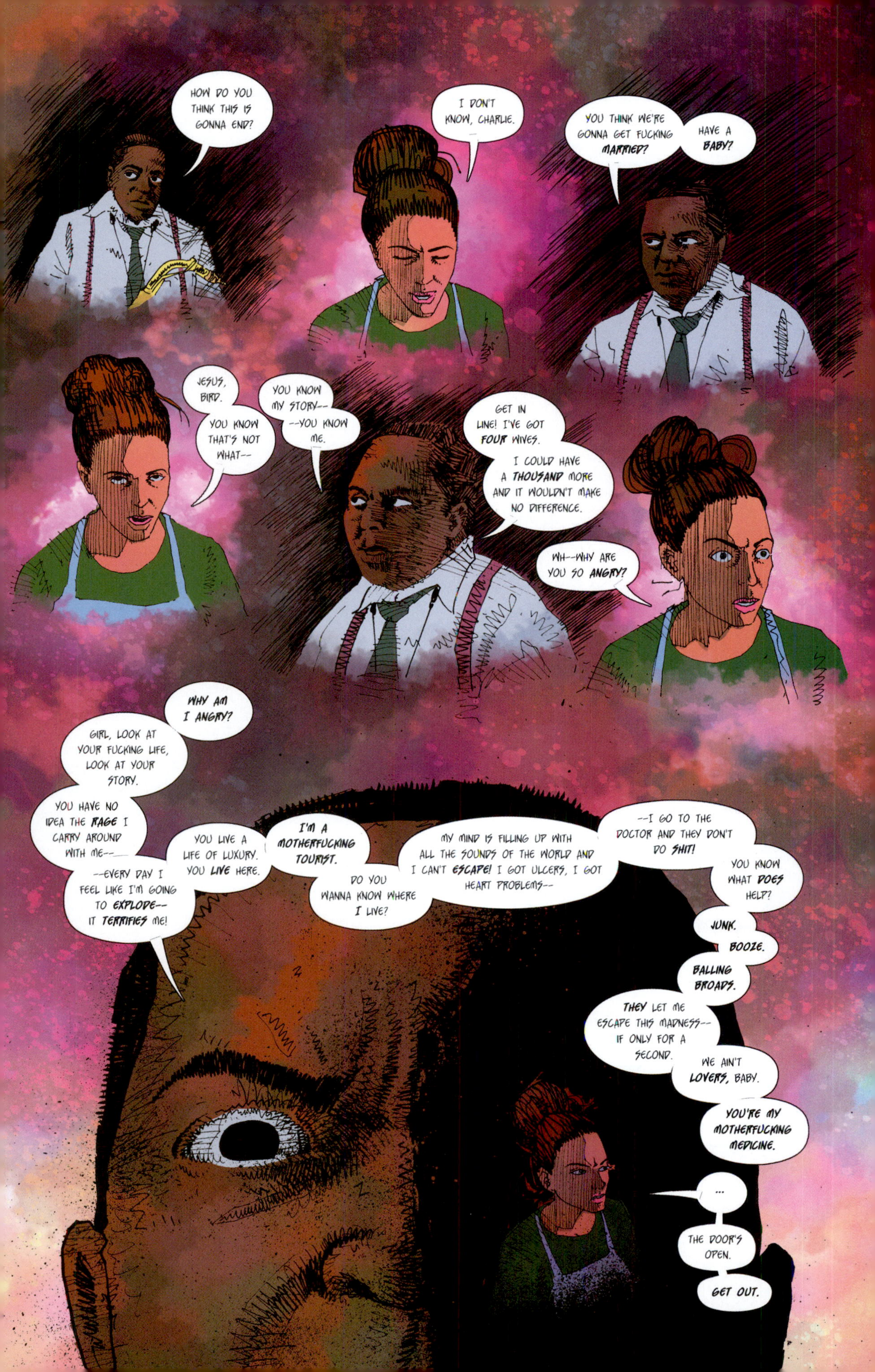
HOW DO YOU THINK THIS IS GONNA END?
I DON'T KNOW, CHARLIE.
YOU THINK WE'RE GONNA GET FUCKING MARRIED?
HAVE A BABY?
JESUS, BIRD.
YOU KNOW THAT'S NOT WHAT--
YOU KNOW MY STORY--
--YOU KNOW ME.
GET IN LINE! I'VE GOT FOUR WIVES.
I COULD HAVE A THOUSAND MORE AND IT WOULDN'T MAKE NO DIFFERENCE.
WH--WHY ARE YOU SO ANGRY?
WHY AM I ANGRY?
GIRL, LOOK AT YOUR FUCKING LIFE, LOOK AT YOUR STORY.
YOU HAVE NO IDEA THE RAGE I CARRY AROUND WITH ME--
--EVERY DAY I FEEL LIKE I'M GOING TO EXPLODE--IT TERRIFIES ME!
YOU LIVE A LIFE OF LUXURY. YOU LIVE HERE.
I'M A MOTHERFUCKING TOURIST.
DO YOU WANNA KNOW WHERE I LIVE?
MY MIND IS FILLING UP WITH ALL THE SOUNDS OF THE WORLD AND I CAN'T ESCAPE! I GOT ULCERS, I GOT HEART PROBLEMS--
--I GO TO THE DOCTOR AND THEY DON'T DO SHIT!
YOU KNOW WHAT DOES HELP?
JUNK.
BOOZE.
BALLING BROADS.
THEY LET ME ESCAPE THIS MADNESS--IF ONLY FOR A SECOND.
WE AIN'T LOVERS, BABY.
YOU'RE MY MOTHERFUCKING MEDICINE.
...
THE DOOR'S OPEN.
GET OUT.

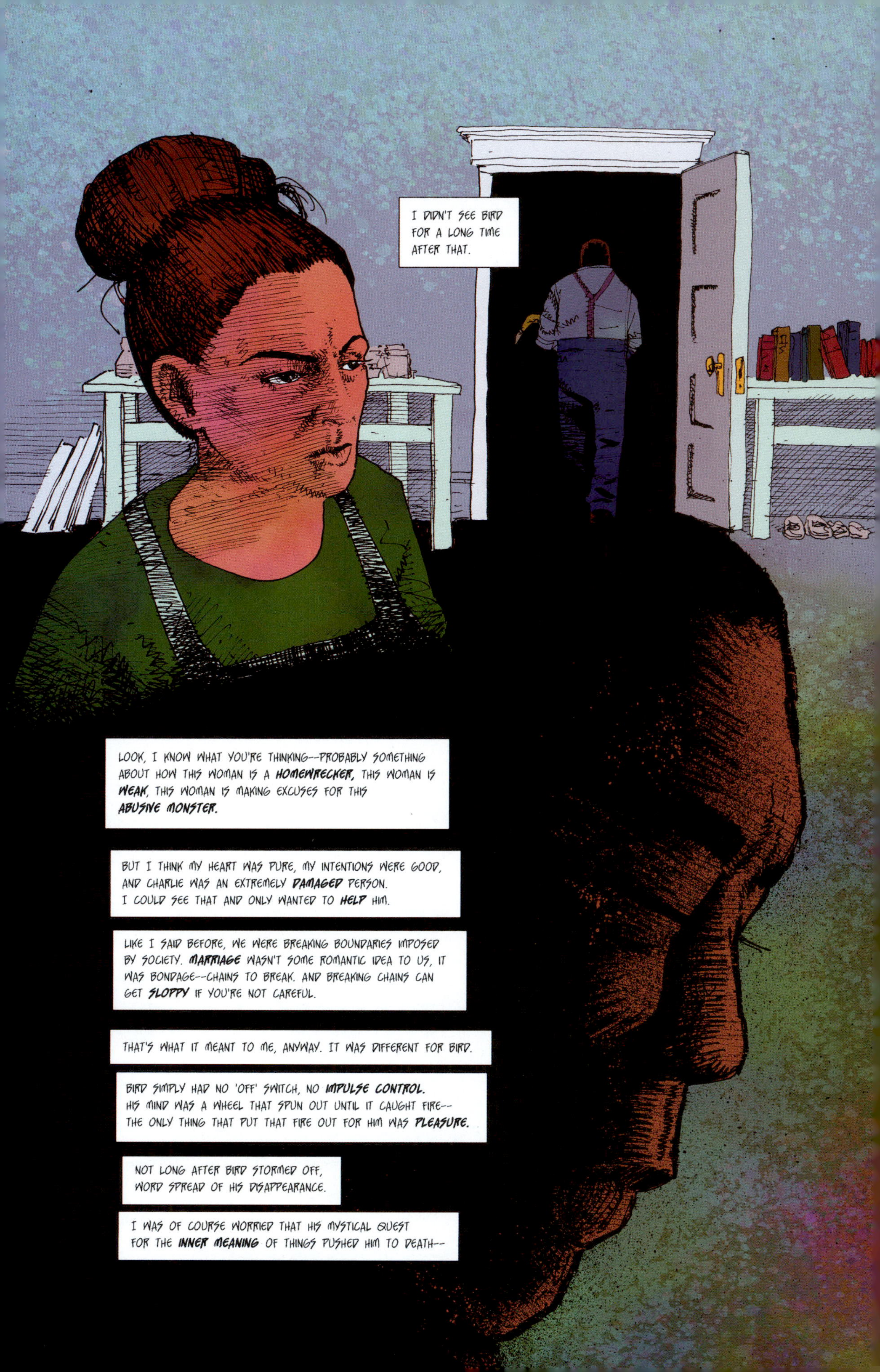
I DIDN'T SEE BIRD FOR A LONG TIME AFTER THAT.
LOOK, I KNOW WHAT YOU'RE THINKING--PROBABLY SOMETHING ABOUT HOW THIS WOMAN IS A HOMEWRECKER, THIS WOMAN IS WEAK, THIS WOMAN IS MAKING EXCUSES FOR THIS ABUSIVE MONSTER.
BUT I THINK MY HEART WAS PURE, MY INTENTIONS WERE GOOD, AND CHARLIE WAS AN EXTREMELY DAMAGED PERSON. I COULD SEE THAT AND ONLY WANTED TO HELP HIM.
LIKE I SAID BEFORE, WE WERE BREAKING BOUNDARIES IMPOSED BY SOCIETY. MARRIAGE WASN'T SOME ROMANTIC IDEA TO US, IT WAS BONDAGE--CHAINS TO BREAK. AND BREAKING CHAINS CAN GET SLOPPY IF YOU'RE NOT CAREFUL.
THAT'S WHAT IT MEANT TO ME, ANYWAY. IT WAS DIFFERENT FOR BIRD.
BIRD SIMPLY HAD NO 'OFF' SWITCH, NO IMPULSE CONTROL. HIS MIND WAS A WHEEL THAT SPUN OUT UNTIL IT CAUGHT FIRE--THE ONLY THING THAT PUT THAT FIRE OUT FOR HIM WAS PLEASURE.
NOT LONG AFTER BIRD STORMED OFF, WORD SPREAD OF HIS DISAPPEARANCE.
I WAS OF COURSE WORRIED THAT HIS MYSTICAL QUEST FOR THE INNER MEANING OF THINGS PUSHED HIM TO DEATH--

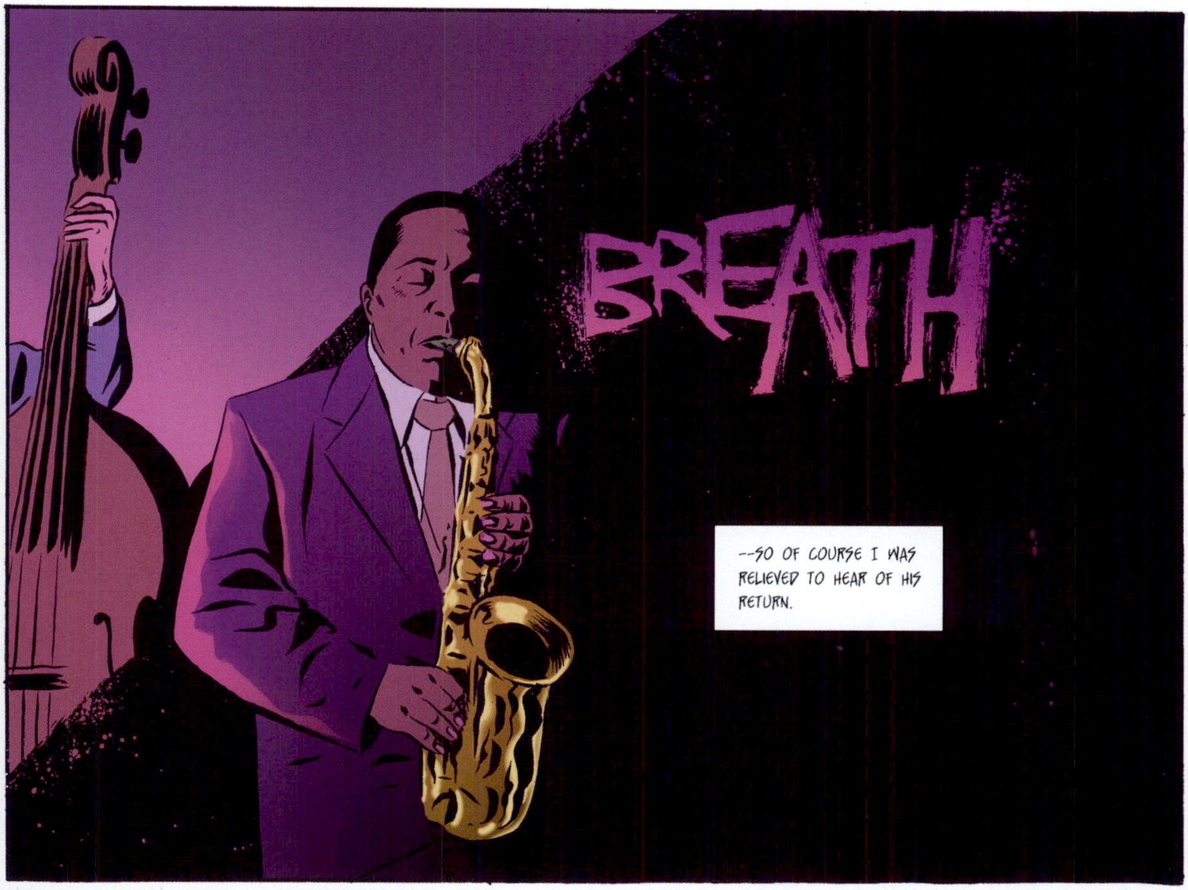
BREATH
--SO OF COURSE I WAS RELIEVED TO HEAR OF HIS RETURN.

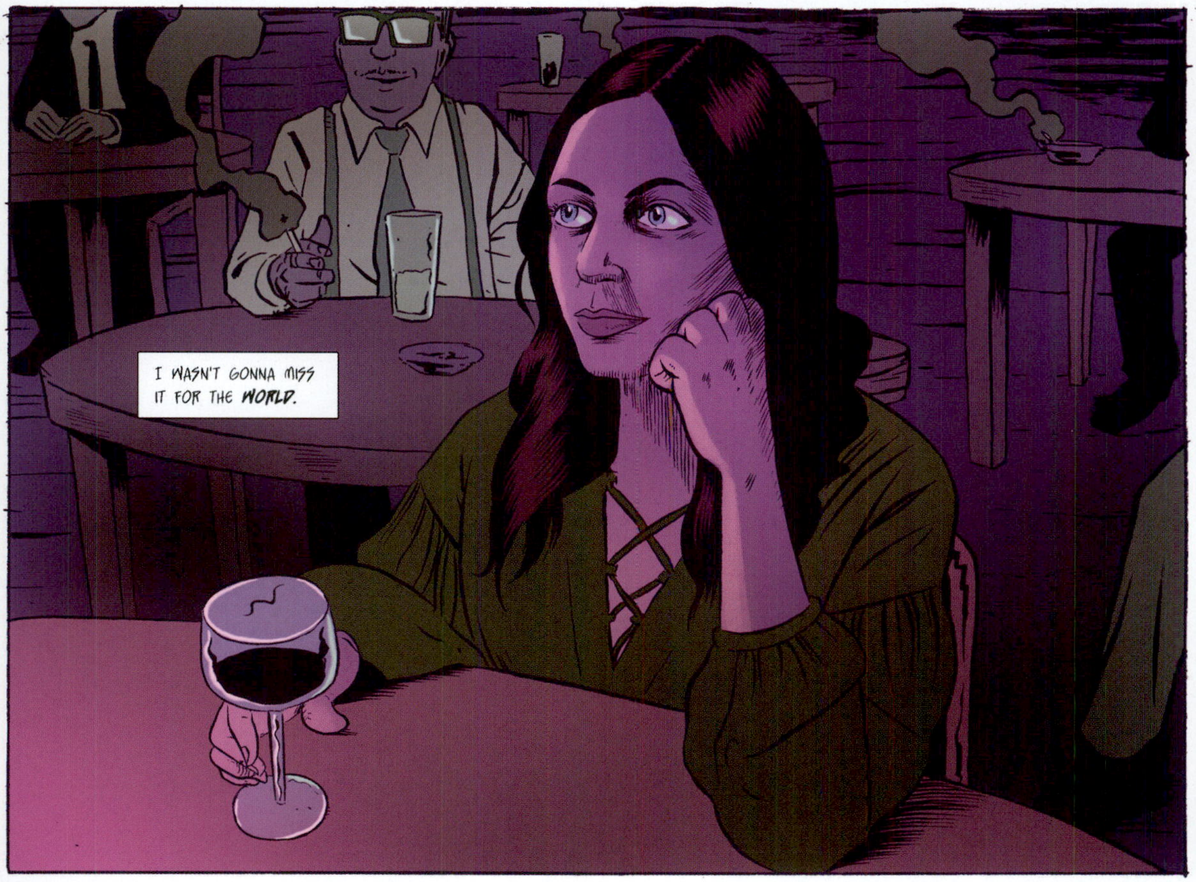
I WASN'T GONNA MISS IT FOR THE WORLD.

CHORUS 5:
coltrane

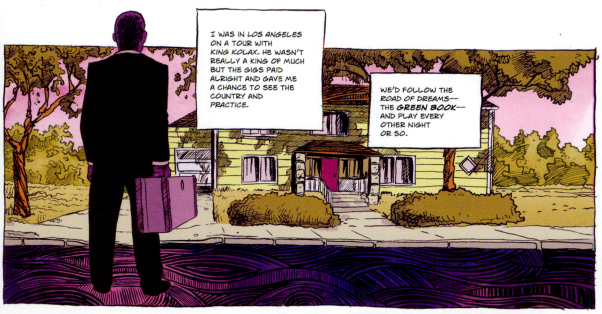

I WAS IN LOS ANGELES ON A TOUR WITH *KING KOLAX.* HE WASN'T REALLY A KING OF MUCH BUT THE GIGS PAID ALRIGHT AND GAVE ME A CHANCE TO SEE THE COUNTRY AND PRACTICE.

WE'D FOLLOW THE ROAD OF DREAMS-- THE *GREEN BOOK*-- AND PLAY EVERY OTHER NIGHT OR SO.

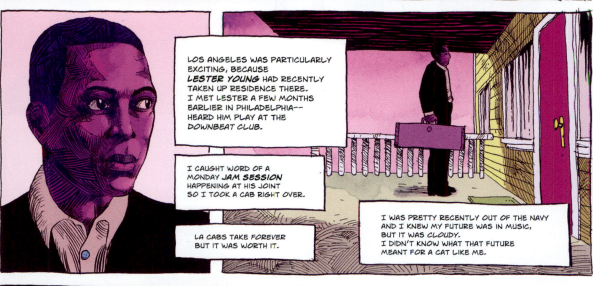

LOS ANGELES WAS PARTICULARLY EXCITING, BECAUSE *LESTER YOUNG* HAD RECENTLY TAKEN UP RESIDENCE THERE. I MET LESTER A FEW MONTHS EARLIER IN PHILADELPHIA-- HEARD HIM PLAY AT THE DOWNBEAT CLUB.

I CAUGHT WORD OF A MONDAY *JAM SESSION* HAPPENING AT HIS JOINT SO I TOOK A CAB RIGHT OVER.

LA CABS TAKE FOREVER BUT IT WAS WORTH IT.

I WAS PRETTY RECENTLY OUT OF THE NAVY AND I KNEW MY FUTURE WAS IN MUSIC, BUT IT WAS CLOUDY. I DIDN'T KNOW WHAT THAT FUTURE MEANT FOR A CAT LIKE ME.

BUT YOU KNOW, SOME DAYS FEEL LIKE THEY'RE POSITIVELY FULL OF THE FUTURE-- MOMENTOUS BEYOND IMAGINING--

--PREGNANT WITH POSSIBILITY.

JOHNNY COLTRANE! COME ON IN!

THIS WAS ONE OF THOSE DAYS.

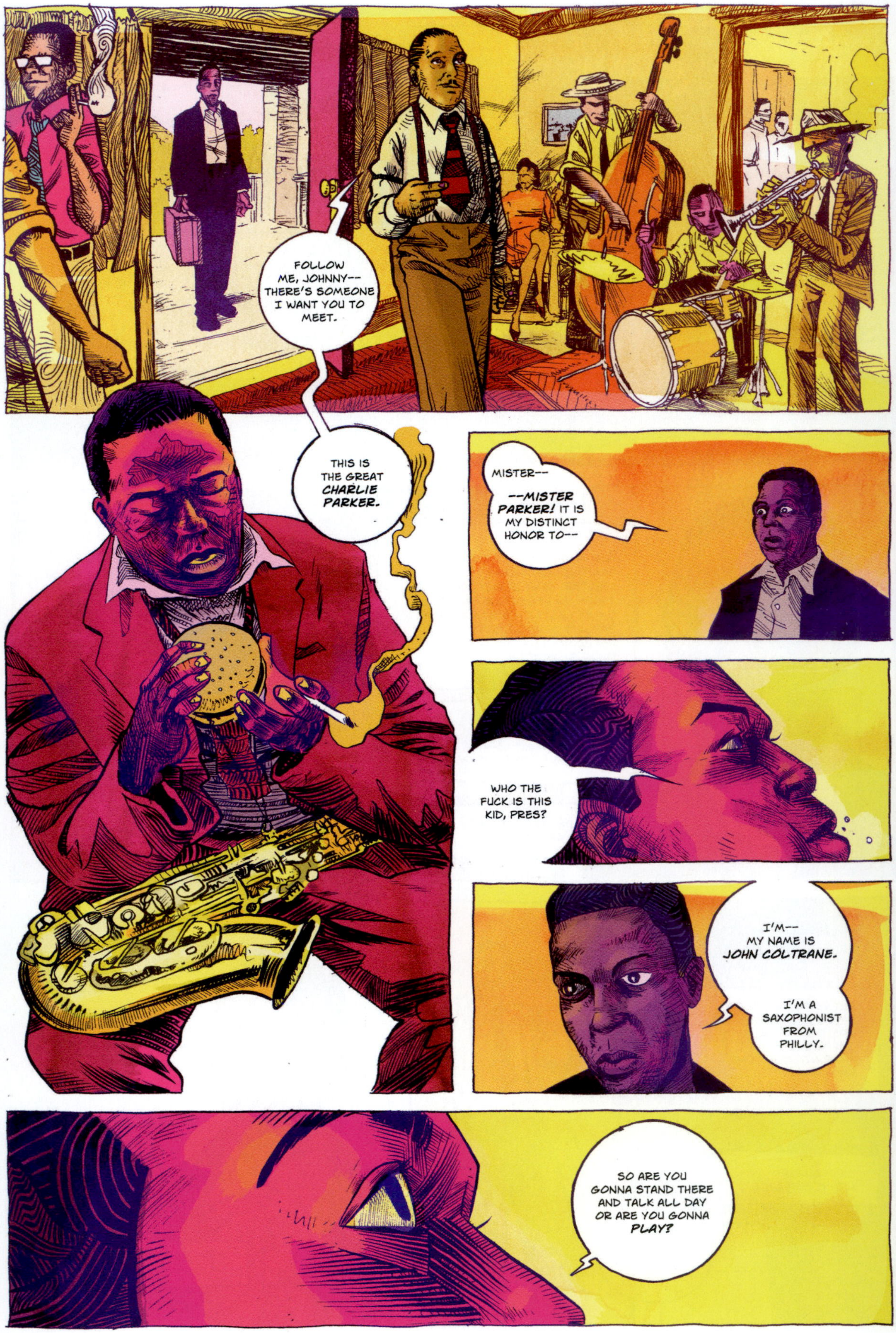
FOLLOW ME, JOHNNY-- THERE'S SOMEONE I WANT YOU TO MEET.
THIS IS THE GREAT CHARLIE PARKER.
MISTER--
--MISTER PARKER! IT IS MY DISTINCT HONOR TO--
WHO THE FUCK IS THIS KID, PRES?
I'M-- MY NAME IS JOHN COLTRANE.
I'M A SAXOPHONIST FROM PHILLY.
SO ARE YOU GONNA STAND THERE AND TALK ALL DAY OR ARE YOU GONNA PLAY?

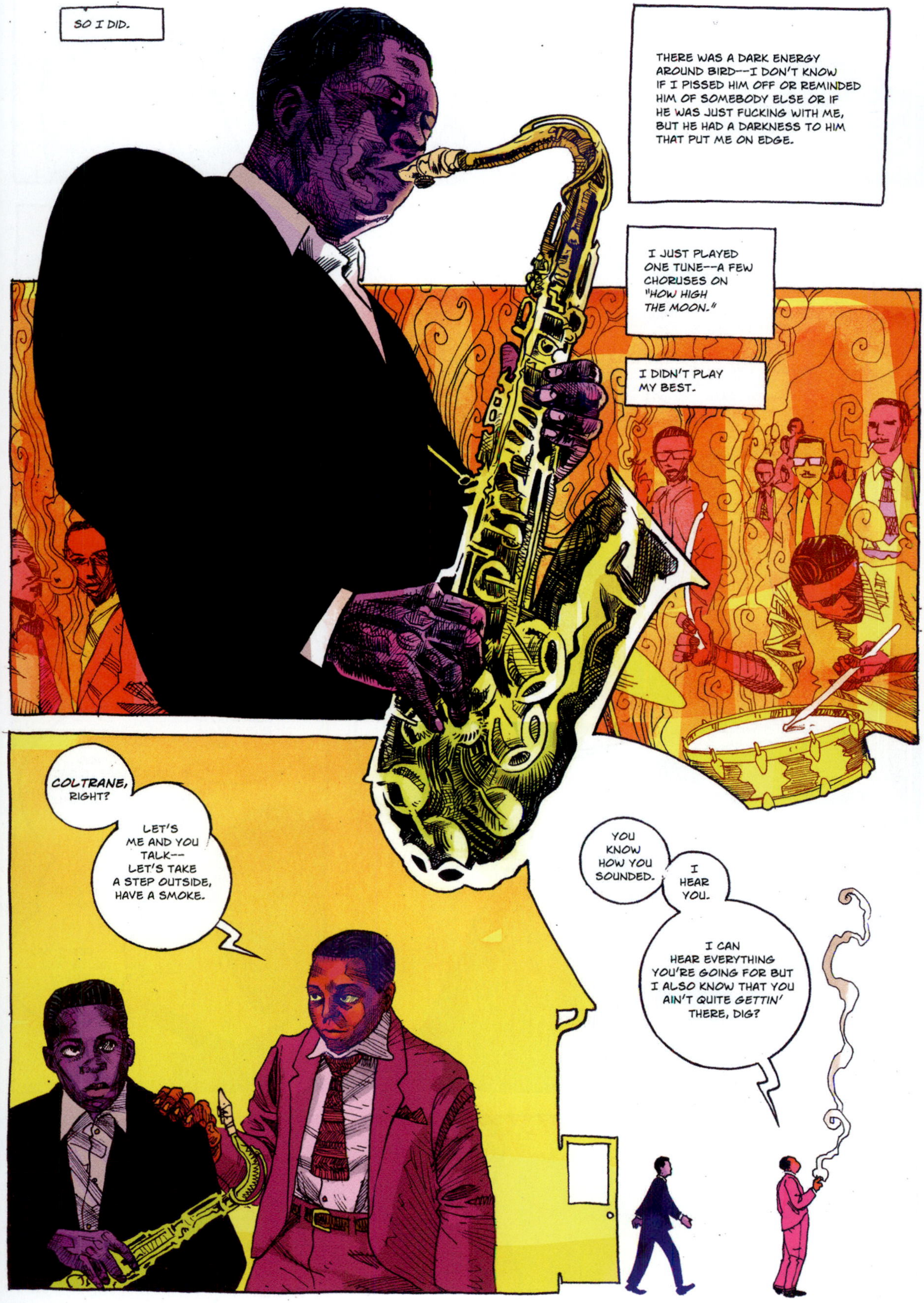

SO I DID.
THERE WAS A DARK ENERGY AROUND BIRD--I DON'T KNOW IF I PISSED HIM OFF OR REMINDED HIM OF SOMEBODY ELSE OR IF HE WAS JUST FUCKING WITH ME, BUT HE HAD A DARKNESS TO HIM THAT PUT ME ON EDGE.
I JUST PLAYED ONE TUNE--A FEW CHORUSES ON "HOW HIGH THE MOON."
I DIDN'T PLAY MY BEST.
COLTRANE, RIGHT?
LET'S ME AND YOU TALK-- LET'S TAKE A STEP OUTSIDE, HAVE A SMOKE.
YOU KNOW HOW YOU SOUNDED.
I HEAR YOU.
I CAN HEAR EVERYTHING YOU'RE GOING FOR BUT I ALSO KNOW THAT YOU AIN'T QUITE GETTIN' THERE, DIG?

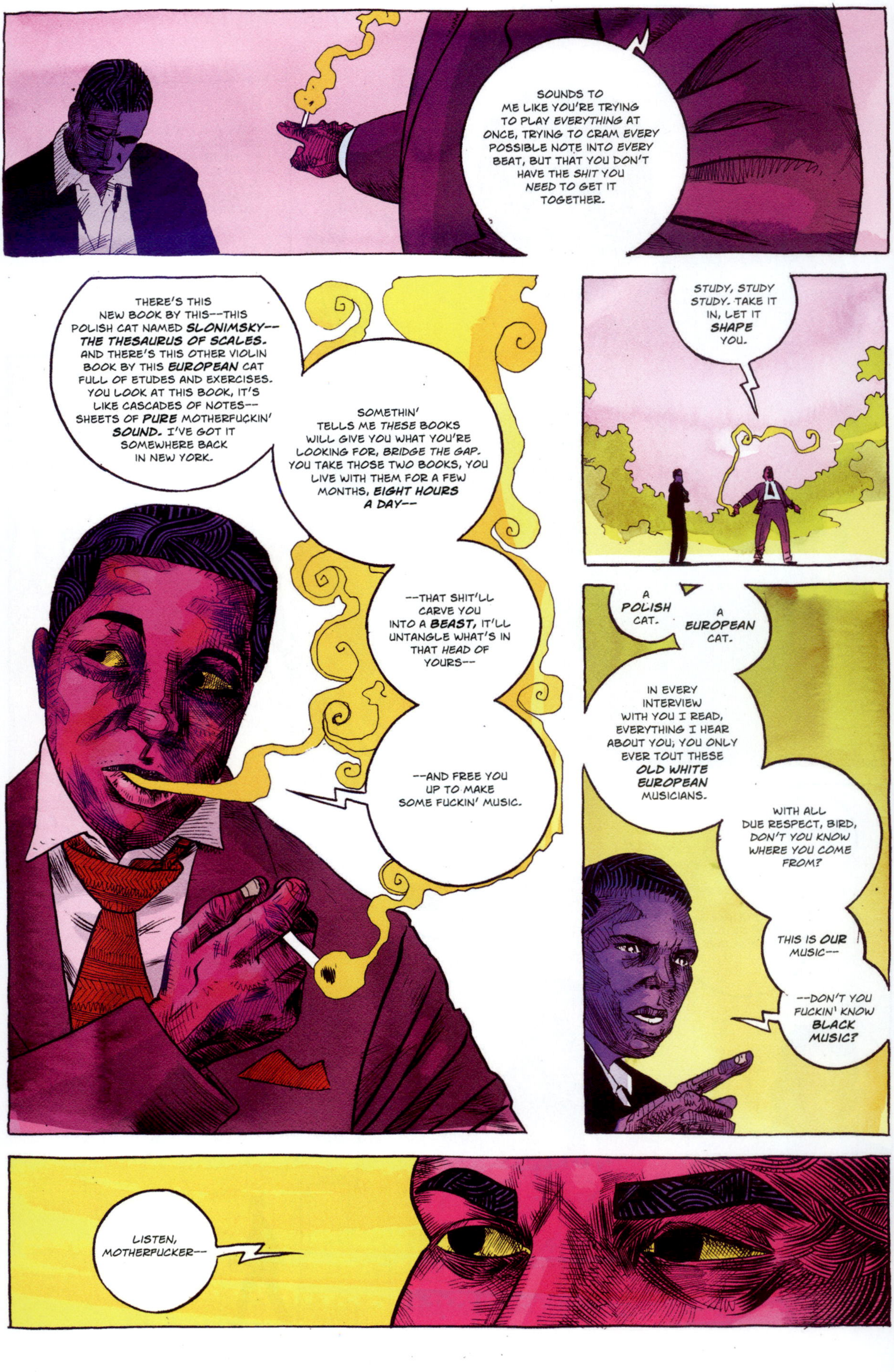
SOUNDS TO ME LIKE YOU'RE TRYING TO PLAY EVERYTHING AT ONCE, TRYING TO CRAM EVERY POSSIBLE NOTE INTO EVERY BEAT, BUT THAT YOU DON'T HAVE THE SHIT YOU NEED TO GET IT TOGETHER.
THERE'S THIS NEW BOOK BY THIS--THIS POLISH CAT NAMED SLONIMSKY-- THE THESAURUS OF SCALES. AND THERE'S THIS OTHER VIOLIN BOOK BY THIS EUROPEAN CAT FULL OF ETUDES AND EXERCISES. YOU LOOK AT THIS BOOK, IT'S LIKE CASCADES OF NOTES-- SHEETS OF PURE MOTHERFUCKIN' SOUND. I'VE GOT IT SOMEWHERE BACK IN NEW YORK.
SOMETHIN' TELLS ME THESE BOOKS WILL GIVE YOU WHAT YOU'RE LOOKING FOR, BRIDGE THE GAP. YOU TAKE THOSE TWO BOOKS, YOU LIVE WITH THEM FOR A FEW MONTHS, EIGHT HOURS A DAY--
--THAT SHIT'LL CARVE YOU INTO A BEAST, IT'LL UNTANGLE WHAT'S IN THAT HEAD OF YOURS--
--AND FREE YOU UP TO MAKE SOME FUCKIN' MUSIC.
STUDY, STUDY STUDY. TAKE IT IN, LET IT SHAPE YOU.
A POLISH CAT.
A EUROPEAN CAT.
IN EVERY INTERVIEW WITH YOU I READ, EVERYTHING I HEAR ABOUT YOU; YOU ONLY EVER TOUT THESE OLD WHITE EUROPEAN MUSICIANS.
WITH ALL DUE RESPECT, BIRD, DON'T YOU KNOW WHERE YOU COME FROM?
THIS IS OUR MUSIC--
--DON'T YOU FUCKIN' KNOW BLACK MUSIC?
LISTEN, MOTHERFUCKER--

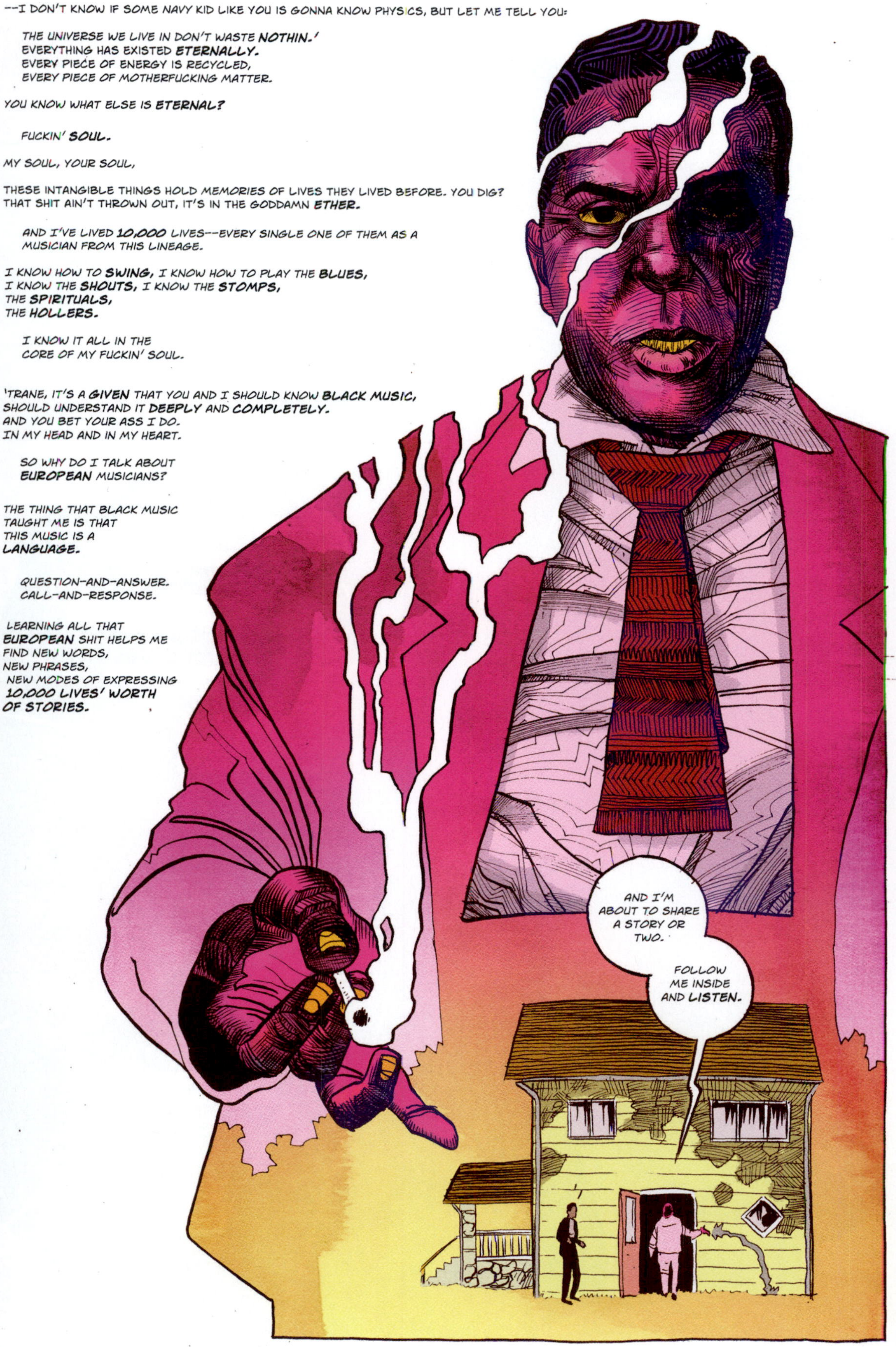
--I DON'T KNOW IF SOME NAVY KID LIKE YOU IS GONNA KNOW PHYSICS, BUT LET ME TELL YOU:
THE UNIVERSE WE LIVE IN DON'T WASTE NOTHIN.' EVERYTHING HAS EXISTED ETERNALLY. EVERY PIECE OF ENERGY IS RECYCLED, EVERY PIECE OF MOTHERFUCKING MATTER.
YOU KNOW WHAT ELSE IS ETERNAL?
FUCKIN' SOUL.
MY SOUL, YOUR SOUL,
THESE INTANGIBLE THINGS HOLD MEMORIES OF LIVES THEY LIVED BEFORE. YOU DIG? THAT SHIT AIN'T THROWN OUT, IT'S IN THE GODDAMN ETHER.
AND I'VE LIVED 10,000 LIVES--EVERY SINGLE ONE OF THEM AS A MUSICIAN FROM THIS LINEAGE.
I KNOW HOW TO SWING, I KNOW HOW TO PLAY THE BLUES, I KNOW THE SHOUTS, I KNOW THE STOMPS, THE SPIRITUALS, THE HOLLERS.
I KNOW IT ALL IN THE CORE OF MY FUCKIN' SOUL.
'TRANE, IT'S A GIVEN THAT YOU AND I SHOULD KNOW BLACK MUSIC, SHOULD UNDERSTAND IT DEEPLY AND COMPLETELY. AND YOU BET YOUR ASS I DO. IN MY HEAD AND IN MY HEART.
SO WHY DO I TALK ABOUT EUROPEAN MUSICIANS?
THE THING THAT BLACK MUSIC TAUGHT ME IS THAT THIS MUSIC IS A LANGUAGE.
QUESTION-AND-ANSWER. CALL-AND-RESPONSE.
LEARNING ALL THAT EUROPEAN SHIT HELPS ME FIND NEW WORDS, NEW PHRASES, NEW MODES OF EXPRESSING 10,000 LIVES' WORTH OF STORIES.
AND I'M ABOUT TO SHARE A STORY OR TWO.
FOLLOW ME INSIDE AND LISTEN.

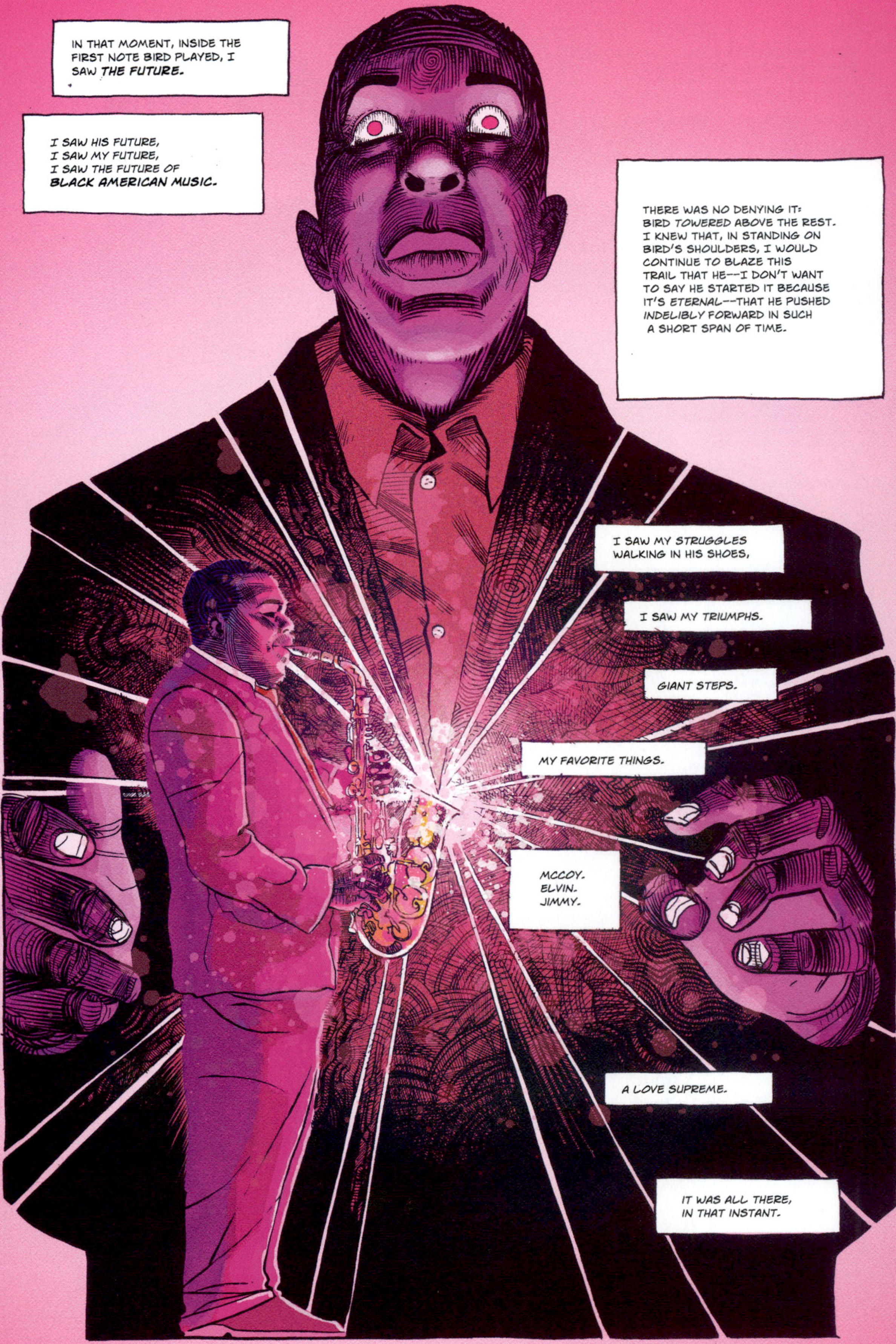
IN THAT MOMENT, INSIDE THE FIRST NOTE BIRD PLAYED, I SAW THE FUTURE.
I SAW HIS FUTURE, I SAW MY FUTURE, I SAW THE FUTURE OF BLACK AMERICAN MUSIC.
THERE WAS NO DENYING IT: BIRD TOWERED ABOVE THE REST. I KNEW THAT, IN STANDING ON BIRD'S SHOULDERS, I WOULD CONTINUE TO BLAZE THIS TRAIL THAT HE--I DON'T WANT TO SAY HE STARTED IT BECAUSE IT'S ETERNAL--THAT HE PUSHED INDELIBLY FORWARD IN SUCH A SHORT SPAN OF TIME.
I SAW MY STRUGGLES WALKING IN HIS SHOES,
I SAW MY TRIUMPHS.
GIANT STEPS.
MY FAVORITE THINGS.
MCCOY. ELVIN. JIMMY.
A LOVE SUPREME.
IT WAS ALL THERE, IN THAT INSTANT.

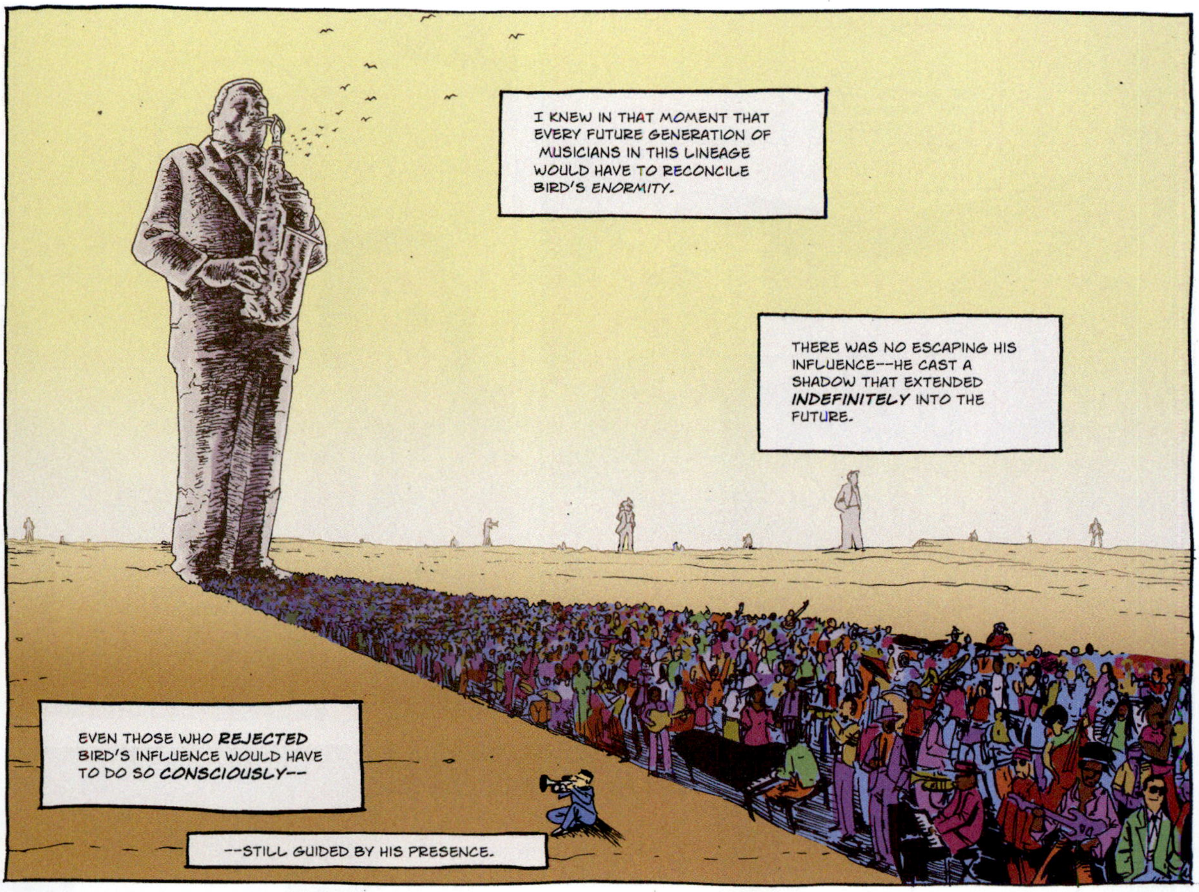
I KNEW IN THAT MOMENT THAT EVERY FUTURE GENERATION OF MUSICIANS IN THIS LINEAGE WOULD HAVE TO RECONCILE BIRD'S ENORMITY.
THERE WAS NO ESCAPING HIS INFLUENCE--HE CAST A SHADOW THAT EXTENDED ***INDEFINITELY*** INTO THE FUTURE.
EVEN THOSE WHO ***REJECTED*** BIRD'S INFLUENCE WOULD HAVE TO DO SO ***CONSCIOUSLY***--
--STILL GUIDED BY HIS PRESENCE.

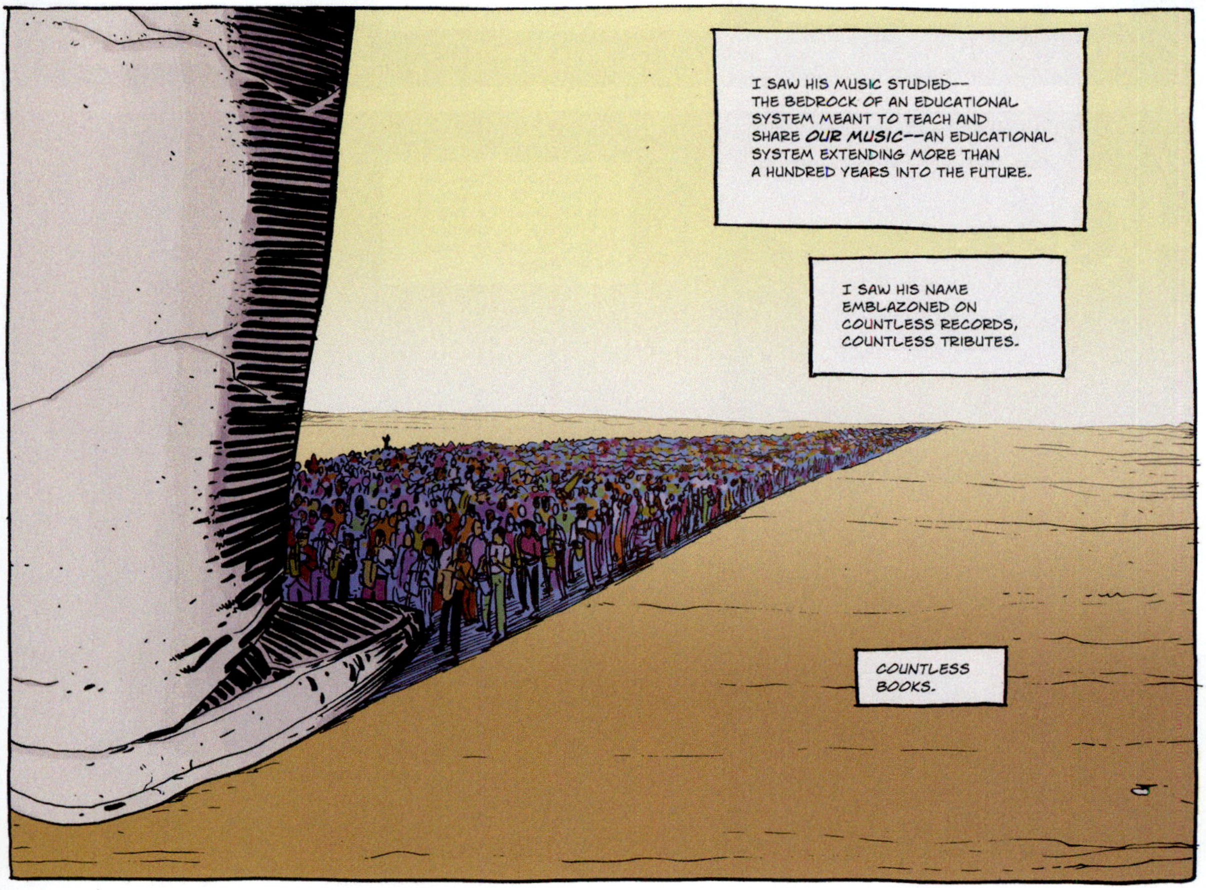
I SAW HIS MUSIC STUDIED--THE BEDROCK OF AN EDUCATIONAL SYSTEM MEANT TO TEACH AND SHARE ***OUR MUSIC***--AN EDUCATIONAL SYSTEM EXTENDING MORE THAN A HUNDRED YEARS INTO THE FUTURE.
I SAW HIS NAME EMBLAZONED ON COUNTLESS RECORDS, COUNTLESS TRIBUTES.
COUNTLESS BOOKS.

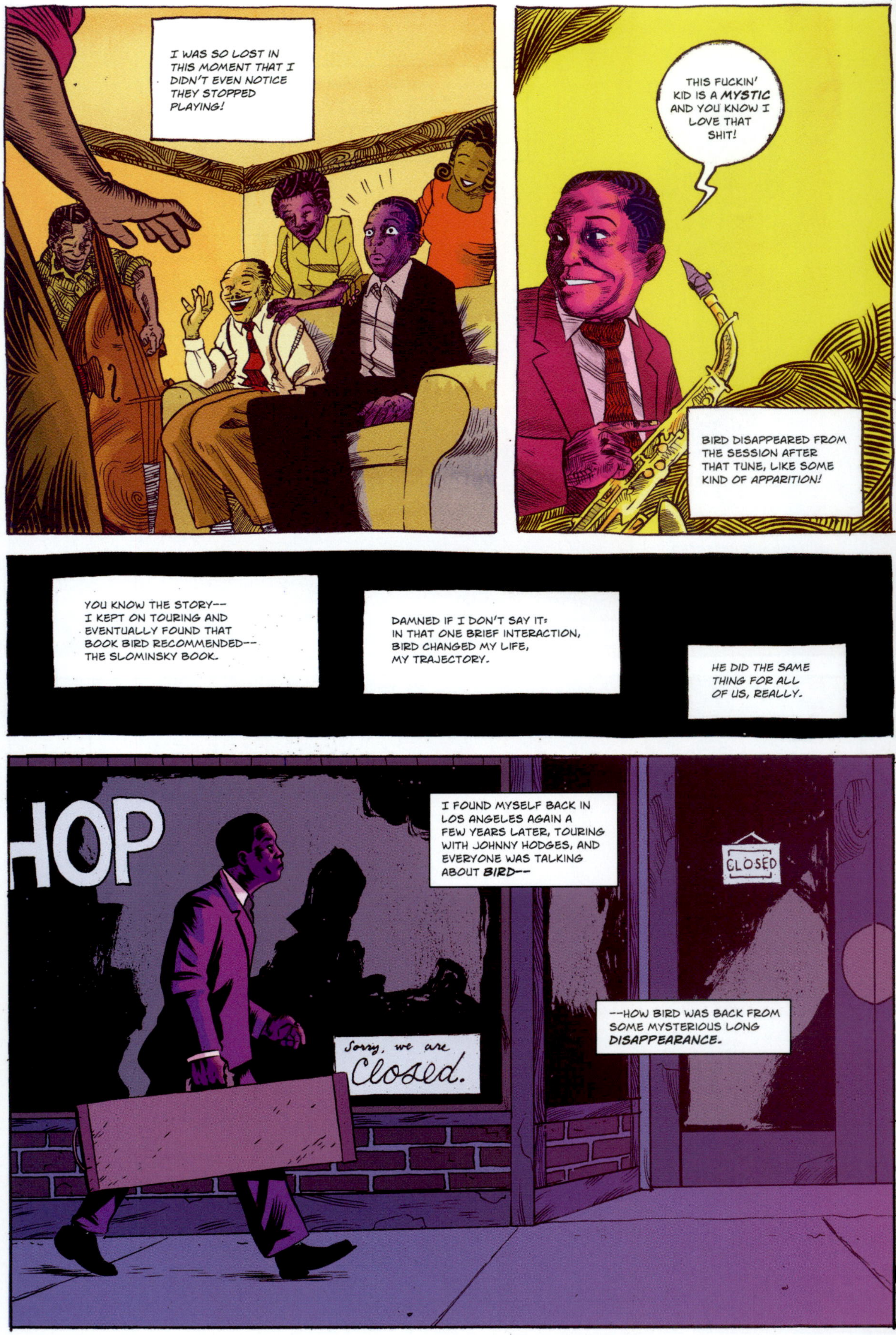
I WAS SO LOST IN THIS MOMENT THAT I DIDN'T EVEN NOTICE THEY STOPPED PLAYING!
THIS FUCKIN' KID IS A MYSTIC AND YOU KNOW I LOVE THAT SHIT!
BIRD DISAPPEARED FROM THE SESSION AFTER THAT TUNE, LIKE SOME KIND OF APPARITION!
YOU KNOW THE STORY-- I KEPT ON TOURING AND EVENTUALLY FOUND THAT BOOK BIRD RECOMMENDED-- THE SLOMINSKY BOOK.
DAMNED IF I DON'T SAY IT: IN THAT ONE BRIEF INTERACTION, BIRD CHANGED MY LIFE, MY TRAJECTORY.
HE DID THE SAME THING FOR ALL OF US, REALLY.
HOP
I FOUND MYSELF BACK IN LOS ANGELES AGAIN A FEW YEARS LATER, TOURING WITH JOHNNY HODGES, AND EVERYONE WAS TALKING ABOUT BIRD--
CLOSED
--HOW BIRD WAS BACK FROM SOME MYSTERIOUS LONG DISAPPEARANCE.
Sorry, we are Closed.

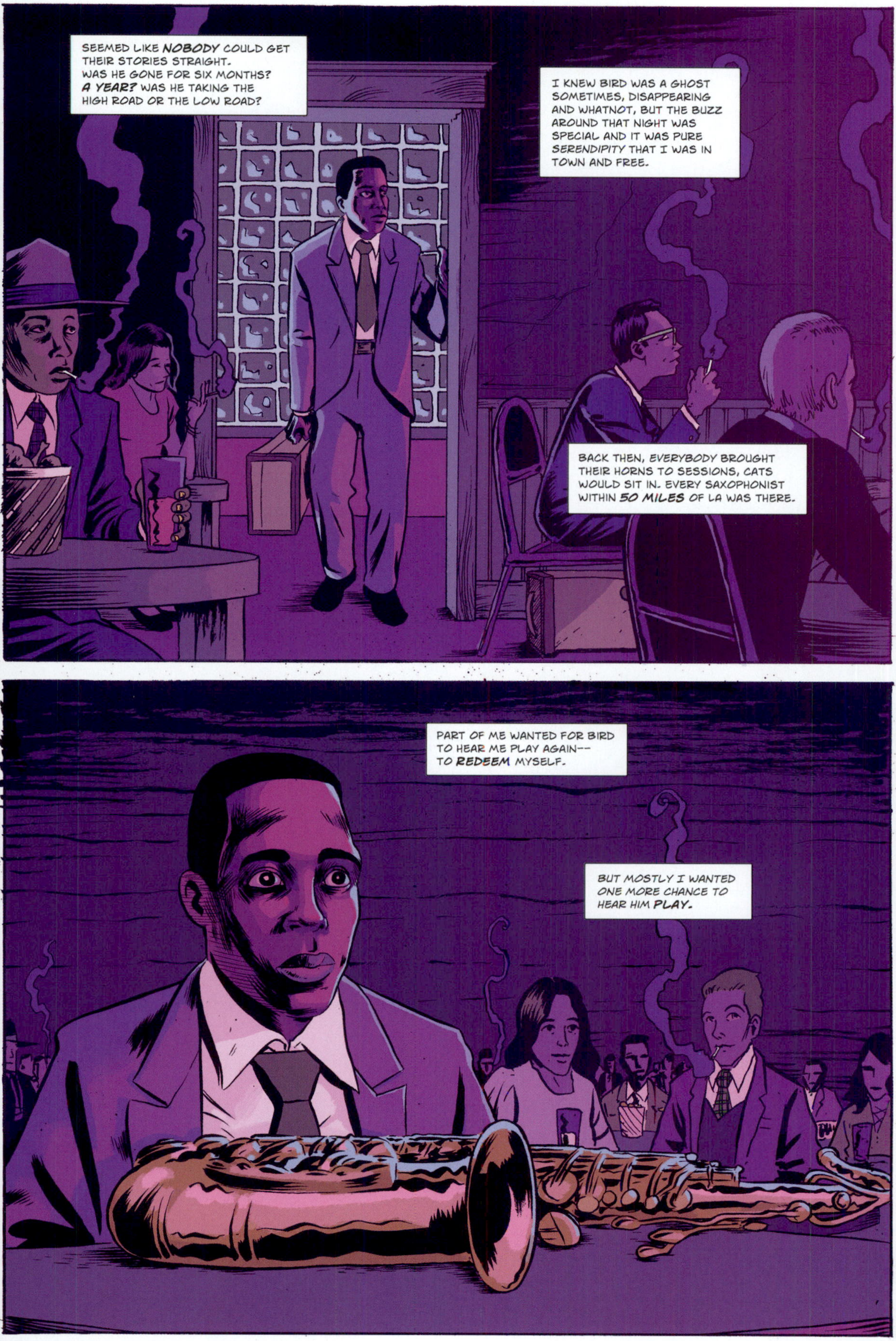
SEEMED LIKE NOBODY COULD GET THEIR STORIES STRAIGHT. WAS HE GONE FOR SIX MONTHS? A YEAR? WAS HE TAKING THE HIGH ROAD OR THE LOW ROAD?
I KNEW BIRD WAS A GHOST SOMETIMES, DISAPPEARING AND WHATNOT, BUT THE BUZZ AROUND THAT NIGHT WAS SPECIAL AND IT WAS PURE SERENDIPITY THAT I WAS IN TOWN AND FREE.
BACK THEN, EVERYBODY BROUGHT THEIR HORNS TO SESSIONS, CATS WOULD SIT IN. EVERY SAXOPHONIST WITHIN 50 MILES OF LA WAS THERE.
PART OF ME WANTED FOR BIRD TO HEAR ME PLAY AGAIN-- TO REDEEM MYSELF.
BUT MOSTLY I WANTED ONE MORE CHANCE TO HEAR HIM PLAY.

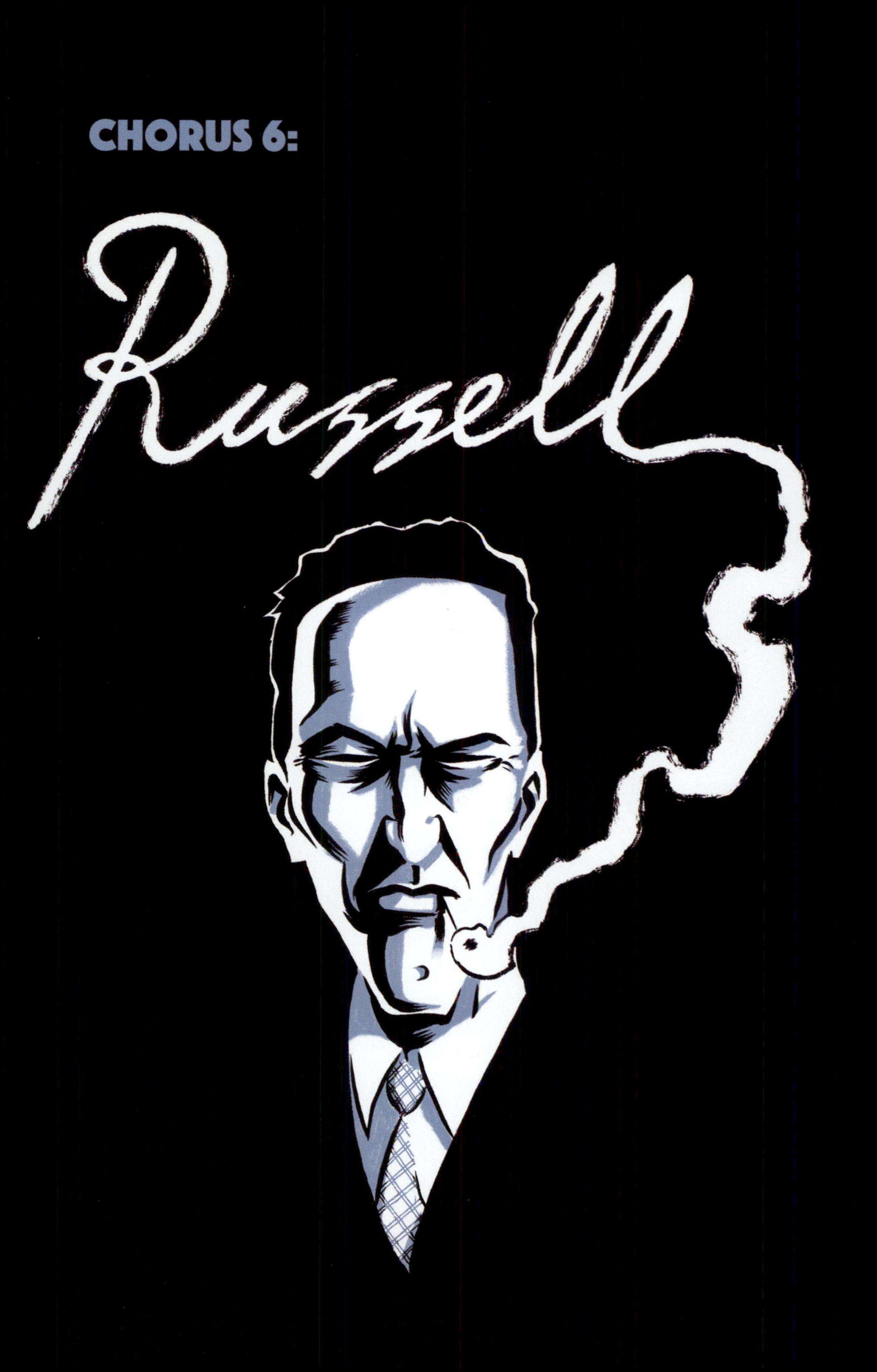
CHORUS 6:
Russell

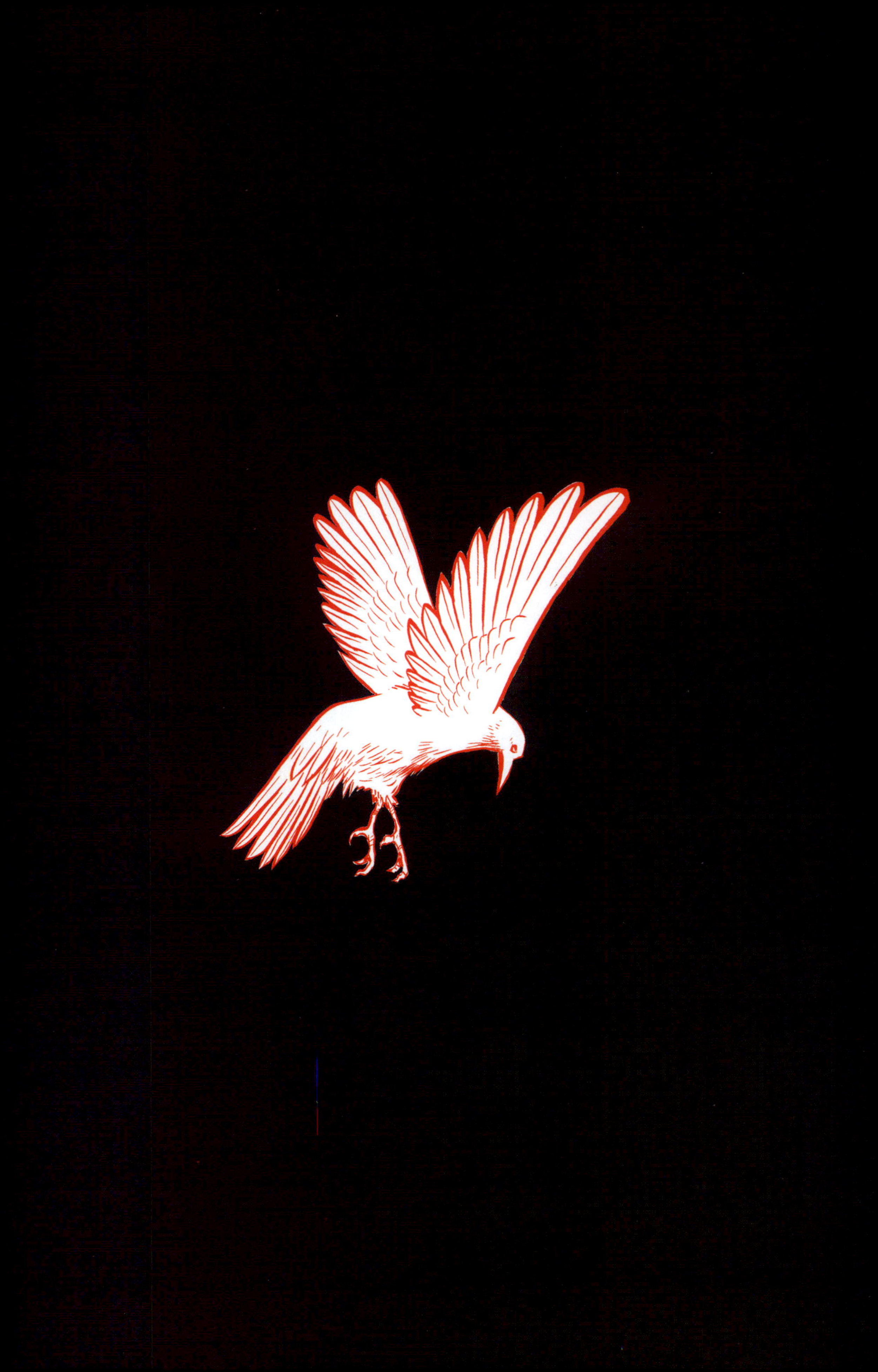

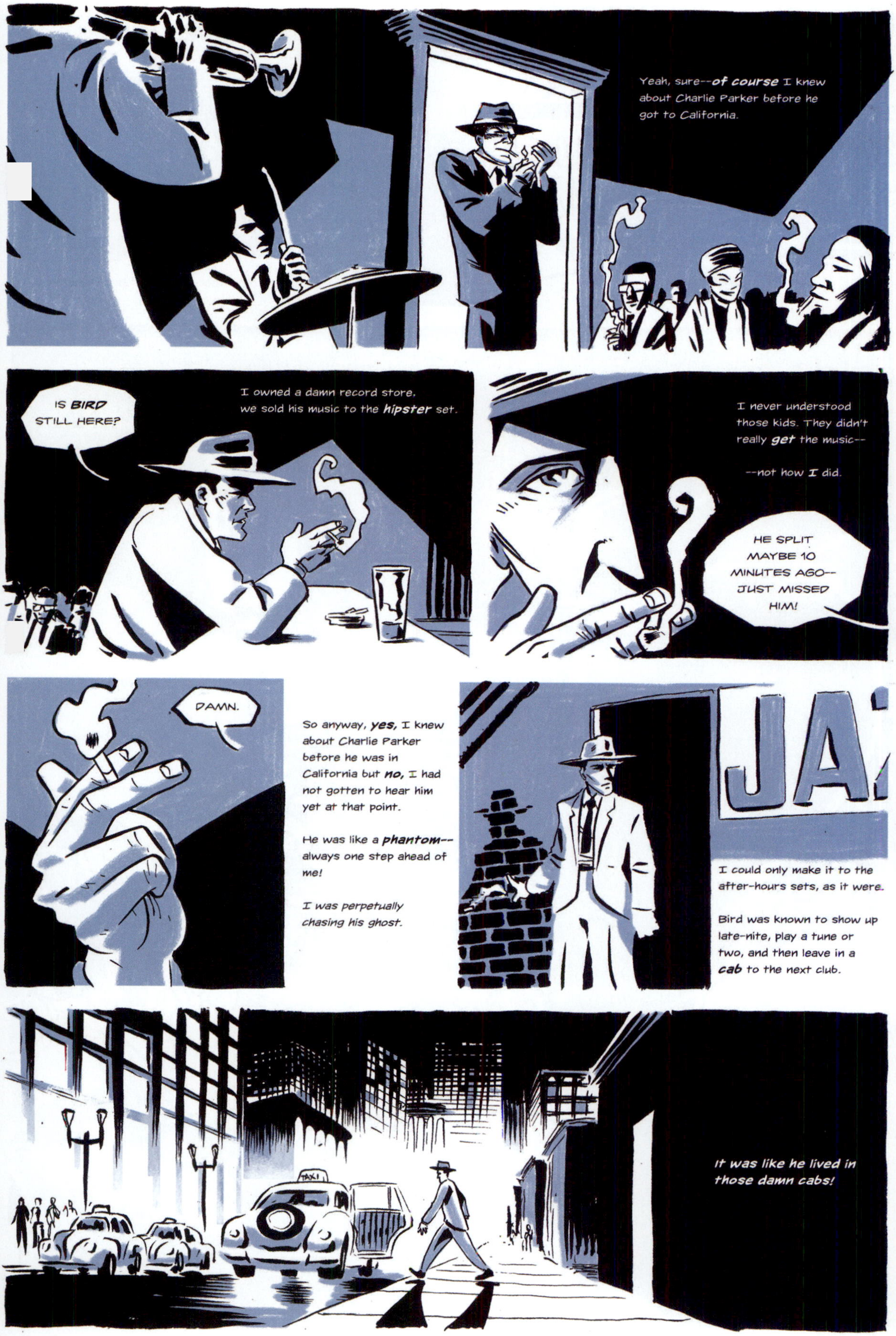
Yeah, sure--of course I knew about Charlie Parker before he got to California.
IS BIRD STILL HERE?
I owned a damn record store. we sold his music to the hipster set.
I never understood those kids. They didn't really get the music--
--not how I did.
HE SPLIT MAYBE 10 MINUTES AGO-- JUST MISSED HIM!
DAMN.
So anyway, yes, I knew about Charlie Parker before he was in California but no, I had not gotten to hear him yet at that point.
He was like a phantom-- always one step ahead of me!
I was perpetually chasing his ghost.
JA
I could only make it to the after-hours sets, as it were.
Bird was known to show up late-nite, play a tune or two, and then leave in a cab to the next club.
TAXI
It was like he lived in those damn cabs!

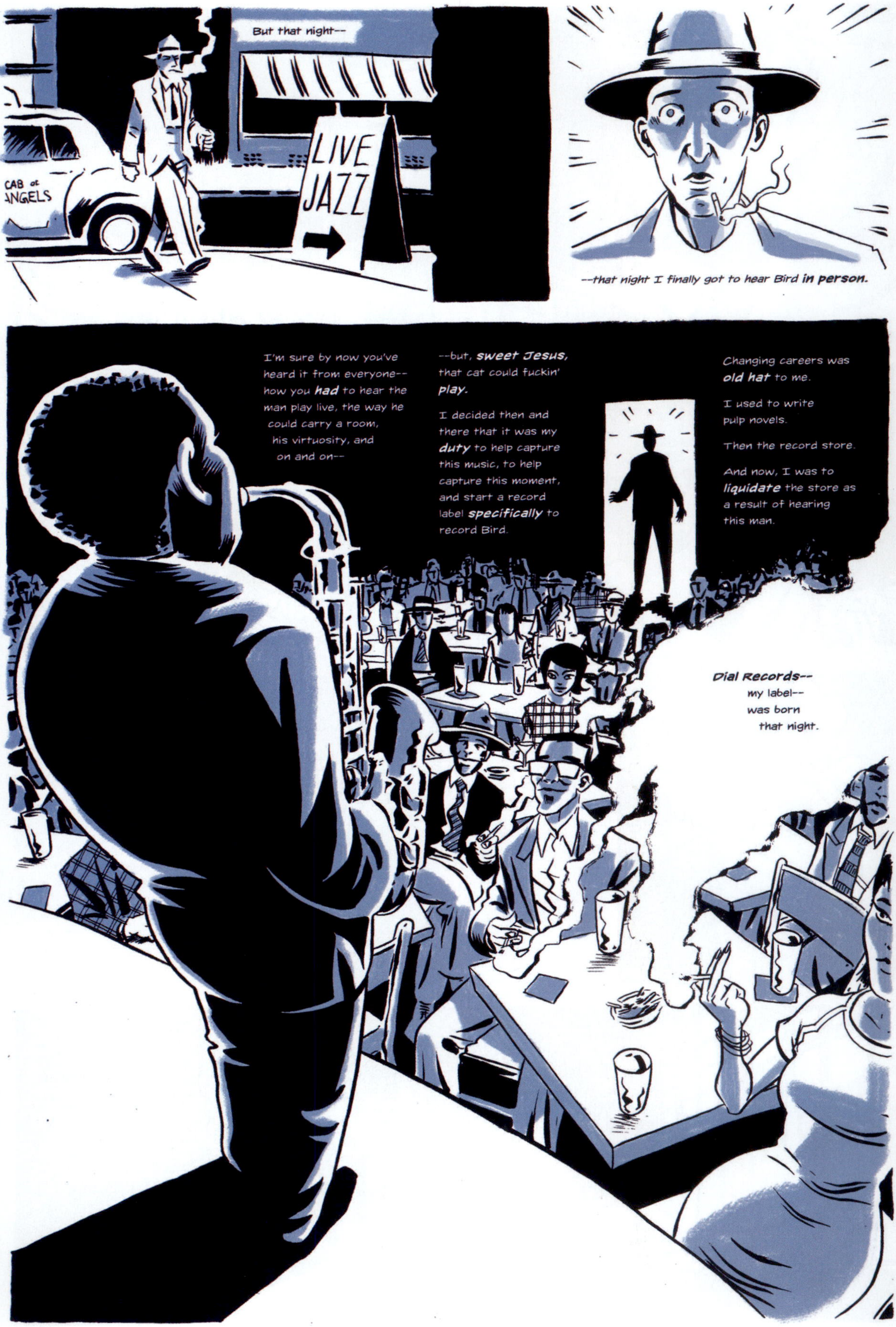

CAB of ANGELS
But that night--
LIVE JAZZ
--that night I finally got to hear Bird **in person.**
I'm sure by now you've heard it from everyone--how you **had** to hear the man play live, the way he could carry a room, his virtuosity, and on and on--
--but, **sweet Jesus,** that cat could fuckin' **play.**
I decided then and there that it was my **duty** to help capture this music, to help capture this moment, and start a record label **specifically** to record Bird.
Changing careers was **old hat** to me.
I used to write pulp novels.
Then the record store.
And now, I was to **liquidate** the store as a result of hearing this man.
Dial Records-- my label-- was born that night.

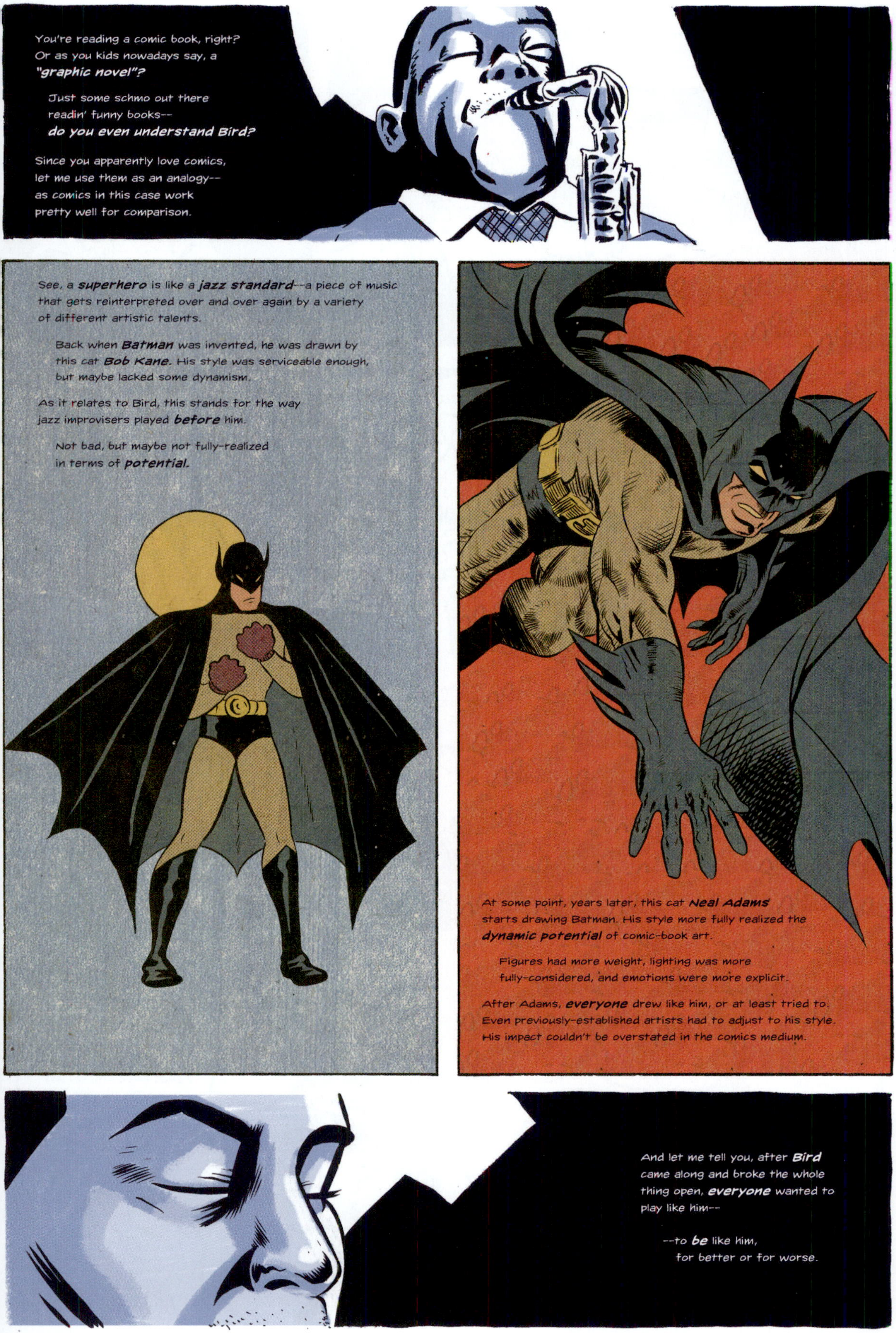
You're reading a comic book, right? Or as you kids nowadays say, a "graphic novel"?
Just some schmo out there readin' funny books-- do you even understand Bird?
Since you apparently love comics, let me use them as an analogy-- as comics in this case work pretty well for comparison.
See, a superhero is like a jazz standard--a piece of music that gets reinterpreted over and over again by a variety of different artistic talents.
Back when Batman was invented, he was drawn by this cat Bob Kane. His style was serviceable enough, but maybe lacked some dynamism.
As it relates to Bird, this stands for the way jazz improvisers played before him.
Not bad, but maybe not fully-realized in terms of potential.
At some point, years later, this cat Neal Adams starts drawing Batman. His style more fully realized the dynamic potential of comic-book art.
Figures had more weight, lighting was more fully-considered, and emotions were more explicit.
After Adams, everyone drew like him, or at least tried to. Even previously-established artists had to adjust to his style. His impact couldn't be overstated in the comics medium.
And let me tell you, after Bird came along and broke the whole thing open, everyone wanted to play like him--
--to be like him, for better or for worse.

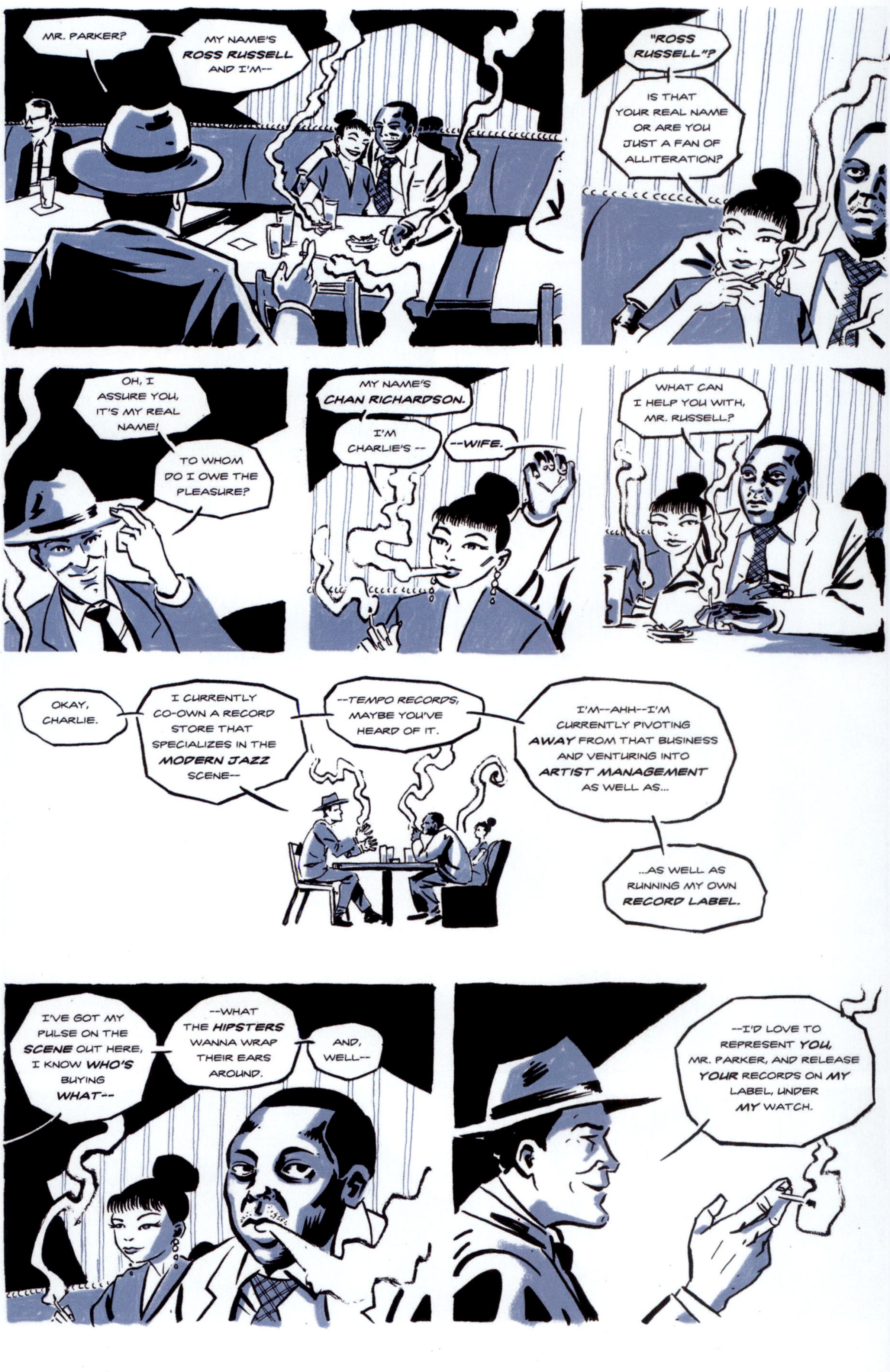
MR. PARKER?
MY NAME'S ROSS RUSSELL AND I'M--
"ROSS RUSSELL"?
IS THAT YOUR REAL NAME OR ARE YOU JUST A FAN OF ALLITERATION?
OH, I ASSURE YOU, IT'S MY REAL NAME!
TO WHOM DO I OWE THE PLEASURE?
MY NAME'S CHAN RICHARDSON.
I'M CHARLIE'S --
--WIFE.
WHAT CAN I HELP YOU WITH, MR. RUSSELL?
OKAY, CHARLIE.
I CURRENTLY CO-OWN A RECORD STORE THAT SPECIALIZES IN THE MODERN JAZZ SCENE--
--TEMPO RECORDS, MAYBE YOU'VE HEARD OF IT.
I'M--AHH--I'M CURRENTLY PIVOTING AWAY FROM THAT BUSINESS AND VENTURING INTO ARTIST MANAGEMENT AS WELL AS...
...AS WELL AS RUNNING MY OWN RECORD LABEL.
I'VE GOT MY PULSE ON THE SCENE OUT HERE, I KNOW WHO'S BUYING WHAT--
--WHAT THE HIPSTERS WANNA WRAP THEIR EARS AROUND.
AND, WELL--
--I'D LOVE TO REPRESENT YOU, MR. PARKER, AND RELEASE YOUR RECORDS ON MY LABEL, UNDER MY WATCH.

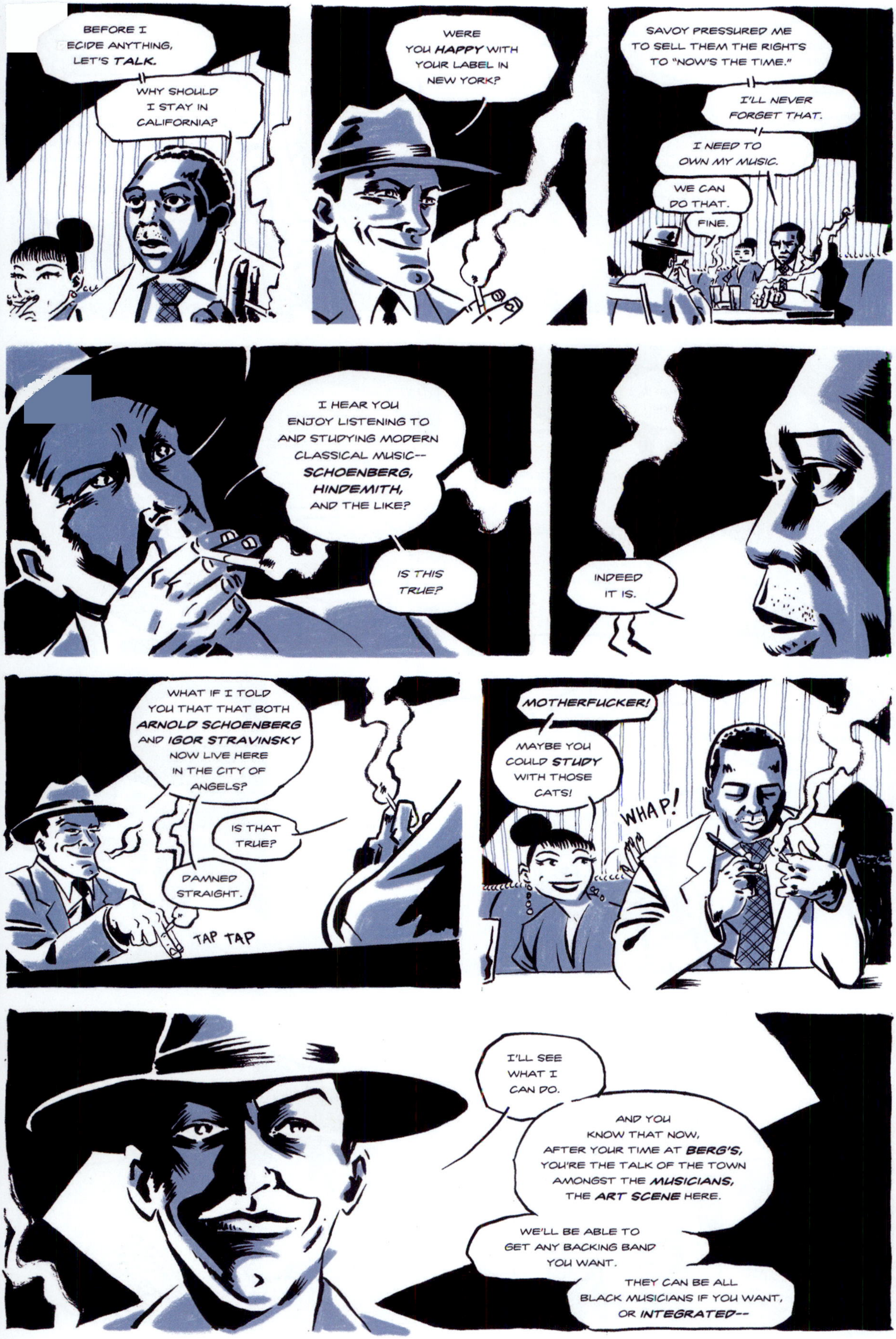
BEFORE I ECIDE ANYTHING, LET'S TALK.
WHY SHOULD I STAY IN CALIFORNIA?
WERE YOU HAPPY WITH YOUR LABEL IN NEW YORK?
SAVOY PRESSURED ME TO SELL THEM THE RIGHTS TO "NOW'S THE TIME."
I'LL NEVER FORGET THAT.
I NEED TO OWN MY MUSIC.
WE CAN DO THAT.
FINE.
I HEAR YOU ENJOY LISTENING TO AND STUDYING MODERN CLASSICAL MUSIC-- SCHOENBERG, HINDEMITH, AND THE LIKE?
IS THIS TRUE?
INDEED IT IS.
WHAT IF I TOLD YOU THAT THAT BOTH ARNOLD SCHOENBERG AND IGOR STRAVINSKY NOW LIVE HERE IN THE CITY OF ANGELS?
IS THAT TRUE?
DAMNED STRAIGHT.
TAP TAP
MOTHERFUCKER!
MAYBE YOU COULD STUDY WITH THOSE CATS!
WHAP!
I'LL SEE WHAT I CAN DO.
AND YOU KNOW THAT NOW, AFTER YOUR TIME AT BERG'S, YOU'RE THE TALK OF THE TOWN AMONGST THE MUSICIANS, THE ART SCENE HERE.
WE'LL BE ABLE TO GET ANY BACKING BAND YOU WANT.
THEY CAN BE ALL BLACK MUSICIANS IF YOU WANT, OR INTEGRATED--

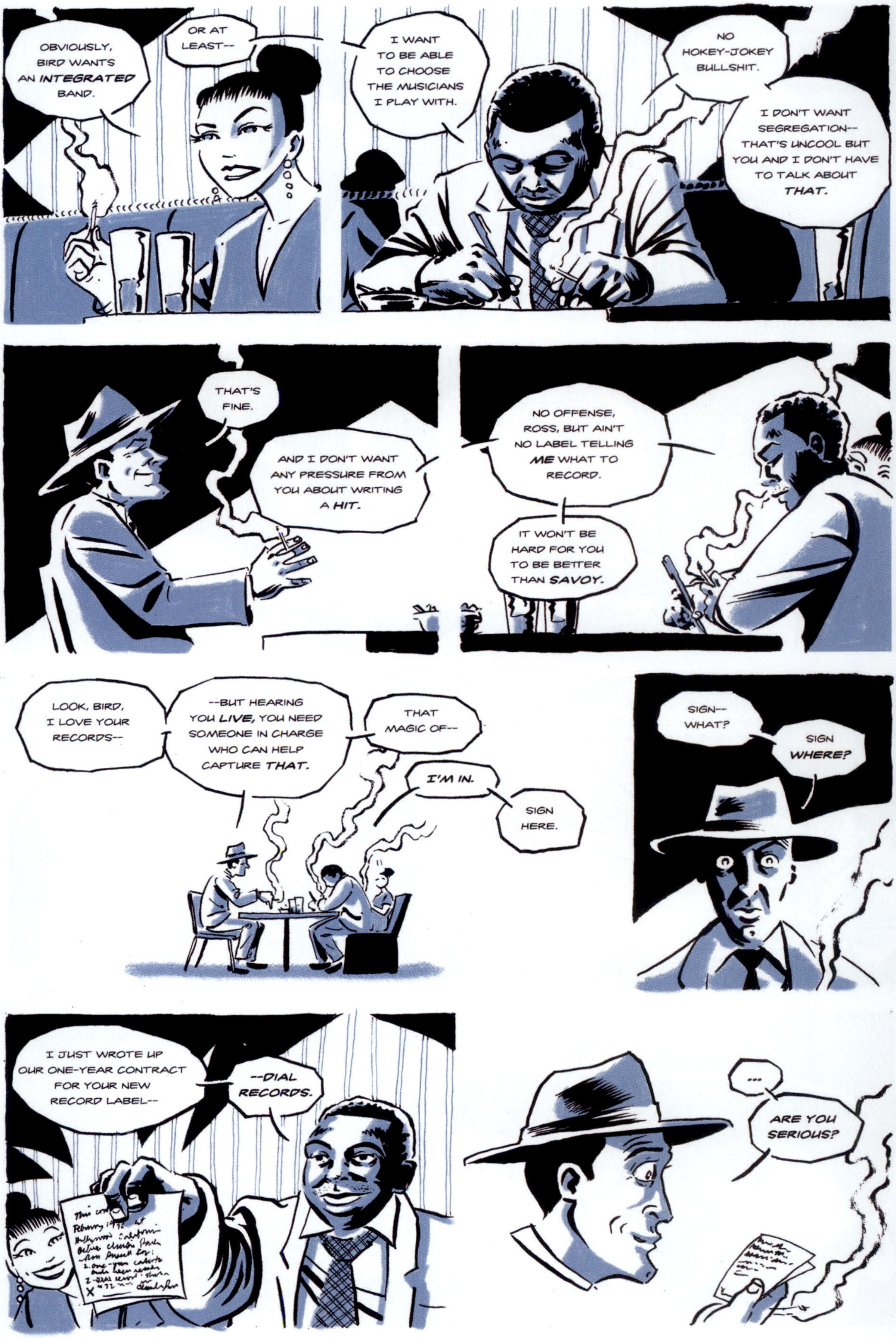
OBVIOUSLY, BIRD WANTS AN INTEGRATED BAND.
OR AT LEAST--
I WANT TO BE ABLE TO CHOOSE THE MUSICIANS I PLAY WITH.
NO HOKEY-JOKEY BULLSHIT.
I DON'T WANT SEGREGATION-- THAT'S UNCOOL BUT YOU AND I DON'T HAVE TO TALK ABOUT THAT.
THAT'S FINE.
AND I DON'T WANT ANY PRESSURE FROM YOU ABOUT WRITING A HIT.
NO OFFENSE, ROSS, BUT AIN'T NO LABEL TELLING ME WHAT TO RECORD.
IT WON'T BE HARD FOR YOU TO BE BETTER THAN SAVOY.
LOOK, BIRD, I LOVE YOUR RECORDS--
--BUT HEARING YOU LIVE, YOU NEED SOMEONE IN CHARGE WHO CAN HELP CAPTURE THAT.
THAT MAGIC OF--
I'M IN.
SIGN HERE.
SIGN-- WHAT?
SIGN WHERE?
I JUST WROTE UP OUR ONE-YEAR CONTRACT FOR YOUR NEW RECORD LABEL--
--DIAL RECORDS.
...
ARE YOU SERIOUS?

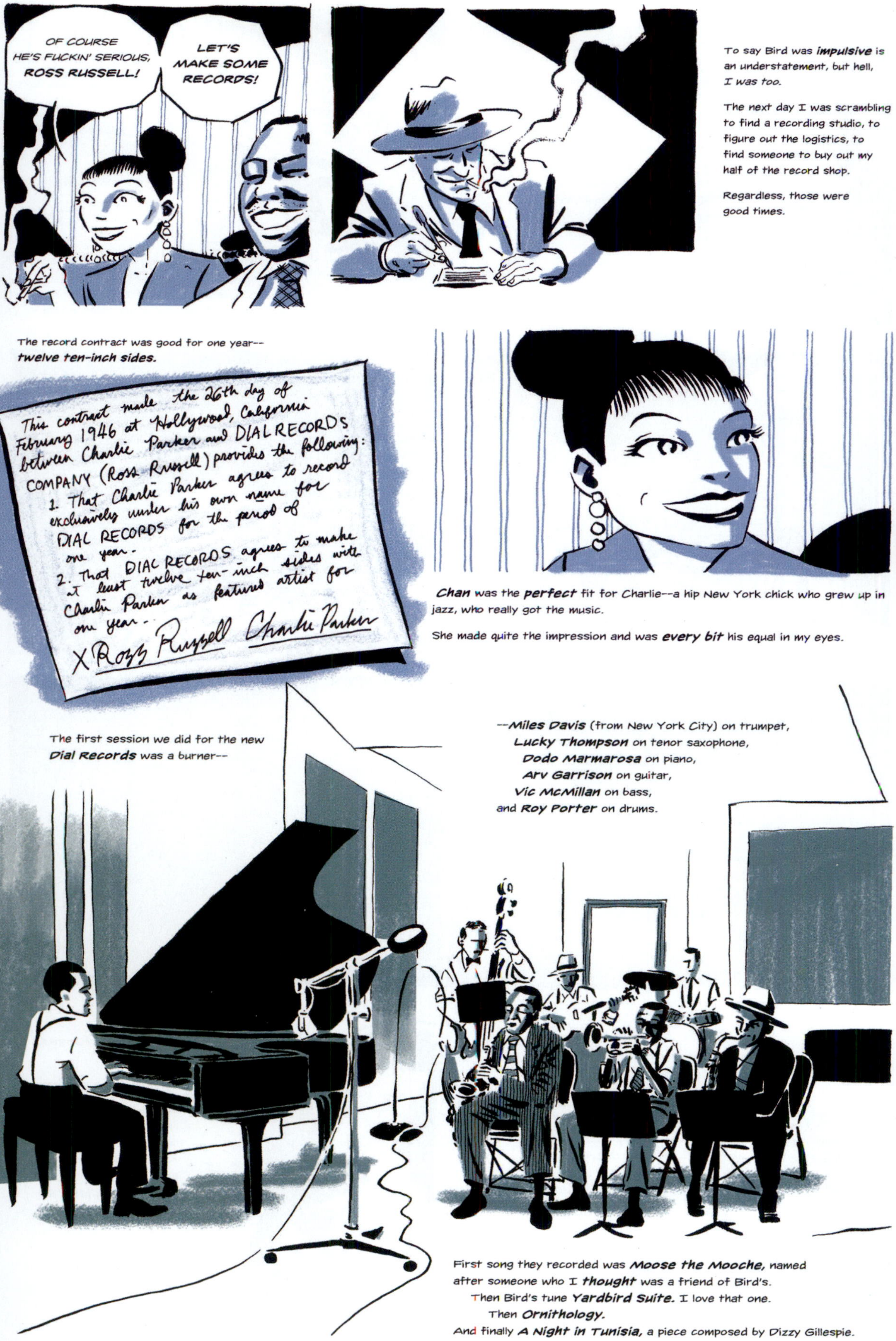
OF COURSE HE'S FUCKIN' SERIOUS, ROSS RUSSELL!
LET'S MAKE SOME RECORDS!
To say Bird was *impulsive* is an understatement, but hell, *I was too.*
The next day I was scrambling to find a recording studio, to figure out the logistics, to find someone to buy out my half of the record shop.
Regardless, those were good times.
The record contract was good for one year-- ***twelve ten-inch sides.***
This contract made the 26th day of February 1946 at Hollywood, California between Charlie Parker and DIAL RECORDS COMPANY (Ross Russell) provides the following:
1. That Charlie Parker agrees to record exclusively under his own name for DIAL RECORDS for the period of one year.
2. That DIAL RECORDS agrees to make at least twelve ten-inch sides with Charlie Parker as featured artist for one year.
X Ross Russell Charlie Parker
Chan was the ***perfect*** fit for Charlie--a hip New York chick who grew up in jazz, who really got the music.
She made quite the impression and was ***every bit*** his equal in my eyes.
The first session we did for the new ***Dial Records*** was a burner--
--***Miles Davis*** (from New York City) on trumpet,
Lucky Thompson on tenor saxophone,
Dodo Marmarosa on piano,
Arv Garrison on guitar,
Vic McMillan on bass,
and ***Roy Porter*** on drums.
First song they recorded was ***Moose the Mooche,*** named after someone who I ***thought*** was a friend of Bird's.
Then Bird's tune ***Yardbird Suite.*** I love that one.
Then ***Ornithology.***
And finally ***A Night in Tunisia,*** a piece composed by Dizzy Gillespie.

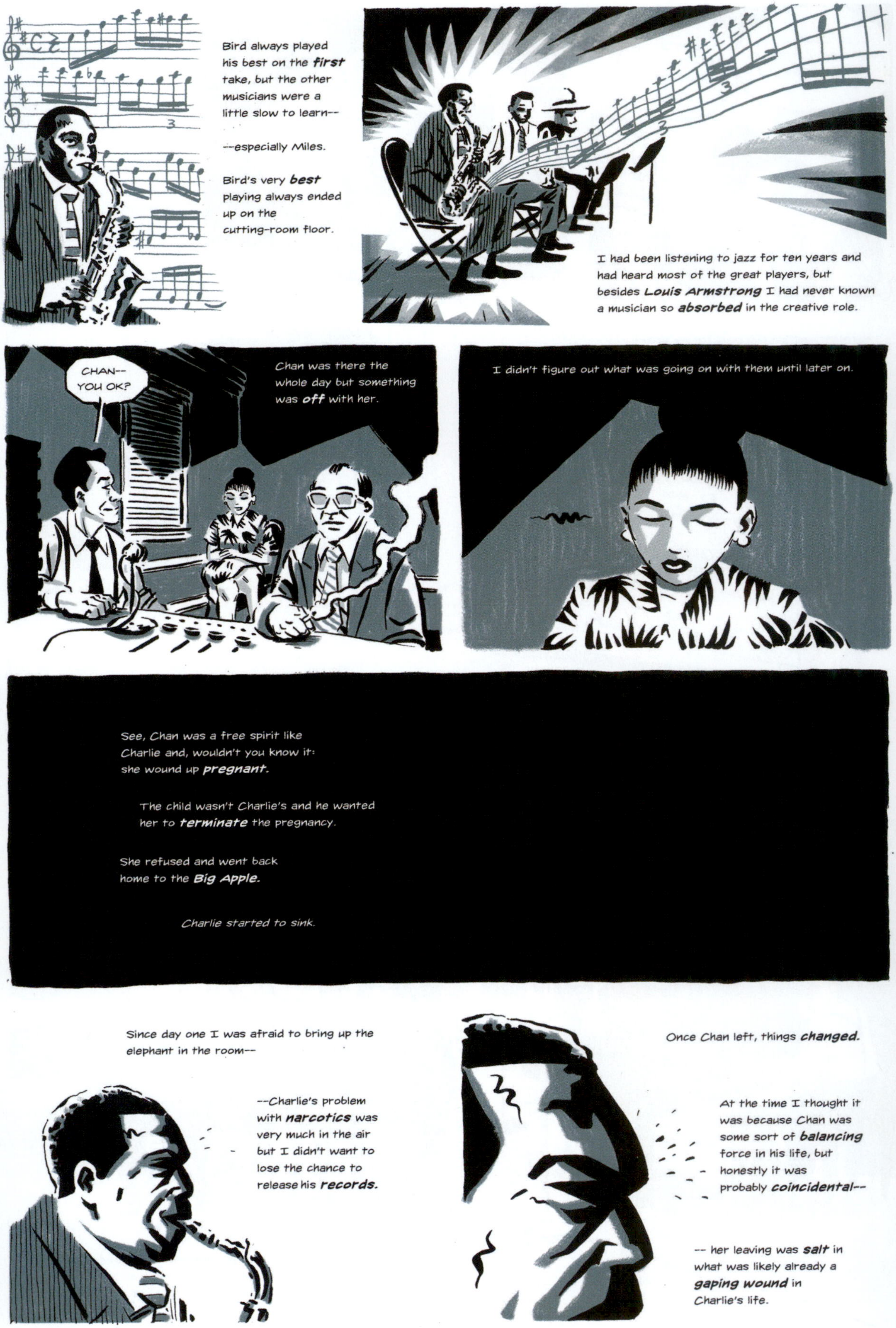
Bird always played his best on the first take, but the other musicians were a little slow to learn--
--especially Miles.
Bird's very best playing always ended up on the cutting-room floor.
I had been listening to jazz for ten years and had heard most of the great players, but besides Louis Armstrong I had never known a musician so absorbed in the creative role.
CHAN-- YOU OK?
Chan was there the whole day but something was off with her.
I didn't figure out what was going on with them until later on.
See, Chan was a free spirit like Charlie and, wouldn't you know it: she wound up pregnant.
The child wasn't Charlie's and he wanted her to terminate the pregnancy.
She refused and went back home to the Big Apple.
Charlie started to sink.
Since day one I was afraid to bring up the elephant in the room--
--Charlie's problem with narcotics was very much in the air but I didn't want to lose the chance to release his records.
Once Chan left, things changed.
At the time I thought it was because Chan was some sort of balancing force in his life, but honestly it was probably coincidental--
-- her leaving was salt in what was likely already a gaping wound in Charlie's life.

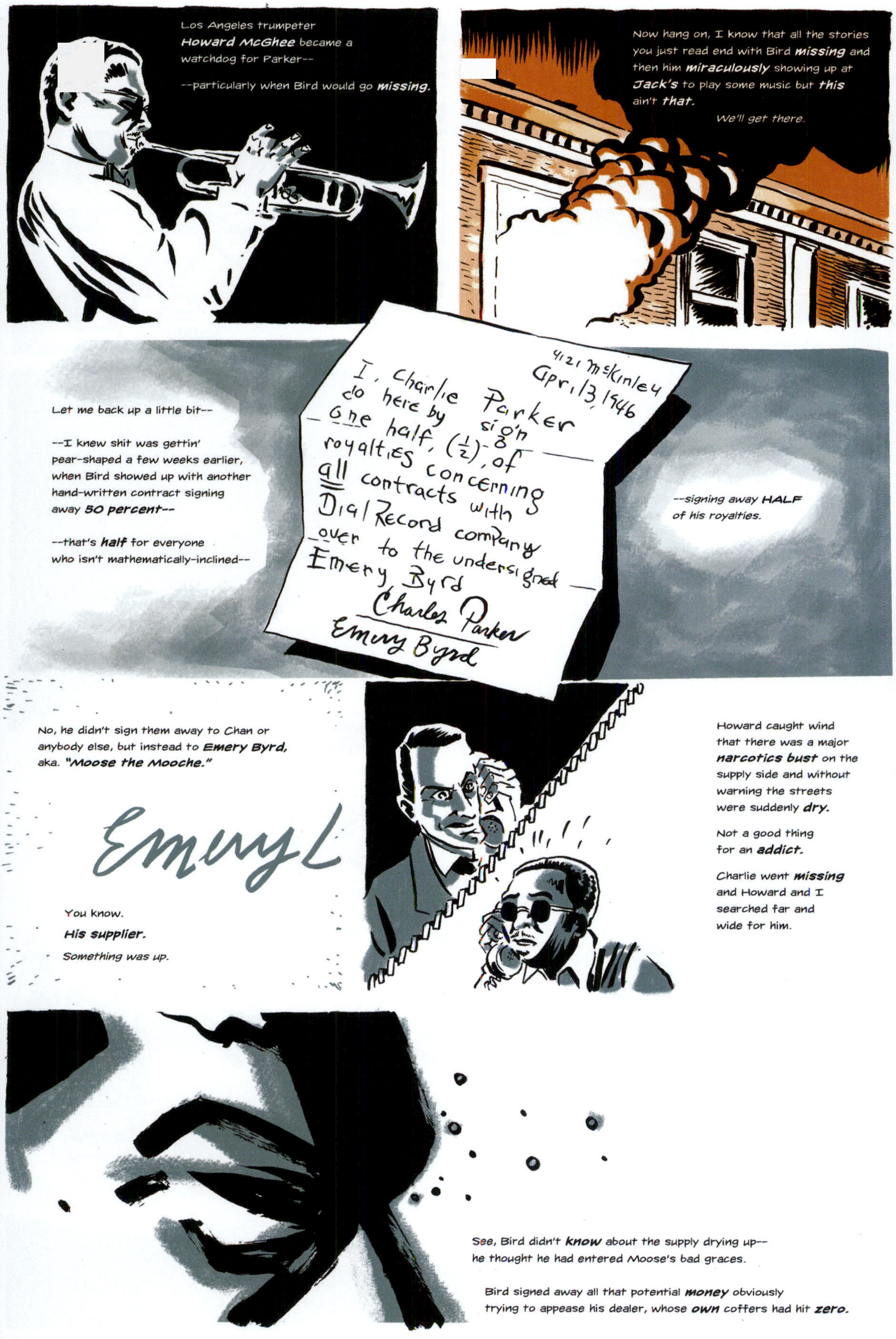

Los Angeles trumpeter
Howard McGhee became a watchdog for Parker--
--particularly when Bird would go missing.
Now hang on, I know that all the stories you just read end with Bird missing and then him miraculously showing up at Jack's to play some music but this ain't that.
We'll get there.
Let me back up a little bit--
--I knew shit was gettin' pear-shaped a few weeks earlier, when Bird showed up with another hand-written contract signing away 50 percent--
--that's half for everyone who isn't mathematically-inclined--
4121 McKinley
Apr. 13, 1946
I, Charlie Parker do here by sign one half, (1/2), of royalties concerning all contracts with Dial Record company over to the undersigned Emery Byrd
Charles Parker
Emery Byrd
--signing away HALF of his royalties.
No, he didn't sign them away to Chan or anybody else, but instead to Emery Byrd, aka. "Moose the Mooche."
Emery L
You know.
His supplier.
Something was up.
Howard caught wind that there was a major narcotics bust on the supply side and without warning the streets were suddenly dry.
Not a good thing for an addict.
Charlie went missing and Howard and I searched far and wide for him.
See, Bird didn't know about the supply drying up--
he thought he had entered Moose's bad graces.
Bird signed away all that potential money obviously trying to appease his dealer, whose own coffers had hit zero.

In this desperate state, Bird started sleeping in an old garage over on McKinley Avenue. At least, this is where Howard found him--likely one of ***many*** flophouses.

It's hard to understand the actions of an ***addict.***

With Bird's supply of dope gone, he turned to ***alcohol.*** This might sound surprising to you dear readers, but this combination--a ***junkie*** with ***no*** supply ***plus*** alcohol--was considerably ***worse*** for Bird than ***heroin alone.***

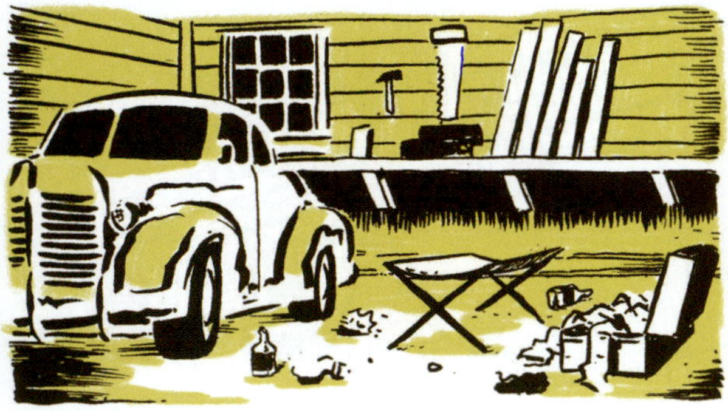

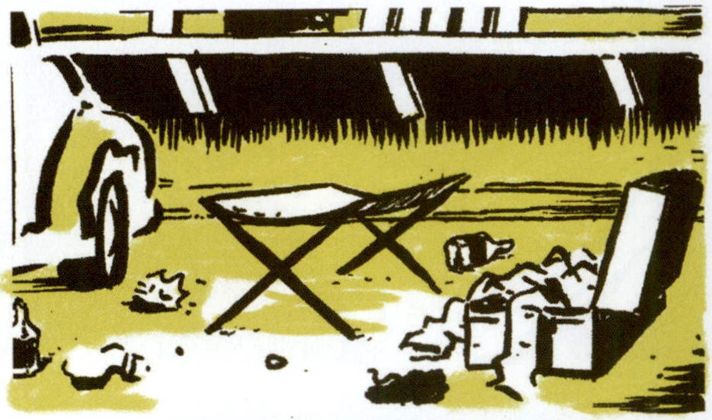

Why?

There was no way alcohol would get Bird as ***high*** as junk would.

But it ***felt*** like it could--if he could just have ***one more drink.***

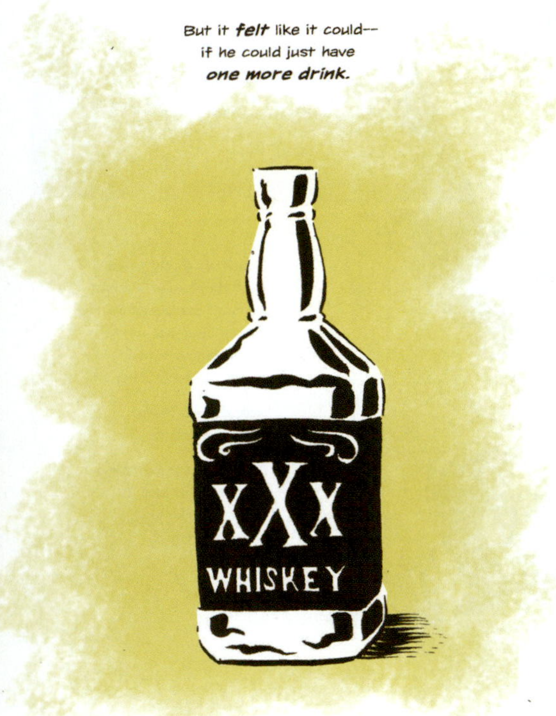
XXX
WHISKEY

*During this time he was drinking a **quart of whiskey** every night.*

No man can attempt to function in that state, much less a ***genius*** like Bird.

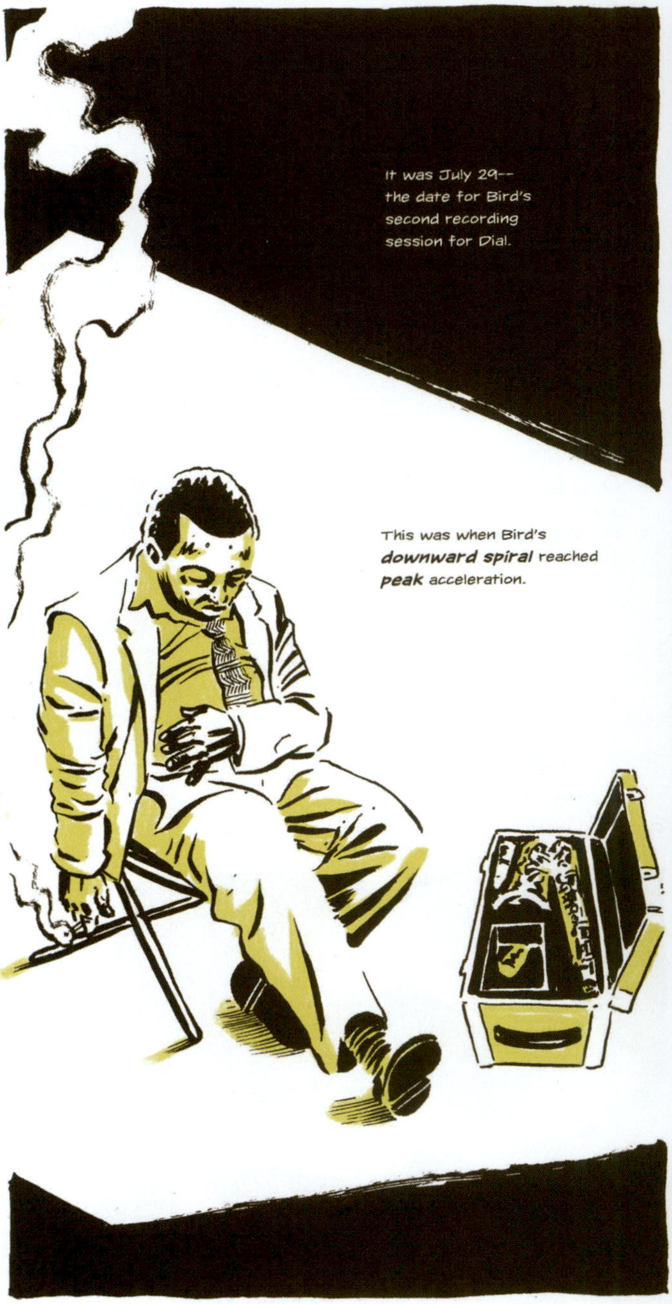
It was July 29--
the date for Bird's
second recording
session for Dial.
This was when Bird's
downward spiral reached
peak acceleration.

BIRD--

--DO YOU WANT TO GET YOUR HORN OUT AND WARM UP ON A FEW SCALES?

SNORT

HUNHH...

WHAT THE FUCK?!

I'D SAY WHAT WE'RE SEEING HERE IS AN *ACUTE* CASE OF *ALCOHOLISM*.

HE--

WE GOTTA CANCEL THIS SHIT!

BIRD CAN'T *PLAY*!

BAM

NO WAY.

I SOLD *EVERYTHING* I HAVE FOR THIS.

GET BACK IN THERE.

GET. BACK. IN. THERE. AND. FUCKING. PLAY!

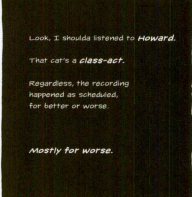

Look, I shoulda listened to *Howard*.

That cat's a *class-act*.

Regardless, the recording happened as scheduled, for better or worse.

Mostly for worse.

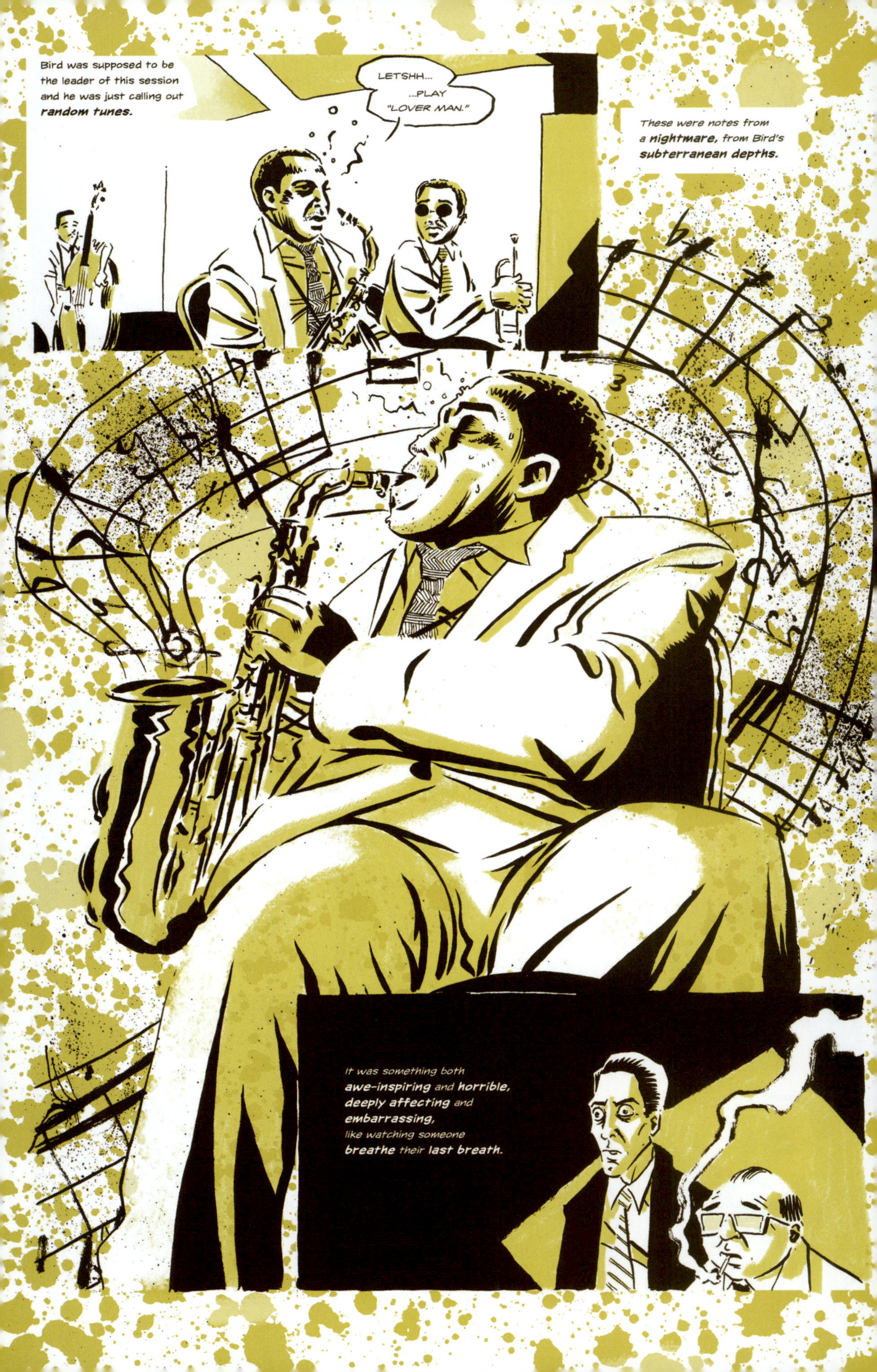

Bird was supposed to be the leader of this session and he was just calling out **random tunes.**
LETSHH... ...PLAY "LOVER MAN."
These were notes from a **nightmare,** from Bird's **subterranean depths.**
It was something both **awe-inspiring** and **horrible, deeply affecting** and **embarrassing,** like watching someone **breathe** their **last breath.**

At the end of the fourth tune,
Bird slumped down in his chair,
passed out.

We woke him up and
put him on a cab
back to his **hotel**
with distinct orders
to get some **rest.**

Howard, in an attempt
to **salvage** what was an
expensive session,
recorded a side of tunes
with the rhythm section.

He sounded great
but was no Bird.

Nobody else was Bird.

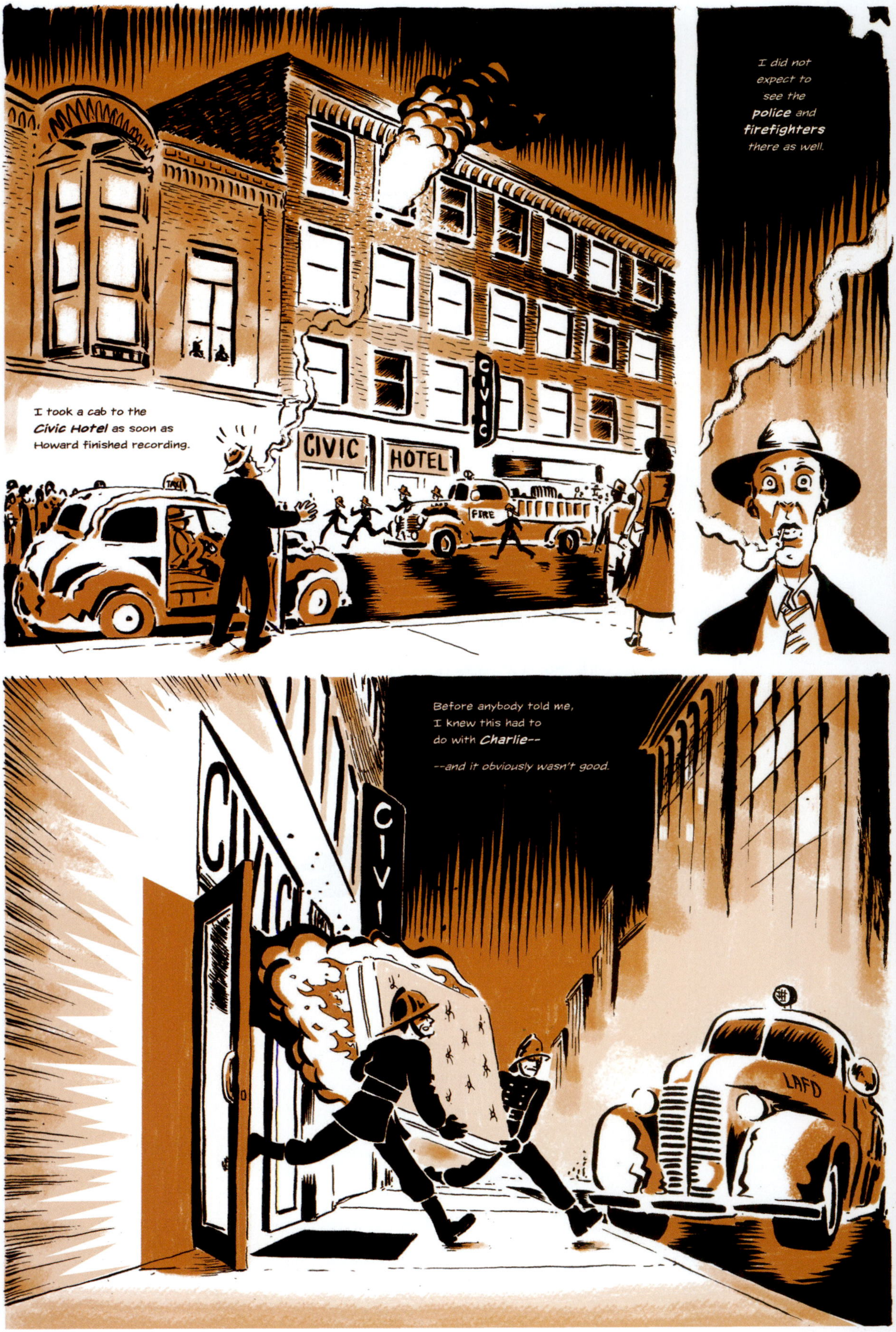
I took a cab to the **Civic Hotel** as soon as Howard finished recording.
CIVIC
CIVIC HOTEL
TAXI
FIRE
I did not expect to see the **police** and **firefighters** there as well.
Before anybody told me, I knew this had to do with **Charlie--**
--and it obviously wasn't good.
LAFD

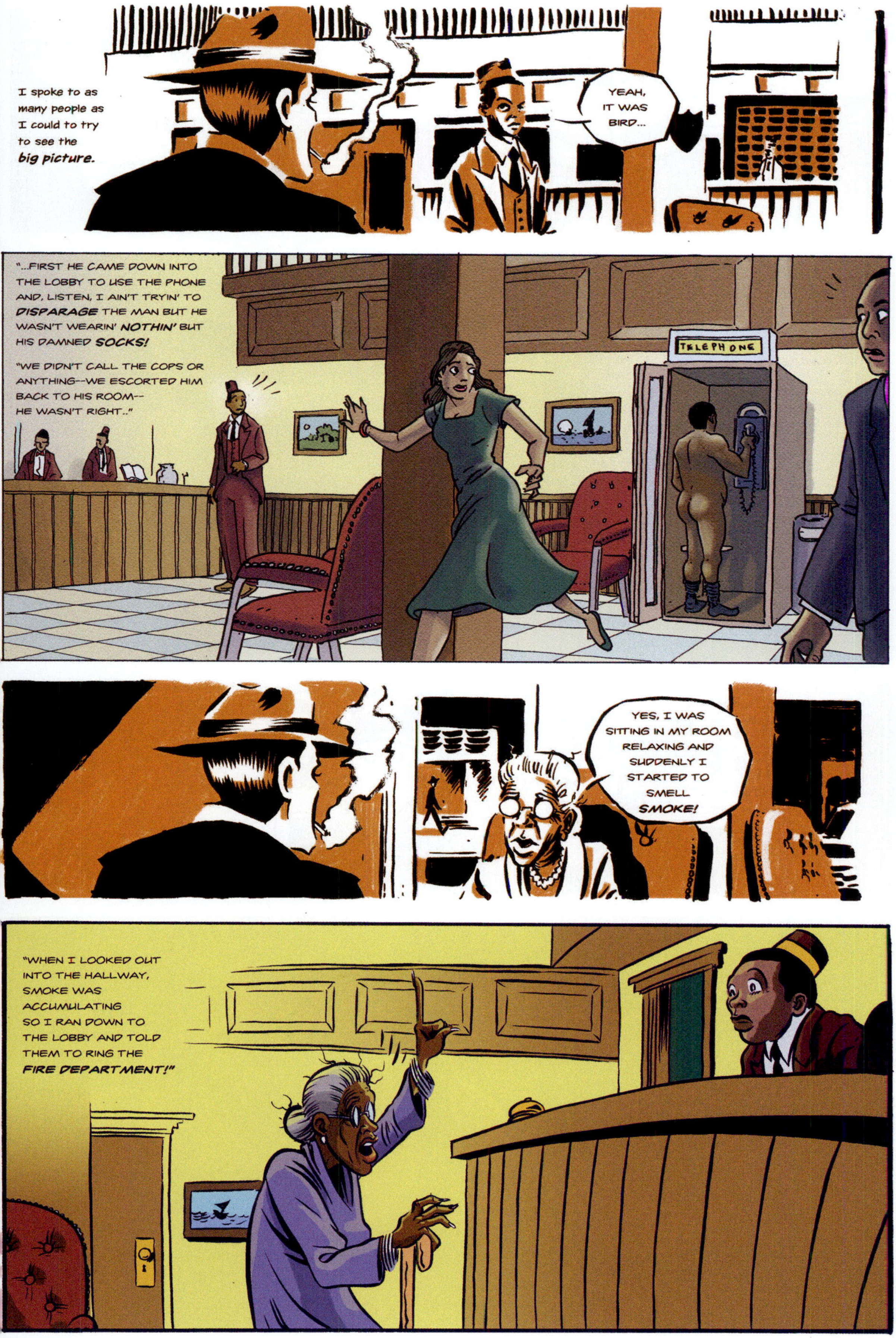
I spoke to as many people as I could to try to see the big picture.
YEAH, IT WAS BIRD...
"...FIRST HE CAME DOWN INTO THE LOBBY TO USE THE PHONE AND, LISTEN, I AIN'T TRYIN' TO DISPARAGE THE MAN BUT HE WASN'T WEARIN' NOTHIN' BUT HIS DAMNED SOCKS!
"WE DIDN'T CALL THE COPS OR ANYTHING--WE ESCORTED HIM BACK TO HIS ROOM-- HE WASN'T RIGHT.."
TELEPHONE
YES, I WAS SITTING IN MY ROOM RELAXING AND SUDDENLY I STARTED TO SMELL SMOKE!
"WHEN I LOOKED OUT INTO THE HALLWAY, SMOKE WAS ACCUMULATING SO I RAN DOWN TO THE LOBBY AND TOLD THEM TO RING THE FIRE DEPARTMENT!"

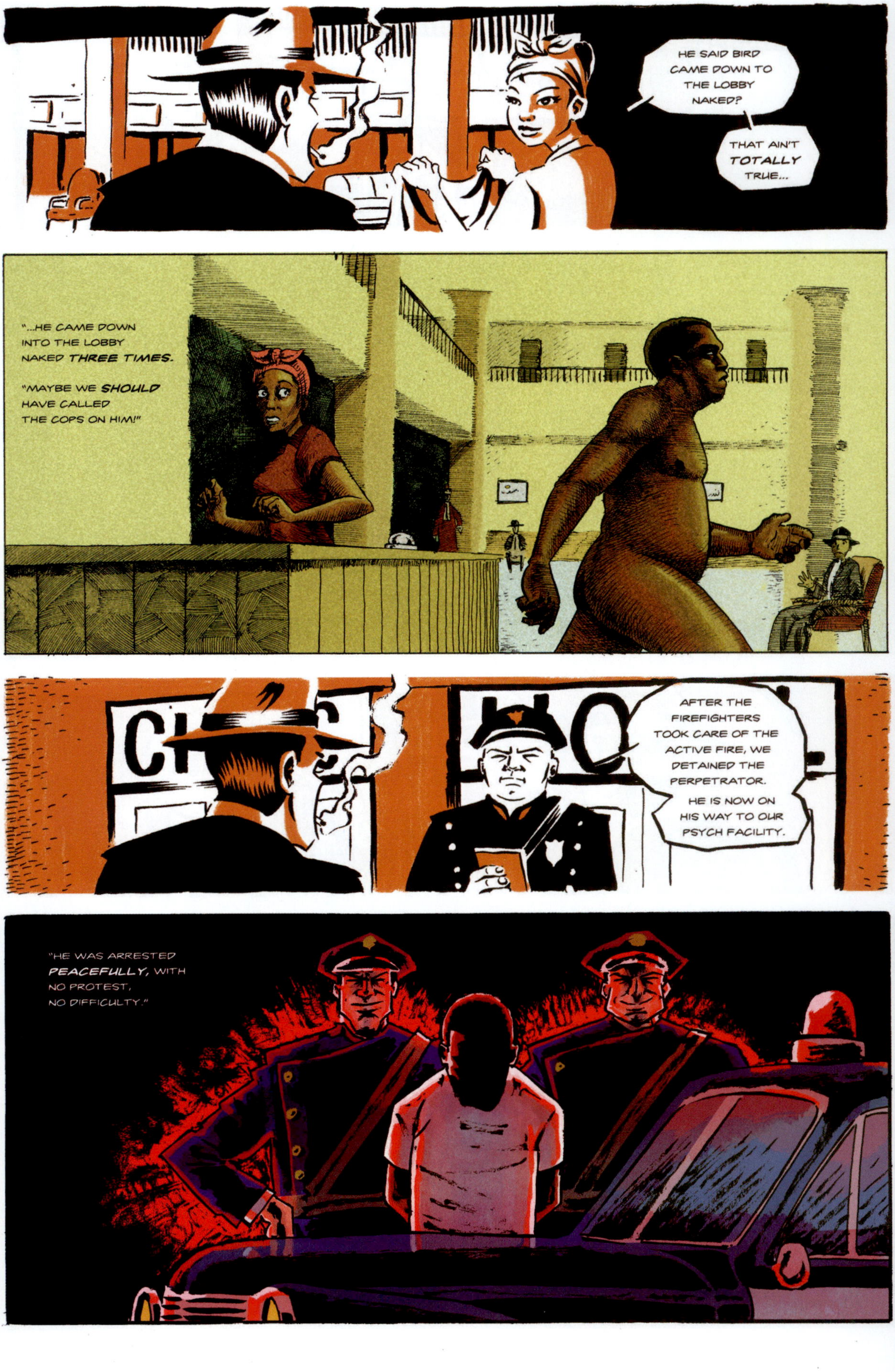

HE SAID BIRD CAME DOWN TO THE LOBBY NAKED?
THAT AIN'T *TOTALLY* TRUE...
"...HE CAME DOWN INTO THE LOBBY NAKED *THREE TIMES.*
"MAYBE WE *SHOULD* HAVE CALLED THE COPS ON HIM!"
AFTER THE FIREFIGHTERS TOOK CARE OF THE ACTIVE FIRE, WE DETAINED THE PERPETRATOR.
HE IS NOW ON HIS WAY TO OUR PSYCH FACILITY.
"HE WAS ARRESTED *PEACEFULLY,* WITH NO PROTEST, NO DIFFICULTY."

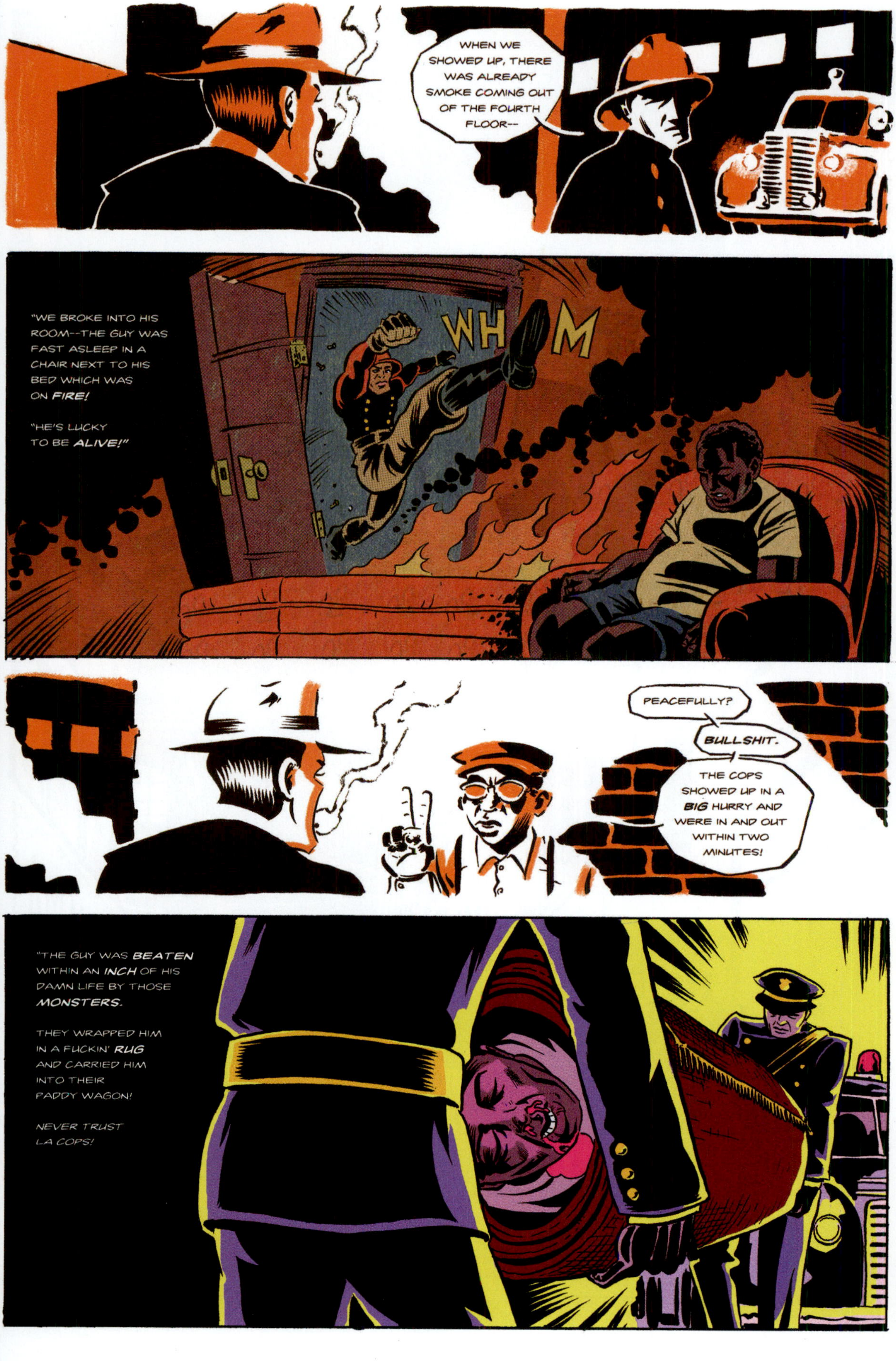

WHEN WE SHOWED UP, THERE WAS ALREADY SMOKE COMING OUT OF THE FOURTH FLOOR--
"WE BROKE INTO HIS ROOM--THE GUY WAS FAST ASLEEP IN A CHAIR NEXT TO HIS BED WHICH WAS ON FIRE!
"HE'S LUCKY TO BE ALIVE!"
WHAM
PEACEFULLY?
BULLSHIT.
THE COPS SHOWED UP IN A BIG HURRY AND WERE IN AND OUT WITHIN TWO MINUTES!
"THE GUY WAS BEATEN WITHIN AN INCH OF HIS DAMN LIFE BY THOSE MONSTERS.
THEY WRAPPED HIM IN A FUCKIN' RUG AND CARRIED HIM INTO THEIR PADDY WAGON!
NEVER TRUST LA COPS!

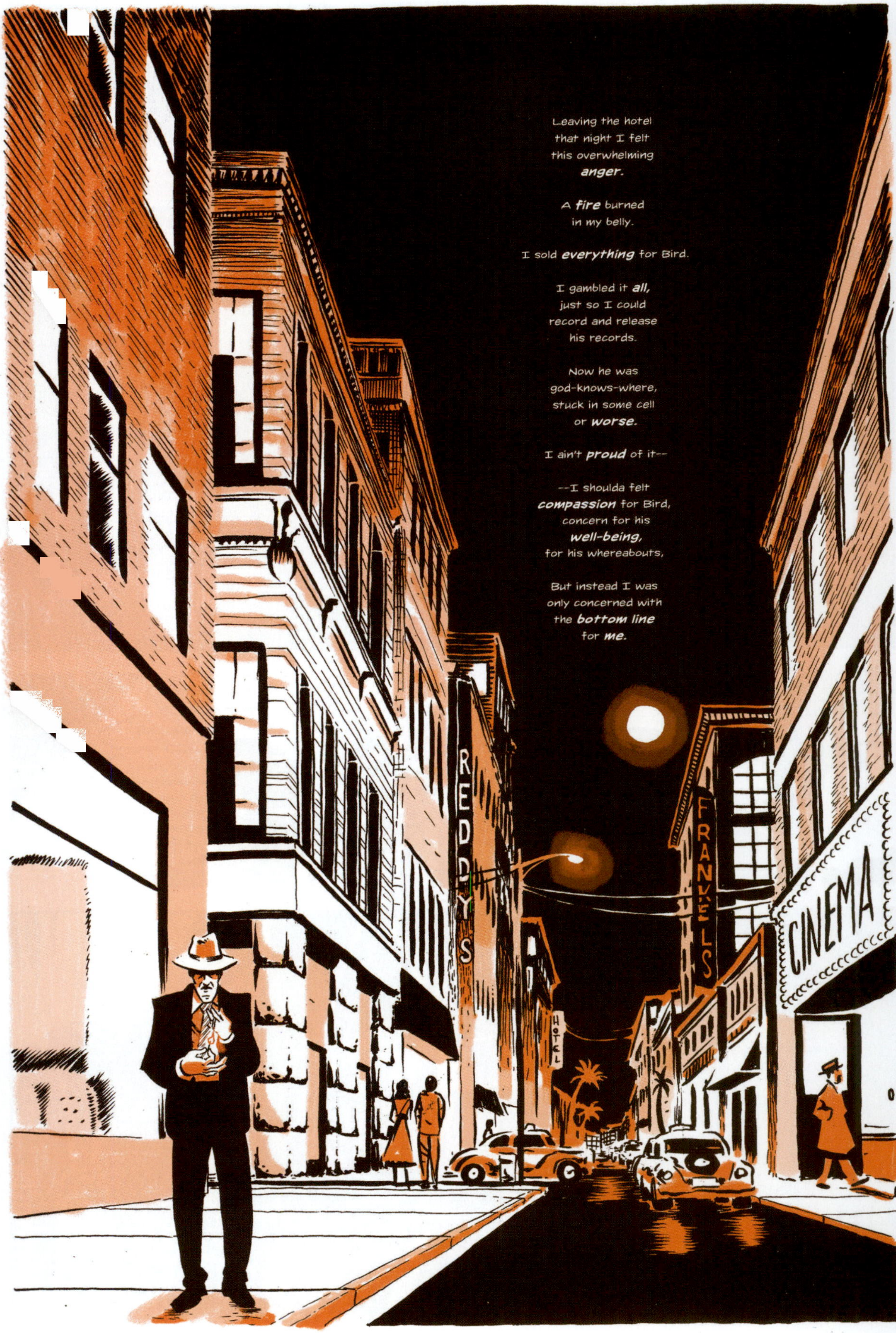
Leaving the hotel that night I felt this overwhelming **anger.**
A **fire** burned in my belly.
I sold **everything** for Bird.
I gambled it **all,** just so I could record and release his records.
Now he was god-knows-where, stuck in some cell or **worse.**
I ain't **proud** of it--
--I shoulda felt **compassion** for Bird, concern for his **well-being,** for his whereabouts,
But instead I was only concerned with the **bottom line** for **me.**
REDDYS
FRANVELS
HOTEL
CINEMA

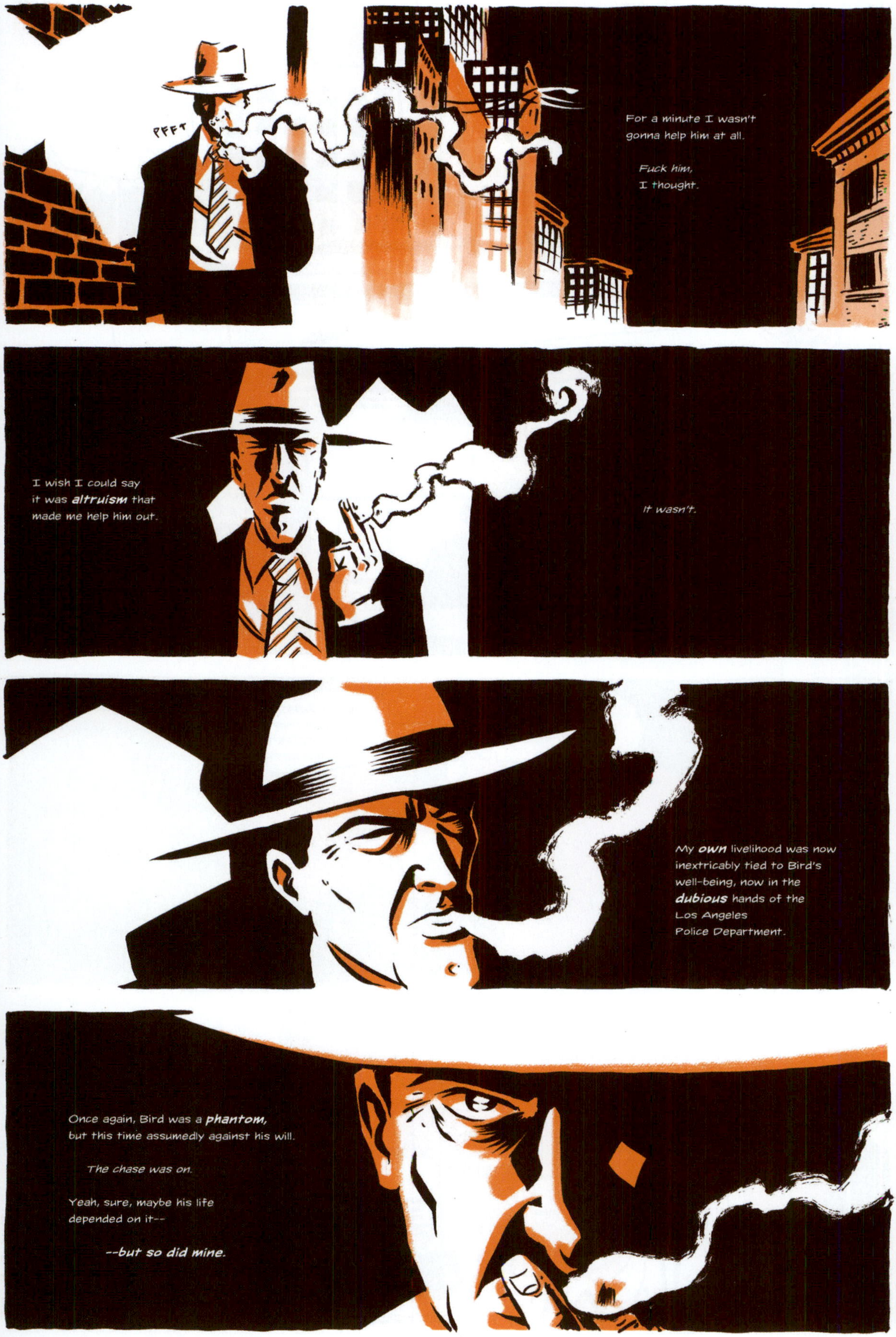
PFFT
For a minute I wasn't gonna help him at all.
Fuck him, I thought.
I wish I could say it was altruism that made me help him out.
It wasn't.
My own livelihood was now inextricably tied to Bird's well-being, now in the dubious hands of the Los Angeles Police Department.
Once again, Bird was a phantom, but this time assumedly against his will.
The chase was on.
Yeah, sure, maybe his life depended on it--
--but so did mine.

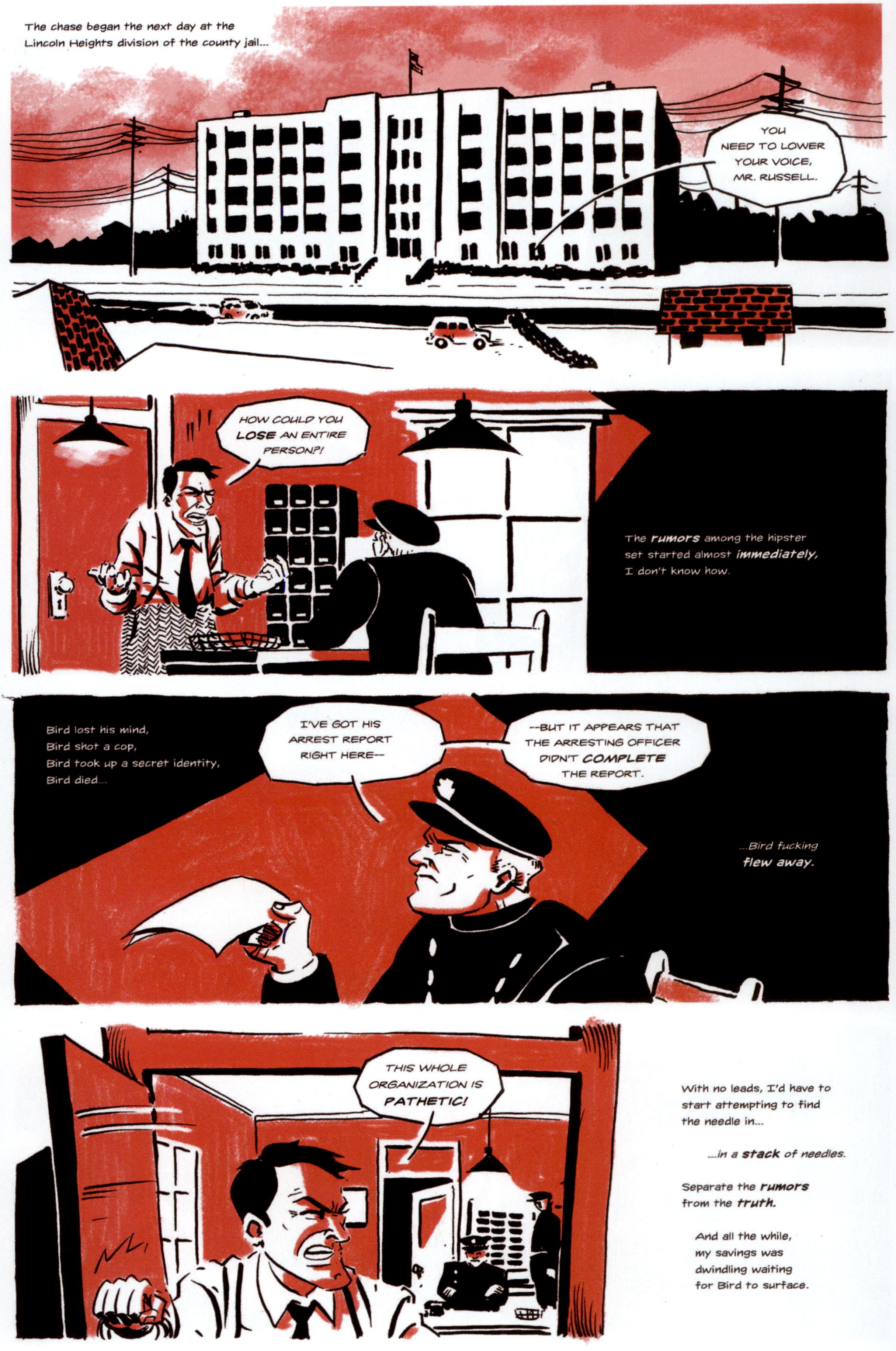
The chase began the next day at the Lincoln Heights division of the county jail...
YOU NEED TO LOWER YOUR VOICE, MR. RUSSELL.
HOW COULD YOU LOSE AN ENTIRE PERSON?!
The rumors among the hipster set started almost immediately, I don't know how.
Bird lost his mind, Bird shot a cop, Bird took up a secret identity, Bird died...
I'VE GOT HIS ARREST REPORT RIGHT HERE--
--BUT IT APPEARS THAT THE ARRESTING OFFICER DIDN'T COMPLETE THE REPORT.
...Bird fucking flew away.
THIS WHOLE ORGANIZATION IS PATHETIC!
With no leads, I'd have to start attempting to find the needle in...
...in a stack of needles.
Separate the rumors from the truth.
And all the while, my savings was dwindling waiting for Bird to surface.

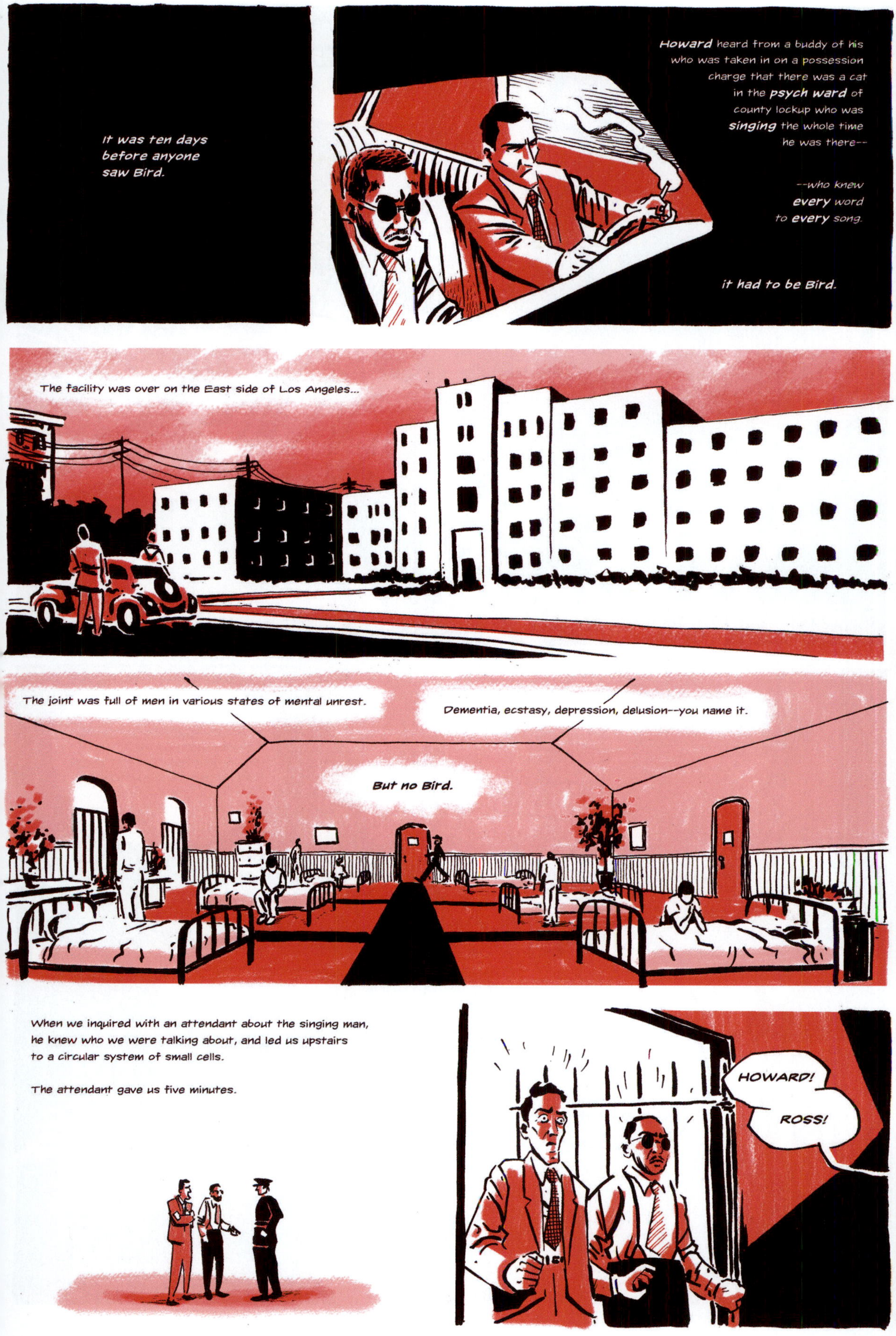
It was ten days before anyone saw Bird.
Howard heard from a buddy of his who was taken in on a possession charge that there was a cat in the psych ward of county lockup who was singing the whole time he was there--
--who knew every word to every song.
It had to be Bird.
The facility was over on the East side of Los Angeles...
The joint was full of men in various states of mental unrest.
Dementia, ecstasy, depression, delusion--you name it.
But no Bird.
When we inquired with an attendant about the singing man, he knew who we were talking about, and led us upstairs to a circular system of small cells.
The attendant gave us five minutes.
HOWARD!
ROSS!

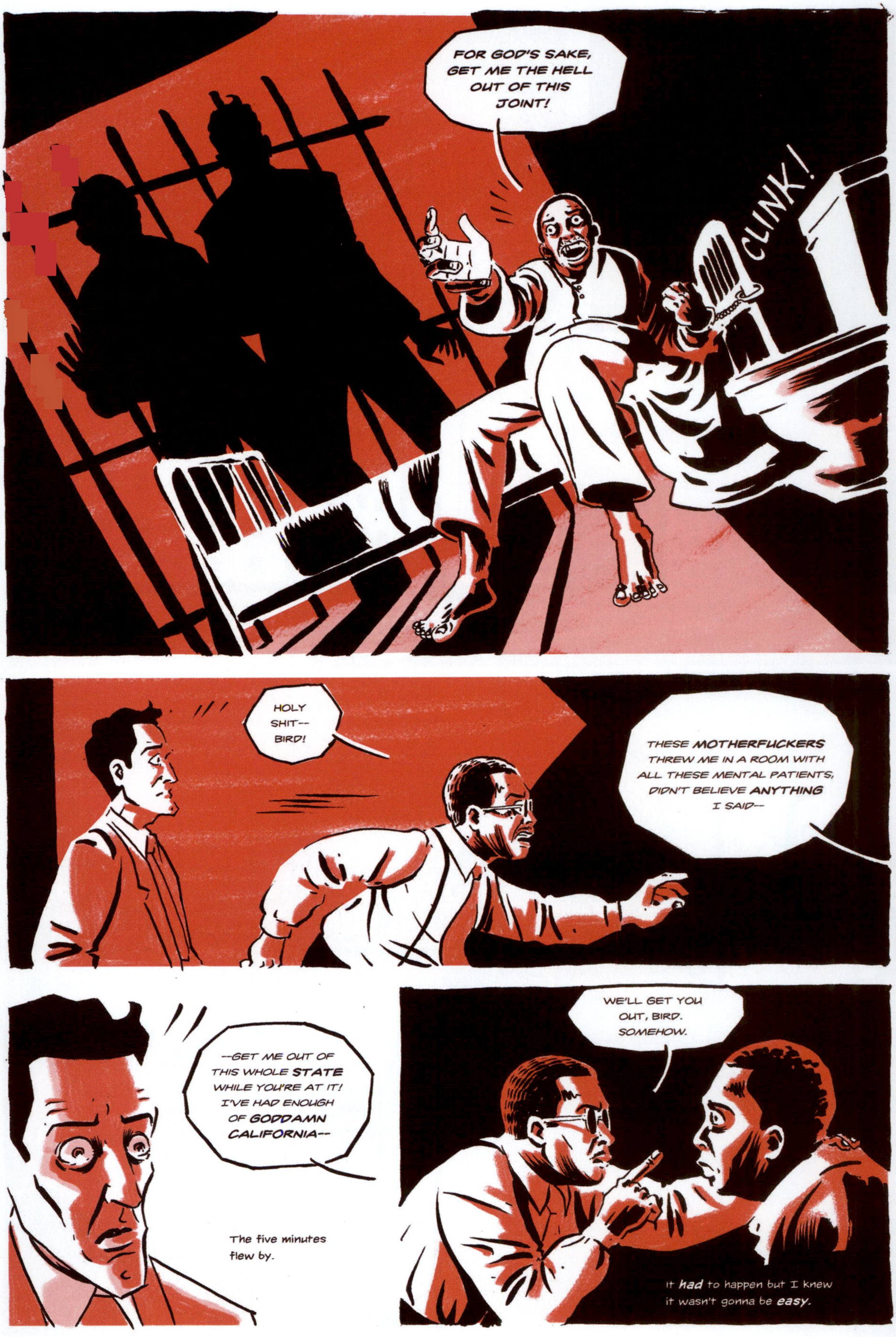
FOR GOD'S SAKE, GET ME THE HELL OUT OF THIS JOINT!
CLINK!
HOLY SHIT-- BIRD!
THESE MOTHERFUCKERS THREW ME IN A ROOM WITH ALL THESE MENTAL PATIENTS, DIDN'T BELIEVE ANYTHING I SAID--
--GET ME OUT OF THIS WHOLE STATE WHILE YOU'RE AT IT! I'VE HAD ENOUGH OF GODDAMN CALIFORNIA--
The five minutes flew by.
WE'LL GET YOU OUT, BIRD. SOMEHOW.
It had to happen but I knew it wasn't gonna be easy.

Good thing I'm the ***Charlie Parker of paperwork.***

I prepared the papers to transfer Charlie's hearing to the docket of the young, liberal judge ***Stanley Mosk*** as opposed to the kangaroo court that inmates of the psychopathic ward usually were party to.

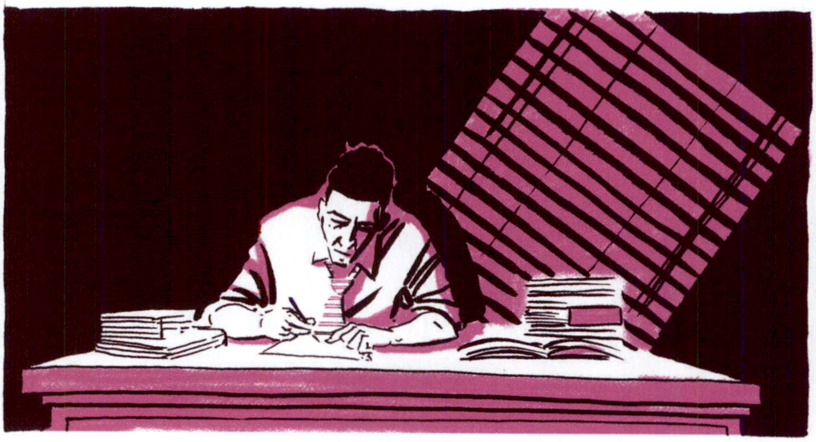

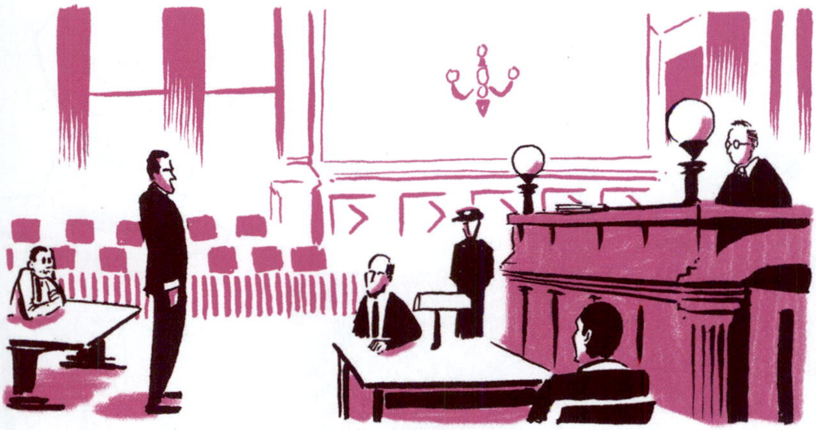

There were three options for these inmates: Norwalk, Patton, or Camarillo.

Norwalk and Patton were more-or-less ***maximum-security*** institutions for the ***criminally insane.***

If Bird ended up in one of those joints, ***forget about it.***

If we couldn't get the charges dropped, ***Camarillo***--the "country club" of mental institutions--was the next best bet.

And after we briefed the judge on Parker's career and contributions to American music, Mosk sentenced him to no less than ***six months*** at ***Camarillo.***

It was the next best thing to dropped charges.

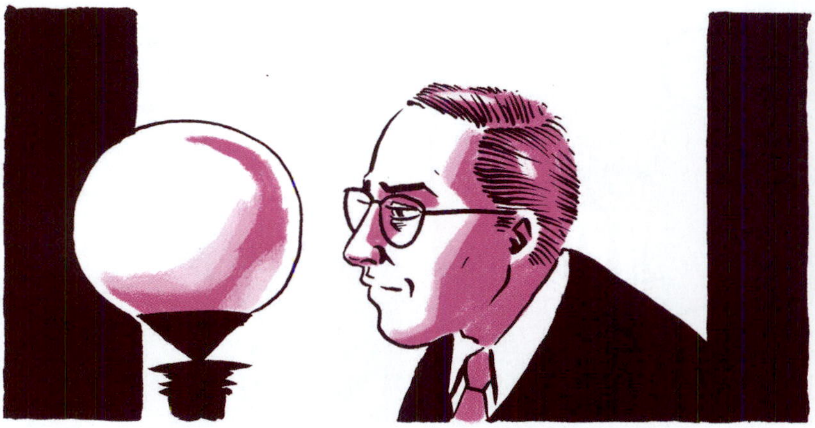

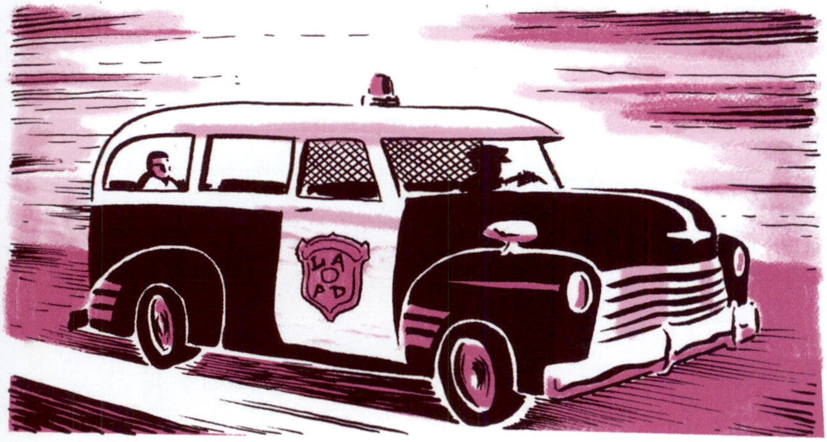
LAPD

The next day Bird was driven to the spot, 70 minutes north of town on a peaceful, docile piece of land overlooking the ocean.

While rumors spread, hope existed.

And, frankly, those rumors had some great ***business potential*** on the back end of this whole fiasco.

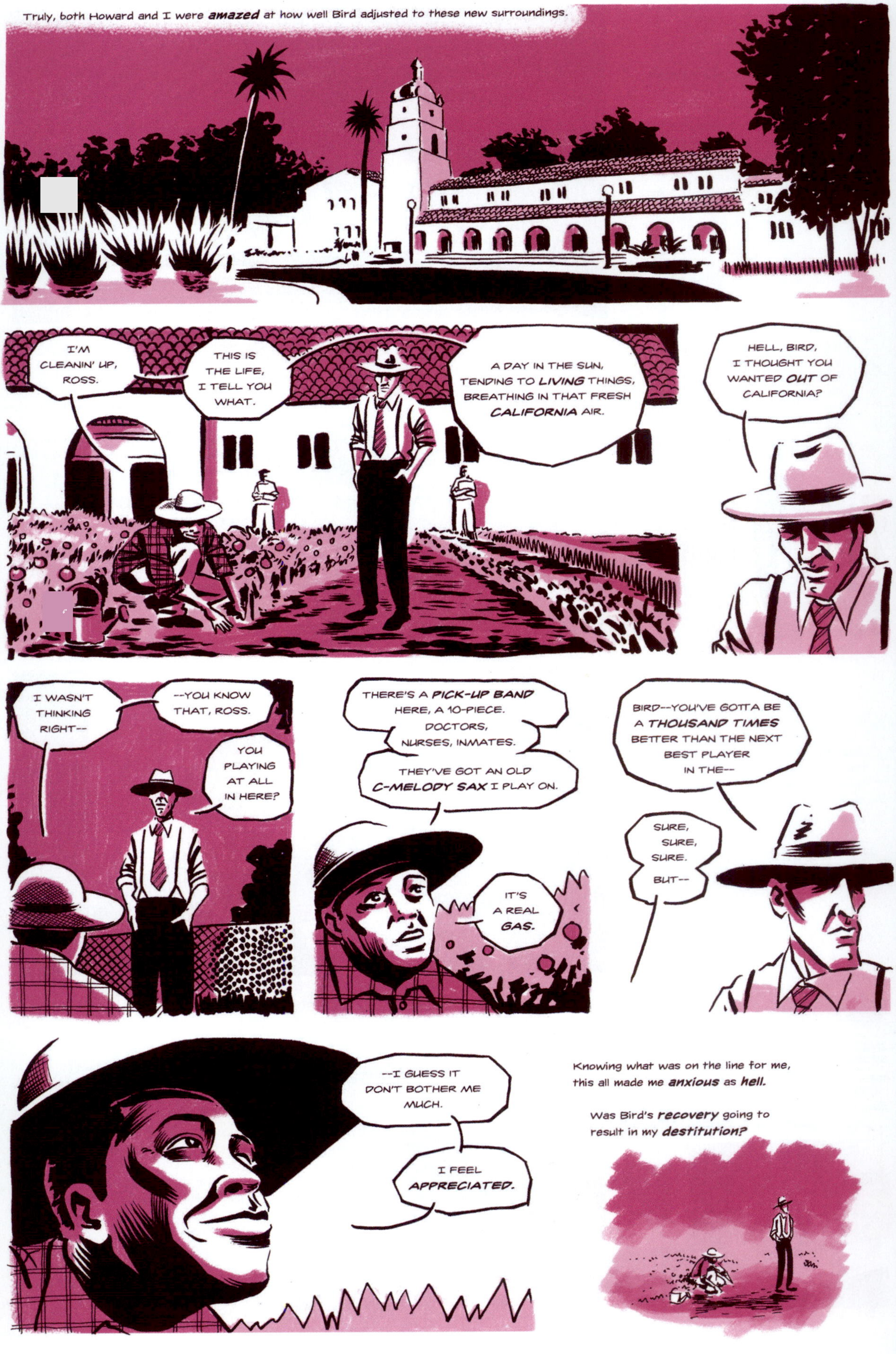

Truly, both Howard and I were **amazed** at how well Bird adjusted to these new surroundings.
I'M CLEANIN' UP, ROSS.
THIS IS THE LIFE, I TELL YOU WHAT.
A DAY IN THE SUN, TENDING TO **LIVING** THINGS, BREATHING IN THAT FRESH **CALIFORNIA** AIR.
HELL, BIRD, I THOUGHT YOU WANTED **OUT** OF CALIFORNIA?
I WASN'T THINKING RIGHT--
--YOU KNOW THAT, ROSS.
YOU PLAYING AT ALL IN HERE?
THERE'S A **PICK-UP BAND** HERE, A 10-PIECE. DOCTORS, NURSES, INMATES.
THEY'VE GOT AN OLD **C-MELODY SAX** I PLAY ON.
IT'S A REAL **GAS**.
BIRD--YOU'VE GOTTA BE A **THOUSAND TIMES** BETTER THAN THE NEXT BEST PLAYER IN THE--
SURE, SURE, SURE.
BUT--
--I GUESS IT DON'T BOTHER ME MUCH.
I FEEL **APPRECIATED**.
Knowing what was on the line for me, this all made me **anxious** as **hell**.
Was Bird's **recovery** going to result in my **destitution?**

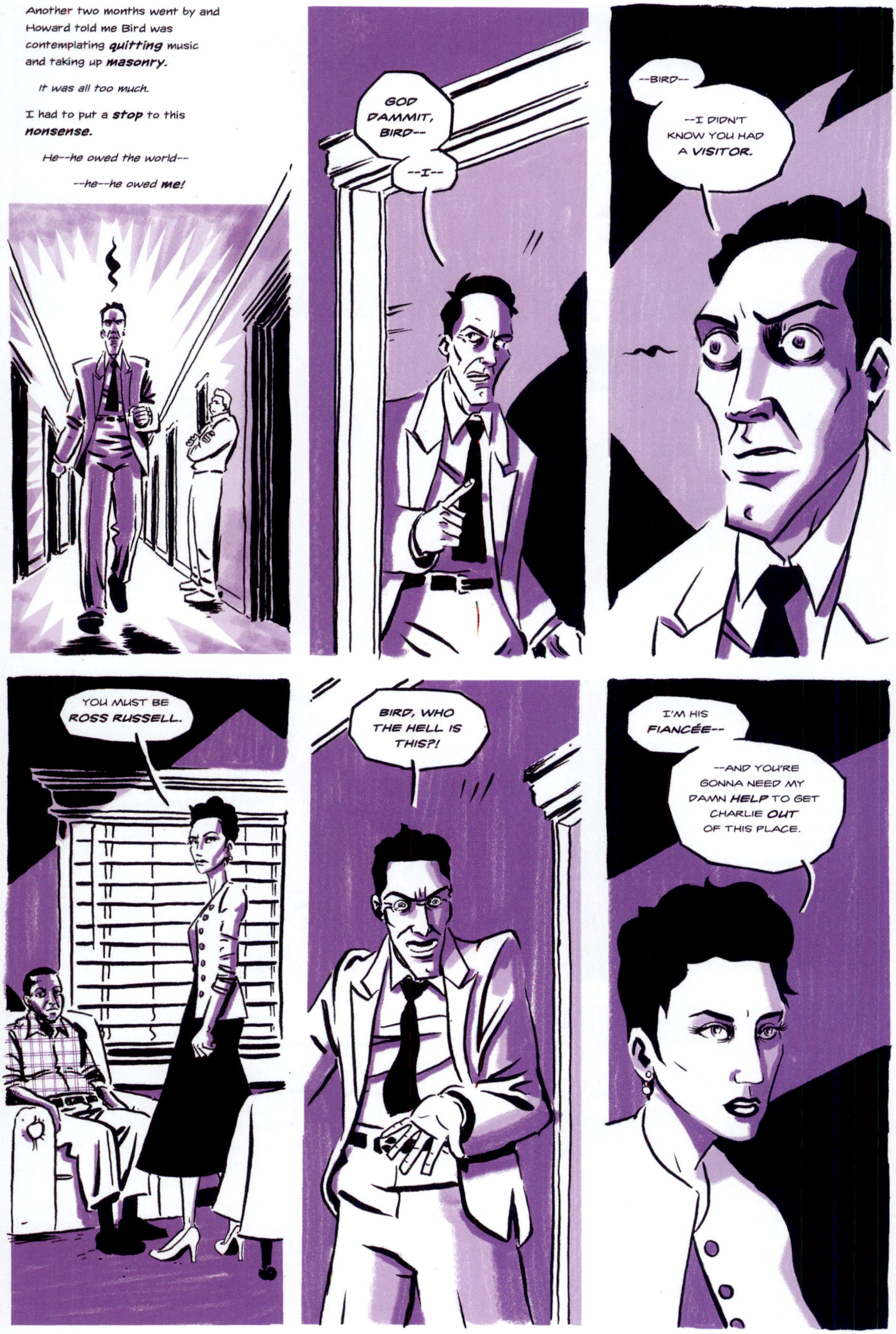
Another two months went by and Howard told me Bird was contemplating *quitting* music and taking up *masonry.*
It was all too much.
I had to put a *stop* to this *nonsense.*
He--he owed the world--
--he--he owed ***me!***
GOD DAMMIT, BIRD--
--I--
--BIRD--
--I DIDN'T KNOW YOU HAD A *VISITOR.*
YOU MUST BE *ROSS RUSSELL.*
BIRD, WHO THE HELL IS THIS?!
I'M HIS *FIANCÉE--*
--AND YOU'RE GONNA NEED MY DAMN *HELP* TO GET CHARLIE *OUT* OF THIS PLACE.

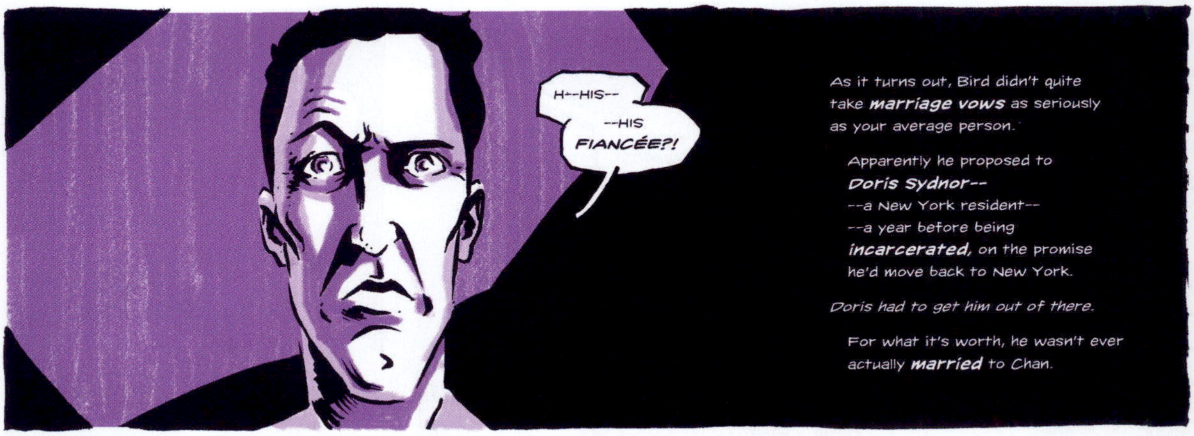
H--HIS--
--HIS FIANCÉE?!
As it turns out, Bird didn't quite take ***marriage vows*** as seriously as your average person.
Apparently he proposed to ***Doris Sydnor--***
--a New York resident--
--a year before being ***incarcerated,*** on the promise he'd move back to New York.
Doris had to get him out of there.
For what it's worth, he wasn't ever actually ***married*** to Chan.

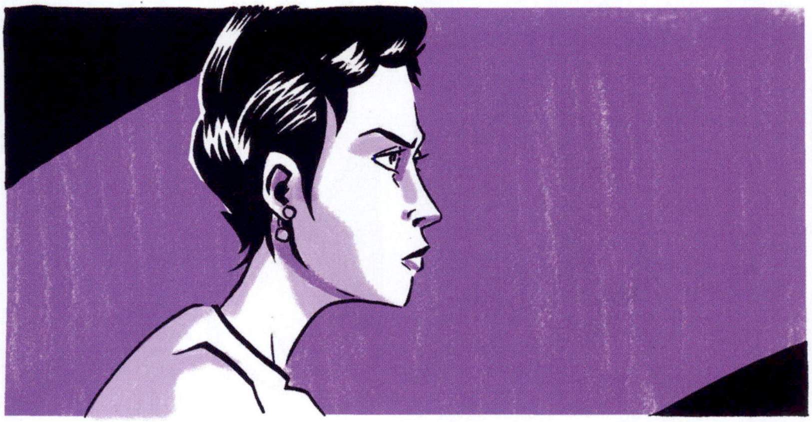

I gotta say, Doris and I, we didn't exactly ***click.***

She was no ***Chan,*** I can tell you that much.

Where Chan was ***sophisticated,*** Doris was ***square.***

Where Chan was ***beautiful,*** Doris was just too ***skinny.***

Where Chan was part of the ***scene,*** Doris wanted ***nothing*** to do with it.

But I couldn't have gotten Bird out of Camarillo and put his life back together without her ***help.***

Doris moved to California a month earlier and was ***waiting tables*** and saving dough.

She recovered all of Bird's personal effects from his various ***flophouses*** around the Los Angeles region.

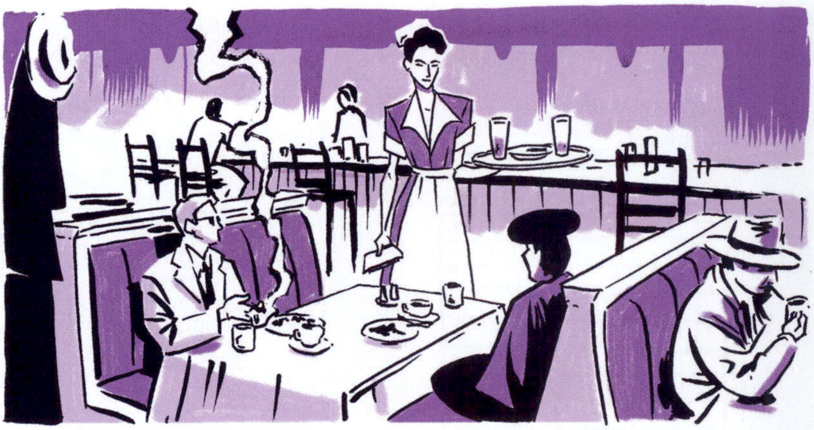

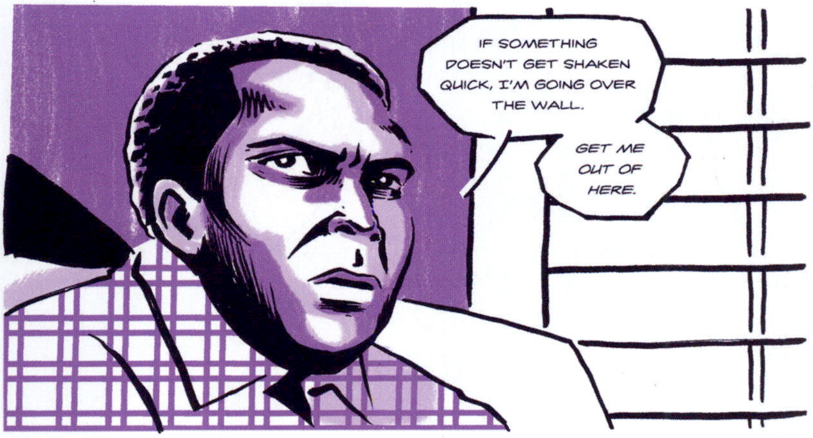
IF SOMETHING DOESN'T GET SHAKEN QUICK, I'M GOING OVER THE WALL.
GET ME OUT OF HERE.

And, miraculously, she got through to Bird that he needed back into the game, back into the music scene.

Somehow, this ***square, plain broad,*** she ***understood.***

I'm guessing she alluded to ***Dizzy's*** meteoric ascent during Bird's sixteen months in California--

*--she probably didn't even do it on **purpose.***

I didn't even have to bring up the god-damned ***masonry.***

Who knows, though?

It all may have been ***coincidental.*** Charlie Parker's return to music was perhaps ***inevitable.***

Horses gotta ***run,*** scorpions gotta ***sting,*** snakes gotta ***bite,*** and Birds gotta ***sing.***

I know this is getting complicated but we're almost there.

The doctors at Camarillo stated that Charlie wasn't ***fit*** for release unless he was under the ***custody*** of a ***California resident.***

Howard and his wife ***refused.***

Doris would've but she had only lived in California for a short time.

That left ***me,*** Ross Russell, owner of Dial Records, as the ***sole*** guardian of one Mr. Charles Parker Jr.

Miraculously it all worked out.

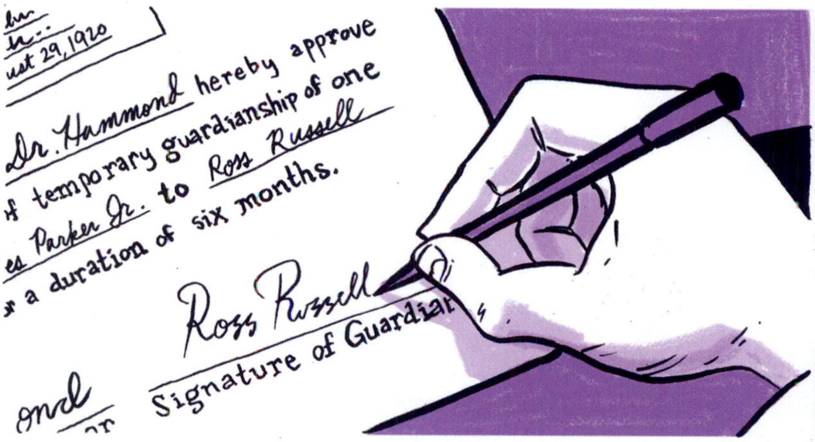
ust 29, 1920
Dr. Hammond hereby approve
f temporary guardianship of one
es Parker Jr. to Ross Russell
a duration of six months.
Ross Russell
Signature of Guardia

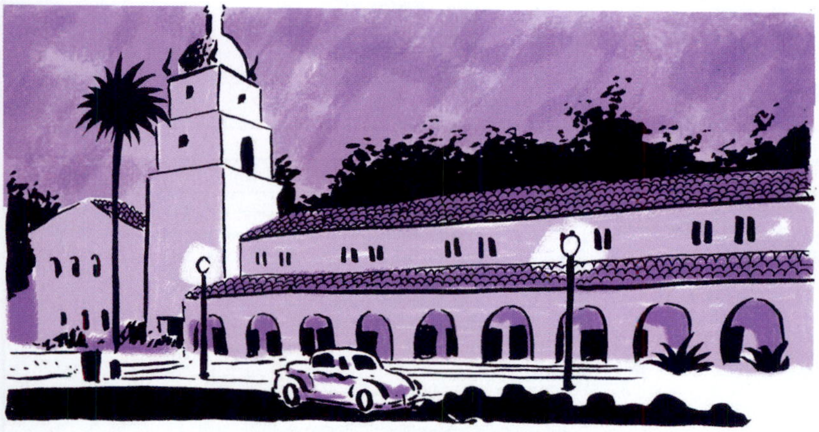

This was a source of ***contention,*** but I showed up with an ***updated*** version of Bird's as-of-yet unfulfilled Dial Records contract for him to sign.

Bird claims I ***made*** him sign but I don't remember doing that.

I was protecting myself as things had gotten ***bleak*** for me.

Bird was a ***confusing*** cat, ***smart*** as hell and ***extraordinarily*** clever.

It's hard to say if the psychiatrists at Camarillo got anywhere with him or if he was just ***fucking*** with them.

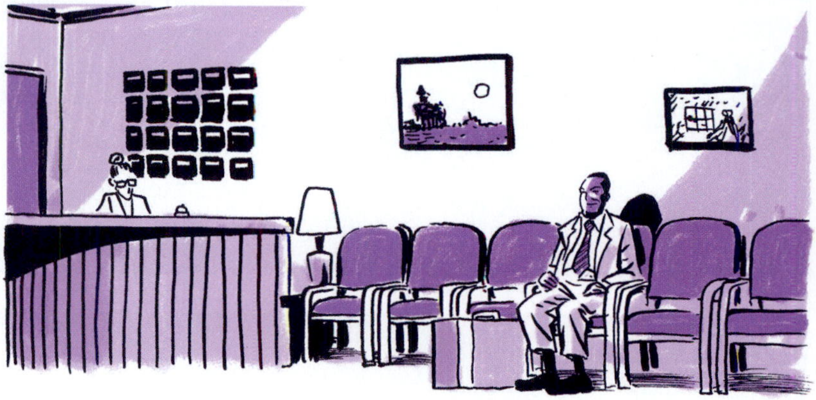

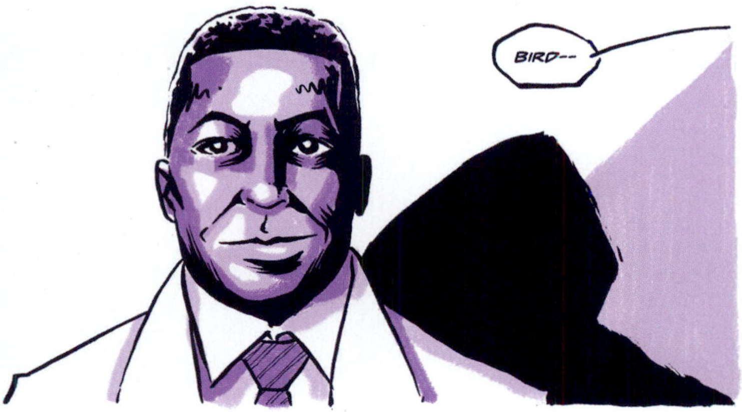
BIRD--

Regardless, it's safe to say that that stretch was perhaps the ***last time*** in Bird's life when he was actually ***clean,*** off dope.

He was ***sharp,*** *he was* ***healthy,*** *and his battery* ***recharged.***

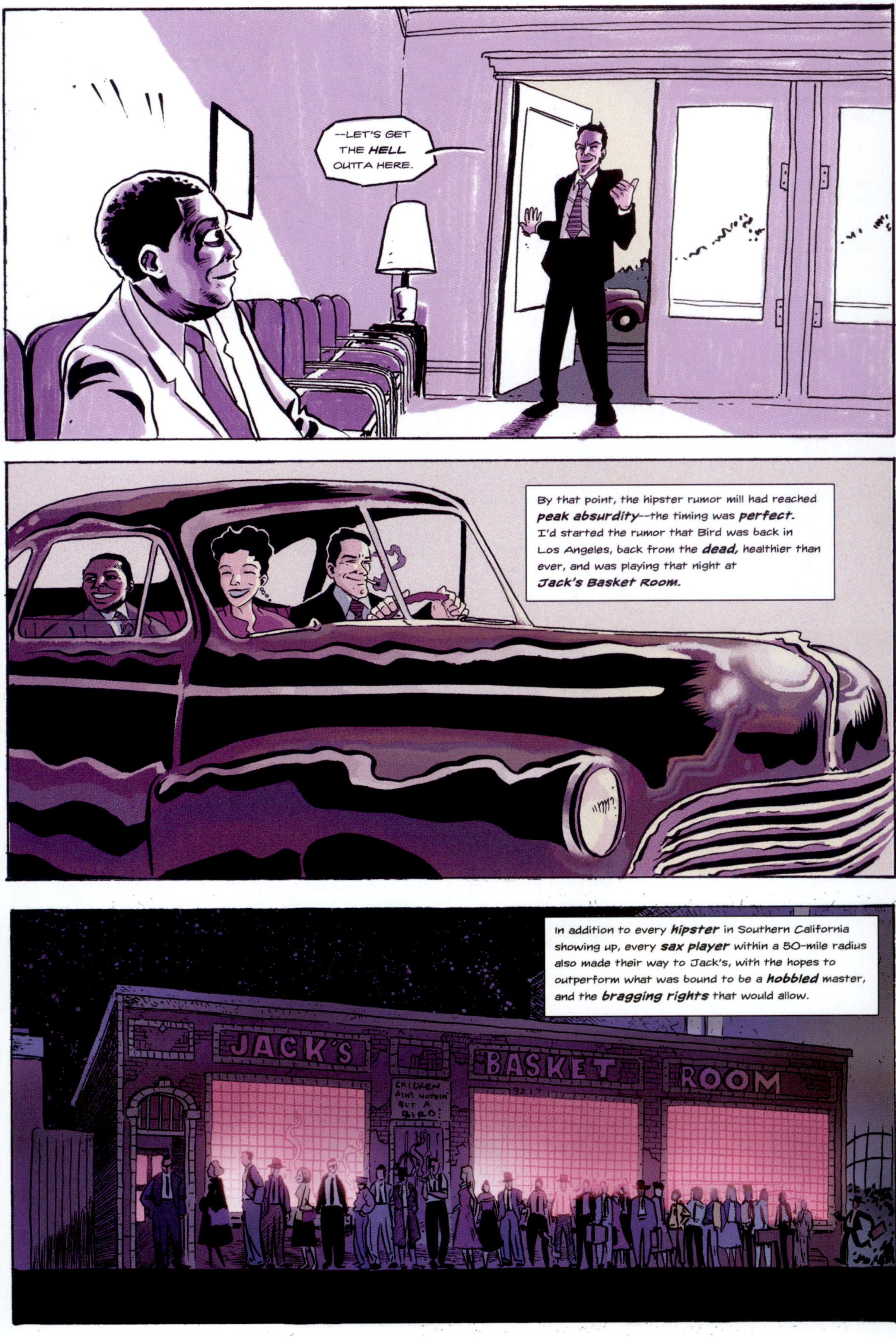
--LET'S GET THE **HELL** OUTTA HERE.
By that point, the hipster rumor mill had reached ***peak absurdity***--the timing was ***perfect.*** I'd started the rumor that Bird was back in Los Angeles, back from the ***dead,*** healthier than ever, and was playing that night at ***Jack's Basket Room.***
In addition to every ***hipster*** in Southern California showing up, every ***sax player*** within a 50-mile radius also made their way to Jack's, with the hopes to outperform what was bound to be a ***hobbled*** master, and the ***bragging rights*** that would allow.
JACK'S BASKET ROOM
CHICKEN AIN'T NUTHIN' BUT A BIRD!

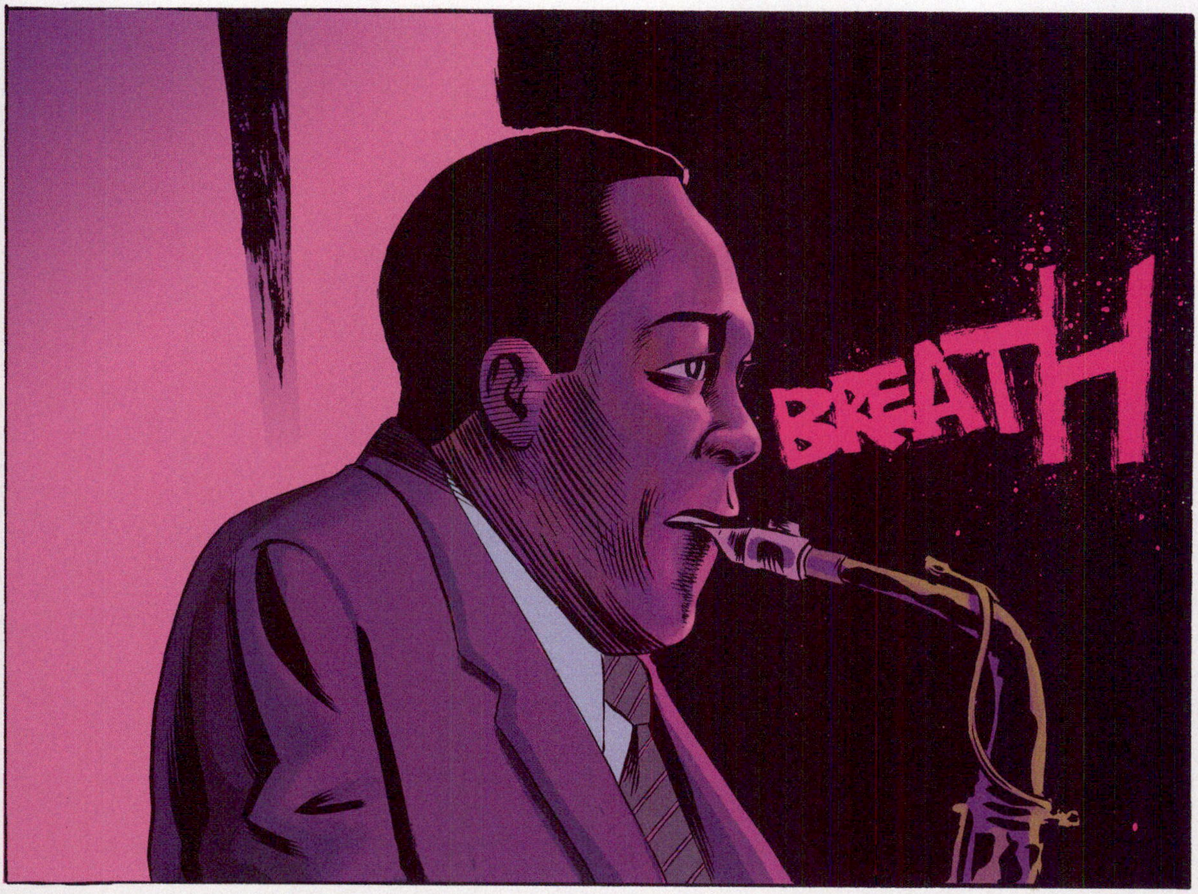
BREATH

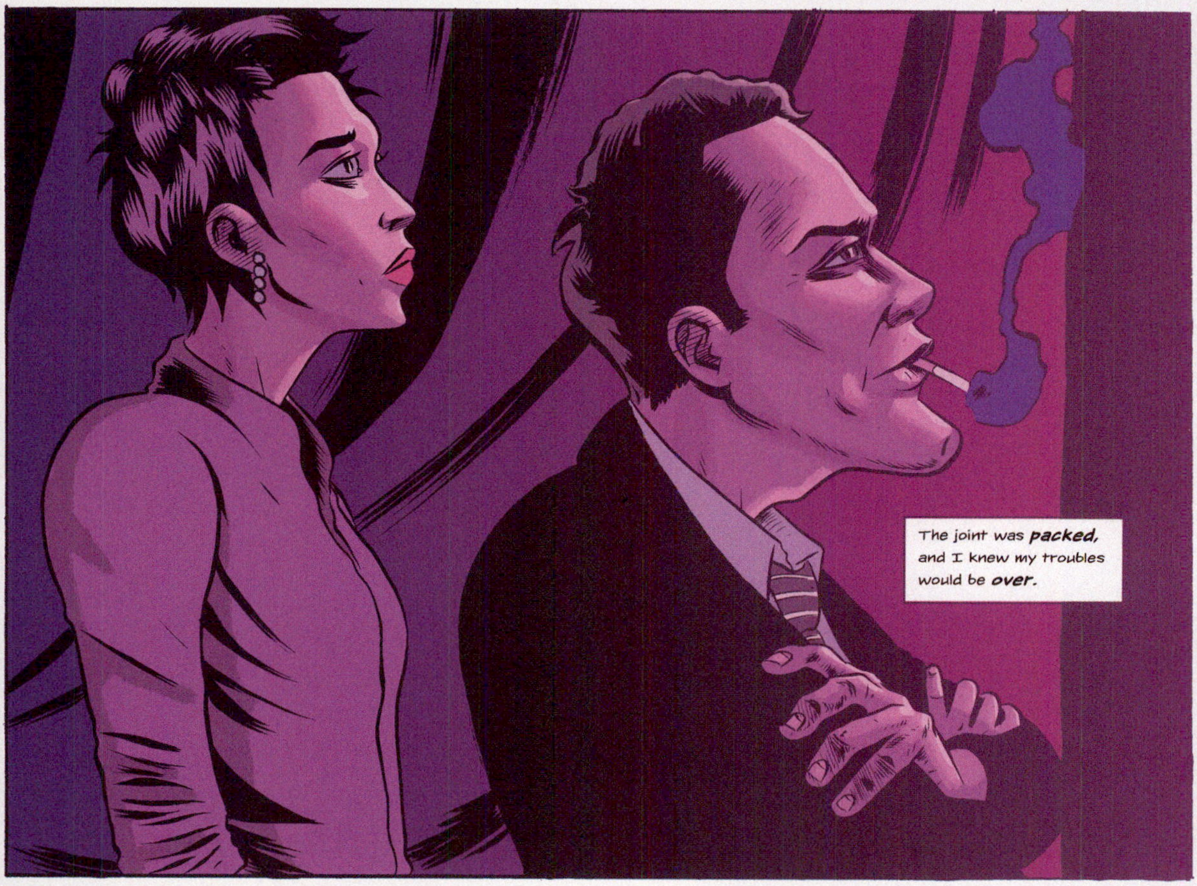
The joint was packed, and I knew my troubles would be over.

OUTRO:

F
F7
C7
D-7
G7

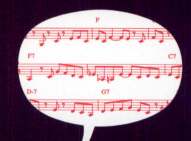

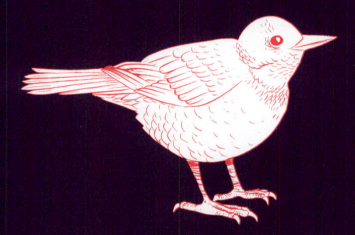

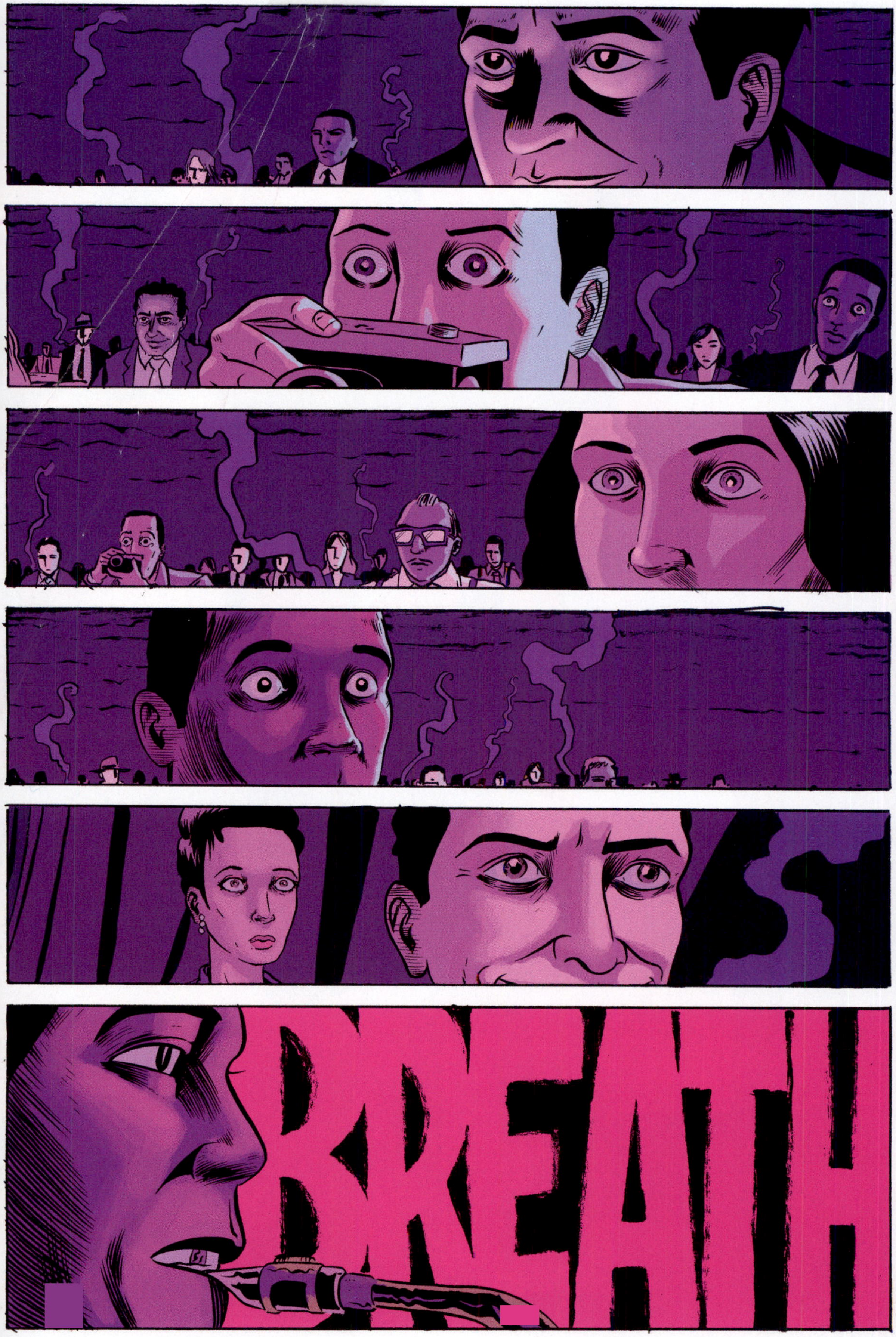
BREATH

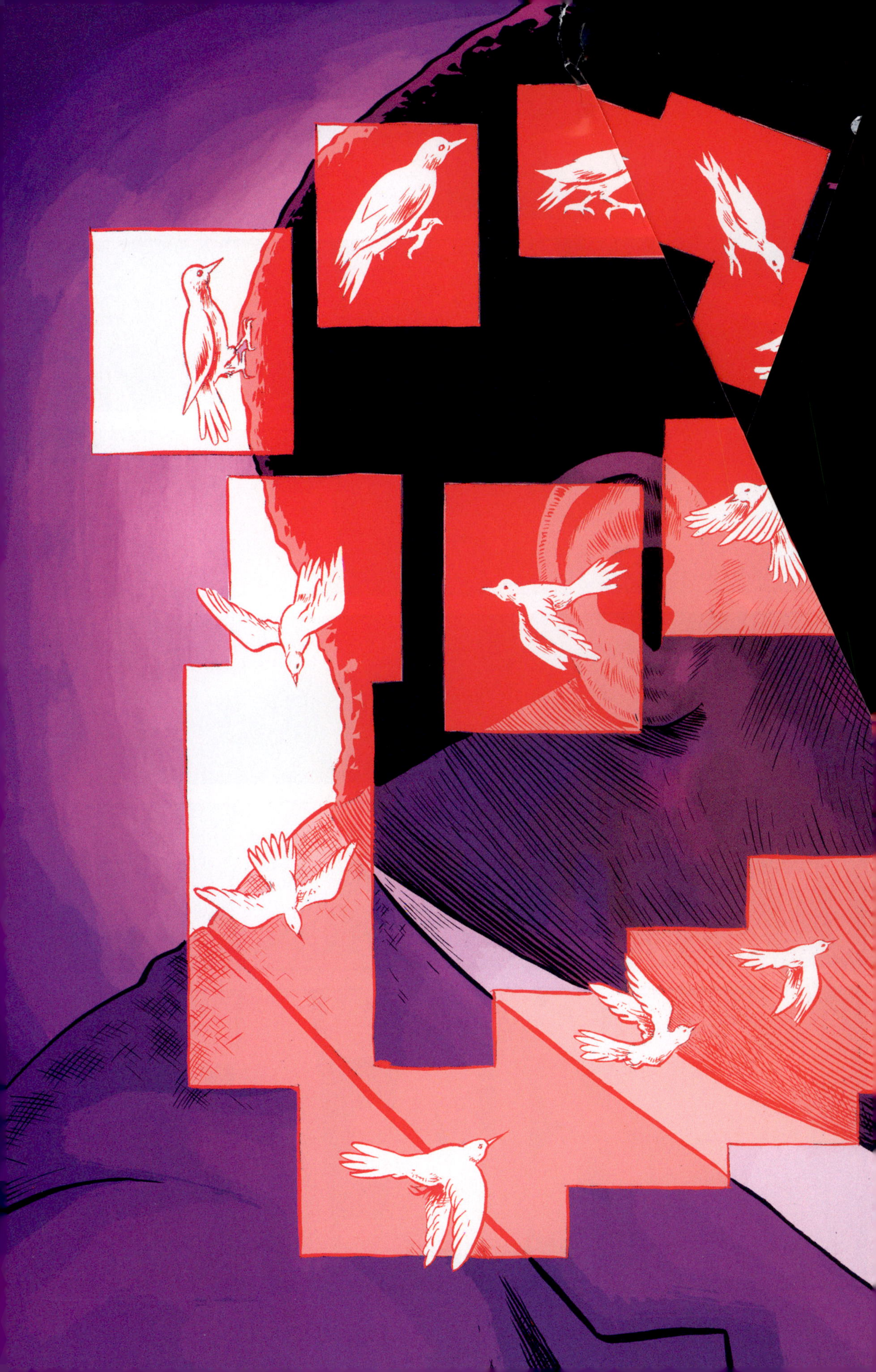

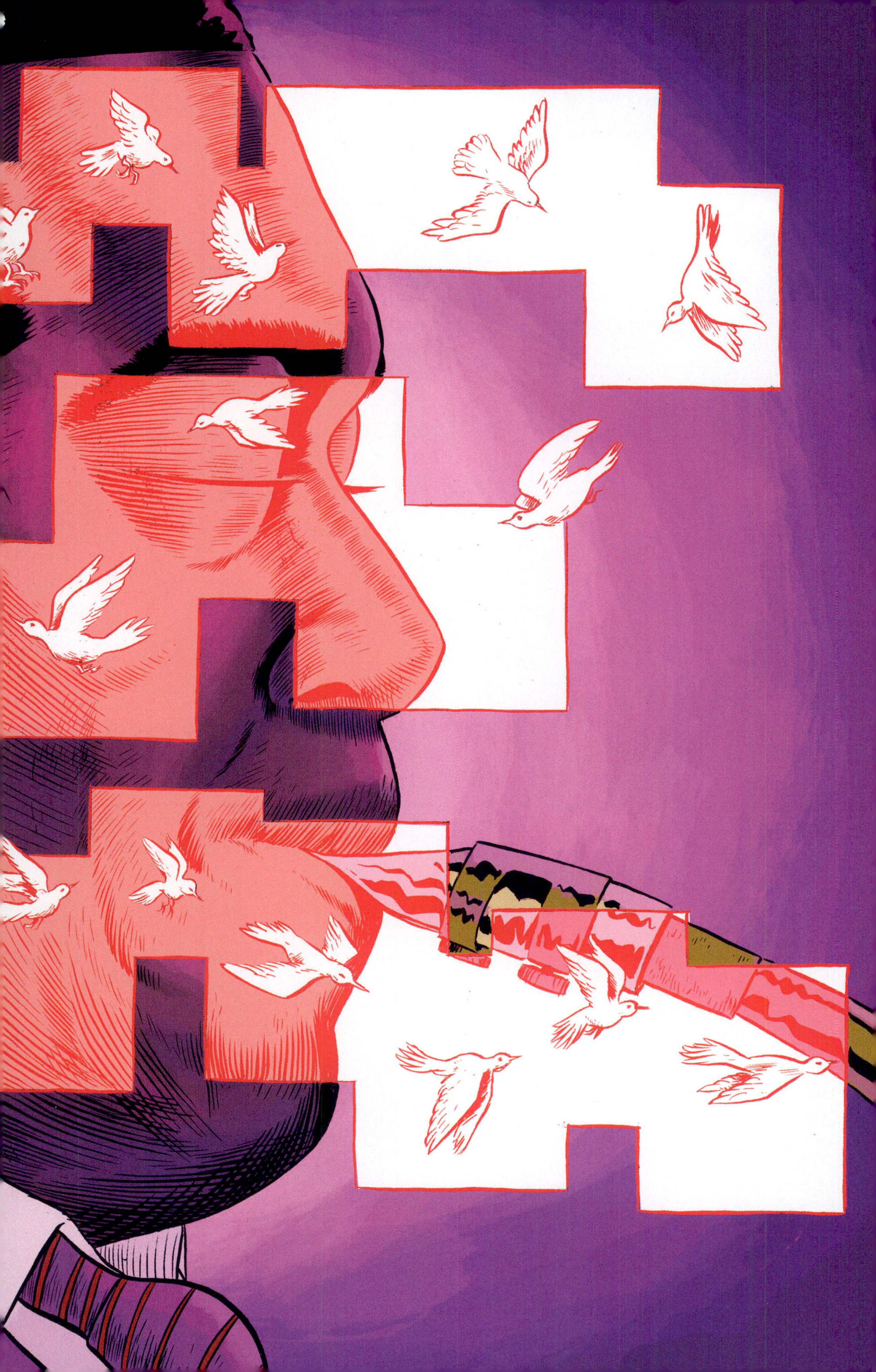

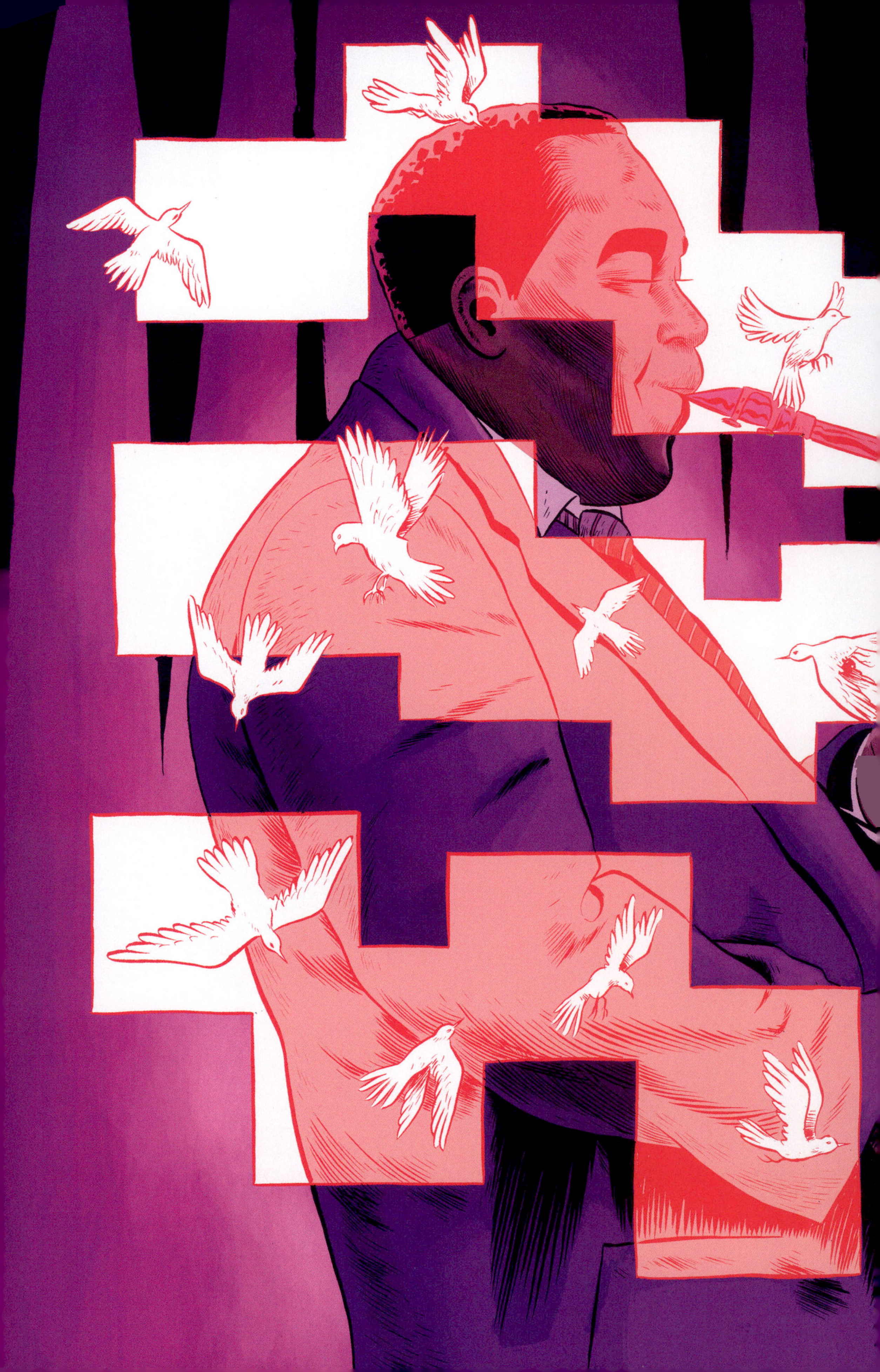

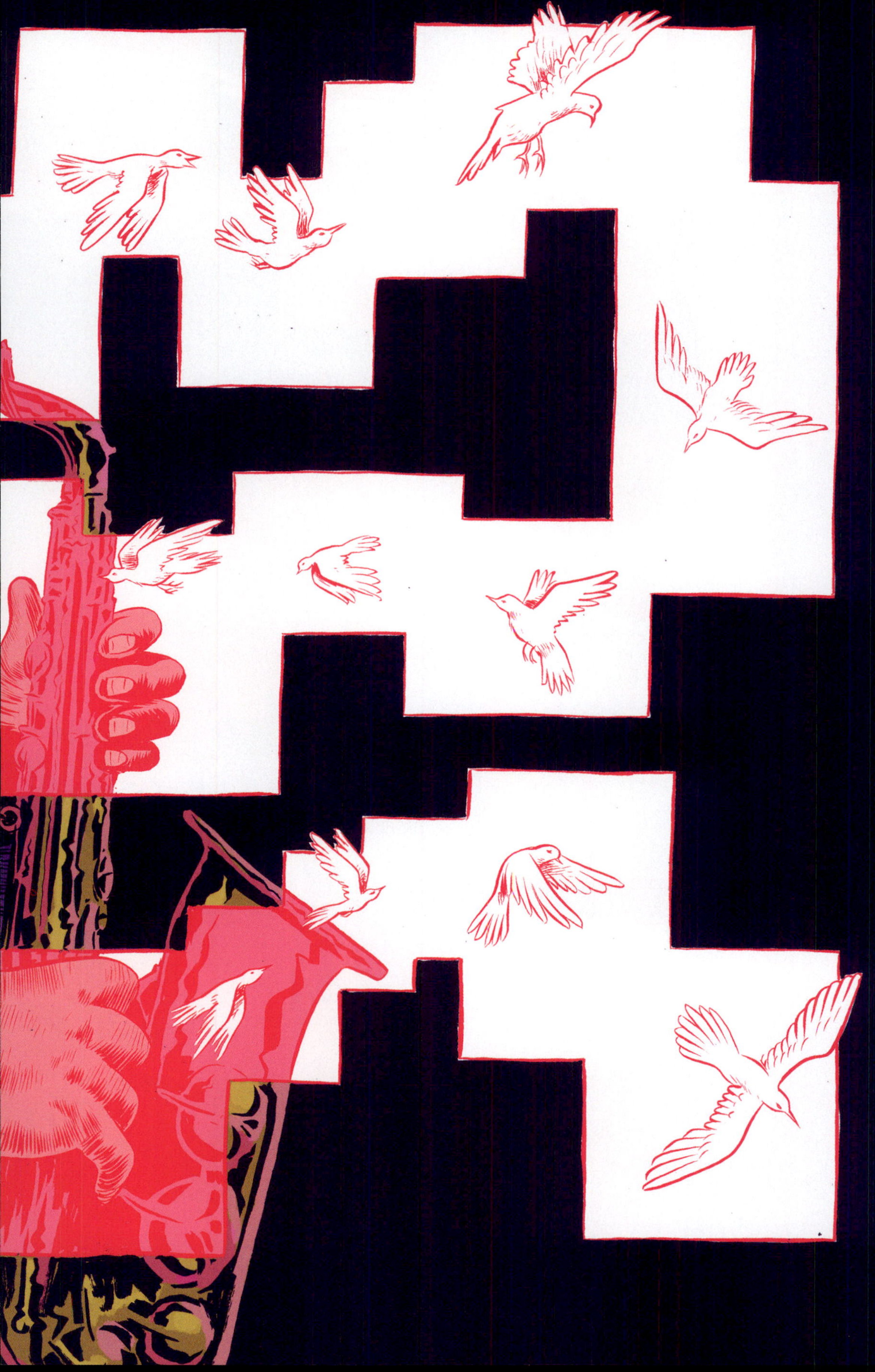

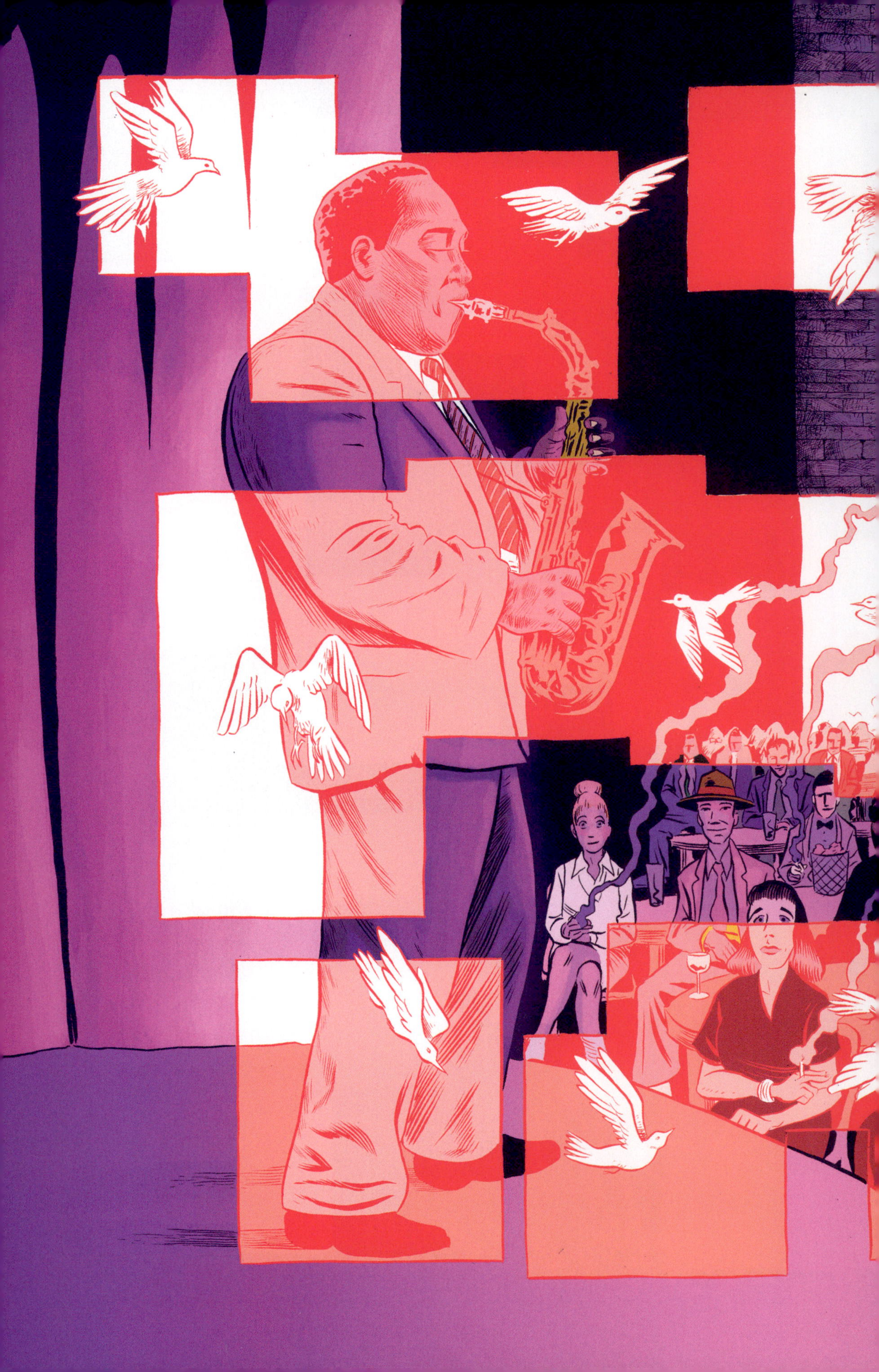

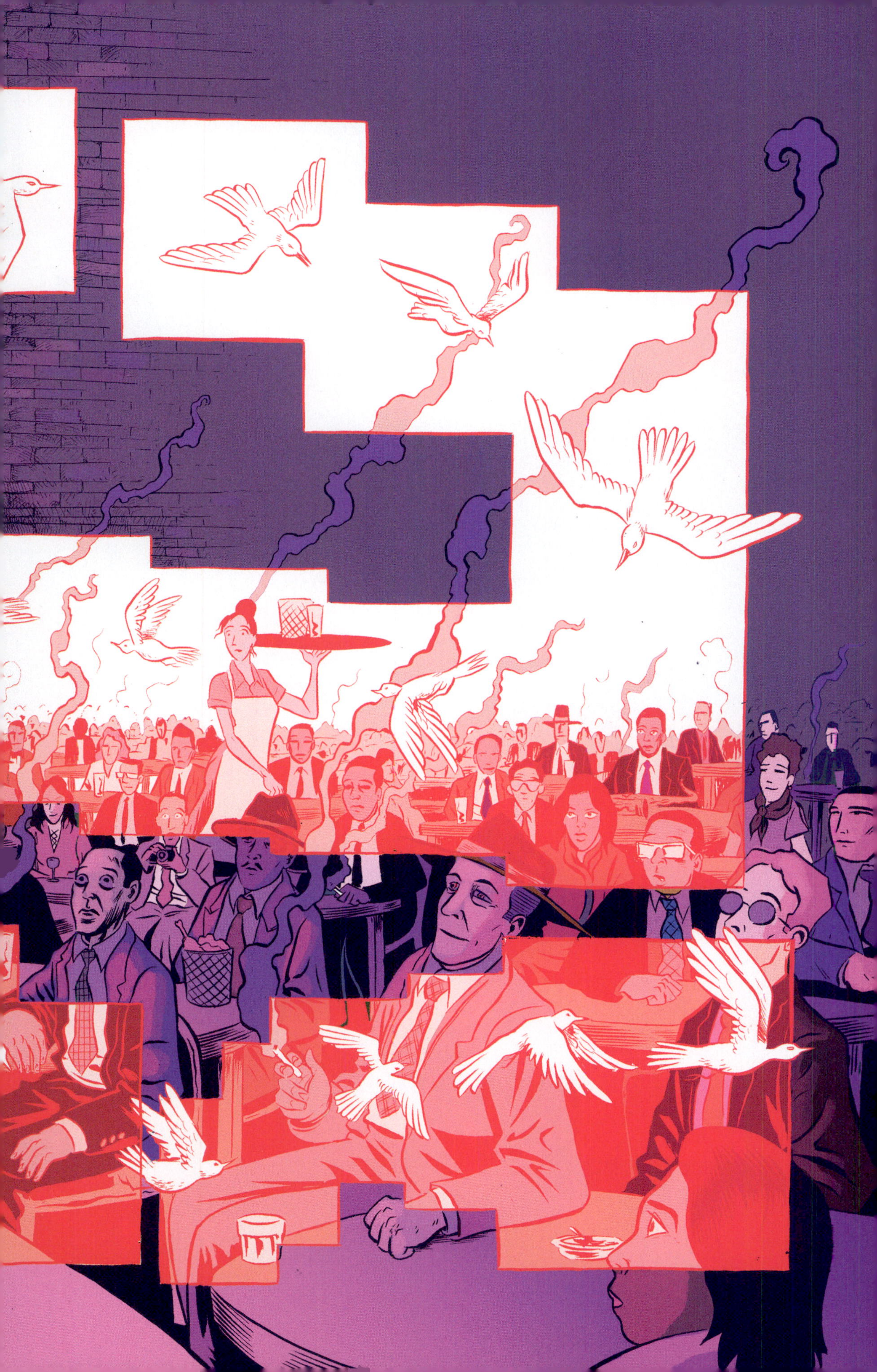

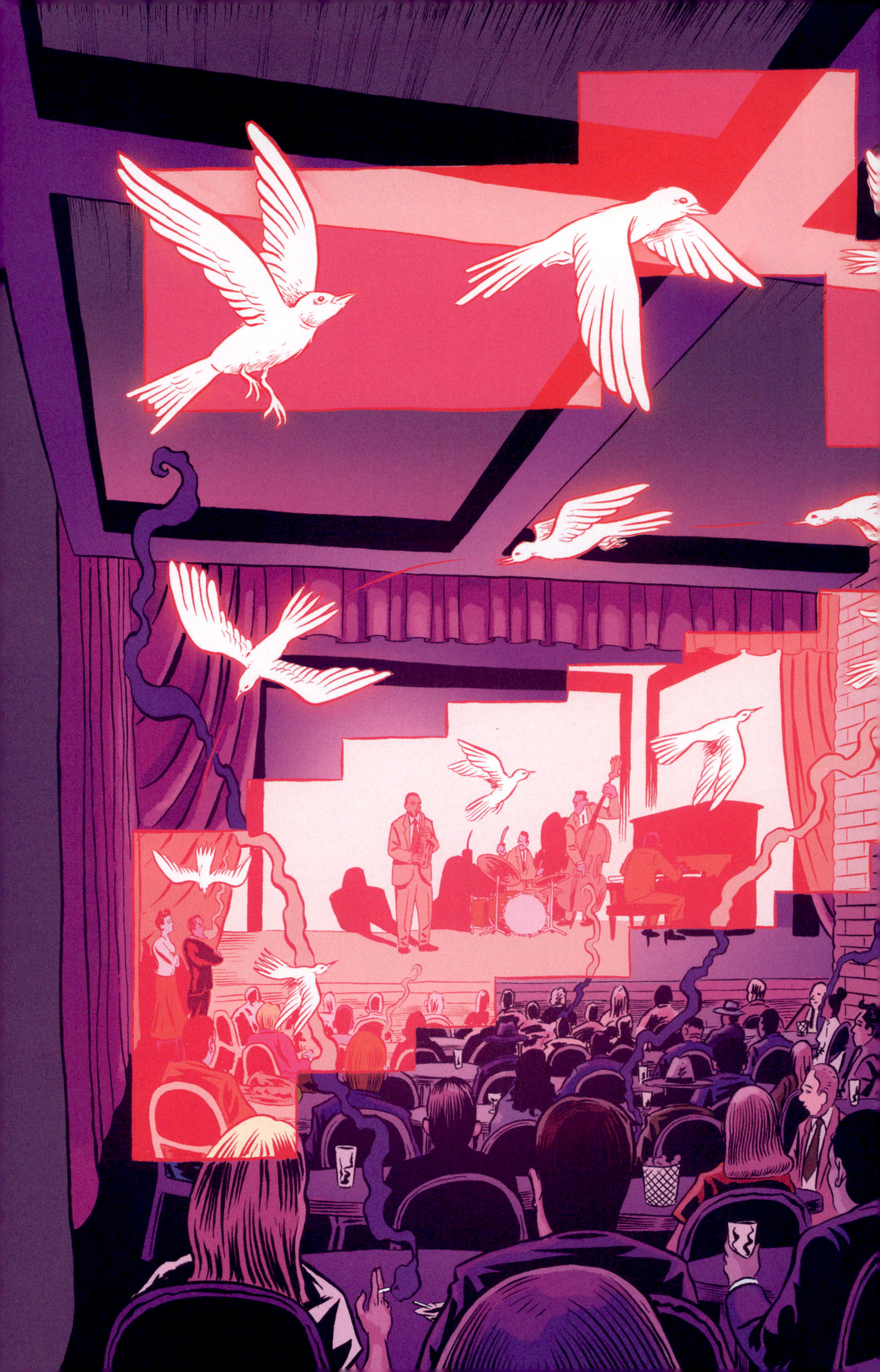

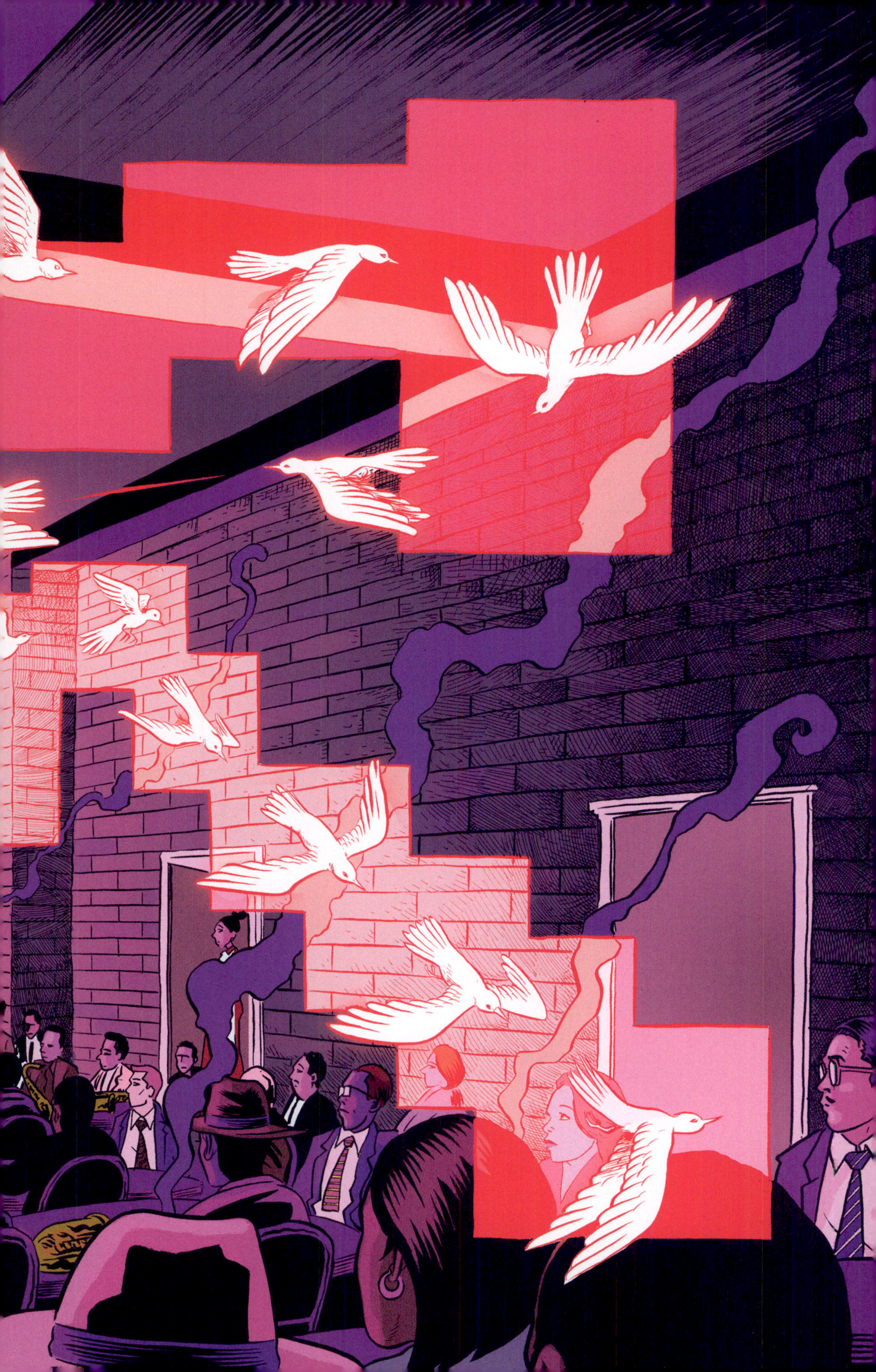

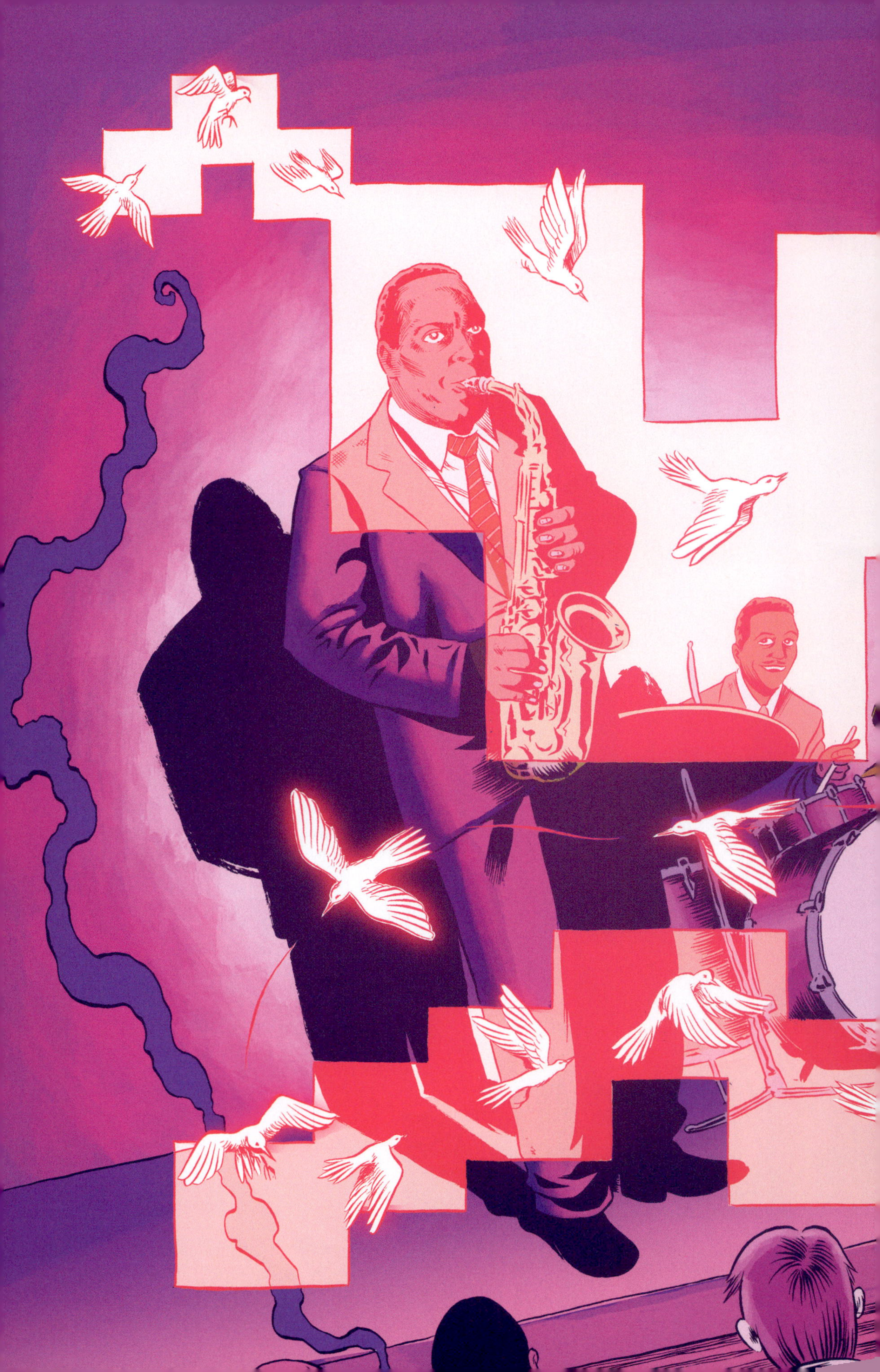

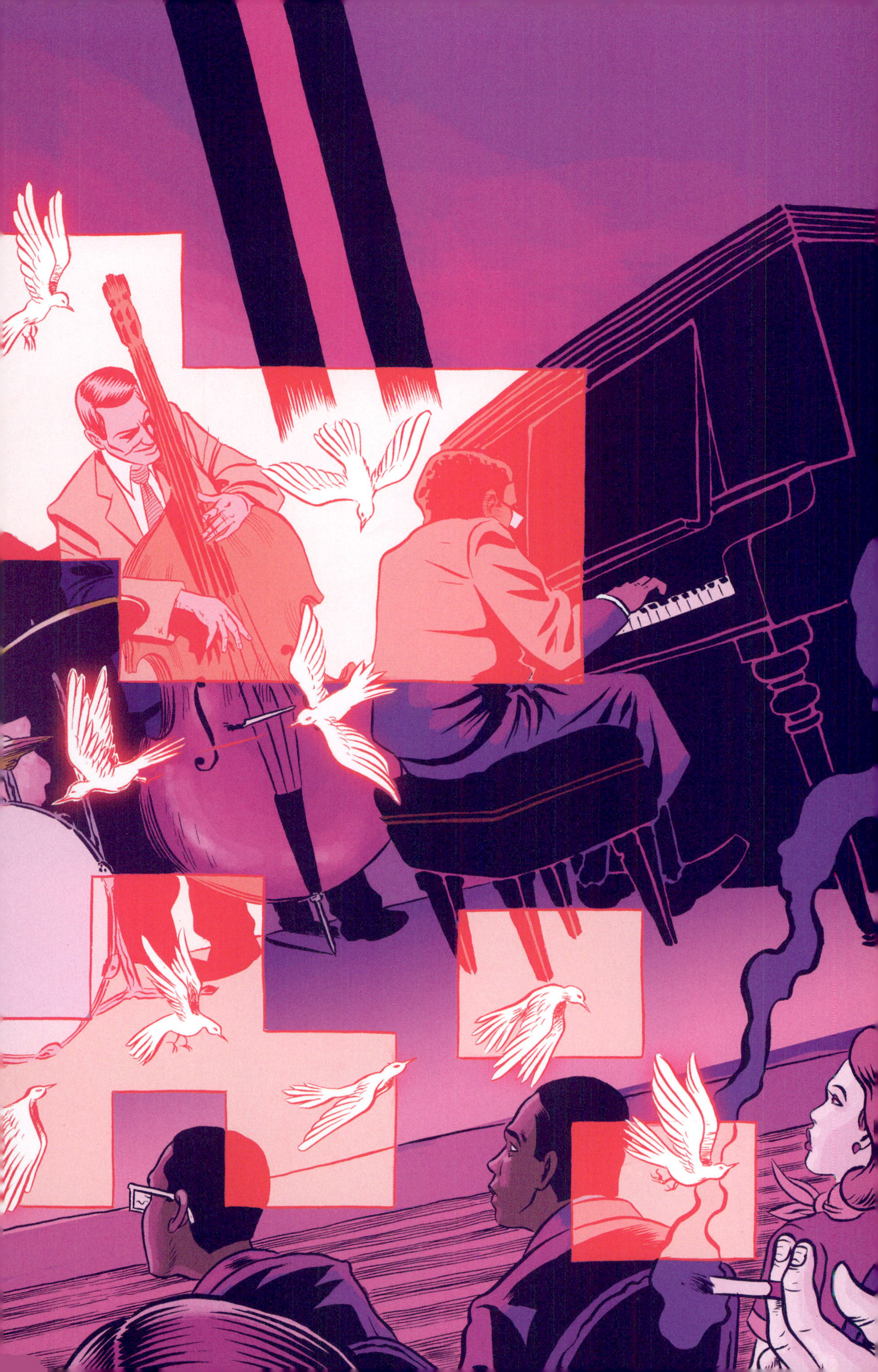

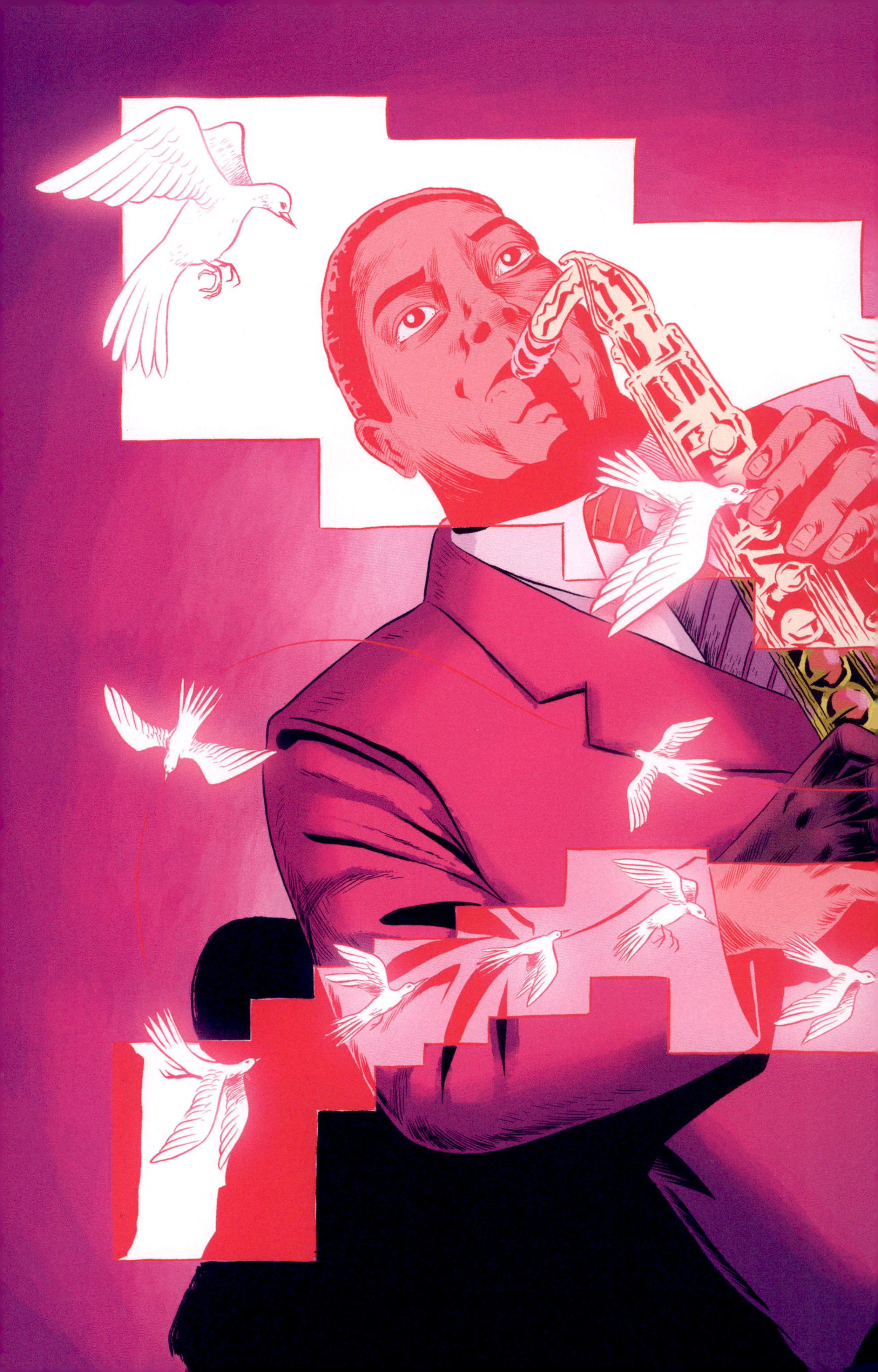

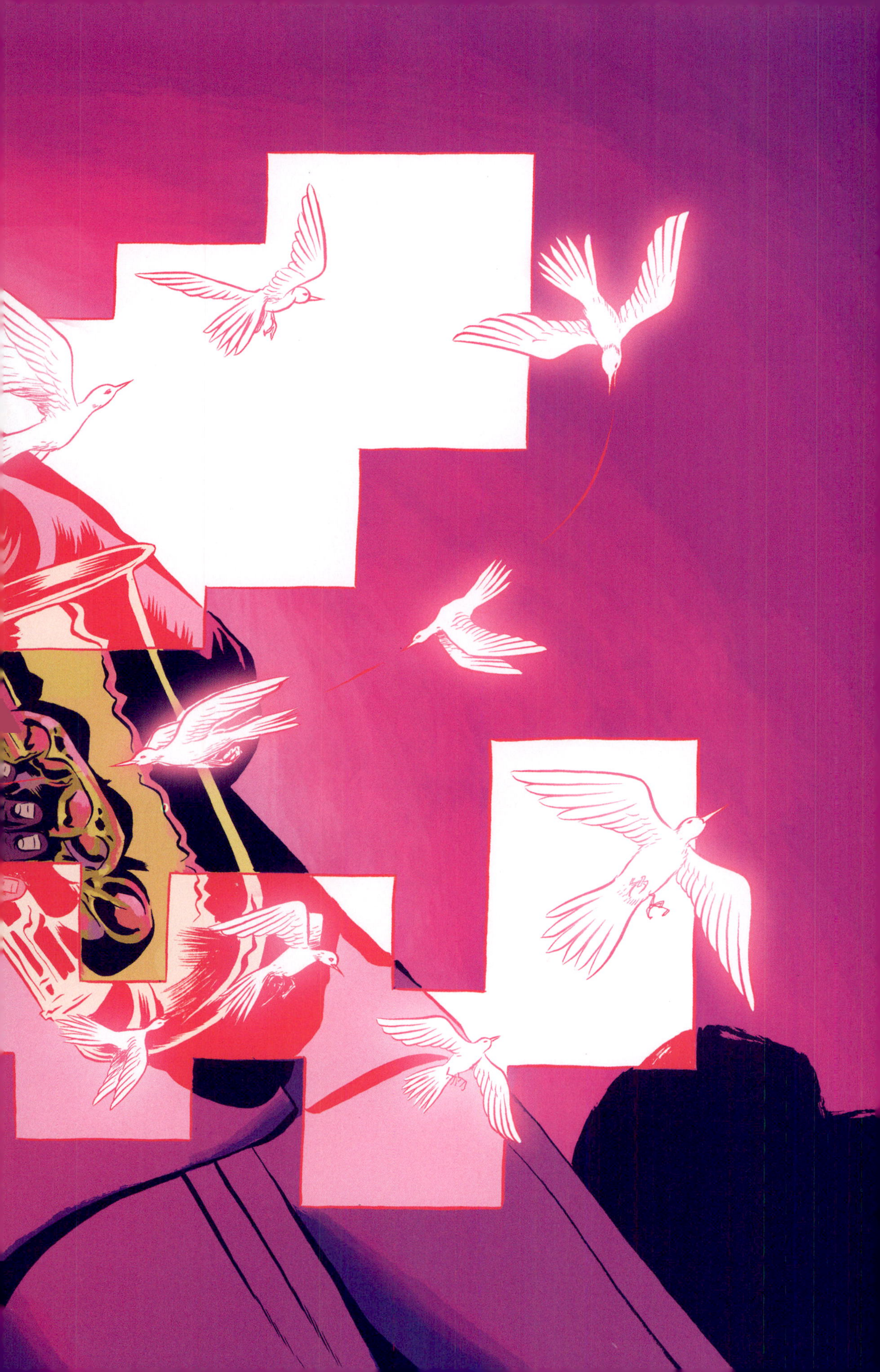

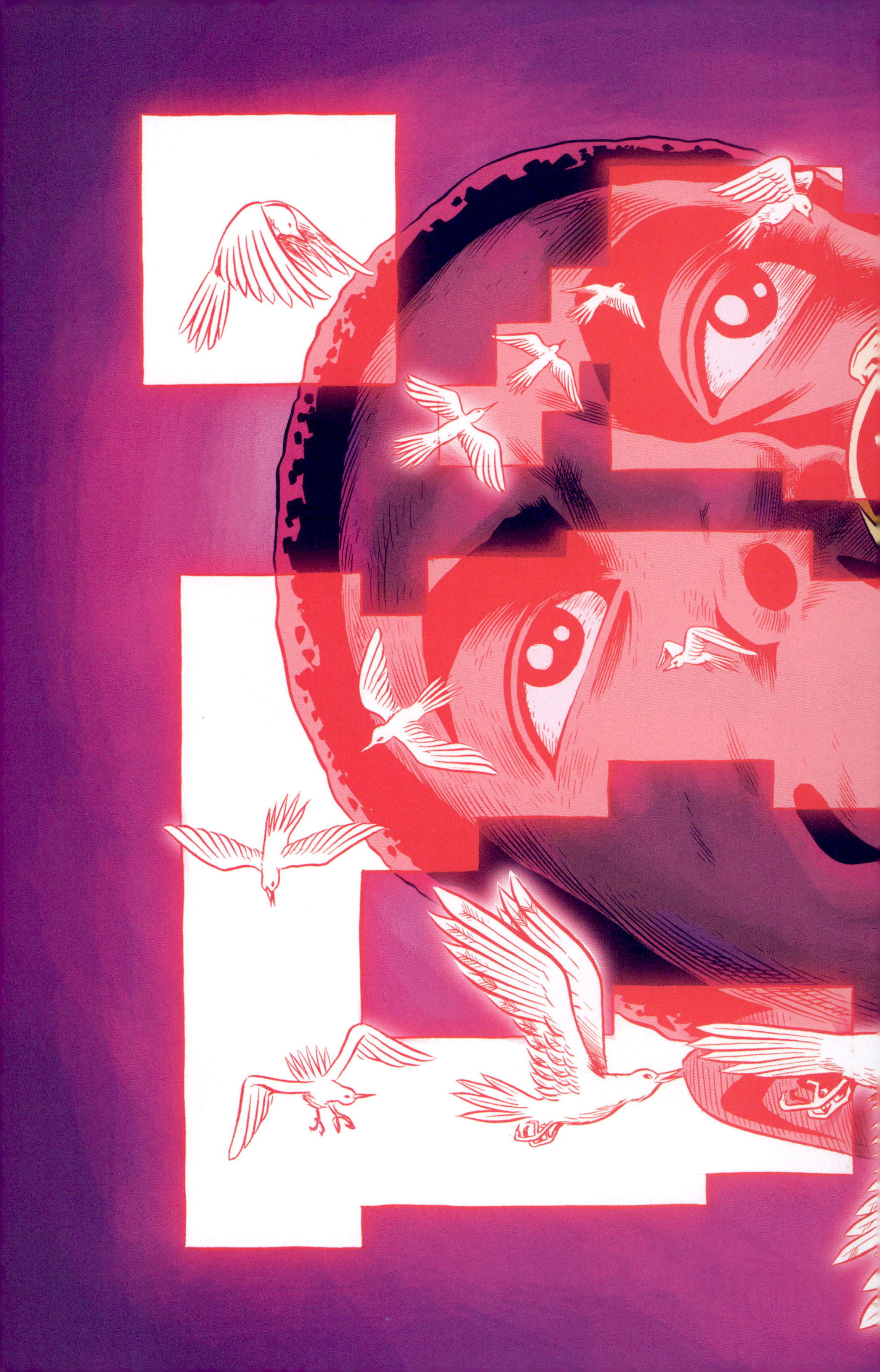

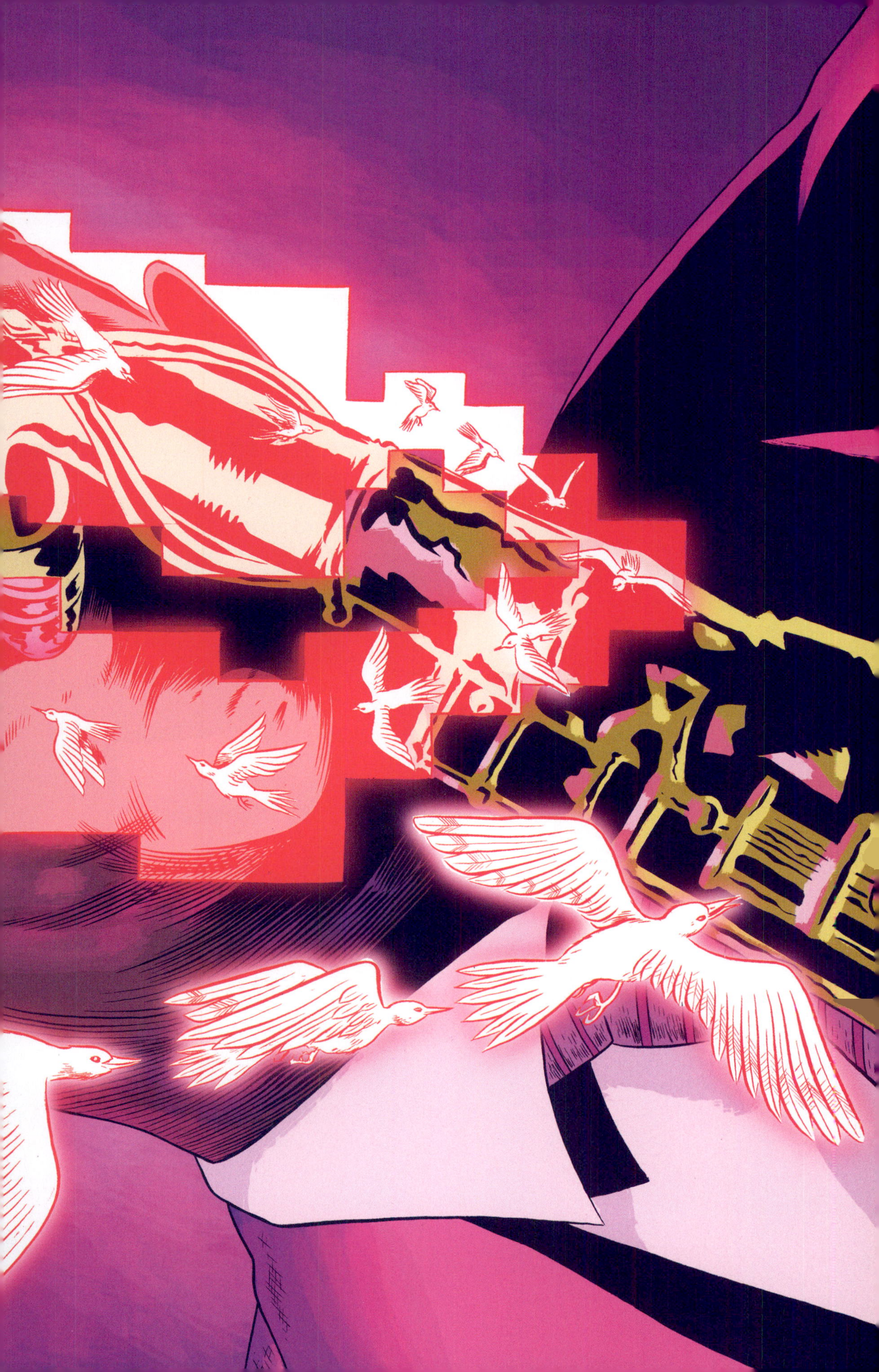

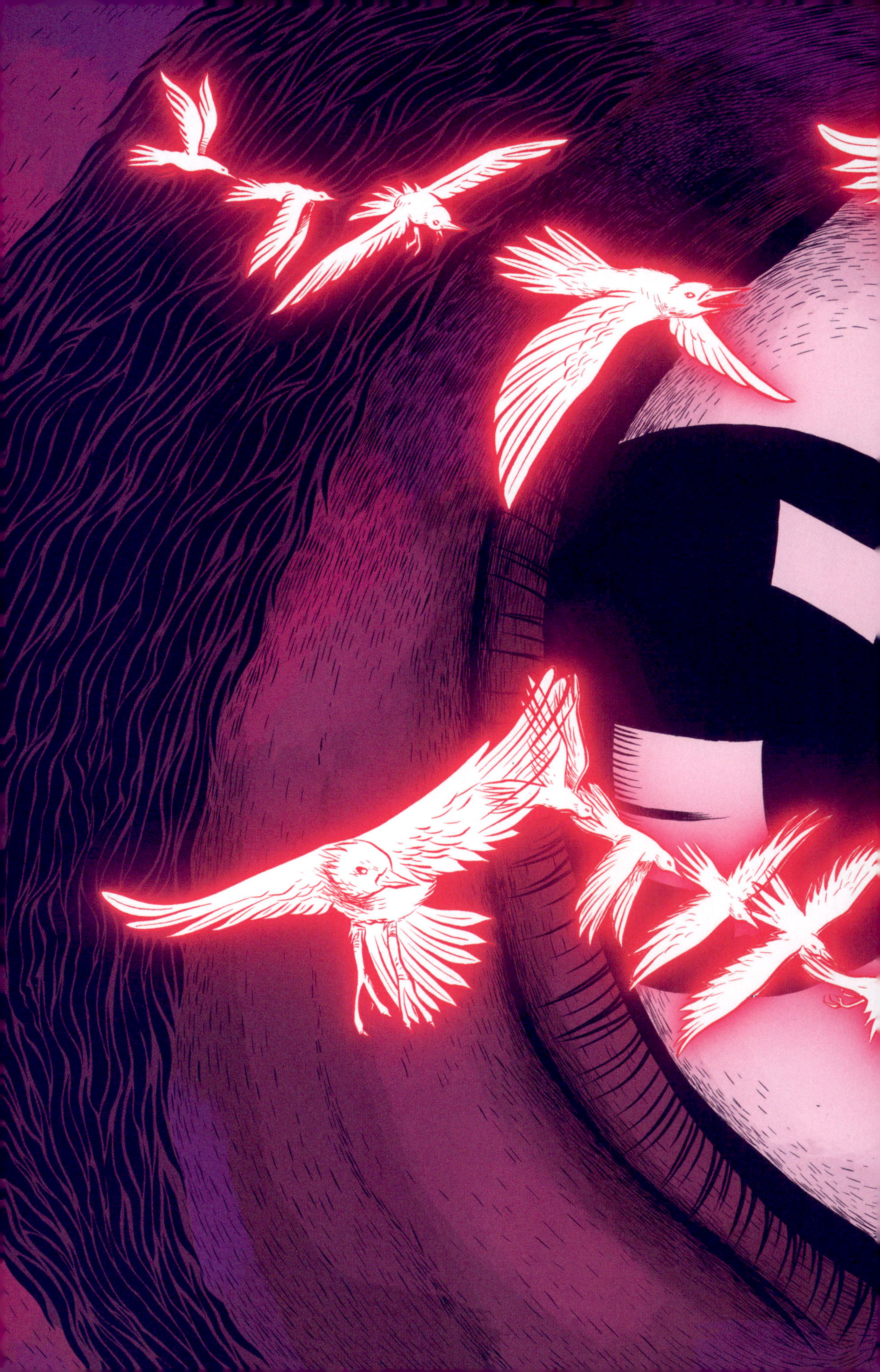

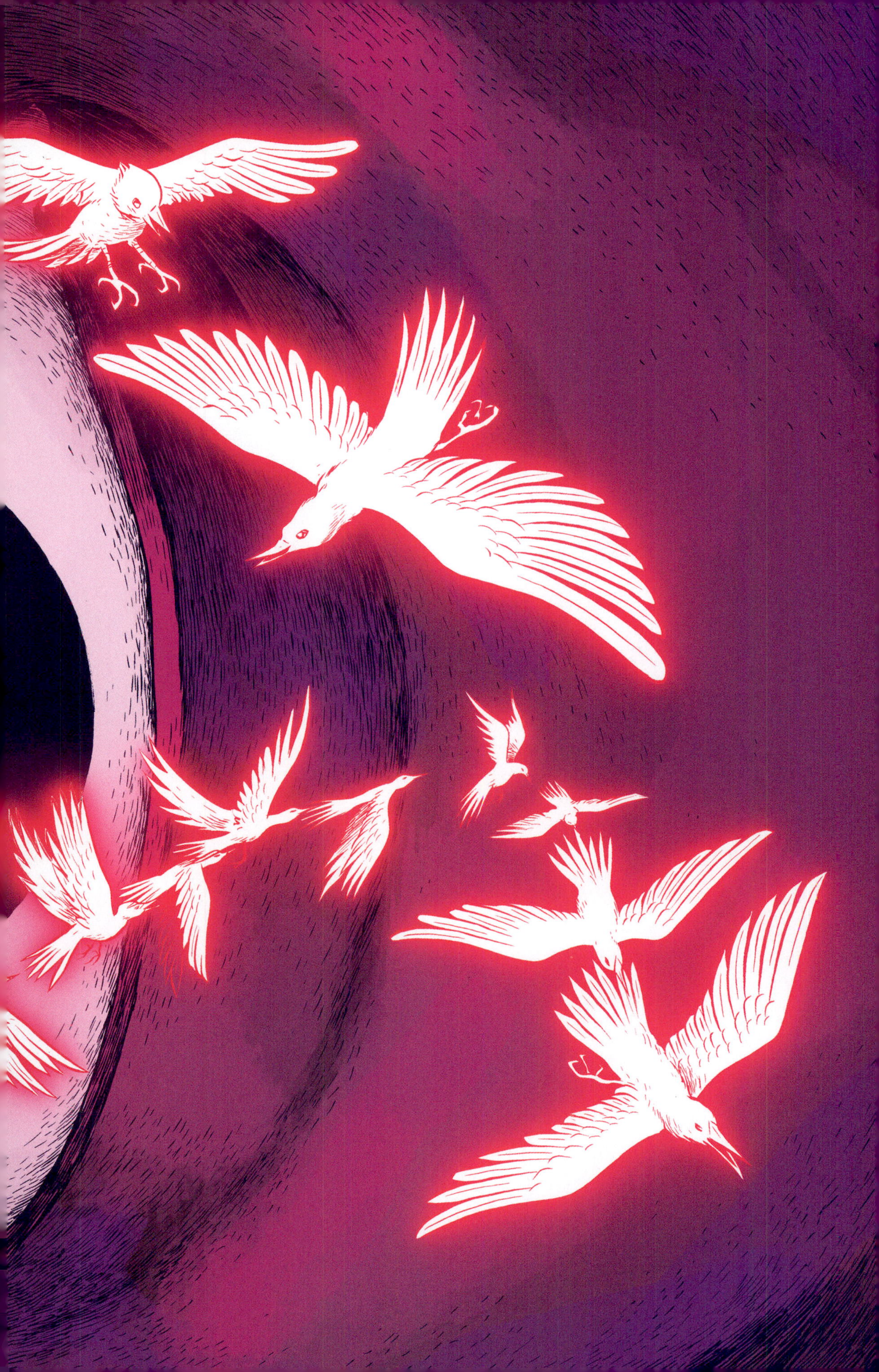

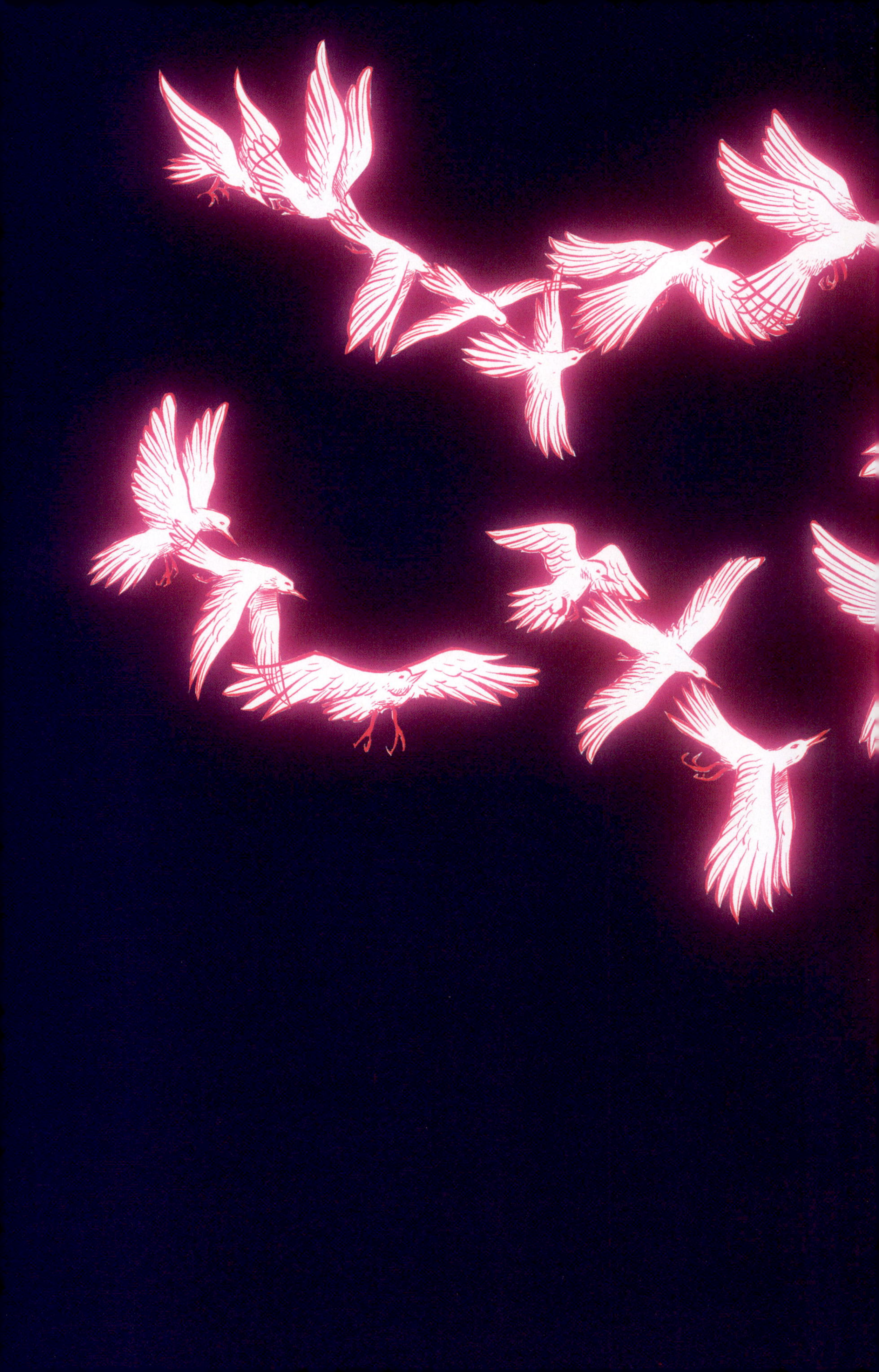

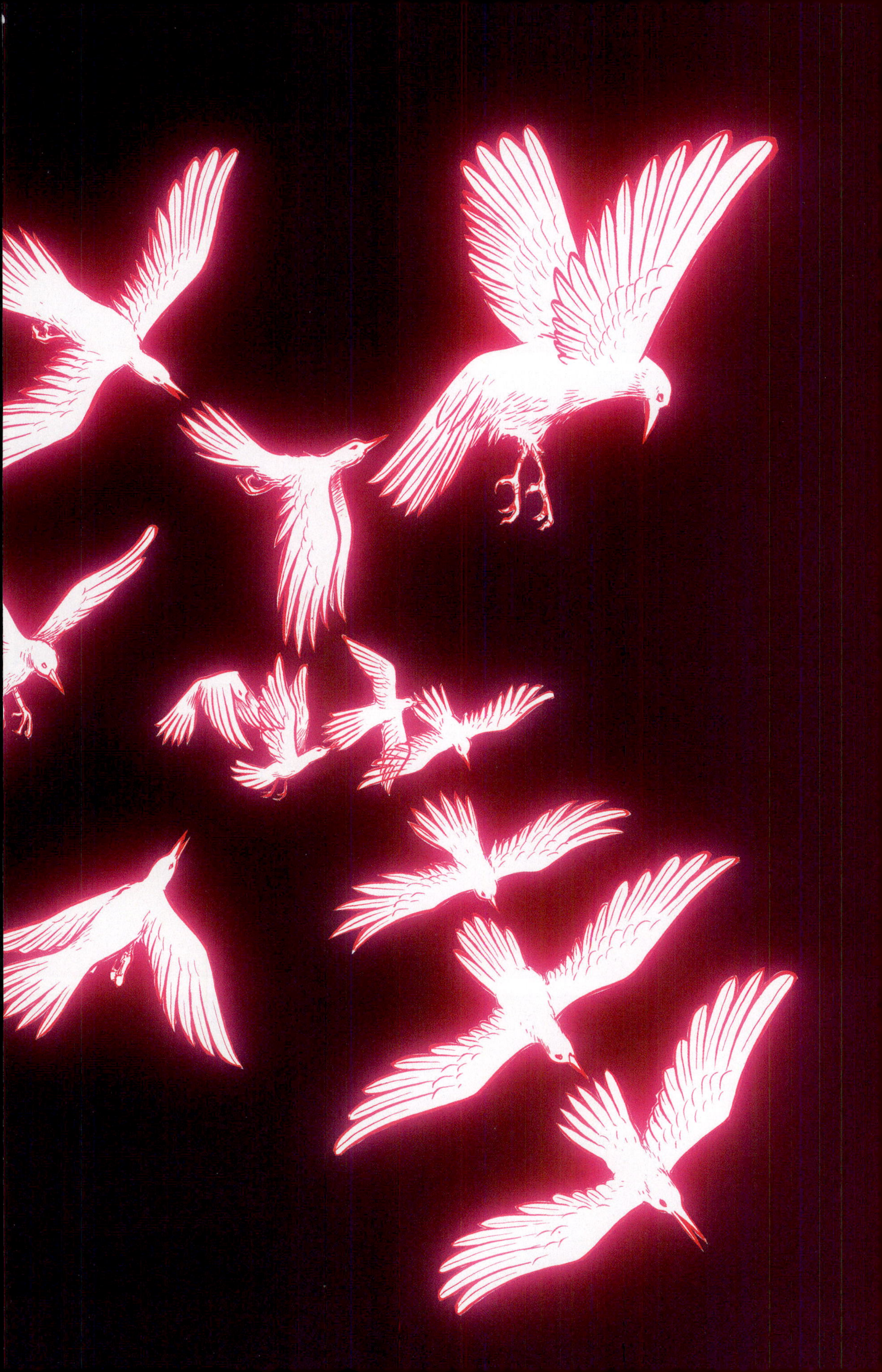

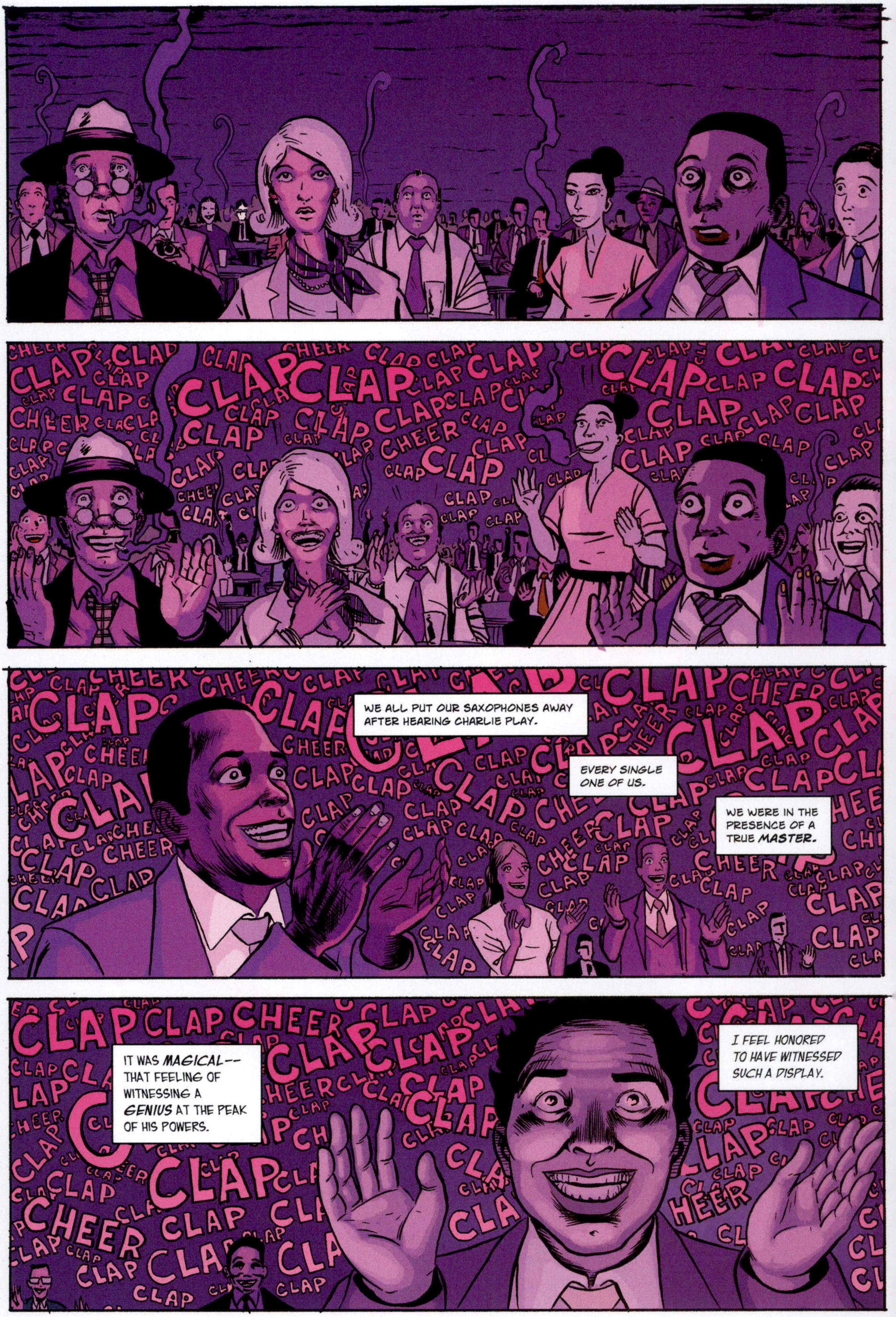
WE ALL PUT OUR SAXOPHONES AWAY AFTER HEARING CHARLIE PLAY.
EVERY SINGLE ONE OF US.
WE WERE IN THE PRESENCE OF A TRUE *MASTER.*
IT WAS *MAGICAL*-- THAT FEELING OF WITNESSING A *GENIUS* AT THE PEAK OF HIS POWERS.
I FEEL HONORED TO HAVE WITNESSED SUCH A DISPLAY.

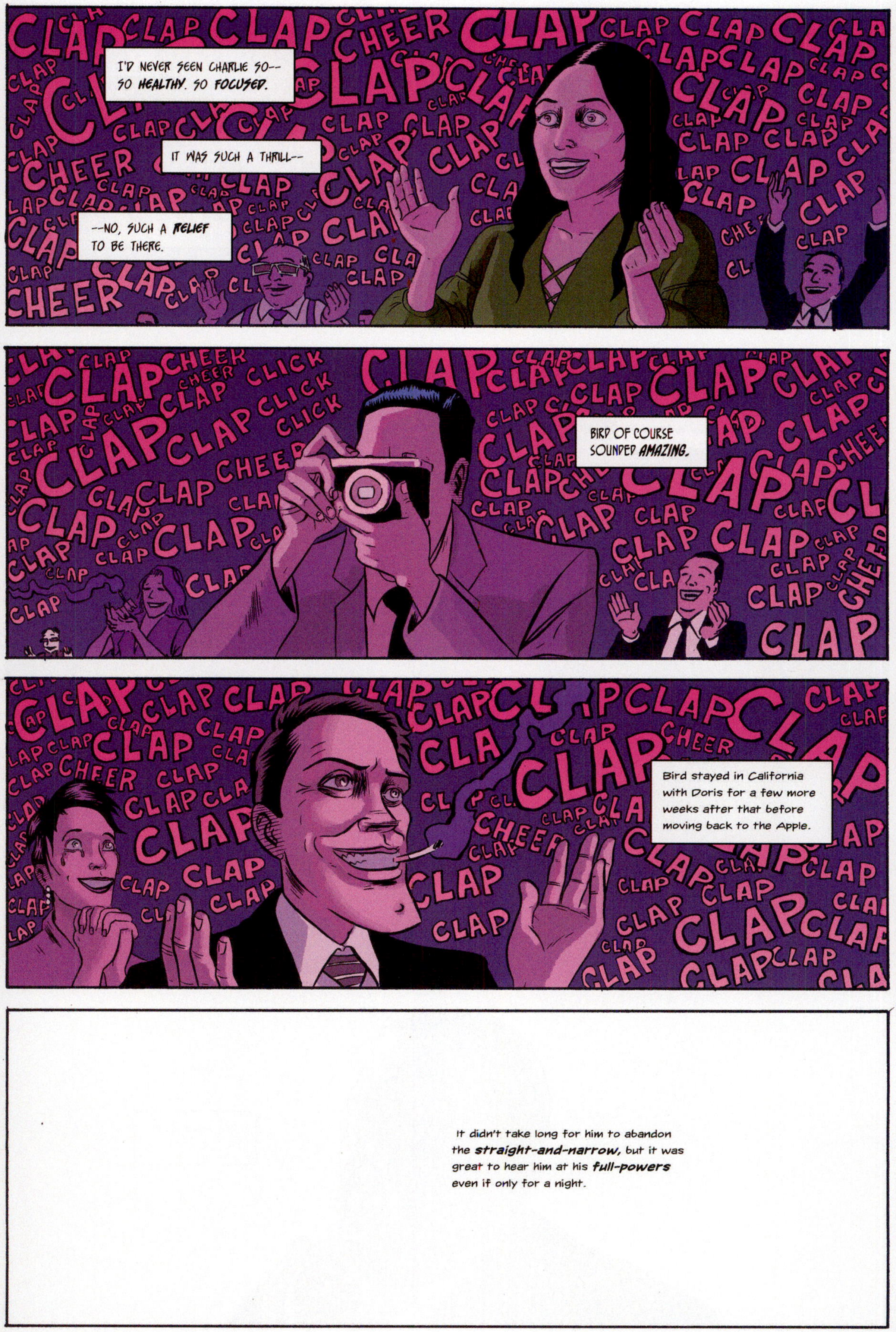
I'D NEVER SEEN CHARLIE SO--
SO HEALTHY. SO FOCUSED.
IT WAS SUCH A THRILL--
--NO, SUCH A RELIEF TO BE THERE.
CLAP
CHEER
BIRD OF COURSE SOUNDED AMAZING.
CLICK
Bird stayed in California with Doris for a few more weeks after that before moving back to the Apple.
It didn't take long for him to abandon the straight-and-narrow, but it was great to hear him at his full-powers even if only for a night.

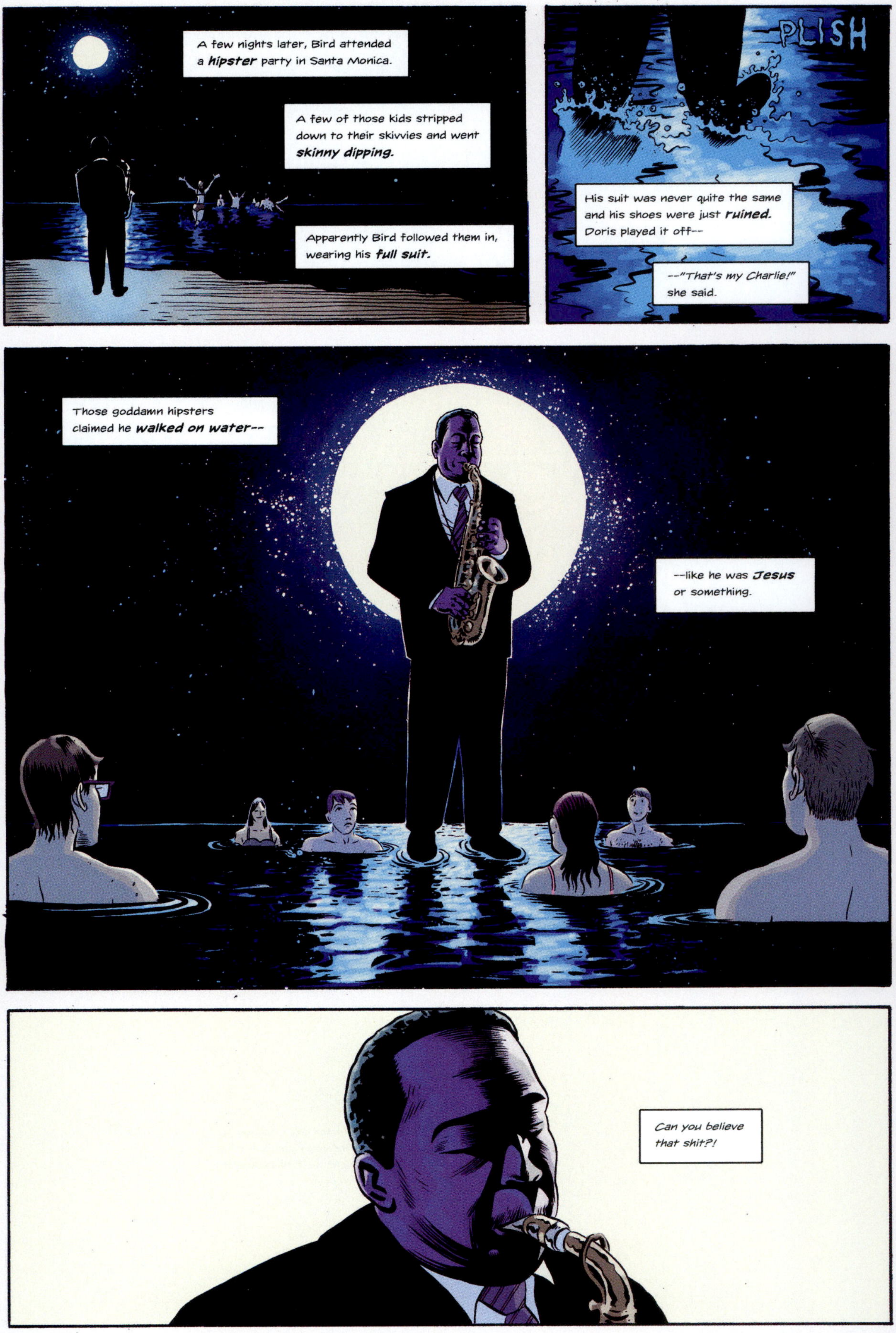
A few nights later, Bird attended a hipster party in Santa Monica.
A few of those kids stripped down to their skivvies and went skinny dipping.
Apparently Bird followed them in, wearing his full suit.
PLISH
His suit was never quite the same and his shoes were just ruined. Doris played it off--
--"That's my Charlie!" she said.
Those goddamn hipsters claimed he walked on water--
--like he was Jesus or something.
Can you believe that shit?!

The End

Afterword/Acknowledgements
by Dave Chisholm

When Josh Frankel and Sridhar Reddy at Z2 Comics approached me with the possibility of creating a graphic novel about Charlie Parker, my brain caught fire. I wanted to make a multifaceted book about Parker, however I didn't want to make a dry documentary-style book--I wanted it to be as much about the legend of Bird as it was about Parker himself. Thankfully, everyone involved agreed on that account! There are so many unbelievable stories about Parker out there--as in, stories that are literally *impossible* to believe. I wanted this book to fold these mythic aspects of the Charlie Parker story into key events from his time in California in a way that took full advantage of the unique storytelling powers of the comics medium. And, frankly, it seems like a story about Parker that doesn't address the legend would be untrue to the spirit of the man.

As tends to happen in the fact-meets-fiction world of biographies/historical fictions involving legendary figures like Charlie Parker, some characters were eliminated or folded into each other, some events are chronologically shifted around, and some events that were not historically well-documented are imaginatively expanded upon--all in the name of speaking to the spirit of Parker the man and Bird the legend as well as crafting a satisfying and pointed narrative arc. If you want to examine the events of this book from another angle, the meticulously detailed liner notes written by John Burton accompanying the *Bird in LA* album released in coordination with this book make for compelling reading.

Big thanks to Josh and Sridhar as well as the Charlie Parker estate management team for not just giving me this opportunity but encouraging me to take some real artistic risks--all in the spirit of Parker.

Thanks to my oldest friend and brilliant artist Peter Markowski for adding the perfect colors to much of this book.

Thanks to Dustyn Payette for your reliable and quality flatting work. This is the most thankless job in comics and you always do a great job.

Thanks to Colin Gordon for the clutch help during the research process as well as for the impeccable transcriptions of Parker's improvised solos that show up in the story.

Thanks to readers Avis Reese, Isaiah Smith, and Kris Johnson for generously providing your insight, wisdom, and empathy.

Thanks to Dusten, Milton, and Rick for your kindness and support through the creation of this book-- your encouragement gave me such a consistent tailwind and helped keep my eyes on the prize and my standards high.

Thanks to my parents Anne and Dan for always spinning the hippest jazz records, encouraging your kids to follow their dreams in the arts, and providing endless patience and support in my dual careers in music and comics.

Thanks to my brother Joe for being my earliest collaborator in both music and comics.

Thanks finally to my wife Elise for the incredible support while I disappeared for the 22 or so weeks it took to make this book. There is literally no way I could have done this book without you.

References

Alexander, BK., Beyerstein, BL., Hadaway, PF., Coambs, R.B. (1981). Effect of Early and Later Colony Housing on Oral Ingestion of Morphine in Rats. Pharmacol Biochem Behav. https://doi.org/10.1016/0091-3057(81)90211-2

Balliett, W. (1976). Bird: The Brilliance of Charlie Parker. The New Yorker. Retrieved October 13, 2019 from https://www.newyorker.com/magazine/1976/03/01/bird-whitney-balliett

Claxton, W. (2005). Jazzlife: A Journey For Jazz Across America in 1960. Cologne, Germany: Taschen Press.

Collette, B. (2000). Jazz Generations. New York: Continuum International Publishing Group.

Duersten, M. (2013). These 3 Books Will Teach You 5 Things You Didn't Know About Charlie Parker. LA Mag. Retrieved September 11, 2019, from https://www.lamag.com/culturefiles/these-3-books-will-teach-you-5-things-you-didnt-know-about-charlie-parker/

Duersten, M. (2014). When Charlie Parker Came to L.A.: The Peaks and Valleys of a Jazz Genius. LA Mag. Retrieved September 11, 2019, from https://www.lamag.com/culturefiles/when-charlie-parker-came-to-la-the-peaks-and-valleys-of-a-jazz-genius/

Giddins, G. (1987, 2013). Celebrating Bird: the Triumph of Charlie Parker. Minneapolis, MN: University of Minnesota Press.

Heckman, D. (1995). JAZZ : Still Chasin' the Bird : Charlie Parker would have turned 75 Tuesday. Sadly, he didn't even make it to 35, but he so influenced the vocabulary of jazz that a new generation of players speaks his language while striving for his eloquence. L.A. Times. Retrieved September 11, 2019, from https://www.latimes.com/archives/la-xpm-1995-08-27-ca-39249-story.html

Hue, C. (2014). The Enduring Mysteries of the Zorthian Ranch. KCET Artbound. Retrieved September 22, 2019, from https://www.kcet.org/shows/artbound/the-enduring-mysteries-of-zorthian-ranch

Iverson, E. (2015). Interview with Wayne Shorter. Do the Math. Retrieved January 20, 2020, from https://ethaniverson.com/interview-with-wayne-shorter

Karlstrom, P. (1997). Oral History Interview with Jirayr Zorthian, 1997 January 28 – July 9. Smithsonian Archives of American Art. Retrieved September 22, 2019 from https://www.aaa.si.edu/download_pdf_transcript/ajax?record_id=edanmdm-AAADCD_oh_216033

Levin, M. (1949). NEW YORK--"Bop is no love-child of jazz," says Charlie Parker. Downbeat Magazine. Retrieved September 11, 2019 from http://jazzprofiles.blogspot.com/2019/05/charlie-parker-1949-downbeat-interview.html

References (continued)

Nolan, T. (2006). William Claxton Puts Jazz in Focus. The Wall Street Journal. Retrieved October 22, 2019 from https://www.wsj.com/articles/SB115213602471998770

Priestley, B. (2005). Chasin' the Bird: the Life and Legacy of Charlie Parker. New York: Oxford University Press.

Reisner, R. (1962). Bird: the Legend of Charlie Parker. New York: Da Capo Press.

Russell, R. (1973). Bird Lives! The High Life and Hard Times of Charlie (Yardbird) Parker. New York: Da Capo Press.

Spitzer, P. (2011). Charlie Parker's Musical Quotes. Retrieved October 22, 2019 from http://peterspitzer.blogspot.com/2011/12/charlie-parkers-musical-quotes.html

Timberg, S. (2014). William Claxton: Eye on Cool. Retrieved October 22, 2019 from http://jazzprofiles.blogspot.com/2014/11/william-claxton-eye-on-cool.html

Vail, K. (1996). Bird's Diary: the Life of Charlie Parker 1945-1955. Chessington, Surrey, UK: Castle Communications plc.

Walker, C. (2014). Everybody Got Naked With Charlie "Bird" Parker at the Wildest Party in L.A. History. LA Weekly. Retrieved September 22, 2019 from https://www.laweekly.com/everybody-got-naked-with-charlie-bird-parker-at-the-wildest-party-in-l-a-history/

White, G. (2001). William Claxton: A Photographic Memory. Retrieved October 13, 2019 from http://digitaljournalist.org/issue0103/claxton_intro.htm

Williams, R. (2010). Charlie Parker: A Genius Distilled. The Guardian. Retrieved September 11, 2019, from https://www.theguardian.com/music/2010/mar/21/charlie-parker-julie-macdonald-sculpture

Schickel, E. (2014). At Zorthian Ranch, a Return to Bohemia. LA Weekly. Retrieved September 22, 2019 from https://www.laweekly.com/at-zorthian-ranch-a-return-to-bohemia/

Woideck, C. (1998). The Charlie Parker Companion: Six Decades of Commentary. New York: Schirmer Books.

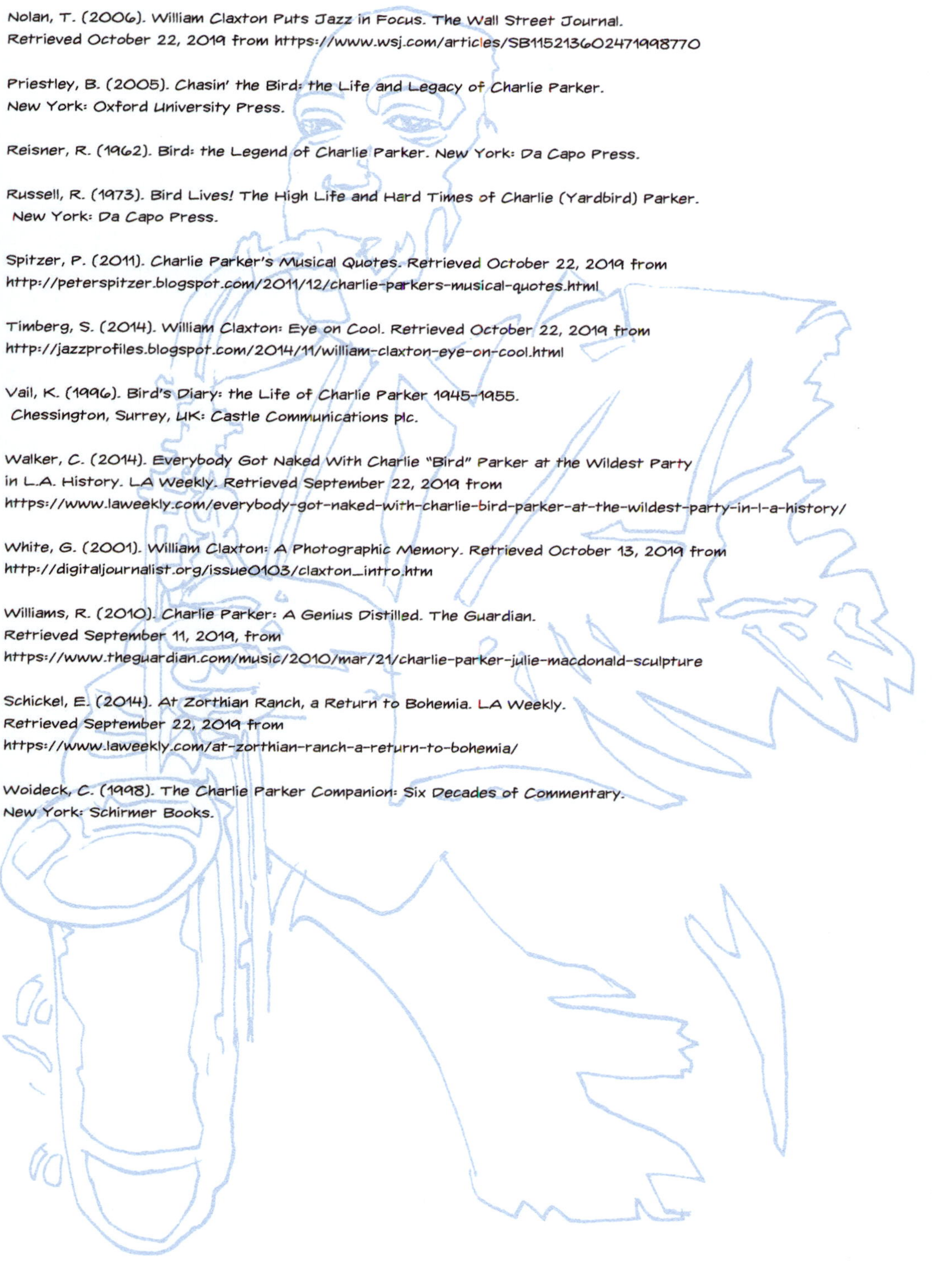

Notes

Introduction

Page 1: The first quote is Parker's favorite quote from *The Rubaiyat of Omar Khayyam.*
The second quote is by jazz composer and bassist Charles Mingus which inspired his
1959 composition "Gunslinging Bird," which is a tribute to Parker. (Russell, 1973, p.338)

Page 3: Jack's Basket Room was a jazz club operated by heavyweight champion Jack Johnson,
later the subject of a documentary with a jazz-fusion score composed and performed by Miles Davis.

Chorus 1: Dizzy

The events of this chapter are documented throughtout Parker books and articles, albeit with frequent
disagreements between historical retellings of these events. I focused on the relationship between
Bird and Dizzy, often folding other figures out of the narrative to maintain that focus.

Page 19: Here Bird is playing through an etude by Marcel Mule, one of many classical saxophone etudes
he was reported to practice.

Page 20: "Ko-ko" is a Parker composition recorded in 1945. The chord changes used for improvisation in this
piece are the same as the chords to the standard "Cherokee," known for its challenging bridge that cycles
through a series of unexpected keys.

Page 21: The composers and musical excerpts here are (from left to right): Claude Debussy and his piece
"Le Fille Au Cheveux Lin," JS Bach and Prelude VII from the first "Well-Tempered Clavier,"
Ludwig Van Beethoven and a bit from the development section of the first movement of his 3rd symphony,
Franz Liszt and the opening chords to his "Ossia arida," Johannes Brahms and his
Intermezzo No. 1, Op.119, and Frederic Chopin and his Prelude in A minor, Op.28, No. 2.
In each of these instances, the composers utilize extended harmony.

Page 22: "Salt Peanuts" is a Dizzy Gillespie composition from 1942.

Pages 24-25: This event most likely occurred in New York City, however it is a perfect encapsulation of the
dynamic between Parker and Gillespie so I transplanted it to Los Angeles.

Page 30: Dizzy's impassioned plea is adapted from Max Roach's recounting of a similar series of events
in New York City. (Priestly, 2005, p 49)

Chorus 2: Zorthian

The events of this chapter are recounted in a few different articles. The topics of discussion between Parker and Zorthian are from my imagination, inspired by Zorthian's wide social circle that included famous physicist Richard Feynman among others. Zorthian was well-known for creating art and s culpture using the scrap from construction sites and other found items, and Bird was well-known for using frequent quotations of famous and often kitschy pieces of music in his improvisation, so this seemed like a reasonable point of connection between these two figures.

Page 34: The Zorthian Ranch is still in operation today, serving as an artist community and Air BnB destination.

Page 35: The Firebird is a ballet composed by Igor Stravinsky. Parker allegedly carried the musical score for this piece in his luggage everywhere he went.

Page 36: I took some liberties in reimagining Zorthian's sculptures. I wanted his ranch to feel utterly alien, a home for the strange.

Page 37: The term "Big Bang" was first used to describe the origin of the universe by English astronomer Fred Hoyle in 1949. It took awhile for it to catch on in the general public, but I imagine Zorthian was hip to it right away!

Page 39: The musical quotations captured here are, beginning at the 1:00 position and going clockwise: "Isle of Capri" by Wilhelm Grosz, "The Man on the Flying Trapeze" by George Leybourne, "Cottontail" by Duke Ellington, "We're in the Money" by Al Dubin and Harry Warren, "Bye Bye Blackbird" by Ray Henderson, and "Tenderly" by Walter Gross. These were all quoted by Parker in recorded improvisations. (Spitzer, 2011)

Pages 44-47: The music excerpt here is from the actual recording of Parker playing "Embraceable You" at the Zorthian Ranch. On the recording you can hear a man yell "Take it off!" in the background.

Chorus 3: Claxton

The events in this chapter are largely pulled from an article about William Claxton on the Jazz Profiles website. The conversation topics between Claxton, his friends, and Parker come from my imagination.

Page 51: The first panel is a re-creation of one of Claxton's most famous photographs featuring one of his favorite subjects: jazz trumpeter Chet Baker.

Page 53: Allegedly, Miles Davis said this to William Claxton when they met. (Nolan, 2006)

Pages 59-60: Parker was an outspoken fan of classical music. His interpretation of Bach's C-minor fugue from The Well-Tempered Clavier comes from my imagination.

Page 61: In the first panel, there are a number of Parker melodies superimposed over each other. I am not going to list them all!

Page 63: The third panel here is a re-creation of a photo Claxton took of Bird with a few of his friends.

Pages 63-64: This passage is referring to the Rat Park experiments. (Alexander, 1981)

Page 65, Panel 2 is a re-creation of another famous photo of Chet Baker taken by Claxton.

Chorus 4: MacDonald

The entirety of this chapter is extrapolated from Julie MacDonald's fascinating page-and-a-half testimonial in the Reisner book. (Reisner, 1962)

Page 69: Julie MacDonald was apparently at the legendary Zorthian party, however it's likely that her and Parker met prior to this event.

Page 74: The art depicted here is "Traverse Line" by Wassily Kandinsky. The line "He truly listened, with mind and heart, and he observed the same way," is taken directly from MacDonald's testimony in the book *Bird: the Legend of Charlie Parker*. (Reisner, 1962, p.138).

Pages 76-77: MacDonald talks about Parker's encounter with this sculpture in the book *Bird: the Legend of Charlie Parker*. (Reisner, 1962, p.140-141).

Page 77-78: The conflict depicted on these pages is from my imagination. Songs depicted on page 77 (from top to bottom): "Lover Man" by Jimmy Davis, Roger Ramires, and James Sherman, "Alone Together" by Arthur Schwartz, "Just Friends" by John Klenner, and "But Not for Me" by George and Ira Gershwin.

Chorus 5: Coltrane

The entirety of this chapter is expanded from a section of the Vail book that briefly documents this meeting: a young John Coltrane goes to a session at Lester Young's Los Angeles residence and jams with Charlie Parker. I knew that I wanted to write a chapter from the point-of-view of an up-and-coming saxophonist, and considering the mystical angle from the MacDonald research, this chapter absolutely needed to be part of this book. (Vail, 1996)

Page 86: Parker recommending the books that allegedly influenced Coltrane's approach comes from the absolutely fascinating interview with post-bop saxophonist Wayne Shorter on Ethan Iverson's *Do the Math* blog. (Iverson, 2015)

Page 87: Parker's soliloquy referencing past lives was inspired by Julie MacDonald's testimonial in the Reisner book. According to MacDonald, Parker expressed interest in past lives among many other things. It seemed to fit his character to adopt this belief if only to teach young John Coltrane a lesson. (Reisner, 1962, p.139)

Pages 88-89: Coltrane most likely heard Charlie Parker play the first time in Philadelphia. For the purpose of this narrative, I transferred that moment to Los Angeles.

Page 91: Coltrane was likely not at Jack's for Bird's return, however in his *Jazz Generations* book, Buddy Collette claims that most sax players in the greater Los Angeles area attended--to me, Coltrane's attendance represents the magnitude of this event.

Chorus 6: Russell

The majority of this chapter stems from Ross Russell's controversial book *Bird Lives.* While Russell's book is certainly a colorful read, it has been criticized for its historical inaccuracy--which speaks to and further fuels the legend of Charlie Parker, muddying the already foggy waters of truth with regards to the truth of Bird. Instead of trying to separate out the truth from the fiction, I leaned into the more noir elements of Russell's presentation while perhaps granting Russell more self-awareness than he displays in his own book.

Page 95: I don't know if Russell was a comic-book aficionado, but this comparison of jazz music with superhero comics was just too fitting to leave out and it fit the tone of Russell's narration-heavy chapter.

Pages 96-98: Adapted from a passage in *Bird Lives.* (Russell, 1973, pp. 208-209)

Page 98: Bird writing the actual contract is a little bit of dramatic flair that didn't likely happen but seemed to fit with Russell's penchant for tall tales.

Page 99: The visual of the contract is adapted from the facsimile of the contract in Bird Lives. (Russell, 1973, 210)

Page 100: The music depicted in the first two panels is Parker's famous solo break on "A Night in Tunisia."

Page 100: Russell's commentary in the second panel is adapted from a passage in *Bird Lives.* (Russell, 1973, p.212)

Page 100: I doubt that Chan was in attendance at this recording session. For the sake of economy of narrative, I rolled the drama all into this one scene.

Page 101: The handwritten contract addendum is adapted from the facsimile of the document in *Bird Lives.* (Russell, 1973, 214)

Page 104: The music depicted here is a transcription of Parker's performance of "Lover Man" from this disastrous session.

Outro

The outro is largely a graphic depiction of the melody to Parker's piece "Relaxin' at Camarillo," (written as a dedication to his time at the mental institution in Camarillo, CA) as well as the first two choruses of his improvisation from the studio version of the piece. If you want to follow along, each two-page spread is four measures of music, just follow the birds around the page!

Page 144: I adapted this account from *Bird Lives.* (Russell, 1973, p.235)

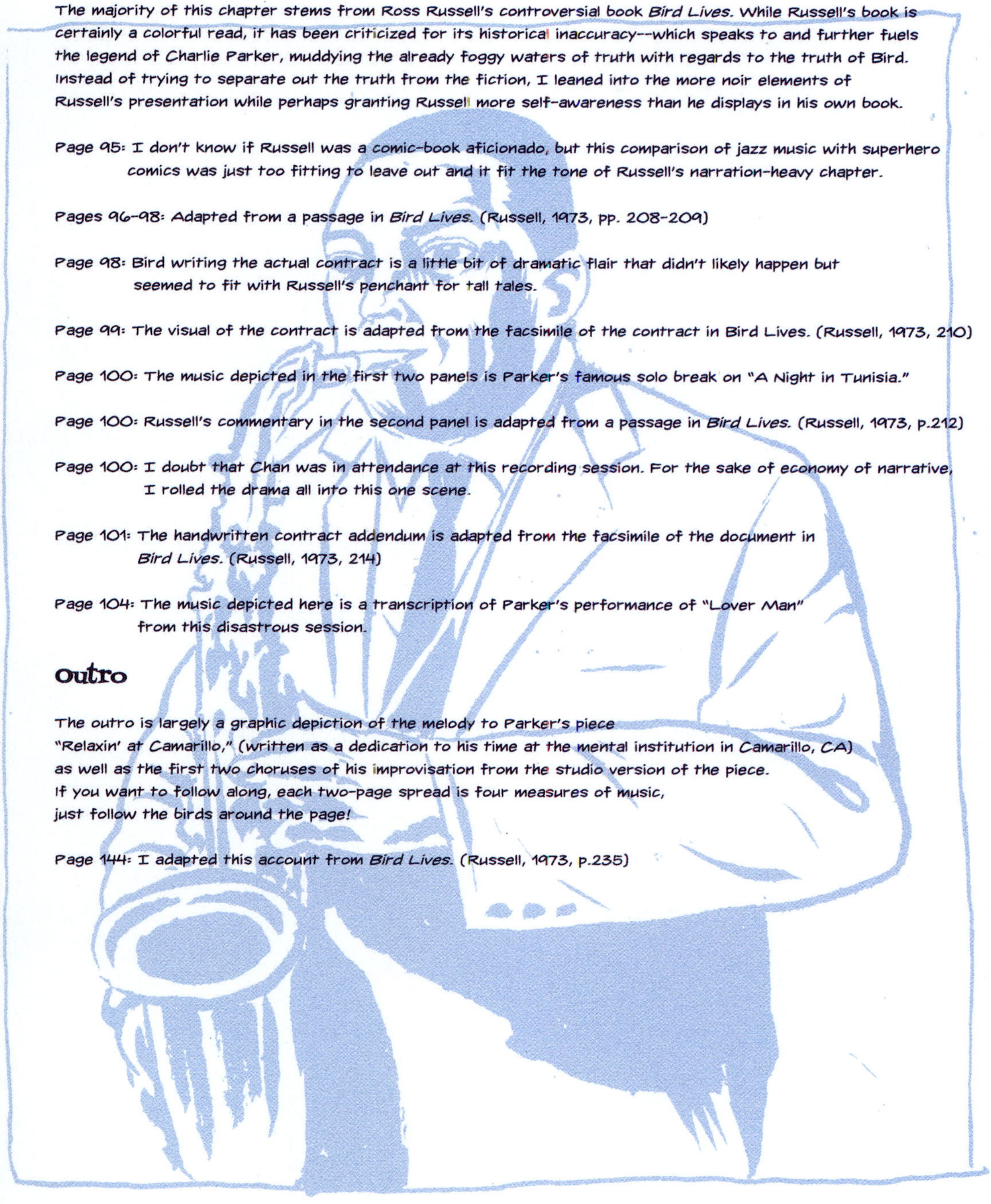

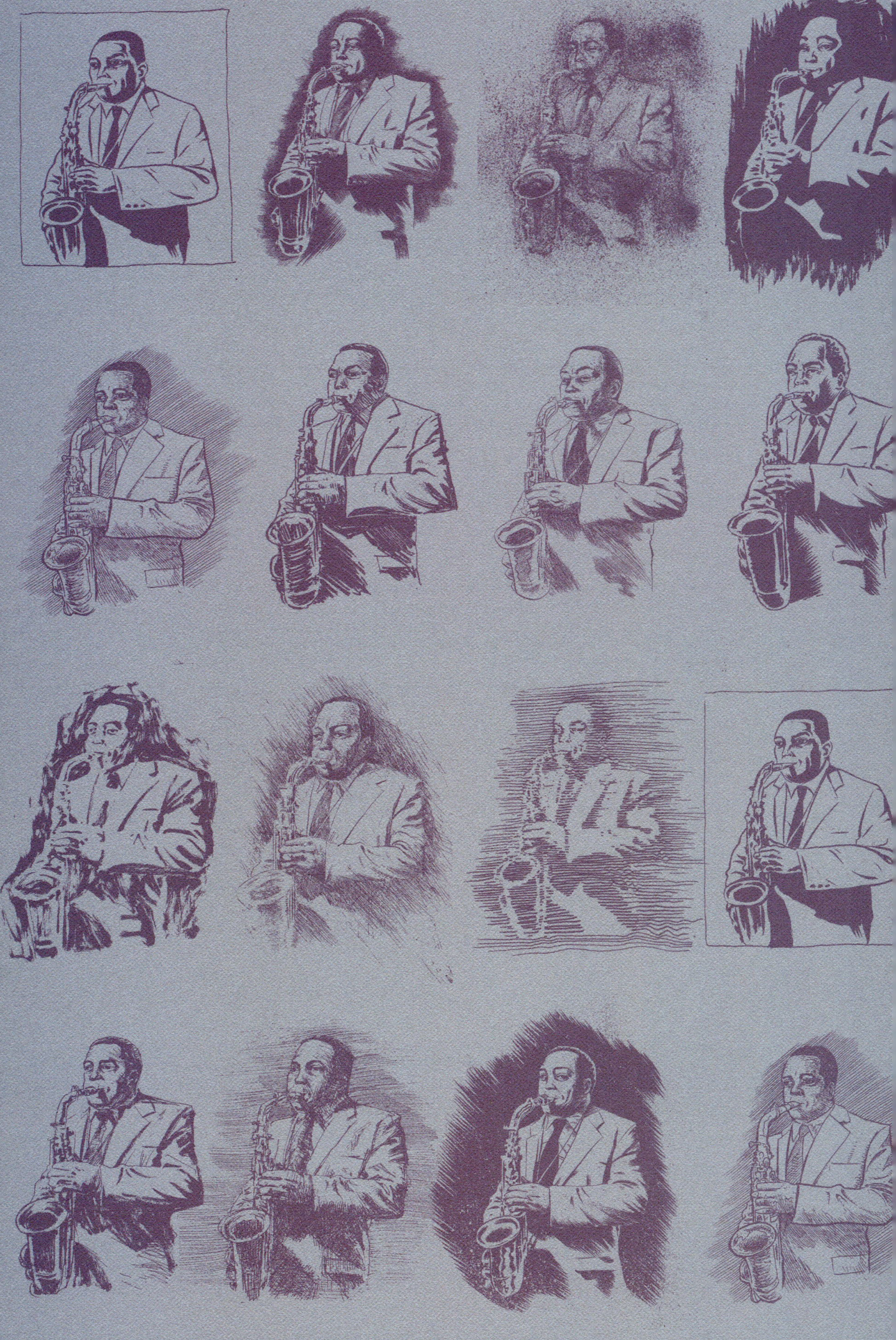

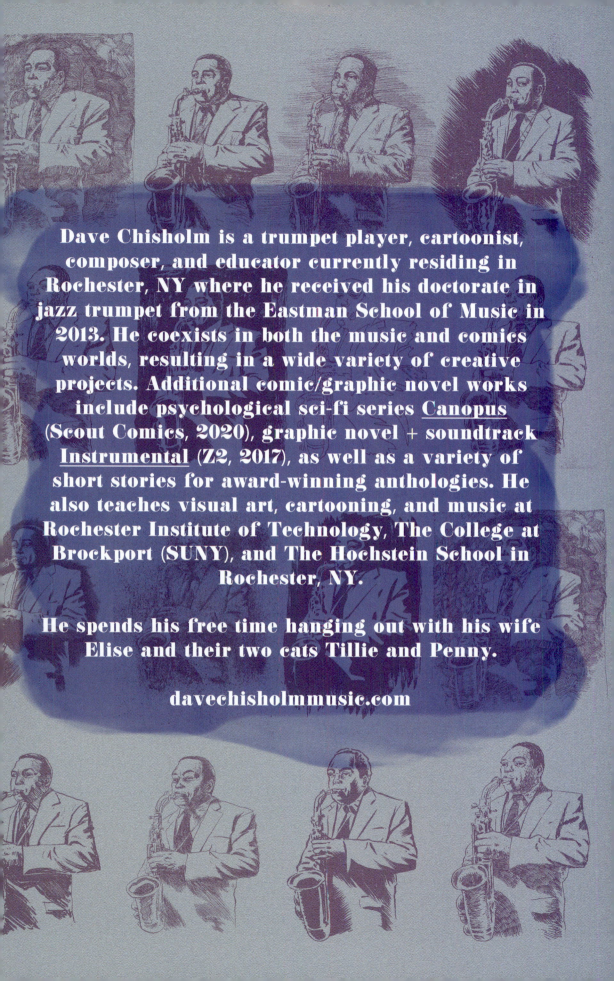

Dave Chisholm is a trumpet player, cartoonist, composer, and educator currently residing in Rochester, NY where he received his doctorate in jazz trumpet from the Eastman School of Music in 2013. He coexists in both the music and comics worlds, resulting in a wide variety of creative projects. Additional comic/graphic novel works include psychological sci-fi series Canopus (Scout Comics, 2020), graphic novel + soundtrack Instrumental (Z2, 2017), as well as a variety of short stories for award-winning anthologies. He also teaches visual art, cartooning, and music at Rochester Institute of Technology, The College at Brockport (SUNY), and The Hochstein School in Rochester, NY.

He spends his free time hanging out with his wife Elise and their two cats Tillie and Penny.

davechisholmmusic.com

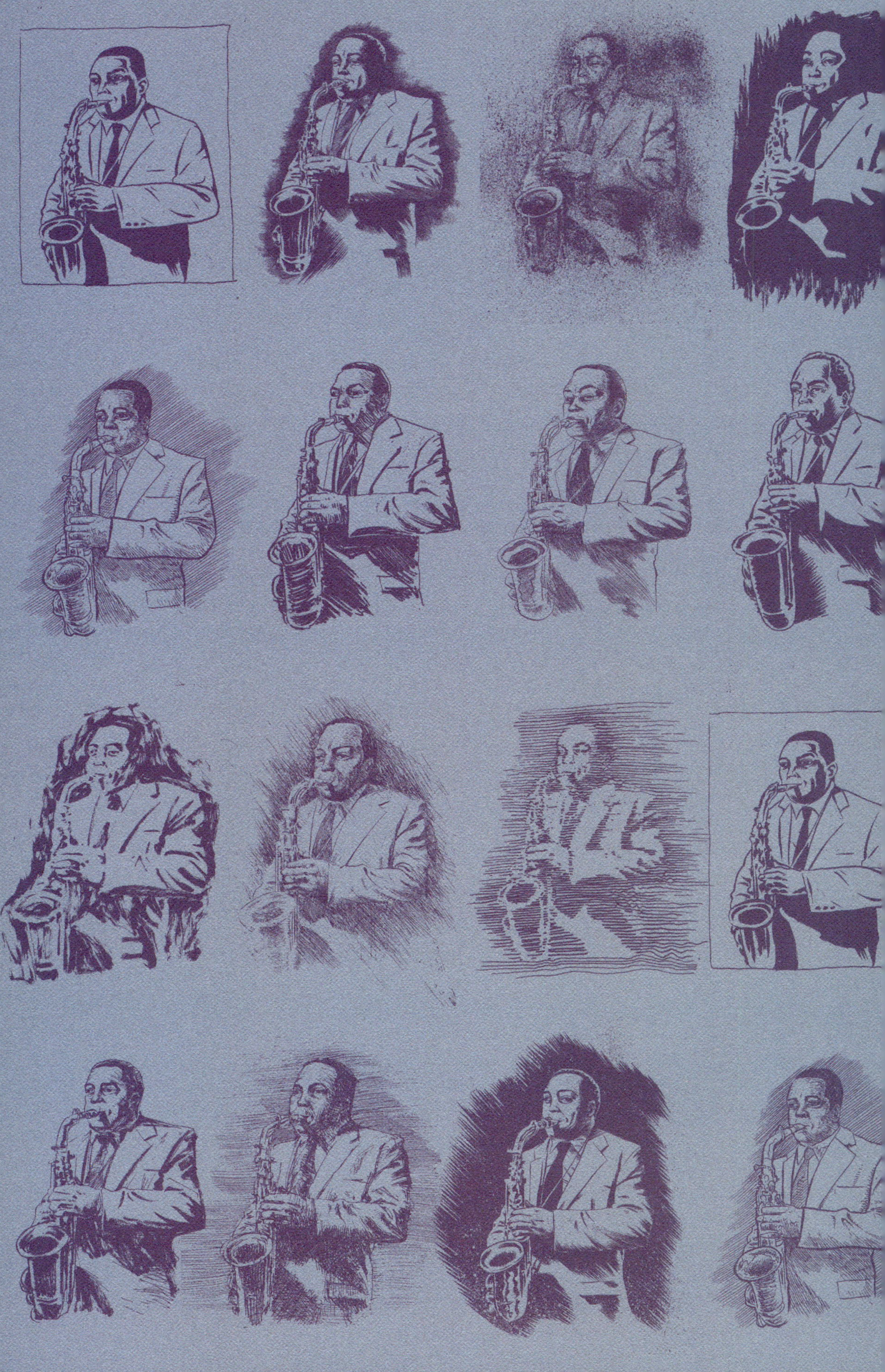